# SEA CHANGE IN LINER SHIPPING

## Related Elsevier books

OUM, PARK & ZHANG
Strategic Alliances of the World's Major Airlines

HENSHER & BUTTON
Handbook of Logistics and Supply-Chain Management

MEERSMAN, Van de VOORDE, & WINKELMANS
World Transport Research: Selected Proceedings of the 8th World
Conference on Transport Research

TURRÓ
Going Trans-European: Towards a Policy of Building and Financing
Transport Networks for Europe

## Related Elsevier journals

Transportation Research Part A: Policy and Practice
*Editor: Frank Haight*

Transportation Research Part E: Logistics and Transportation Review
*Editor: Wayne K Talley*

Transport Policy: Journal of the World Conference on Transport Research
Society
*Editors: Moshe Ben-Akiva, Yoshitsugu Hayashi and John Preston*

Free specimen copies available on request

# SEA CHANGE IN LINER SHIPPING

## REGULATION AND MANAGERIAL DECISION-MAKING IN A GLOBAL INDUSTRY

### Mary Brooks

Centre for International Business Studies
Dalhousie University, Halifax, Nova Scotia, Canada

PERGAMON
An Imprint of Elsevier Science
**Amsterdam – Lausanne – New York – Oxford – Shannon – Singapore – Tokyo**

ELSEVIER SCIENCE Ltd
The Boulevard, Langford Lane
Kidlington, Oxford OX5 1GB, UK

First edition 2000

Library of Congress Cataloging in Publication Data
A catalog record from the Library of Congress has been applied for.

A catalog record from the British library has been applied for.

ISBN: 0 08 043428 2

⊗ The paper used in this publication meets the requirements of ANSI/NISO Z39.48-1992 (Permanence of Paper).

Printed in The Netherlands.

to Sir J. Graham Day
mentor and friend,
your faith was appreciated

# TABLE OF CONTENTS

# Acronyms

| | | | | |
|---|---|---|---|---|
| AA | American Airlines | | ESC | European Shippers' Council |
| ACCOS | Advisory Commission on Conferences in Ocean Shipping | | EU | European Union |
| | | | FAK | freight all kinds |
| ACL | Atlantic Container Line | | FCL | full container load |
| ACTA | Associated Container Transportation (Australia) | | FEFC | Far East Freight Conference |
| | | | FMC | Federal Maritime Commission |
| ANL | Australia National Line | | FTC | Federal Trade Commission |
| ANZDL | Australia New Zealand Direct Line | | GATT | General Agreement on Tariffs and Trade |
| APL | American President Lines | | GBP | pounds sterling (£) |
| ASC | Australian Shippers' Council | | GDP | gross domestic product |
| ASK | available seat kilometres | | HHI | Herfindahl-Hirschman Index |
| ATKs | available tonne kilometers | | IA | independent action |
| ATFI | Automatic Tariff Filing and Information System | | IC | Illinois Central |
| | | | ICC | Interstate Commerce Commission |
| BA | British Airways | | IJV | international joint venture |
| BN | Burlington Northern | | IPO | initial public offering |
| BNSF | Burlington Northern Santa Fe | | JIT | just-in-time |
| CEO | Chief Executive Officer | | JV | joint venture |
| CIFFA | Canadian International Freight Forwarders Association | | KCS | Kansas City Southern |
| | | | LCL | less than container load |
| CGM | Compagnie General Maritime | | Marad | Maritime Administration (US Department of Transportation) |
| CMA | Compagnie Maritime d'Affretment | | | |
| CMB | Compagnie Maritime Belge | | MISC | Malasian International Shipping Corp. |
| CN | Canadian National | | MOL | Mitsui O.S.K. Line |
| CNW | Chicago & Northwestern | | MSC | Mediterranean Shipping Co. |
| CP | Canadian Pacific | | MSP | Maritime Security Program |
| CRS | computer reservation system | | MTC | Maritime Transport Committee (OECD) |
| CSC | Canadian Shippers' Council | | NAA | North Atlantic Agreement |
| CSX | CSX | | NAEC | North America east coast |
| CWA | Cooperative Working Agreement | | NAWC | North America west coast |
| DG IV | Directorate IV—Competition Policy | | NITL | National Industrial Transportation League |
| DG VII | Directorate VII—Transport | | | |
| DoJ | Department of Justice | | NLG | Dutch guilders |
| EC | Commission of the European Communities | | NOL | Neptune Orient Lines |
| | | | NS | Norfolk Southern |
| ECU | European currency unit | | NTA | National Transportation Agency |
| EDI | electronic data interchange | | | |
| EEC | European Economic Community | | | |

| | | | |
|---|---|---|---|
| NTARC | National Transportation Act Review Commission | STB | Surface Transportation Board |
| NVOCC | Non-Vessel Operating Common Carrier | SUNAG | Scandinavia UK North Continent Arabian Gulf |
| NYK | Nippon Yusen Kaisha | TAA | Trans-Atlantic Agreement |
| OECD | Organization for Economic Cooperation and Development | TACA | Trans-Atlantic Conference Agreement |
| | | TEU | twenty-foot equivalent unit |
| OOCL | Orient Overseas Container Line | TMM | Transportacion Maritima Mexicana |
| P&OCL | P&O Containers Limited | TPL | third party logistics (supplier) |
| P&O | Peninsular & Oriental Steam Navigation Company | TSA | Transpacific Stabilization Agreement |
| | | TVR | time-volume rate |
| ROCE | return on capital employed | TWRA | Transpacific Westbound Rate Agreement |
| ro-ro | roll on roll off | UASC | United Arab Shipping Company |
| RPKs | revenue passenger kilometers | UNCTAD | United Nations Conference on Trade and Development |
| RTKs | revenue tonne kilometers | | |
| RTW | round the world | UP | Union Pacific |
| SAS | Scandinavian Airlines System | USEC | US east coast |
| SCEA | Shipping Conferences Exemption Act | USL | United States' Lines |
| SCL | Safmarine Container Line | USWC | US west coast |
| SF | Atchison, Topeka & Santa Fe | VSA | vessel sharing agreement |
| SLCS | St. Lawrence Coordinated Service | WCSA | west coast South America |
| SP | Southern Pacific | WTO | World Trade Organization |
| SPI | Society of the Plastics Industry | | |

# KEY LEGAL CITATIONS

## CANADIAN

*Combines Investigation Act*, R.S.C. 1970, C. 23.

*Competition Act* R.S.C. 1985, c. C. 34.

*Air Canada Public Participation Act*, R.S.C. 1985 (4th Supp.), C. 35.

*Shipping Conferences Exemption Act of 1987*, R.S.C. 1985 (3rd Supp.), C. 22.

*Canada Transportation Act*, S.C. 1996, C. 10.

*CN Commercialization Act* , S.C. 1995, C. 24.

*National Transportation Act, 1987*, R.S.C. 1985 (3rd Supp.), C. 28.

## EUROPEAN

*Treaty Establishing the European Economic Community (EEC)*, 25 March 1957, 298 UNTS 11; 4 EYB 412; U.K.T.S. 15 (1979); Cmnd. 7480; JOF 2 Feb. 58; 1958 RTAF 5; 12 Vert A 134 [Treaty of Rome].

Council Regulation (EEC) 954/79, concerning the ratification by Member States of, or their accession to, the *United Nations Convention on a Code of Conduct for Liner Conferences, Official Journal of the European Communities*, 1979 L 121, 1.

Council Regulation (EEC) 4056/98 of 22 December 1986 laying down detailed rules for the application of Articles 85 and 86 of the Treaty to maritime transport, *Official Journal of the European Communities*, 1986 L 378, 4.

Council Regulation 4064/89, *Official Journal of the European Communities*, 1989 L 395, 1, as corrected by *Official Journal of the European Communities*, 1990 L 257, 13.

Commission Decision of 19 October 1994 relating to a proceeding pursuant to Article 85 of the EC Treaty (IV/34.446 – Trans-Atlantic Agreement), *Official Journal of the Commission of the European Communities*, L 376, 4.

Decision of the Council and Commission of 10 April 1995 concerning the conclusion of the Agreement between the European Communities and the Government of the United States of America regarding the application of their competition laws, *Official Journal of the European Communities*, 1995, L 95, 45.

Commission Regulation (EC) 870/95 of 20 April 1995 on the application of Article 85(3) of the Treaty to certain categories of agreements, decisions and concerted practices between liner shipping companies (consortia) pursuant to Council Regulation (EEC) No 479/92, *Official Journal of the Commission of the European Communities*, 1995, L 89, 7.

Commission Decision of 16 September 1998 relating to a proceeding pursuant to Articles 85 and 86 of the EC Treaty (Case No. IV/35.134: Trans-Atlantic Conference Agreement), *Official Journal of the Commission of the European Communities*, L 95, 1.

See also Appendix C.

## INTERNATIONAL

*United Nations Convention on a Code of Conduct for Liner Conferences,* UN Doc TD/Code 11/Rev. 1 and Corr. 1; 13 ILM 917; U.K.T.S. 45 (1987).

## US

*Shipping Act, 1916*, ch. 451, s. 1, 39 Stat. 728.

*Convention on International Civil Aviation of 7 December 1944*, United States Department of State publication 2282.

*Federal Aviation Act of 1958*, Pub. L. 85-726 72 Stat. 731.

*Hart-Scott-Rodino Antitrust Improvements Act of 1976*, Pub. L. 94-435, 90 Stat. 1383.

*Airline Deregulation Act of 1978*, Pub. L. 95-504, 92 Stat. 1705.

*Railroad Revitalization and Regulatory Reform Act of 1976*, Pub. L. 94-210, 90 Stat. 31.

*Staggers Rail Act of 1980*, Pub. L. 96-448, 94 Stat. 1985.

*Shipping Act of 1984*, Pub. L. 98-237, 98 Stat. 67.

*Ocean Shipping Reform Act of 1998*, Pub. L. 105-258, 112 Stat. 1908.

# LIST OF TABLES AND FIGURES

# ACKNOWLEDGEMENTS

Academics are a privileged group in society. How many others are able to take the time necessary to write a book such as this, and receive a salary and the support of their colleagues while doing it? In today's global trading environment, fewer and fewer individuals have the support of their employers and society to put their thoughts and insights on paper. This book serves to consolidate the learning I had over the past 20 years of being an observer, although not always a dispassionate one, of this industry.

For the luxury of that time, I would first and foremost like to thank Dalhousie University. The University provided me not only with the time, but its Board of Governors and its Centre for International Business Studies provided the financial support necessary to make the trips to Washington, in the case of the former, and Paris and Brussels in the case of the latter.

Time and financial support were not the only gifts that made this book possible. The Federal Maritime Commission generously gave me office space and access to anything I requested during my time in the US capital. FMC staff encouragement of my critical eye was unequivocal. Bob Blair, Karen Gregory, Florence Carr and Austin Schmitt of the Bureau of Economics and Agreement Analysis, among others, were incredibly generous with their time and moral support. The Commissioners, and in particular Delmond Won and Judy Hsu, gave me the access that led, I hope, to understanding.

In Canada, support from Transport Canada, the Canadian Transportation Agency and Industry Canada was always forthcoming. Now that Canada is in the midst of a regulatory review of its shipping conference legislation, I hope that they will feel that their cooperation was warranted!

On the European side of the Atlantic, Serge Durande, David Wood and Charles Williams provided me with their time, a very valuable commodity in the days leading up to the TACA decision in September 1998. They were among many who made me feel welcome in Brussels; both Chris Welsh of the European Shippers' Council and Alfons Guinier of the European Shipowners' Association made time for me and gave me access to materials to ensure that I understood their viewpoints even in the midst of litigation. Wolfgang Hubner of the OECD assisted me with understanding the disharmony that exists in today's conference regulation.

Several people also generously reviewed early drafts of chapters and provided advice. Particularly I would like to thank Robert G. Blunden and Pramodita Sharma for their comments on Chapter 2, Graham Fraser and Brian Fitzgibbon for comment on Chapter 4, Jim Blaze for assistance on Chapter 5, Ken Button and John Rowcroft on Chapter 6, and Gerald Robertson and Russell Weil for Chapter 9. They may not agree with what I written or concluded but they took their role of providing constructive criticism to heart and I am very thankful.

My appreciation is not limited to those directly involved or interviewed. My stay in Washington was made more enjoyable by the evenings organized by Robert and Eslyn Banks, and the model railroaders who meet at Crew Heimer's home; running model trains with a glass of wine in hand is an enjoyable introduction to the business of railroading!

I am most thankful to *Containerisation International*, Drewry Shipping Consultants and UNCTAD, who did not extract a pound of flesh for the use of their data. While many permissions were granted at no or modest cost, I am disappointed with the many publishers who saw the permissions process as an opportunity to extract monopoly prices for minuscule phrases and quotes. Because of them, you the reader have not been presented with the full and rich tapestry of thinking in the words they were originally expressed.

At home, I'd like to thank the many students who, over the years, have challenged my ideas in the classroom and helped me refine my views of managerial decision-making. More recently, Roberta Morrison has been invaluable in assisting in the finalization of the book and the seemingly never-ending task of getting permissions, Tonya Flood with the indexing process, and Janet Lord has suffered the vagaries of manuscript preparation. Above all, my husband has provided the sanctuary and the sanity needed to complete this book. I hope that you find it a stimulating read and are moved to work towards balanced and effective regulation, a climate for competent decision-making by managers in this global industry.


Mary R. Brooks

# 1

# INTRODUCTION TO THE LINER SHIPPING INDUSTRY AND ITS REGULATION

## INTRODUCTION[1]

Transport policy is undergoing major changes which transcend national boundaries. These changes are typified by the reform of regulatory regimes in many countries and influenced by both developments within the sector and factors outside of transport. General patterns of liberalization and privatization can be observed within the sector and trade liberalization and the globalization[2] of demand industries have been well documented. Concurrent with this changing business climate must be a re-examination of competition policy as it relates to liner shipping. Moreover, there are unique competition policy features for this industry, which is a global one by any definition. Yet it faces divergent, national regulation. From both regulatory and commercial perspectives, the path of progress wanders through a minefield of regulatory disharmony towards a standard set of rules governing firms in the liner shipping industry.

Within the Organization for Economic Cooperation and Development (OECD), there has been significant philosophical divergence over the last decade with regards to what constitutes an effective competition policy for this industry. Asian businesses now effectively control almost 50% of the world's largest liner fleets and Asian governments, with the exception of Japan, have a laissez-faire attitude towards merger and alliance activity, which encourages monopoly power and its abuse. It is "survival of the fittest" at its extreme. The World Trade Organization has been unable to find consensus on maritime services regulation. Efforts by the OECD have not succeeded in moving the issue forward.

The North Atlantic trade lane provides an excellent illustration of the dilemma facing lines and regulators. On the North American side of the trade route, Canada and the United States have competition policies that differ in the way they deal with innovative business relationships, generally called alliances in North America (but called consortia by the European regulators). More important, the US rules are in conflict with those on the European side of the route. The

---

1  Some of the material in this chapter is based on work originally published in Brooks (1998). ©1998 by the University of Chicago. All rights reserved. Used with permission. It has been updated for use here.

2  The meaning of globalization is discussed later in this chapter.

negotiation of cooperative agreements between regulators, for example the ones across the north Atlantic, is only a first step.

Meanwhile, the situation is currently being resolved by litigation, but litigation only applies national laws, while the activity and situation are transnational in nature. The solution is to harmonize the international regulatory environment to promote effective transnational competition. The dilemma is to find the balance point on the scale so that regulators neither tip the balance towards destructive competition or abuse of dominant position, nor over-regulate the industry so that gains from trade liberalization are lost. As the US and Europe are at the ends of two of the three largest trade routes, the opportunity to resolve differences here offers the potential to set a new transnational standard.

Eventually, a harmonized regulatory climate for this industry will only come about through political and diplomatic efforts, as other avenues appear stalled. Recognizing this, this book puts forward a view of liner shipping regulation from a managerial perspective. The hope is that public policy interests will see the benefits liner companies desire from the positions they take and that a common understanding will ensue. It advocates a position that does not endorse one country's regulatory approach over another but seeks to find common ground based on principles.

This chapter seeks to set the stage for consideration of the issues and frameworks that must be used to examine those issues. It begins with background information on the industry and its current players, and relates the history to date of liner shipping regulation by three regulatory authorities on the north Atlantic trade route.[3] The chapter concludes with a discussion of globalization. First, what is liner shipping, what is a conference and why do conferences have unique exemption on a global basis from the competition rules that apply to other industries?

## WHAT IS LINER SHIPPING?

Since the earliest days of the British Empire, owners of ships plying the globe realized the benefits they could offer trading interests if known, reliable sailing schedules could be established. The development of the steam engine removed the unreliability of winds from trip planning and the ability to offer a scheduled (called liner) service was born. Unlike tramp (or unscheduled) vessels, liners plied the trade routes from the United Kingdom to Asia and back on a regular basis. Iron ships with steam engines conferred benefits the jet engine would later give airlines—the business would be able to predict its transit times better and schedules would become more reliable. However, the rapid expansion of the business led many shipowners to chase too little cargo and, finding that fixed costs were high, liner operators tried cutthroat marginal pricing to secure business. In 1875, to stem the instability of the business, the UK/Calcutta Conference was born. Four years later, John Samuel Swire founded the first Far Eastern conference—the Agreement for the Working of the China Trade, Outbound and

---

3    Although the three have similar policy objectives, there is some disharmony in the regulations that have developed to deal with the industry, the specifics of which will be dealt with in greater detail in Chapter 9.

Homebound—and became known as "the Father of Shipping Conferences."[4] He worked hard to develop a model system of cargo and revenue pooling that was the feature of the early conferences, and brought stability to the Europe–Far East trade.

In order to understand the topic of liner shipping regulation, it is best to start by defining the term liner conferences. While the book discusses specific definitions of a conference in Chapter 8 and Appendix D, for the purposes of introducing the concept, the definition found in Chapter 1 of the UNCTAD *Code of Conduct for Liner Conferences* is satisfactory:

> *a group of two or more vessel-operating carriers which provides international liner services for the carriage of cargo on a particular route or routes within specified geographical limits and which has an agreement or arrangement, whatever its nature, within the framework of which they operate under uniform or common freight rates and any other agreed conditions with respect to the provision of liner services.*

Because the early conferences employed a common tariff and attempted to control capacity and pool revenue, they came under the scrutiny of both British and American regulatory authorities. In the United Kingdom, the *Report of the Royal Commission on Shipping Rings* (United Kingdom, 1909) concluded that the conference system should be supported, approved deferred rebating, but urged that shippers' bargaining power should be strengthened. In the United States, Congress initiated an investigation that resulted in the Alexander Report (House Committee on Merchant Marine and Fisheries, 1914). The report, which also supported the conference system, led to the *Shipping Act, 1916*, with a separate legal regime exempt from antitrust, and an oversight body separate from the Department of Justice to administer the regime. The conference system was to be an open one with membership restrictions prohibited, unlike any other in the world. Both of these investigations determined that liner shipping conferences possess such uncommon features that they should be exempt from competition legislation. As a result, traditional competition policy guidelines applicable to most land-based industries have not been applied to liner shipping.

Until the early 1980s, conferences were the dominant form of inter-organizational structure developed to control destructive competition in the liner shipping industry. However, in the past two decades, conference membership in many jurisdictions has eroded. The market share of conference operators has been declining steadily. For example, by 1997, independents carried only 53.6% of Canada's liner trade (Transport Canada, 1998). In Australia, the conference share dropped by 13% inbound and 16% outbound in the decade prior to 1993, but remained more than half of Australia's total liner trade at the time of the Part X study (Part X Review Panel, 1993:4, Table 1.2). Even the strongest and most successful conference, the Trans-Atlantic Conference Agreement (TACA), was reported to have lost 4% market share eastbound and 2% westbound in 1997, declining to 64% and 66% of the traffic respectively (Fabey, 1998). Although the market share of conferences has diminished, today's competition watchdogs are witnessing a realignment of business in all sectors of the economy with the growth of strategic

---

4    Those interested in history are recommended to read Jennings (1980).

alliances.[5] There is also a round of merger and acquisition activity on a scale not previously seen.

This book explores whether, given these developments, the antitrust exemption for conferences should still exist. Arguments in favour of exemption often focus on the global nature and capital intensity of the business, and the ability of owners to move capital assets from one legal jurisdiction to another and avoid disclosure through the judicious use of international holding companies and tax havens. Arguments against exemption point to the globalization of the business and the need for consistent treatment of all industries. This book investigates the nature of the industry, comparing it with other asset-intensive networked service industries, and searches for common ground in regulatory philosophy. In this chapter, the foundation is laid with a review of the key players, the basic features of the industry and its regulation.

## THE LINER SHIPPING INDUSTRY

In most other industries involving capital-intensive networked services, the firm is a single entity. In shipping, because of the dilemma of sister ship arrest,[6] there has been a tendency towards one-ship companies with undisclosed ownership, particularly in the tramp sector. Because of the scheduled nature of liner service, ownership disclosure is less of an issue for liner companies. However, the risk level of the business and the significant presence of family interests has made it one with few publicly traded companies.[7]

Since containerization developed as a new way of packaging goods for transport, the growth in volumes carried has been relentless. (See Table 1.1.) Even in poor economic times there has been the tendency to try and move more and more goods by this means. The growth rate has been faster than that of trade as a whole, because the method results in less damage and affords greater security for the goods than other forms of general cargo transport. The growth of just-in-time production and delivery systems and the advent of supply chain management have enhanced the attractiveness of this form of transport. Drewry (1996:40) estimates the container share of general cargo rose from 20.7% in 1980 to 30.1% in 1985, 35.1% in 1990 and 41.6% in 1994. The company forecasts that the penetration of containers into the general cargo market will rise to 53.8% in 2000 (Drewry, 1996:46).

Table 1.2 illustrates that container ships make up significantly less than 10% of the world's fleet. However, it is a critical sector as it carries the world's manufactured goods trade, competing predominantly with air cargo in this activity. There is no particular pattern as to where

---

5    Throughout the book, the term strategic alliance is used in its broadest sense and implies a full range of business relationships, including joint marketing agreements and equipment-sharing agreements. Both later in this chapter and in the next, strategic alliances will be discussed and defined in greater detail.

6    When authorities are unable to arrest a ship for a violation, they may arrest a similar ship owned by the same company in its place.

7    Only P&O and NYK made it into the Global 500 ranking by *Fortune* in 1997. By 1998, NYK had disappeared. However, trading companies Mitsui (of Mitsui OSK Lines), Hyundai (parent of the shipping line of the same name) and Preussag (parent of Hapag-Lloyd) were ranked as was CSX (parent of Sea-Land).

ships are flagged, but the developed country flags have a larger share of container shipping than the average. Because the business is a scheduled one, where service patterns are determined and advertised, it is not surprising to see that flags of convenience[8] have less than average registry as ship owners see less need for anonymity in this sector of the business.

**Table 1.1: Growth in World Container Trade**

| Year | Total TEU (in millions) | % increase |
|------|------------------------|-----------|
| 1973 | 15.0 | |
| 1974 | 16.2 | 8.0 |
| 1975 | 17.4 | 7.4 |
| 1976 | 20.2 | 16.1 |
| 1977 | 23.0 | 13.9 |
| 1978 | 26.5 | 15.2 |
| 1979 | 34.3 | 29.4 |
| 1980 | 38.7 | 12.8 |
| 1981 | 41.9 | 8.2 |
| 1982 | 43.8 | 4.5 |
| 1983 | 47.5 | 8.5 |
| 1984 | 54.6 | 15.0 |
| 1985 | 57.2 | 4.8 |
| 1986 | 62.2 | 8.7 |
| 1987 | 68.3 | 9.8 |
| 1988 | 75.4 | 10.4 |
| 1989 | 82.0 | 8.8 |
| 1990 | 87.4 | 6.6 |
| 1991 | 95.8 | 9.6 |
| 1992 | 105.2 | 9.8 |
| 1993 | 115.3 | 9.6 |
| 1994 | 128.3 | 11.3 |
| 1995 | 135.0 | 5.2 |
| 1996 | 147.3 | 9.1 |

Note:   TEU = twenty-foot equivalent unit
Source:  Data from *Containerisation International Yearbook*, various years.

In the liner shipping sector, three main trades make up a significant share of the traffic carried (Table 1.3). The transpacific is the largest, followed by the Europe/Asia trade and then the transatlantic. The rest of the traffic is widely disbursed, accounting for the existence of hundreds of carriers in the market.

---

8    A ship is treated as a person in law and therefore is declared to have the nationality of the country in which it is registered (flag). A flag of convenience is a country that provides certain tax benefits and regulatory concessions to foreign shipowners in return for their patronage of the shipping register.

**Table 1.2: Allocation of Liner Shipping by Country of Registry**

| Flag | Total Fleet | Container Ships | Share |
|---|---|---|---|
| Developed market-economy countries | 202,993,571 | 17,851,308 | 8.8% |
| Central & Eastern Europe & former USSR | 29,044,654 | 499,158 | 1.7% |
| Open-registry | 339,455,621 | 17,113,417 | 5.0% |
| Socialist countries of Asia | 27,079,927 | 1,704,756 | 6.3% |
| Other developing countries | 147,491,877 | 8,813,499 | 6.0% |
| Other unallocated | 12,113,522 | 2,784,546 | 23.0% |
| World total | 758,179,172 | 48,766,684 | 6.4% |

Source: Created from data published in UNCTAD (1998:117-120).

**Table 1.3: The Main Liner Trades (in 000 TEUs)**

| | Asia/USA total | Europe/USA total | Asia/Europe total |
|---|---|---|---|
| 1995 | 7,480 | 2,656 | 5,140 |
| 1996 | 7,624 | 2,640 | 5,726 |
| 1997F | 8,164 | 2,832 | 6,146 |

Source: Created from data published in UNCTAD (1998:48, Table 31).

The picture of corporate strategy in the industry has changed significantly over the years, not surprising given the tremendous growth experienced in the volume of traffic. The companies involved have also evolved; there have been many mergers, numerous companies exiting the business, and many changing the nature of business they do. Table 1.4 offers a ranking of the leading operators worldwide.

In 1980, many of these companies operated ships, made money on the sale and purchase market, and may have owned their vessels jointly with other companies on the list. The absence of sister ships in many fleets and the lack of consistency about what their core business was would have branded the companies in the industry as opportunistic. That is not the pattern today. The industry has evolved and with it has come more strategic thinking and professional management.

Table 1.4 presents the Top 20 carriers, comparing their 1998 TEU carrying capacity with that listed just three years earlier.[9] What is particularly striking to industry watchers is the growing share held by the largest carriers worldwide. Booz-Allen & Hamilton (1990) noted that the Top 20 carriers controlled 26% of the TEU capacity in 1980 and predicted that the number in

---

[9]   1995 was the first year *Containerisation International Yearbook* ranked the top carriers, although the monthly magazine *Containerisation International* has been doing it for much longer for its subscribers.

1995 would be 50%. Although the dominance of these firms appeared to be overestimated at the time, the Top 20 reported by *Containerisation International* controlled 38.8% of TEU capacity in 1990, 41.6% in 1992, 43.7% in 1993, 46.2% in 1994 and almost 50% in 1995.[10] By 1997, the Top 20 controlled 50.7% of the world fleet.

Given the trade press coverage of alliances, it would be easy to conclude that alliances are a relatively new phenomenon in the industry. This is not the case. Mahoney (1990) tabulated and identified 54 consortia operating on 25 trade routes with 143 companies engaging in some sort of vessel sharing arrangements. Even more important, in 1990 it was estimated that the main trades supported at least 12 major consortia (Clancy, 1995). Today it is clear that number is too high.

The pivotal year in the restructuring of the industry was 1995. The Global Alliance between APL, OOCL, MOL and Nedlloyd (with side arrangements with CGM and MISC) was announced. The alliance configuration included services in the transpacific, Europe–Asia and Asia–east coast North America and moved the industry beyond cooperation on a single route basis. However, the key trade route of the transatlantic was missing and so the service was not truly a "global" one. P&O also announced that it would join the already established Hapag-Lloyd/NYK/NOL grouping, active in the Asian trades. This left Maersk, one of Europe's three operators in the top eight, a free agent on the north Europe/Asia trade. As the second largest carrier in the world at the time, Maersk had the capacity to go it alone but, given the overwhelming economic advantages of consortia participation, opted for a closer relationship with Sea-Land, a company with which it already had an established relationship.[11] By August of 1995, four alliances had been announced: (1) Maersk and Sea-Land,[12] (2) the Grand Alliance of NYK/P&O/Hapag-Lloyd/NOL,[13] (3) the Global Alliance of APL/Mitsui O.S.K./Nedlloyd and OOCL,[14] and (4) the alliance of Hanjin/DSR-Senator/Cho Yang expected to be in operation by 1998 (Bonney, 1995). With these, the industry entered a new phase, one where the key industry players sought to reach global markets for customers desiring global services.

---

10   Fossey (1990, 1995) and various issues of *Containerisation International*.

11   This relationship is discussed in greater detail in Chapter 4.

12   The Sea-Land Maersk alliance (with no clever accompanying name) was wide-ranging in nature with service on Far East Mid-east/US, transpacific, Europe/Asia, Asia/US east coast, US/South America and the north Atlantic through the existing vessel sharing agreement. The two had a history of cooperation which is detailed in Chapter 7.

13   The Grand Alliance covered three major trades—transpacific, Asia/US east coast, and Asia/Europe. However, the partners also offered by 1996 a Suez service Asia/North America east coast (FMC Agreement Number: 203-011503).

14   Although called the Global Alliance, it was far from "global" as it was an agreement to put ships predominantly on Asia/Europe and Asia/US trades.

**Table 1.4: Top 20 Container Operators 1998 and 1995**

| 1998 Rank | Company | 1998 Total TEU | 1995 Rank [1] | 1995 Total TEU |
|---|---|---|---|---|
| 1 | Maersk | 346,123 | 2 | 186,040 |
| 2 | Evergreen/Uniglory Marine | 280,237 | 3 | 181,982 |
| 3 | P&O Nedlloyd | 250,858 | | |
| | Nedlloyd | | 6 | 119,599 |
| | P&O | | 8 | 98,893 |
| 4 | Mediterranean Shipping Co. (MSC) | 220,745 | 10 | 88,955 |
| 5 | Hanjin (incl. DSR-Senator) | 213,081 | | |
| | Hanjin | | 9 | 92,332 |
| | DSR-Senator | | 14 | 75,497 |
| 6 | Sea-Land Service | 211,358 | 1 | 196,708 |
| 7 | Cosco | 202,094 | 4 | 169,795 |
| 8 | APL/NOL | 201,075 | | |
| | APL | | 11 | 81,547 |
| | Neptune Orient Lines/PUL | | 16 | 63,469 |
| 9 | NYK/TSK | 163,930 | 5 | 137,018 |
| 10 | Mitsui-OSK Line | 133,681 | 7 | 118,208 |
| 11 | Hyundai | 116,644 | 18 | 59,195 |
| 12 | Zim | 111,293 | 12 | 79,738 |
| 13 | CP Ships | 105,322 | NR | |
| 14 | CMA (incl. CGM) | 91,600 | | |
| | CMA | | 20 | 46,026 |
| | CGM | | NR | |
| 15 | Hapag-Lloyd Containerline | 90,879 | 15 | 71,688 |
| 16 | OOCL | 90,063 | 19 | 55,811 |
| 17 | K Line | 89,717 | 13 | 75,528 |
| 18 | Yangming | 79,840 | 17 | 60,034 |
| 19 | United Arab Shipping | 59,331 | NR | |
| 20 | SCL [2] | 55,584 | NR | |
| | Top 20 Total (share of total fleet) | 3,113,455 | (53%) | |
| | Total Fleet | 5,878,214 | | |

Notes:  NR = Not Ranked

(1)  1995 was the first year the *Yearbook* undertook to rank the carriers.

(2)  SCL is a merger of Safmarine and CMB Transport. The CMB share was acquired in July 1998 by Safmarine and the company renamed to Safmarine Container Lines.

Source:  1995 data are from Fossey (1995:56). 1998 data are from *Containerisation International Yearbook 1999* (6-7, Table 3).

**Table 1.5: Alliances and Vessel Slots 1995**

| *Alliance* | *Operator* | *Committed to Alliance* | *Total Fleet* |
|---|---|---|---|
| Global Alliance | APL<br>Mitsui-OSK<br>Nedlloyd<br>OOCL | 77 vessels | 187 vessels<br>375,165 slots |
| Grand Alliance | Hapag Lloyd<br>NOL<br>NYK<br>P&O | 60 vessels | 182 vessels<br>371,068 slots |
| Maersk/Sea-Land | Maersk<br>Sea-Land | 175 vessels | 206 vessels<br>382,748 slots |
| Tricon/Hanjin | Cho Yang [1]<br>DSR-Senator<br>Hanjin | 60 vessels | 95 vessels<br>200,843 slots |

Notes:   (1) Not in Top 20.

It should be pointed out, however, that commitment to alliances varied (Table 1.5). For example, the Global Alliance represented a deployment of only one-third of the vessels operated by its partners; likewise the Grand Alliance's vessels were also one-third the total partners operated. The greatest commitment to alliance usage was represented by the Sea-Land Maersk alliance, at 175 vessels deployed of the 206 possible. There was at least recognition in some alliances that if the maximum benefits were to be extracted from the alliance, it should not be of short duration. Longer term relationships would encourage mutually beneficial invest-ments in similar-sized ships that would exploit the vessel schedule and slot-sharing synergies of the partners. The Global Alliance was fixed to 2005 in the transpacific, while it was in effect until 2001 in Asia/east coast North America and Asia-Europe.

P&O Nedlloyd dealt with their problems through merger.[15] The merger posed a problem for the new company as to which alliance agreement it would honour. Once it chose the Grand Alliance, the newly merged NOL/APL opted to join the restructured Global Alliance. As OOCL was not included in the new Global Alliance, it became a participant in the Grand Alli-ance. OOCL's strength in the China and southeast Asia market provided better balance within the Grand Alliance rather than duplicating the strength of its former alliance partner, APL/NOL. In the final analysis, there has been a natural balancing in the process of realignment.

The pattern of mergers and alliances changed dramatically between 1995 and 1998 and has, in all likelihood, not reached its final configuration. Of the Top 20, 13 are involved in one of the

---

15   This merger is studied in detail in Chapter 7.

large-scale cooperative agreements noted in Table 1.6.[16] The efforts by the large carriers to gain control over costs and service offerings resulted in service realignments globally. The five new global groupings dominated the Top 20 and accounted for 28% of the TEU on offer in 1998. All alliances in Table 1.6 now offer services on the three main trade lanes.

## Table 1.6: Changing Alliances

| Alliance | 1995 Members | 1997 Members (December) | 1998 Vessel Deployment |
|---|---|---|---|
| Global Alliance | APL | APL (NOL) | 90 vessels |
| | Mitsui-OSK | Hyundai | 325,487 TEU |
| | OOCL | Mitsui-OSK | |
| | Nedlloyd | | |
| Grand Alliance [1] | Hapag Lloyd | Hapag Lloyd | 93 vessels |
| | NOL | MISC [2] | 350,197 TEU |
| | NYK | NYK | |
| | P&O | OOCL | |
| | | P&O Nedlloyd | |
| Maersk/Sea-Land | Maersk | Maersk [3] | 167 vessels |
| | Sea-Land | Sea-Land | 438,089 TEU |
| Tricon/Hanjin (United Alliance) | Cho Yang [4] | Cho-Yang [4] | 85 vessels |
| | DSR-Senator | DSR-Senator | 277,000 TEU |
| | Hanjin | Hanjin | |
| Cosco/K-Line/ Yangming [5] | | Cosco | 65 vessels |
| | | K-Line | 212,714 TEU |
| | | Yangming | |

Notes:  (1) The original Grand Alliance agreement was cancelled 29 July 1996.
 (2) On certain routes only (very limited participation).
 (3) By Feb. 1998, only Maersk's Australian and African services lie outside its alliance with Sea-Land.
 (4) Not in Top 20.
 (5) This alliance is much looser than the others, with alliance members engaging primarily in slot exchanges, often without vessel sharing or schedule management.

Source:  1998 deployment data as reported by Fossey (1998).

Alliance participation does not necessarily mean conference participation; conference participation varies by trade lane and so complicates the picture. Even Sea-Land, a strong supporter of the conference system and traditionally a conference member on all the major trade lanes, entered the Canada-Europe trade as a non-conference operator in 1997. Conference member-

---

16  In contrast to route-specific slot charters.

ship and alliance membership serve different purposes; this is an important distinction that should influence the way they are regulated.[17]

Of significant interest in the industry is the rate at which carriers are adding capacity. The capacity being added far outstrips the growth in the business. In Europe, Maersk strove to improve its position, steadily climbing to first place through an impressive record of building new post-Panamax ships. By 1998, Evergreen and Maersk had the most TEU on the order book, but others in the Top 20 are focusing on growing their capacity too. (See Table 1.7.) Hyundai made it to 11th place by the fall of 1997. The Asian Crisis hit the Korean carriers particularly hard and Hyundai made it through the financial crisis by selling a number of its ships and leasing them back. OOCL had a dramatic decline (it ranked 7th in 1992 and 19th in 1995) that it has attempted to stall through ordering new vessels. The only one outside the Top 20 operating the large post-Panamax vessels is the Malaysian International Shipping Corporation (Fossey, 1995).

**Table 1.7: Top 20's Contracted Newbuildings as of 1 September 1998**

| Top 20 Rank | Company | TEU on order |
|---|---|---|
| 2 | Evergreen/Uniglory Marine | 89,404 |
| 1 | Maersk | 81,256 |
| 3 | P&O Nedlloyd | 39,630 |
| 9 | NYK/TSK | 37,150 |
| 15 | Hapag Lloyd Containerline | 33,600 |
| 6 | Sea-Land | 31,000 |
| 7 | Cosco | 24,684 |
| 16 | OOCL | 22,000 |
| 4 | Mediterranean Shipping | 20,250 |
| 10 | Mitsui-OSK | 10,000 |
| 17 | K Line | 6,912 |
| 5 | Hanjin | 5,300 |
| 14 | CMA/CGM | 4,400 |

Note:    APL, NYK, Hyundai, Zim, CP Ships, United Arab, and SCL did not appear on the list of those ordering new tonnage.

Source:  Data provided by *Containerisation International Yearbook 1999.*

As this book focuses on the growth strategies of these carriers, it is worth examining carrier behaviour over the past three years. In 1995-96 Asian carriers Cosco, Yangming and Evergreen steadily expanded their capacity and Hyundai Merchant Marine expressed aspirations to be in the Top 10 by 2000. Both Cosco (a state-controlled carrier from the People's Republic of

---

17   This point is discussed further in Chapter 9.

China) and Evergreen (a Taiwanese carrier) also grew rapidly, preferring to follow a "go-it-alone" strategy. In spite of this approach by some of the largest, many of the firms opted to grow through an alliance strategy. By February 1998, *Containerisation International* noted that Evergreen and Mediterranean Shipping Company were the only two standing alone (Fossey, 1998).

As for the shape of future liner shipping networks, the structure of the competing consortia is not yet stable. There will be continuing distress as a result of the penetration of post-Panamax vessels on major trade lanes and the overall injection of capacity at a foolhardy rate, one far exceeding the growth rate in containerizable trade.

## A HISTORY OF CONFERENCE REGULATION

Most world governments seek to control the presence of market power through antitrust legislation, but most OECD countries provide conferences and consortia in the liner shipping industry with immunity from antitrust legislation.[18] This section will examine conference regulation in three jurisdictions—the US, Canada and the European Union.

### Regulation in the US

The introduction of the *Shipping Act of 1984* was a watershed event in US regulation of shipping conference activity. It introduced the concepts of independent action and service contracts as the means to limit the market power of the conferences. The Act was reviewed in 1989 by the Federal Maritime Commission (FMC), with its report favouring the maintenance of the status quo, including the system of open conferences.[19] Despite some complaints by shippers that conferences had been using the Act to thwart meaningful negotiations between conferences and shippers, a critical mass of interest in changing the Act was not achieved. That changed in April 1992 when the newly-formed conference Trans-Atlantic Agreement (TAA)[20] announced a 19% capacity reduction westbound in order to increase prices, necessary because the industry had combined 1991 losses of US$250 million on the route, slot utilization was running at a mere 60% and freight rates had fallen below 1980 levels (Toll, 1992).

The TAA had a number of features that proved problematic as will be evident from later discussion of the EC regulatory climate. First, it divided carriers into two groups with differing rate-making authority mandated for each. One group consisted of conference members of predecessor conferences (plus OOCL) while the other included significant non-conference operators. Second, there was a capacity management regime implemented westbound **only**. Third, it

---

[18]  A detailed review of the differences in a number of national laws appears in the report of the Part X Review Panel (1993:43-8).

[19]  Federal Maritime Commission (1989). The history of US conference regulation prior to the introduction of the *Shipping Act of 1984* is detailed in Part I of this report.

[20]  FMC Agreement Number 202-011375. The members are listed, as of November 1992, in Table 1.8.

imposed strict rules on service contracts, and fourth, granted inland rate-making authority. All four of these issues raised immediate concerns and shippers' complaints quickly appeared.[21]

The FMC moved swiftly to modify the TAA's plans, seeking revisions and getting enough to be satisfied with the operational design of the TAA in August 1992 so that it would become effective 31 August 1992. European shippers were not pleased and moved quickly against the TAA. A process to suspend the TAA was initiated by the European Shippers' Council.

In the United States, shippers were not satisfied with the FMC approval and strengthened their lobbying efforts to remove antitrust immunity for liner conferences. In 1994, 17 large shippers and the National Industrial Transportation League complained about the TAA to the FMC, which resulted in an investigation being launched. On 5 July 1994, the TAA revised its agreement, renaming it the Trans-Atlantic Conference Agreement, and filed it with the FMC. The TACA made changes, eliminating the two-tier pricing structure and altering restrictions on capacity management; it also reduced notice on independent action, and lowered volume limits on service contracts in an effort to address concerns about anti-competitive activity (Porter, 1994; Weil, 1995). The FMC forced concessions in return for its approval: the elimination of capacity management, no volume limits on service contracts, and even further reductions in notice for independent action (Beargie, 1994). All of these concessions resulted in TACA being compliant with the *Shipping Act of 1984*. According to Canna (1994:43), the changes to capacity management made TACA "look a lot like any other conference, which at this stage in its legal struggles is just what it needs."

In September 1995, the US House of Representatives passed the *Ocean Shipping Reform Act of 1995* to amend the *Shipping Act of 1984*. The Act sought to eliminate tariff and contract filing, and government tariff enforcement and regulation, although it would retain the current system of oversight and filing requirements for carrier agreements. There was considerable concern and debate in the trade press about the ability of large shippers to put small shippers at a disadvantage through confidential contracting. Although the Act passed the House, it subsequently stalled in the Senate.

On 10 March 1997, Senator Hutchison, with co-sponsors Lott, Gorton and Breaux, introduced Senate 414 to amend the *Shipping Act of 1984*. The new bill attempted to balance the interests that defeated the *Ocean Shipping Reform Act of 1995* with those seeking changes. The bill passed the Senate in 21 April 1998 and had to pass the house unamended to become law. On 4 August, S414 passed the House after removing controversial veterans' burial and death benefits. As it was changed, it returned to the Senate, running against the US election time constraints. On 1 October 1998 the Senate passed the *Ocean Shipping Reform Act of 1998* for implementation 1 May 1999. The US had made substantial changes in its regulatory approach to conferences. The principal changes in the new legislation affect service contracts and tariff filing and, as will be discussed in Chapter 9, have moved the US in some measure closer to Europeans. However, significant regulatory gaps remain.

---

21   For an excellent discussion of the legal issues with respect to the TAA, see Weil (1995).

## Regulation in Canada

In Canada, the *Shipping Conferences Exemption Act, 1979* had granted conferences exemptions from the antitrust investigation powers of the *Combines Investigation Act*. Anti-trust legislation was altered in 1986 with the passage of the *Competition Act*. Concurrently, with the passage of the *Shipping Act of 1984* in the US, and the move for regulatory reform in other transport sectors in the period 1985 to 1987, conferences and their exemption were put under the microscope. The result was the *Shipping Conferences Exemption Act of 1987*, which underwent a five-year review in 1992. The outcome of that review was to recommend the Canadian government revisit the Act if and when the US removes antitrust protection from conferences. Regulators in Canada informally admit that the matter of conference regulation in Canadian trades has a low priority given the significant presence of non-conference lines in the market. Only in the wake of regulatory reform in the US has conference regulation in Canada begun to be discussed. A consultation paper suggesting various options has been released for comment.

## Regulation in Europe

On the European side, conference regulation has followed quite a different path from that of the US, driven in part by Europe's internal efforts to cooperate more deeply and broadly within its own community. Competition rules for Member countries of the European Union were laid down in the *Treaty of Rome*, and therefore fall under the Competition Directorate of the Commission (DG IV) rather than the Transport Directorate (DG VII).

Transport policy was one of the three original common policies of the European Community; however, the provisions of the *Treaty of Rome* did not establish common principles for implementation. Therefore, the transport sector within the EU today has been characterized as one with significant government intervention and "a confused network of bilateral and multilateral inter-state agreements."[22] This was due, in part, to the differing views of Europe's Member States on the process of market liberalization. For example, one area of debate was whether the harmonization of competition rules should come before or after market liberalization. The Benelux countries argued in favour of market liberalization first while Germany and Italy, in order to protect their transport companies, wished to liberalize only after the competition rules were harmonized.

There was, in the era following the promulgation of the *Treaty of Rome*, considerable debate about its application to the transport sector and whether transport regulations ran counter to the universality principles embodied in the Treaty. This debate is carefully detailed in Ortiz Blanco and van Houtte (1996, Chapter 2) and by Wilks (1992). When the Member States sought to endorse the principles found in the *United Nations Convention on a Code of Conduct for Liner Conferences* (hereinafter referred to as the UNCTAD Code), approved 6 April 1974, they needed to address the question of how this convention would fit with the provisions of

---

[22] Ortiz Blanco, L. and B. van Houtte (1996:4-5), *EC Competition Law in the Transport Sector*. By permission of Oxford University Press.

the Treaty. Many European countries had become signatories to the UNCTAD Code, which was in direct conflict with some of the principles of the *Treaty of Rome*. Council Regulation (EEC) 954/79 allowed Member States to ratify the UNCTAD Code providing they made specific reservations[23] so that the existence of conferences would not breach Community competition rules and would allow the continuation of the shipping industry's status as self-regulating. The Regulation recognized the stabilizing role of conferences in assuring reliable services to shippers. It also enabled the UNCTAD Code to come into force in 1983, and began the long process of discussion about appropriate competition rules for conferences.

As the acquisition of greater power by DG IV progressed throughout the 1980s, the authority's activities gradually expanded into sectors not previously subject to competition rules. Neither maritime nor air transport was completely subject to the competition rules as, on the maritime side, they did not apply to cabotage or tramp shipping while, on the air side, they only applied to intra-Community transport. Extra-Community international air transport remained under the purview of individual governments. In addition, the focus of activity by DG IV shifted from vertical to horizontal agreements and, therefore, to issues of price-determination, market share and abuse of dominant position.

According to Brooks and Button (1992), the current regulatory climate for liner shipping began with the release of the 'First Package' of maritime measures by the Commission (European Communities Commission, 1985a) in 1985, just prior to the publication of the *Cockfield Report* (European Communities Commission, 1985b).[24] The *Cockfield Report*, which set out the conditions perceived necessary for the achievement a Single European Market, clearly indicated that changes in Community maritime policy would be necessary. The 'First Package' regulations were generally accepted by the Council of Ministers in December 1986 for entry into force 1 July 1987. In particular these were:

- Council Regulation (EEC) 4055/86 of 22 December 1986 applying the principle of freedom to provide services to maritime transport between Member States and between Member States and third countries.
- Council Regulation (EEC) 4056/86 of 22 December 1986 laying down detailed rules for the application of Articles 85 and 86 [covering Competition Policy] of the Treaty [of Rome] to maritime transport.
- Council Regulation (EEC) 4057/86 of 22 December 1986 on unfair pricing practices in maritime transport.
- Council Regulation (EEC) 4058/86 of 22 December 1986 concerning coordinated action to safeguard free access to cargoes in ocean trades.

These measures were intended to improve the competitive structure of the European shipping industry and its ability to counteract unfair competition from third countries (Erdmenger and

---

23  Ortiz Blanco and van Houtte (1996) enumerates these in Chapter 4 of their book.

24  A second set of measures, the "Positive Measures Package" was released in 1989 and more directly focused on operating conditions in the industry, and therefore this package will not be discussed.

Stasinopoulos, 1988; UK House of Lords Select Committee on the European Communities, 1986; Kreis, 1990). They were successful; providing the Commission with the power to react to predation or unfair rate-setting by third party ship owners, such as in the case involving Hyundai Merchant Marine of Korea on the Europe–Australian trade (Anonymous, 1990). The measures and the subsequent Hyundai case were persuasive to Eastern bloc shipowners who changed their strategies without legal proceedings being required.

Rather than implementing the Treaty's competition rules, Council Regulation 4056/86 sought to give legal form to the political compromise respecting the liner conference system's *status quo*,[25] i.e., accepting exemption from antitrust investigation for conferences. While Council, Regulation 4056 granted a block exemption to liner conferences, this exemption did not apply to carriers' non-transport activities or, as argued later, transport activities in other sectors such as inland transport. Article 1(3)(b) of Council Regulation 4056/86 adopts the definition of conferences found in Chapter 1 of the UNCTAD Code (Ortiz Blanco and van Houtte, 1996:109).

While Council Regulation 4056/86 provided block exemptions to the full force of the competition rules for liner conferences, safeguards to ensure that this privilege was not abused were put in place. Specifically, conferences (1) must not discriminate between ports or shippers on non-justifiable economic grounds; (2) should consult shippers on matters of common interest; (3) where they have 'loyalty agreements' with their customers, these should fulfill reasonable criteria; (4) should publish tariffs; (5) should not act in a predatory manner towards competitors.

The regulations accepted that shippers want to move goods of any size and type at their convenience and that liner conferences are the most efficient way of doing this. The block exemption for conferences was also designed "to give fair consideration to the interest of users," especially the shippers' councils, and the precedent of the Hyundai case has protected users against predatory pricing.

As in the US, the Commission noted that firms in the industry were moving towards more cooperative agreements and, in 1986, DG IV's policy review with regard to consortia[26] was initiated. An interim report, issued in January 1988, concluded that there was no evidence to justify a block exemption for consortia. In 1990, the UK House of Lords, which had undertaken its own examination, issued a report calling for urgent further clarification (UK House of Lords Select Committee on the European Communities, 1990). The primary argument was that consortia were becoming the market practice which, rather than large conferences like the Far East Freight Conference, might be important to counter the rapidly growing large operators, like Sea-Land and Evergreen (Bott, 1990).

As noted previously, the formation of the TAA in the early 1990s led to significant complaints. The TAA was notified to the Commission on 28 August 1992. (Such notification protected the TAA members from EC penalties until the legality of the agreement could be

---

25  Ortiz Blanco and van Houtte (1996:256). Its Chapter 4 details the unfolding of events.

26  Consortia are defined in Appendix D after Chapter 8.

determined.) The Commission argued that the TAA was not a conference because its pricing practices were not uniform (there were two tiers), that capacity limits were illegal under Council Regulation 4056/86, and that inland pricing authority was beyond the scope of Council Regulation 4056/86 and violated Council Regulation 1017/68.

Two major events in the ensuing confrontation between the Commission and the conferences were the Commission's ruling of 19 October 1994 against the TAA and the banning of price-setting on multimodal rates by the Far Eastern Freight Conference (applicable to all conferences) in December 1994. On 9 March 1995, the Luxembourg-based Court of First Instance granted a stay of the decision prohibiting inland rate-making on the grounds that such a prohibition could compromise market stability. Members of TACA could quote a common multi-modal tariff. This competitive advantage was short-lived with the passing into force of Commission Regulation 870/95 on 20 April 1995.

Commission Regulation 870/95 signaled the EU's recognition that consortia rather than conferences would be the dominant form of liner shipping business serving Europe. The rules grant immunity from antitrust regulation to a long list of activities typical of joint ventures; it is critical to note that price-fixing is not on the list. These rules, with a five-year life span, clarify the conditions consortia must meet in order to be granted a block exemption from competition policy application; these conditions differ from the ones that apply to conferences. Like US liner shipping regulation, Commission Regulation 870/95 encourages independent action and service contracts but it does not accept extensive inland cooperation or broad-based capacity management. The rules apply to all consortia (cooperative agreements) ranging from slot-swapping to highly integrated vessel sharing arrangements. Under Commission Regulation 870/95, consortia are not able to impose penalties on members that withdraw, are not allowed to manage capacity except for seasonal fluctuations, and must allow members that engage in joint marketing to engage in independent marketing with notice. Consortia members may also offer service packages tailored to the needs of individual shippers.

On 21 June 1995, the European Commission lifted TACA's antitrust immunity, exposing TACA carriers to fines for collective rate-making on inland transport. The Competition Directorate outlined six reasons why the Commission considered TACA practices anti-competitive: (1-4) price agreements between members on maritime transport, port activities, inland transport services for multimodal shipments, and maximum freight forwarder compensation; (5) agreements on slot-sharing, space charters and equipment exchanges; and (6) the terms and conditions of entering into service contracts with shippers (Canna, 1995). The ruling forced TACA members to redefine their operations to meet the new regulations affecting consortia.

In addition to the passage of Commission Regulation 8709/95, 1995 was a critical year for conferences in Europe as Karel van Miert established the Multimodal Group (also known as the "Wise Men") to examine the inland pricing issue.[27] For the next two years the process moved through a series of hearings as the Europeans awaited their report as well as the results

---

27   Their findings are reported in detail in Appendix D (Inland Rates).

of another case, the SUNAG case on the Far Eastern Freight Conferences' use of inland pricing. That case was resolved through an out-of-court settlement in 1998 and the Commission then focused its attention clearly on TACA. On 16 September 1998, the Commission released its decision, levying fines of US$318 million against the 15 member lines of TACA for their abuse of dominant position in the transatlantic trade (Table 1.8). The Commission ruled that TACA induced potential competitors to join TACA (thereby altering the competitive structure of the market), violated rules on service contracts and fixed inland prices. An appeal followed.

### Table 1.8: TAA/TACA Members and Fines

| TAA Members November 1992 (% Share) | TACA Members September 1997 | EU Fine Assessed in millions of ECU |
|---|---|---|
| Atlantic Container Line (7.8%) | Atlantic Container Line | 6.88 |
| CGM (2.5%) | | |
| Cho Yang (2.6%) | Cho Yang [2] | 13.75 |
| DSR-Senator (4.5%) | DSR-Senator [2] | 13.75 |
| Hapag-Lloyd (10.3%) | Hapag-Lloyd | 20.63 |
| | Hanjin Shipping [1] | 20.63 |
| | Hyundai [2] | 18.56 |
| Maersk (10.9%) | Maersk | 27.50 |
| Mediterranean Shipping (6.0%) | Mediterranean Shipping | 13.75 |
| Nedlloyd (4.7%) | as P&O Nedlloyd | (below) |
| | Neptune Orient Lines [1] | 13.75 |
| | NYK | 20.63 |
| OOCL (8.2%) | OOCL | 20.63 |
| P&O Containers (8.8%) | as P&O Nedlloyd | 41.26 |
| Polish Ocean Lines (8.0%) | Polish Ocean Lines [2] | 6.88 |
| Sea-Land (9.5%) | Sea-Land | 27.50 |
| | Tecomar [2] | 6.88 |
| | Transportacion Maritima Mexicana [2] | 6.88 |

Notes:  (1)  Left TACA prior to the fine announcement.
        (2)  Have since withdrawn from TACA.

Source:  Roberts (1992:1A) for TAA member shares. Fine data from the European Commission (1998), *Commission Refuses to Exempt the TACA and Fines its Members*, press release IP/98/811, 16 September.

Since then, TACA has contemplated turning itself into a discussion agreement (Freundmann, 1998), a course of action that would be illegal in Europe. The Box Club[28] proposed to the

---

28  The Box Club is a group of CEOs of the major shipping lines; a list of its members appears in Appendix A to this chapter.

Commission that they would accept the abolition of inland pricing on European trades if the EC were to grant immunity for port-to-port contracts involving multiple carriers. Cho Yang announced its departure from TACA in August 1998 and others have followed since. As of September 1998, there were nine independents on the north Atlantic route (Freundmann, 1998), with the potential to neuter the effectiveness of TACA as a conference. In the early days after it was first formed, TAA lines controlled 83.8% of US/northern Europe traffic (Roberts, 1992); by mid-1998 the share held had dropped to 63% (Davison, 1998:49). A new conference, the North Atlantic Agreement (NAA) involving all but two independents (Mitsui OSK Lines and Evergreen) was announced in early 1999 but stalled shortly after.[29] As of press time, the future of TACA remains uncertain, but discussions with regulators continue.

Conferences have a block exemption from antitrust scrutiny for certain activities, and consortia have a block exemption for another list of activities.[30] The European Shippers Council (ESC), in choosing whether the existence of both block exemptions is in the best interests of the users of the services, decided to call for the removal of the block exemption on conferences as its preferred route (Maloney, 1995). What should be done is the subject of Chapter 9.

## POLICIES ON MERGERS AND COOPERATIVE AGREEMENTS

In the US, competition policy affecting liner shipping companies is dealt with specifically via the *Ocean Shipping Reform Act of 1998*; parameters are not established in a general competition policy and then liner companies exempted from the application of that policy, as is the case in the EU and Canada.

In the **US**, recognition of new cooperative forms of business relationships in this industry happened much earlier than in the other two jurisdictions with the passage of the *Shipping Act of 1984*. That situation has not changed with the new legislation. A consortium of two or more carriers may be classified as either a "joint venture" or as a "cooperative working agreement" (subject of Section 4 of the *Ocean Shipping Reform Act of 1998*). A consortium is a joint venture, according to Section 10 (e) of the Act, if the agreement creates a joint service and operates as a single carrier.

If the relationship is determined to be a joint venture under Section 10, it will be subject to review to determine if it would have the potential for substantially reducing competition in a trade as a whole. Efficiency gains expected may be sufficiently compelling to counter arguments about abuse of market power.

> Since such an agreement can enable carriers to raise necessary capital, attain economies of scale, and rationalize their services, joint ventures may result in more effective and efficient service being provided in a trade. (Ullman, 1995:62)

---

[29] The European Commission was waiting for the new FMC rules to be laid down while the FMC sought more information from the NAA; that information did not materialize and the agreement was withdrawn.

[30] But that does not mean complete exemption without review. Each consortium or conference must apply for the exemption (Evans, 1994).

It has been noted that, in general, if the US Department of Justice Merger Guidelines were applied to a consortium, one involving 10% of the market would be deemed legal, 20% probably legal, and even at 30% or 40% the efficiencies in support of its legality might be proved.[31]

If the alliance does not operate under its own name, publish its own tariffs, or issue its own bills, then it will not be viewed as a single common carrier (joint venture) but as a cooperative working agreement. The new global alliances, as currently structured, are considered to be cooperative working agreements.

Alliance agreements may be quite far-reaching, as seen in Table 1.9. What is not included in an agreement is just as important as what is. Alliances usually maintain individual sales operations and individual vessel ownership along with associated maintenance management and insurance. The alliance members are free to set prices outside the alliance structure (although they may be set by a conference of which alliance participants are members).[32] Most important, alliances are not usually involved in revenue, cargo or profit (loss) sharing pools. As will be discussed in greater detail in Chapter 4, they predominantly exist to deal with operations—asset deployment and service integration—so that the customer receives the service desired. There is no way, under US law, that strategic alliances in the liner industry can be confused with either joint ventures or mergers.

### Table 1.9: Sample Conditions in an Alliance Agreement

- Coordination of sailings, including: numbers of vessels and total capacity, sailing schedules, service frequency, ports served and rotation, feeder arrangements, and notice of changes in vessel allocation.
- Reciprocal space chartering, including terms of its provision, and advertisement of its availability.
- Contracting with and co-ordination with suppliers of equipment, terminals and ancillary services.
- Maintenance of individual marketing and sales offices.
- Joint development of documentation and data systems.
- Conditions of withdrawal from agreement.
- Duration of agreement.
- Conditions determining breach of agreement.

As for policies on cooperative agreements in **Europe**, the previous section noted that Europe's policy on consortia was linked to its policy on conferences, both specific to the shipping

31  Advisory Commission on Conferences in Ocean Shipping (1992:83). Larger market shares may be acceptable in the context of liner shipping consortia because such ventures are less complete and permanent than full mergers and because they are capable of producing pro-consumer efficiencies that must be factored into the analysis (ACCOS, 1992:88, footnote 141).

32  Under EC Regulation (Commission Regulation 870/95), alliances are prohibited from price-fixing and therefore alliance members must be a member of a conference to agree on prices.

industry. With the passage of Commission Regulation 870/95, a clear separation of the two types of entities became evident and the European approach was discussed in that section.

The EU examines different business arrangements using guidelines specifically for that business structure. Under EU law, a merger results when one or more undertakings acquire, whether by purchase of securities or assets, by contract or by any other means, direct or indirect control of the whole or parts of another.[33] In order to be reviewed under Council Regulation 4064/89, it must also have a "community dimension," which is achieved in circumstances in which the world turnover of the parties equals or exceeds ECU 5 billion and the turnover of at least two of the parties is ECU 250 million or more. In determining the acceptability of the merger, the Commission will examine whether the merger creates or strengthens a dominant position and results in impeding effective competition in a substantial part of the common market.[34]

Under the European definition of a merger, a consortium could rarely, if ever, be regarded as a merger. This is primarily because a consortium agreement tends to contain clauses with respect to its termination and, therefore, the consortium does not meet a permanence test applied to mergers. Because consortium members may transfer their assets or abandon opportunities to enter into other agreements on other routes, it is clear to the Commission that a consortium is not a merger (Kreis, 1990).

A consortium may, however, resemble a joint venture (JV). Under European law, JVs may be deemed to be "concentrative" in nature, or "coordinations" aimed at achieving efficiency gains. Those set up to coordinate the competitive behaviour of independent undertakings are excluded from merger control regulation but are examined under Council Regulation 17/62 of 21 February 1962. A concentration occurs when control is obtained, including those situations in which control is gained via a contractual agreement that enables one or more partners to jointly control the assets of a partner (Götting and Nikowitz, 1990). A concentration is determined to exist where several enterprises are brought together in a permanent form so that their economic independence is lost. The Commission has held that concentrations that contribute to European Community objectives by bringing about desirable changes in industrial structure should not be prohibited, only those that create excessive market power (Bellamy and Child, 1987). There has been subsequent refinement, but the principles have essentially remained unchanged.

The key difference between cooperative and concentrative JVs appears to be the existence of the phrase "performing on a lasting basis."[35] For this reason, the global liner shipping consortia are also clearly not concentrations as defined by the Commission, but are seen to be coordinations, with the limits to their activities specified under Commission Regulation 870/95.

---

33  Defined in Article 3 of Council Regulation 4064/89.

34  Under Article 2 (2) according to Evans (1994).

35  Article 3(2) Council Regulation 4064/89 of 21 December 1989 on the control of concentrations between undertakings. *Official Journal of the European Communities*, 1990 L 395, 1. A lasting basis is seen to be at least five years but the entity must be autonomous to be a JV. Miguel A. Peña C. (1998), personal interview, Commission of the European Communities, 8 July.

In **Canada**, Industry Canada (1995) issued a bulletin on its own interpretation of strategic alliances as mergers under its merger guidelines (Consumer and Corporate Affairs, 1991). The Competition Bureau in Canada has tended to take a broad view of the definition of a merger to include strategic alliances in which there is a significant interest between the parties. For example, this may be a situation in which there is co-production of a product (although market-ing activities may be maintained as separate entities) or in which production may be separate but marketing is undertaken jointly.

> *Where it is found that one firm's decisions in respect of pricing, purchasing, distribution, marketing or investment are materially influenced by another firm, a significant interest may be deemed to have been acquired or established.*[36]

Speaking simply, vessel sharing arrangements with their implicit capacity focus might be determined to be co-production of the service, even though the carriers maintain separate marketing entities. Therefore, the Bureau could deem the consortium to be a merger but has concluded that most strategic alliances do **not** raise market power issues under the *Competition Act* (Industry Canada, 1995).

As for the reality of the Canadian situation, there has not been an examination of cooperative agreements by the Bureau. In the absence of firm regulations, if discussion agreements and other cooperative groups file copies of their agreements according to the requirements of SCEA with the Canadian Transportation Agency, they have been considered *de facto* as conferences in Canada.

In conclusion, global liner shipping alliances (consortia) as they are currently evolving in the industry are not seen as "mergers" under either EU or US legislation. They may be treated as mergers under the existing strategic alliance guidelines of Canada's Competition Bureau but, as their status is neither specifically included nor excluded under the *Shipping Conferences Exemption Act of 1987*, how they will be treated is not entirely clear.

## IS THIS THE GLOBALIZATION OF SHIPPING?[37]

The common man has heard plenty about the globalization of trade, of banking and even of the airline business. Is the move towards alliances in the shipping industry really only the "globali-zation" of shipping? The term "globalization" has a specific meaning as used in the book and clarification is required.

Globalization, as it is used today in the management literature, was first introduced by Levitt (1983) as an observation about markets and the approach by which companies could address these markets. He called on companies to ignore superficial national and regional differences

---

[36]  Industry Canada (Competition Bureau), 1995:11. Reproduced with permission of the Minister of Public Works and Government Services Canada, 1999.

[37]  An earlier version of these thoughts on globalization appeared in an invited lecture, *Globalization and Liner Shipping*, for the Bureau of Transport and Communication Economics, Canberra, Australia, 28 July 1995.

and treat the world as a single market. Promoting the search for commonalties rather than differences, he encouraged companies to develop market-specific products only after they had failed to find the commonalties necessary for the global marketing of standardized products.

Before Levitt's article about the potential for standardization strategies in international market-ing turned marketing managers on their ears, most struggled with trying to service divergent customer wants by sourcing locally or developing products specific to each country market. The truly global products today are found in niches where customer mobility is high, the need is technologically standardized worldwide, or where product adaptation costs are so prohibi-tively high the product is only available in a standard format. Kodak film, McDonald's fast food service, Louis Vuitton luggage, and Macintosh computers are examples of global products today.

Beyond Levitt's globalization of markets (and one might conclude a standardization of pro-ducts and services offered to that market), there is also the globalization of production. In this case, a company identifies the locale offering greatest competitive advantage for either the total production process or, in the case of car production, for modules of the process, and builds its global products in that location until the location-specific advantages securing the production to the site shift to a new location. Any country can compete as the site for production, distri-bution, research and development or management operations for global firms; whether it will be successful or be able to sustain the competitive advantage is, of course, a separate issue. For many of the customers of liner shipping companies, the globalization of production and distribution is the path to survival as they face the imperative of having to produce a globally-competitive product or being ousted from their once secure domestic market by foreign competition.

This book is about liner shipping companies that serve traders in a global marketplace; the nature of trade is becoming global and there are manufacturers that seek to serve a marketplace global in scope. The application of location-specific advantages to liner shipping is limited primarily to tax and ship management elements. The advent of the flag of convenience meant shipping was one of the first industries to become "globalized." Inputs to the development of the service are purchased from the most cost-effective source; mobility of assets and the ability to source labour (seafarers) and capital equipment (ships, containers and the like) from the most advantageous seller also mark shipping as a global business. Liner shipping has been less "free" due to conference legislation but not less global. The relevance of globalization of production and distribution more affects the liner companies' customers as the service offering is decoupled from the managerial location.[38] Hence liner firms may make the decision to offer their services in a market with a global geographic scope in order to serve the needs of global traders (Table 1.10). This approach may still not extend to the thinner routes, as evident from a random selection of these (Table 1.11).

---

38  Decoupling is a term often found in service management literature. In the production and distribution of a product, these functions are physically linked and therefore coupled locationally. As the service is intangible and not necessarily produced in the location from which it is managed or distributed, the production and distribution functions are considered "decoupled."

**Table 1.10: Operators on Principal Trade Routes 1998**

| Top 20 Operator | Europe/ Far East | Europe/ NAEC | Far East/ NAWC | Far East/ NAEC |
|---|---|---|---|---|
| Maersk | ✓ | ✓ | ✓ | ✓ |
| Evergreen | ✓ | ✓ | ✓ | ✓ |
| P&O Nedlloyd | ✓ | ✓ | ✓ | ✓ |
| Sea-Land | ✓ | ✓ | ✓ | ✓ |
| Cosco | ✓ | ✓ | ✓ | ✓ |
| Hanjin | ✓ | ✓ | ✓ | ✓ |
| NOL/APL | ✓ | ✓ | ✓ | ✓ |
| Mediterranean Shipping | ✓ | ✓ | | |
| NYK/TSK | ✓ | ✓ | ✓ | ✓ |
| Mitsui-OSK | ✓ | | ✓ | ✓ |
| Hyundai | ✓ | | ✓ | ✓ |
| Zim | | | ✓ | ✓ |
| Yang-Ming | ✓ | ✓ | ✓ | ✓ |
| CMA-CGM | ✓ | ✓ | | ✓[4] |
| OOCL | ✓ | ✓ | ✓ | ✓ |
| CP Ships | ✓[1] | ✓[2] | | ✓[3] |
| K-Line | ✓ | ✓ | ✓ | |
| Hapag Lloyd | ✓ | ✓ | ✓ | ✓ |
| Cho Yang | ✓ | ✓ | ✓ | ✓ |
| SCL | | | | |

Notes:    (1) Contship
               (2) Canada Maritime, Cast, Contship, Lykes
               (3) Contship
               (4) Minimal deployment this route.

Source:   Based on information provided by *Containerisation International Yearbook 1998*:201-11.

Does this mean that most liner shipping firms will therefore seek global status? The short answer is no. Most liner firms are regional or niche players in the supply of liner shipping and do not have the financial wherewithal or managerial inclination to follow this approach. As an example, Atlantic Container Line, a regional player on the north Atlantic, has a niche strategy of sticking to a route where it has the competitive advantage of thoroughly understanding the needs of the customers and offering specialized equipment and ships to meet those needs. There are many examples of geographic and equipment niches sought by liner firms. Conclusion: only some liner firms seek global market scope and customers that trade globally.

Porter (1980:275), in recognizing the increasing transboundary nature of business and in order to explore the nature of competition between firms for which the business arena was global, defined a global **industry** as "one in which the strategic positions of competitors in major geographic or national markets are fundamentally affected by their overall global positions."[39] More important than definitions, however, is the understanding of how companies that are seeking greater global integration will respond strategically, the topic of several chapters in this book.

Furthermore, it is important not to confuse globalization with the acquisition of market power; a firm can be global in its management philosophy without seeking market control. The existing trends in slot chartering and strategic partnerships in liner shipping can be expected to become even more established in the global marketplace. The regulators' interest is to identify those firms for which global does reflect a strategy of market dominance and abuse of that position.

**Table 1.11: Operators on Selected Minor Trades 1998**

| *Top 20 Operator* | *South Africa/ South America east coast* | *Australasia/ North America west or east coast* | *Caribbean/ South America west coast* | *Far East/ South America east coast* |
|---|---|---|---|---|
| Maersk | ✓ | | ✓ | |
| Evergreen | | | | |
| P&O Nedlloyd | ✓ | ✓ | | ✓ |
| Sea-Land | | | ✓ | |
| Cosco | ✓ | | | |
| Hanjin | ✓[1] | | ✓[1] | |
| NOL/APL | | | | |
| Mediterranean Shipping | | | | |
| NYK/TSK | ✓ | | ✓ | ✓ |
| Mitsui-OSK | ✓ | | ✓ | ✓ |
| Hyundai | | | | |
| Zim | | | | |
| Yang-Ming | | | | |
| CMA-CGM | | ✓ | ✓ | |
| OOCL | | | | |
| CP Ships | | ✓[2] | ✓[3] | |
| K-Line | | | | ✓ |
| Hapag Lloyd | | | | |
| Cho Yang | | | | |
| SCL | ✓ | | | |

Notes:   (1)  Through DSR Senator
         (2)  Contship and ANZDL
         (3)  Lykes

Source:  Based on information provided by *Containerisation International Yearbook 1998*:201-11.

---

[39] Source: *Competitive Strategy: Techniques for Analyzing Industries and Competitors* by Michael E. Porter. ©1980 by The Free Press, a division of Simon & Schuster, Inc. Reprinted with permission of the publisher.

## ABOUT THIS BOOK

The economic pressures driving downsizing and outsourcing in many business sectors in the 1990s are also felt in liner shipping. Firms have come to realize that inter-corporation cooperation, ranging from slot charter[40] agreements and vessel sharing arrangements through to full-fledged alliances, offers far greater economic benefits than possible merely through conference membership (Brooks *et al.*, 1993). The situation has been exacerbated by the global trends of deregulation[41] and trade liberalization. Chapter 2 will examine the economic and strategic management literature to explore the theoretical underpinnings of structural options for growth that are available to liner firms. Chapter 3 will apply one of these theories to liner companies to explore the nature of the industry and provide a model of managerial decision-making which includes consideration of those strategic options for growth. Chapter 4 will examine the key operational issues that face liner shipping companies and identify successful operational strategies. These three chapters set the scene so that the reader has an understanding of both the theoretical literature and the day-to-day realities faced by liner shipping firms.

The middle of the book—Chapters 5 to 7—explores whether or not there are lessons for liner shipping companies from the strategic options to growth chosen by the firms profiled in these chapters. Each chapter focuses on a different industry, chosen for its relative similarity to the liner shipping industry. The industries are all globalizing, capital intensive, networked service industries. They share some significant features—all face derived demand,[42] mobile assets and substantial fixed costs. Chapter 5 focuses on railway mergers and alliances, Chapter 6 on airline alliances (both simple and global), and Chapter 7 focuses on the full range of structural options used by the liner industry. In each of these chapters, some industry background is provided and then a number of case studies are presented to illustrate the key decisions made in keeping with the model proposed in Chapter 3.

The industries chosen for Chapters 5 to 7 are those with the greatest number of lessons for liner shipping. While the regulatory climate for each is significantly different, the choice of growth option has been driven by the regulatory climate, the nature of the business and managerial preferences of the firm's management. These are the three drivers on which the book is focused. Why were these industries chosen? Financial services, freight forwarding and telecommunications were also considered. The capital intensive nature of financial services and their networks drew some interest but was quickly eliminated as it appeared that the cost of capital was the largest driver of success, not a major issue for liner shipping companies. The

---

40  A slot is a measure of ship space; one slot will accommodate one TEU, or twenty foot equivalent container (20' x 8' x 8'). The calculation of slot cost is illustrated in Table 3.5. A slot charter is an agreement to charter (read lease) a specific number of slots (a space to hold a single TEU) on another carrier's vessel.

41  According to Høj *et al.* (1995), the reasons for the trend within OECD countries towards deregulation have been: (1) recognition that traditional regulatory instruments can result in serious efficiency losses (limiting entry can contribute to higher costs and prices and regulations on conduct may limit innovation); (2) changing technologies cause re-evaluation of traditional policy tools; (3) globalization of economies has increased international competition; and (4) shift in public ownership in network services (privatization can improve internal efficiencies).

42  Transport demand is secondary to (i.e. derived from) the demand for goods (trade).

freight forwarding industry presented the weakest case for inclusion and did not fit with the others—only some of the businesses could be considered capital intensive and networked; the remainder could be as small as a single person brokering global deals. It did not adequately match the characteristics sought for comparison. Finally, the telecommunications business was the last to be eliminated; it is currently undergoing a sea change brought on by both deregulation and market liberalization, but the relative strength of resellers and the porosity of industry boundaries made for muddy comparisons. How does the cable television or Internet or telecom company define its market and how much overlap is there? The two contrasting industries—air and rail—were ultimately selected because they reflect choices made by companies much larger than today's liner operators, and provide excellent illustrations of the major structural choices liner companies face today: merger and acquisition, joint venture, global strategic alliance or simple alliance. Each of these will be defined in the course of Chapter 2.

Finally, the last two chapters—Chapter 8 and 9—focus on the dilemmas authorities face in the regulation of liner shipping. For example, most liner companies work in two or more countries—each with a different set of regulations which are often contradictory. It is extremely important to the business community in general that business uncertainty generated by divergent regulation be reduced; otherwise companies will divert their resources from efficiency-maximizing strategies to those intended to reduce regulatory risk at the price of societal welfare. Therefore, the purposes of these two final chapters are: (1) to explore competition policy issues surrounding the regulation of liner shipping, and (2) to identify the primary areas of convergence and divergence in national approaches to liner shipping regulation, and develop a set of guiding principles that may be both workable for the industry and acceptable to regulators.

Given the current industry trends towards alliances and corporate concentration through merger, the business environment will become increasingly more complex. Litigation, the current solution to conflicting national laws, must give way to the only truly workable solution: harmonization of the regulatory environment. Without such harmonization, we may see in this industry what has happened in the aerospace industry with the merger of McDonnell Douglas and Boeing; the EC has issued the terms and conditions under which it will find a non-EC merger acceptable. From a commercial risk management perspective the uncertainty and risk associated with a situation makes it extremely difficult for businesses to undertake strategic planning and for investors in such companies to assess the risk of their investment. In the long run, the regulatory climate should reflect the global nature of the industry. This book seeks to make the first steps in that direction.

# Appendix A

# Members of the Box Club

A. P. Møller—Maersk Line

Atlantic Container Line AB

Australian National Line Limited*

Blue Star Line Ltd.*

CMA-CGM Group
    Compagnie Maritime d'Affretement*
    Compagnie General Maritime

Cho Yang Shipping Co. Ltd.

China Ocean Shipping (Group) Co.

CP Ships Holding Inc.
    Canada Maritime Limited
    Cast Line Limited
    Contship Containerlines Limited
    Lykes Lines Limited
    Ivaran Lines
    ANZDL Limited

Crowley Maritime Corp.

Evergreen Marine Corp.

Hamburg-Südamerikanische

Hanjin Shipping Co. Ltd.
    DSR-Senator Lines GmbH*

Hapag-Lloyd Container Linie GmbH

Hyundai Merchant Marine Co. Ltd.

Italia di Navigazione, SpA

Kawasaki Kisen Kaisha, Ltd.

Malaysian International Shipping
    Corporation Berhad

MSC Mediterranean Shipping Company SA

Mitsui O.S.K. Lines Ltd.

National Shipping company of Saudi Arabia

Neptune Orient Lines Ltd.
    APL Limited*

Nippon Yusen Kaisha (NYK Line)

Orient Overseas Container Line Ltd.

P&O Nedlloyd BV/P&O Nedlloyd Limited

Sea-Land Service Inc.

South African Marine Corporation Limited

Transportacion Maritima Mexicana SA
    de CV

United Arab Shipping Co. (S.A.G.)

Wan Hai Lines Ltd.

Wilh. Wilhelmsen SA

Yangming Marine Transport Corp.

Zim Israel Navigation Co. Ltd.

---

Note:    * Company has been purchased.

Source:    Cooperative Working Agreement Number 203-010099, as of 22 December 1998.

# 2

# LITERATURE AND THEORIES ON
# FIRM STRUCTURE AND MARKET BEHAVIOUR

## INTRODUCTION

Most research on the liner shipping industry has offered a one-dimensional perspective, reflecting national policies from one side or the other of the north Atlantic. It has taken a predominantly economic viewpoint and drawn regulatory conclusions from this context. The regulatory view of the industry will be discussed in detail in Chapters 8 and 9. This chapter will examine literature underpinning the competition analyst's view as presented in Chapter 8 as well as evaluate management theory in preparation for the chapters on managerial decision-making and the case studies that appear in the intervening chapters. The intention in this chapter is to paint the background so that the individual elements of the rest of the book have a context in which to be seen.

This chapter begins with a review of the key elements of both economic and strategic management literature on firm behaviour before attempting to reconcile the two. It then moves forward to examine the relationship structures that have evolved. It is at this point that the range of structures—from mergers to simple agreements—are defined so as to be used more precisely. The chapter will then introduce research into structural failure and success, examining what has been written about the factors that play a role in generating these outcomes. This book seeks to take the reader beyond pricing and conference structure into the nature of alliances and mergers in today's global business environment.

## THE ECONOMIC LITERATURE

The basic proposition of the economic literature on firm behaviour and performance are that man is rational but opportunistic, and makes decisions based on profit-maximizing objectives; that supply and demand determine the price paid in the market; and that the firm is the result of the economies arising from the division of labour, the specialization of activity, and the organizational structure to perform specific tasks. It is the proposition of the book that these three central themes do not fully explain the current behaviour of firms and their choice of strategic direction in pursuing growth.[1] The economic literature provides a partial explanation and a starting point.

## Industrial Organization (IO) paradigm

In the Industrial Organization (IO) paradigm, the performance of **markets** is based on both the conduct of buyers and sellers in the particular market and the structure of the market. Originally conceived by Mason (1939, 1949) and extended by Bain (1959),[2] Heflebower (1954) and Sosnick (1958), the industrial organization model proposed by Scherer (1970) has become the classic illustration of the IO approach. In this paradigm, the basic conditions of supply and demand in the market influence the market structure which, in turn, affects conduct—the combined actions of the firms in the marketplace. These actions, in turn, influence the performance of the market and feedback to affect market structure as well as the basic supply and demand conditions.

While market structure and the resulting firm conduct had feedback loops influencing the basic conditions in the market, Scherer's model had no feedback effects from the performance of the market as a result of firm conduct. Perhaps this was due to Bain's belief that published data on business conduct were incomplete and unreliable and, therefore, there were serious obstacles to testing any hypotheses about the output of firm conduct. While Scherer did not agree with this particular proposition of Bain's, his model also does not connect market performance arising from firm conduct back to market structure. However, the IO paradigm provided the foundation for the subsequent development of the strategic management literature and its strategy-conduct-performance theory discussed later in this chapter.

From this foundation, various theories of industrial organization evolved. Davies (1990:106-119) provided an excellent review of these in the context of the legislative reform of liner shipping in the 1980s. He noted that, within IO economics, there are three distinct schools of thought: the neo-Chicago/UCLA analysis of efficient market structures, game-theoretic analysis[3] (including the theory of the core), and the theory of contestable markets. It has been hotly debated by maritime economists as to whether these last two are appropriate as a foundation for liner shipping regulation.

---

[1]   For example, profit-maximizing may only be one of many goals of the firm and, in today's commercialization moves by government, it may not be an objective at all. A firm may engage in "satisficing" behaviour in order to ensure long-run survival of the firm. For a further evaluation of the premises, see Cyert and March (1963: chapter 2).

[2]   Bain (1959) did not give much weight to the variable of conduct which became key to later discussions of the paradigm.

[3]   Game theory seeks to explain that strategic choices may be influenced by the structure of payoffs arising from competitive actions. Axelrod (1984) undertook a significant analysis of game theory, explaining its basis in the prisoner's dilemma, its key tenets and using these to develop a theory of cooperation. He explored its application to a myriad of situations from warfare to computer-based instruments.

The **neo-Chicago/UCLA** school is organic in thinking; "survival of the fittest" and "natural selection" as Darwinian concepts form its central propositions. Firms and markets are efficient because they have been shaped by market forces, which are more pervasive than in other IO models. Market domination is the result of superior performance. Its detractors noted that market imperfection must exist or the superior performance cannot be sustained; the imperfection would work to prevent successful duplication of the superior performance.[4] The approach also does not appear to provide any opportunity to explore pro-competitive regulatory intervention. However, a variant of this school, as proposed by the population ecologists (Hannah and Freeman, 1977), will be explored later as it does hold some promise in explaining organizational evolution.

In the **game theoretic** approach, firm choices are assumed to be independent, not cooperative. Deterministic models of this school, such as the theory of the core,[5] assume a small number of players thinking logically and acting rationally. Button and Nijkamp (1998) provide, in an appendix to their paper, a graphical explanation of why some empty core situations may emerge in network industries like transportation. Simply stated, the "core" is the set of equilibrium outcomes in game theory; when competitive equilibrium does not exist, it is because the "core" of the market may be empty. That is, equilibrium is not possible and there will never be stability. This situation is argued to be more likely, according to Sjöstrom (1989), when suppliers' minimum average costs demonstrate limited variability, when demand is less elastic, and when excess capacity exists—all conditions acknowledged to be present in the liner shipping market.

Sjöstrom (1989) and Pirrong (1992) have argued that under free market conditions, the liner shipping market will not achieve equilibrium and therefore stability must be imposed.[6] Conferences are seen as agreements which industry players impose on their own performance as a result.[7] Sjöstrom (1989:1161) reasoned that the longevity of conferences and support by the buyers of the services suggested that conferences were an efficiency-enhancing mechanism rather than just a means of extracting monopoly rents. He concluded that because market forces cannot achieve equilibrium and therefore produce a sustainable price, industry members are forced to cooperate in imposing an artificial equilibrium. Without agreements in some form

---

4   This has been addressed by Galbraith and Kazanjian (1978) and others in the strategic management literature who noted that superior performing firms are those that seek new innovation knowing that, ultimately, all existing superior performance will be replicated by astute firms.

5   The theory of the core is best explained by Sjöstrom (1989).

6   Core theory advocates also argue that, in the airline industry, once the airport slot is assigned, the airline has monopoly power and that, in shipping, berth guarantees might do the same thing. Unlike airport capacity where severe congestion rations slots, port capacity is over-built and so berth allocation will not grant a virtual monopoly. As transit time is much more unpredictable due to weather, flexibility in the port system must be greater. The problem of port congestion is unlikely to be an issue in the foreseeable future except, perhaps, in a few key locations. Even so, port authorities are often quick to find government funds to build more facilities at the slightest hint of relocating business.

7   Philosophically this also raises the argument that if industry players act independently then how can the cooperative activity of conferences happen unless imposed by government. It is the industry, not government, that has sought antitrust immunity for conferences.

(conferences or alliances) between industry players, Pirrong (1992) concludes that instability and competitive chaos would exist.

On the other hand, Sjöstrom (1989) pointed out that with more heterogeneous firms, the core is less likely to be empty. He noted that he was unable to test the "heterogeneity of the firm" because there is not an operational definition of heterogeneity. Firms in the shipping industry are widely dissimilar, ranging from small companies with chartered-in ships and family businesses to large diversified enterprises seeking to circle the globe with their own assets. In the liner shipping industry, those entering into global strategic alliances do not appear to be so divergent. This theory, with the high number of theoretically possible outcomes (a consequence of the number of players in the market), has not been rigorously tested, hence the debate.

The third school promulgates the theory of **contestable markets**, first explored by Baumol *et al.* (1982) and based on the competitive consequences of potential entry. The theory of contestable markets has been explored for its relevance to liner shipping most thoroughly by Davies (1984, 1986, 1990) and Gilman (1994). A contestable market is one in which the barriers to entry by new sellers are very low. The existence of potential (not actual) competition, and therefore the height of barriers to entry and exit, determines the contestability of the market.[8]

Perfect contestability has three features: absence of sunk costs (given the charter market to buy or dump capacity), symmetrical positioning of entrant and incumbent (both have the same access to inputs and markets), and price sustainability.[9] If any of these are violated, the applicability of the theory is called into question. While Davies (1986) concluded from his study of the Canadian market from 1976-1979 that the Canadian market was highly contestable,[10] he also noted that the existence of closed conferences violated the principles of market contestability (Davies, 1990:159).

Davies (1990) indicated that in liner shipping all firms face the "common cost" problem.[11] These unattributable fixed costs force firms to recognize that it is in the long-run interest of all firms to engage in revenue maximization through differentiated pricing of differing cargoes. (See Zerby and Conlon (1978) for an illustration of this.) There is widespread recognition throughout the industry that differentiated pricing is the most efficient in this market.[12]

---

8    The issues of barriers to entry and exit for this industry are dealt with in Chapter 3.

9    The last of these issues will arise again in Chapter 8 during an examination of the ability to impose a sustainable price rise. At the end of the day, the ability to impose a price rise that is sustainable is the mark of an industry whose markets fail to protect the public interest.

10   Jankowski (1989) argued that the high level of entries and exits were a sign of unprofitable companies failing, indicating that the market was not contestable.

11   On the other hand, Jansson and Schneerson (1987:223) argued that this problem on large volume routes with a large number of vessels in service has been aggressively exaggerated.

12   Such recognition will ensure that FAK pricing does not succeed in the longer term. FAK or freight all kinds pricing is undifferentiated; all boxes are charged the same price regardless of their contents. A variant of this is the commodity box rate where the existing tariff structure is simplified but it then ceases to meet the "one price" expectation of FAK pricing. (See Chapter 4 for a discussion of this factor.)

One of the key underpinnings of contestability theory is that all players in the industry have similar cost bases. This is a very bold assumption that is not borne out in the marketplace. Shipping is very capital intensive, and it makes a difference whether assets are owned or chartered (leased). In recessions, charter payments can be higher than mortgage payments (resulting in a higher fixed cost to cover) which can, in turn, be higher than the on-going maintenance costs (variable costs) of fully depreciated, mortgage-free older container vessels. There is also the complication of firm structure to alter the cost bases. Firms can alter their structure through diversification into related and unrelated businesses as a means of managing their risk. The strategies of large multinational firms may vary widely as does their ability to manage varying returns on assets. To assume that a firm with its own greenfield marine terminal faces the same terminal charges as one using a full cost recovery, common-user terminal or one using a government-subsidized facility is exceedingly bold. Wide variability in cost bases is, in fact, the explanation for the short-term instability in the industry.

While the entry and exit issues will be dealt with in Chapter 3, new entrant and incumbent symmetry is also suspect as a premise. There is a tendency to forget the investment in terminals and sales organizations that cannot be readily acquired or forgone. Carriers require time and must absorb sunk costs in order to establish customer patronage, although these may be arguably less if the carrier is already well-known because of a "global presence" and established operations in an adjacent market.

The contestability theory has not been accepted by some maritime economists, particularly Jankowski (1989), Gilman (1994) and Heaver (1993); by regulators (Federal Maritime Commission, 1989, and the European Commission[13]); or by industry (according to McConville, 1994).[14] The primary problem with acceptance of the theory of contestable markets lies in the issue of thin routes, and the underlying assumptions about ease of market entry and exit. They are not considered to reflect even a simplified reality. There is also the complication that no one in this industry has agreed on what constitutes a "relevant market." It is difficult to argue about market entry and exit when the concept of market is defined differently by all debaters.[15]

Scherer and Ross (1990:89-102) note that market structure is determined by economies of scale, growth, chance and government policy; the last includes procurement policies, loan guarantees, antitrust and patent laws, tariffs, environmental taxes and so on. These policies may have negative as well as positive consequences. The assumption underlying the industrial organization literature is that the public interest may be enhanced, in cases of market failure, by appropriate government regulation. However, the nationalization of businesses and the severe regulations imposed in the post-WWII era have failed; market forces in the modern

---

13  Commission Decision of 16 September 1998 relating to a proceeding pursuant to Articles 85 and 86 of the EC Treaty (Case No. IV/35.134: Trans-Atlantic Conference Agreement), *Official Journal of the Commission of the European Communities*, L95, 9.04.1999, 1.

14  Although this was generally true at the time McConville (1994) drew his conclusions, TACA drew heavily on the work of Davies, Sjöstrom and Pirrong in the legal defense of its policies.

15  As market definition is the central feature of the competition analyst's approach, it is dealt with in Chapter 8.

economy have grown in importance. As deregulation and privatization continue to occur, the role of regulation must be re-examined.

Firms in this industry are not homogeneous, although there is some question about whether the service produced is a commodity. Any argument put forward in support of a particular element of regulation in this industry should not be based on theories that assume identical firms; such an assumption is not relevant in the current deregulated, market-driven, globalized business environment of the 20th century. There is need of an alternative philosophical approach, one that contemplates the changing dynamics of firm behaviour in a deregulated and liberalized global trading environment.

> *Of course in the real world the trade cycle and the secular forces affecting the evolution of the industry ... will simultaneously influence corporate behaviour and performance.*[16]

## Transaction Cost Analysis and Internalization

Economic theory views integration as a way of reducing transaction costs. Coase (1937) argued that the main cost of transacting in the marketplace is that of learning and haggling over the terms of trade. (Any businessperson would agree that this has not changed in the 60 years since Coase's work was published.) Integration, vertical or horizontal, relocates the risks and the costs of the transacting relationship to within the firm (internalizing it), thereby reducing them. If these risks and costs remain outside the firm, they are gradually mitigated through the implementation of a contractual relationship between the parties.

Internalization theory holds that multinationals grow through foreign direct investment, mergers, or acquisitions in preference to joint ventures or strategic alliances because ownership affords a reduction in transaction costs and enhances the ability of the firm to extract rents from both tangible and intangible assets (Buckley and Casson, 1976; Dunning, 1979; Rugman, 1981). However, internalization theory does not fully explain the reasons for the emerging organizational structures of many capital-intensive global businesses, as seen in Chapter 1 for the shipping industry. The question to be explored in this book is why?

Williamson (1975, 1985) examined transaction costs in the principal-agent relationship and argued that transaction costs are particularly important when economic agents make relationship-specific investments. He noted that firms try to overcome transaction costs by integrating vertically, thereby transforming the market into a hierarchy. By 1985, Williamson's thinking had evolved; he accepted that intermediate forms (such as joint ventures and strategic alliances) could also create frameworks for transactions. Ring and Van de Ven (1992) concluded that this is a dynamic process and that varying combinations of risk and trust will lead

---

[16]   Davies, J. E. (1990:172), *Legislative Change on the North American Liner Trades: A Study of Causes and Consequences*, Ottawa: Transport Canada Economic Analysis. Reproduced with permission of the Minister of Public Works and Government Services Canada, 1999.

transacting parties to choose among four governance structures for their dealings: discrete contracting, recurrent contracting, relational contracting and then hierarchical arrangements.[17]

Mytelka (1991) argued that the internalization theory does not consider the possibility that rents may be appropriated from intangible assets without ownership of the assets. Her work focuses on the cooperative arrangements so evident in high-technology industries, in which it is extremely important to extract the knowledge-based advantages from the relationship. In the case of liner shipping, it might be argued that the sheer capital requirements of the industry deter ownership on the scale necessary to acquire the benefits sought. Tight alliances may allow firms to extract the advantages of merger without completing a merger while such benefits cannot be extracted from looser arrangements. Later in this chapter, the rationale for alliance development will be explored further.

In a contractual agreement (as opposed to a merger), it is highly likely that incomplete contracts will result, because of the high cost of the contract between parties and the pressure of time for its negotiation. That is, there will be some property rights which are not entirely clear.[18] Ambiguity leads the asset owner to exercise control, potentially not in a manner that is mutually beneficial; in an alliance, such exercise of control may cause an unstable relationship to deteriorate and ultimately dissolve. In an acquisition, control of all assets goes to the acquiring entity, called the bidding firm (as opposed to the target firm) in this book. This is another key benefit of internalization over contract-based relationships.

In the transaction cost approach, internalization will take place when it will lower costs for the firm but internalization is not always the best course of action. Internalization only occurs when the result will be a more efficient operation; otherwise, the firm will outsource the activity, possibly entering into incomplete contracts to achieve the desired efficiencies. Williamson (1985) recognized that there will be circumstances in which alternative structures will succeed. Relationships in the globalized world have ceased to be simple. The simple buyer–seller model of business relationships has evolved into a complex web of activity, including horizontal relationships for mutual gain, and business structures that are less able to be neatly categorized.

Williamson (1975) considered that the firm and the market had distinct boundaries. Networks and alliances alter that situation. Gomes-Casseres (1996:3) explained that these collaborative structures blur the boundary between the traditional firm and the traditional market. They reside between the firm and the market combining features of both.

> *Like firms, alliances are ways to govern incomplete contracts between economic actors; like markets, alliances represent decision-making mechanisms in which no one firm has complete authority, and negotiation is the norm.*[19]

---

17  Relational contract-based forms are alliances, partnerships, coalitions, franchises, research consortia and networks. Hierarchical forms imply that mergers or acquisitions have taken place to internalize the transaction costs.

18  For a discussion of incomplete contracts, see Hart (1995:160-4).

19  From *The Alliance Revolution* by Benjamin Gomes-Casseres. © 1996 by the President and Fellows of Harvard College. Reprinted by permission of Harvard University Press.

Today, firms are more porous; soft alliances are part of the web of relationships and equity-based alliances are no longer the only option available to firms choosing not to internalize activities through integration.

There is another explanation for the myriad of organizational structures present today—population ecology. This school of thought is based on the neo–Chicago/UCLA principles of "survival of the fittest" and answers the question of why so many types of organizational structures develop. Hannah and Freeman (1977) proposed that organizations, faced with strong internal pressures and environmental variation (such as might be imposed by multiple jurisdictions), develop differing varieties of excess capacity to provide flexibility in their growth options. Such a view moves the economic literature closer to the strategic management literature, the subject of the next section of this chapter.

Lu and Lake (1997) argued that institutional economics (as presented by Williamson 1975, 1985) provides an important but not entirely adequate explanation for international joint ventures (IJVs) as the relationships in IJVs are more complex than contemplated by the transaction cost perspective. Institutional forces can be deployed by state-linked agencies using regulatory measures to shape or sanction IJV behaviour or to define standards for industry to follow. The problem is that current regulation is set by institutional economics. Dunning (1997) has suggested that capitalism has entered a new phase, that there is a shift from hierarchical capitalism (based on internalization theory) to alliance capitalism, the latter requiring firms to engage in a network of cooperative relationships to extract the most benefits from globalization. In spite of liberalization, countries still have boundaries but competition between firms does not,[20] and hence there is a need to discuss market power and constraints on that power in a broader context as firms globalize their activities. This requires a new platform for regulatory design.

## THE STRATEGIC MANAGEMENT LITERATURE

Unlike the economic model of industrial organization, the strategic management literature is based on the assumption that man is both rational and emotional, and therefore decisions may not always focus on profit-maximizing objectives. The literature proposes a more complex model and is more tolerant of what may be a "right" approach given these conditions. The strategic management literature grew out of microeconomics and sought to explain firm behaviour, drawing not only on economics but on theories from the sociology and psychology literature. However, it could not go down this path in isolation because firm behaviour is influenced by the nature of the industry in which it competes.

Chandler (1962) proposed that structure (of the organization) should reflect the product-market strategy of the firm. That is, organizational structure follows strategy.

---

[20]  This idea was best captured by Ohmae (1989b).

*Strategy can be defined as the determination of the basic long-term goals and objectives of an enterprise, and the adoption of courses of action and the allocation of resources necessary for carrying out these goals.* (Chandler, 1962:13)

Galbraith and Kazanjian (1978) believed Chandler's approach was too narrow and that just matching strategy and organization structure was not all that was required. "[S]trategy must be matched with a compatible, congruent configuration of organizational structure, process, systems, and people for effective financial performance to result." (Galbraith and Kazanjian, 1978: xvii) Performance of the firm was also a product of industry structure and strategy. (See Figure 2.2 for the model they proposed, a model in which firm performance is measured only in financing terms, rather than more broadly as is the practice today.)

## Figure 2.1: Variables Related to Firm Economic Performance

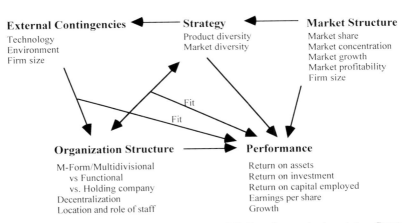

Source:   J. R. Galbraith and R. K. Kazanjian (1978:29, Figure 3.1). From *Strategy Implementation: Structure, Systems and Process, 2nd edition*. Reprinted with permission of South-Western College Publishing, a division of Thomson Learning. Fax 800 730-2215.

They concluded that not all structural forms are effective tools in implementing corporate strategy. Strategic management theory is built on the premise that the process of value creation in mergers and acquisitions, or cooperative arrangements, requires strategic fit between the parties involved. Strategic fit exists when synergies within the combined resources of the firms result in enhanced market power, or economies of scale (larger size or volume increases productivity) or of scope (doing a greater variety of tasks is more efficient than doing fewer). This leads to the concept that firms succeed through superior performance based on their ability to garner market power or cost advantages or offer superior service which creates value for the customer, all based on a concept of fit.

Goold and Campbell (1998) examined the concept of synergy in today's business environment. They concluded that synergy, or the ability of two or more units working together to produce greater value than would be possible by working apart. Synergy takes one of six forms: shared know-how, shared tangible resources, pooled negotiating power, coordinated strategies, vertical integration, and combined business creation. To share know-how would likely mean leakage or erosion of what makes a liner company a superior performer. Shared tangible resources are really only applicable to terminals and ships. Negotiating power is not a key driver for strategic success, while coordinating strategic responses to shared competitors is. The last two imply more than being involved in an alliance and have been successfully implemented in this industry.

Effectiveness of the structure is a function of "fit," or how consistent or congruent all of the organization dimensions are with the strategy. Understanding the firm's core skills is an important component of strategy formulation because fit results if these core skills are matched correctly to strategy.

Competitive advantage accrues to the firm with early strategy-structure fit; the competitive advantage is eroded over time as other firms seek to gain a better fit. If a firm then changes its strategy, it might therefore change its structure. (Incremental changes in strategy may not require structural change.) As explained by Galbraith and Kazanjian (1978), in Stage A, the firm develops a strategy which then must have its structure, Structure A, in keeping with Chandler (1962). If the firm adapts to a changing market environment (market structure) and adopts Strategy B, but retains Structure A, the mismatch leads to a decline in performance, which provokes the firm to develop a new structure, Structure B, resulting in improved performance due to fit. They further argue that only under competitive conditions will performance decline with such a mismatch. If a competitive environment does not exist, as might happen in the case of regulatory failure intended to provide such a competitive marketplace, a firm with Strategy B and Structure A might well maintain its performance with a mismatch.

It is particularly interesting to note that Galbraith and Kazanjian's model shows strategy in a two-way relationship with organization structure. There is very little research that examines the impact of organization structure on firm strategy. This will be examined further in Chapter 7 in the case of the P&O Nedlloyd joint venture.

The dilemma for management in the liner shipping firm then becomes one of managing growth within the broader geographic scope mandated by today's global trading environment. How will that growth be achieved? What organizational structures will provide the best framework for managing the enterprise through growth? If this model of firm behaviour is accepted, the role of the regulator is one of ensuring that the marketplace remains competitive by providing an environment that encourages firm evolution with the consequent outcome of matched strategy and organization structure, thereby exerting further pressure on competing firms to innovate.

Porter (1979, 1980) applied the economist's IO paradigm to the firm, changing the terminology and, as a result, made a significant contribution to the strategic management literature. His analysis of the key elements of industry structure, now commonly known as the Five Forces

Model, has become a classic managerial tool of professional managers seeking to make decisions about how to position their firms in the marketplace.

By using Porter's Five Forces Model, each firm can analyze the structure of its industry and, through the knowledge gained, understand the five forces—power of buyers and suppliers, threats of new entrants and substitutes, and the competitive rivalry these four produce—which shape strategy. Rather than explain this model further here, it will be used at the beginning of Chapter 3 to examine the liner shipping industry prior to developing the new model this book uses to explain liner company strategies and, in particular, their choice of alliance or other structural options.

Based on his analysis of the competitive forces and their impact on industry structure, Porter (1980, 1985) concluded that firms develop three generic strategies to respond competitively to the situation they face: cost leadership, differentiation and focus. (To avoid confusion, this approach will be called Porter's Three Generics.) Implicit in Porter's Three Generics is that firms may choose to respond to a changing industry environment on two dimensions, by seeking cost leadership or differentiation on one and by deciding about the scope of that response (narrow or broad) on the other. It follows then that resource deployment by the firm defines the firm's distinctive competence.

These two concepts provide a framework for examining an industry and a firm's response to that industry at a point in time. They do not explain what happened before that point in time or what will happen after the firm responds to the situation. They do, however, provide a tool for understanding the firm's current competitive environment, the bases on which competition takes place, and suggest strategies that may be developed in response. Their application to the liner shipping industry is developed further in Chapter 3.

Porter (1986) then developed an extended framework (the Global Framework) for global industries. It proposed that the strategies of his Three Generics may be further refined geographically, as global or country-centred in scope. While differentiation or focus strategies may recognize the global market, some country-centred strategies will continue to be developed. The two country-centred strategies of "national responsiveness" or "protected markets" reflect the existence of some governments' measures to protect domestic companies from global competitors, the local reality facing many global industries. In this way, Porter wove in the element of regulatory impact on company strategy.

Shelter-based strategies do not build on firm-specific advantages to achieve satisfactory economic performance, but rely on regulation to protect them from competition. When a firm attempts to impose artificial barriers on foreign competitors through government standards regulation or seeks to protect a domestic market via a differential application of subsidies, it is engaging in a shelter-based strategy. Liner shipping firms employ a shelter-based strategy when they expend resources lobbying for change to legislation instead of investing in innovation and the development of resource or capability-based competitive advantage.

Porter (1986:48) clearly accepted that the shelter-based strategies may emerge as part of the protected industries or national responsiveness strategy (depending on the chosen scope of the firm). Shelter-based strategies are considered as acceptable by some firms when regulatory authorities signal that the market may engage in them without fear. While the demise of shelter-based strategies is a target of current regulatory reform in many markets, too many liner firms appear to rely on shelter-based strategies rather than meet competition in a positive way.

In recent years, the strategic management literature has broadened its base further by taking a resource-based view and attempting to move beyond approaches like Porter's with its industrial economics foundation and its focus on industry characteristics. For example, Rugman and Verbeke (1993) argued that neither Porter's Three Generics nor his Global Framework are sufficiently robust to address international firm strategies; they posited that it is critical to examine firm-specific advantages to fully understand managerial decision-making. The resulting debate underscored the divergence of the two streams of thought, those based on IO paradigm and industrial economics and those based on a behaviouralist approach.

Barney (1986) argued that the nearly exclusive focus by strategists on the combination of products and markets obscured the relevance of a firm's resources as a key component of strategy formulation. What are resources? They are both tangible (assets including financial resources) and intangible—employee knowledge and skill, organizational processes, brand image or firm reputation, and so on. A firm's capability is its ability to use the competencies it achieves as a result of combining and organizing its resources. According to Teece *et al.* (1990), a firm's current capabilities greatly influences its ability to develop new capabilities and the rate at which it can build those capabilities to engage in competence-based competition (Hamel and Heene, 1994). The primary research exploring core competencies was Pralahad and Hamel (1990) and this was, according to Sanchez and Heene (1997), the stream of research that secured the middle ground between applied industrial economics as proposed by Porter and the behaviouralists.

In closing this discussion on the strategic management literature, it is useful to note that even the definition of strategy is not fully agreed. Chandler's (1962) view was updated by Andrews (1971) and then Mintzberg (1978) proposed that strategy was a pattern of objectives and plans in the case of the former or of decisions in the case of the latter; both agreed that strategy was action-oriented. Normann and Ramírez (1993:65) incorporated the concept of value creation into their definition of strategy. They also extended it to include value creation based on the firm's position in the value constellation rather than the value chain. (The term constellation is defined later.) They argued that the creation of value within the constellation is based on the reconfiguration of roles to enhance the fit between competencies and customers. The means to achieve value for the firm, alliance or constellation is its strategy; consistency leads to effectiveness.

As a concluding thought, there has been a tendency in the strategic management literature to consider that the value chain is linear. Perhaps this is no longer the case and a value tree might be a more appropriate term. Successful value creation may take place in different ways on different paths within companies at the branch or root end of the tree but all activities undertaken flow through the trunk either from or to those branches or roots. The trunk may contain more than one path.

## COMMENTARY ON THE ECONOMIC AND STRATEGIC MANAGEMENT LITERATURE

To the IO economist, firms do not have strategy and can only achieve supernormal profits if they gain market power. This is too simplistic. IO economics does not explain the pattern of firm decision-making that takes place within a firm—decisions about scale and scope of activities, internal and external relationships, or indeed, how the firm chooses to relate to its buyers. It is the interface between market structure and organization structure that is central to understanding the role of liner shipping regulation. Firms are no longer individually responsive; in acting collaboratively they have developed and refined their strategic thinking. Response is no longer necessarily direct.

Transaction cost economics has been a useful foundation. It explains when non-market transactions will arise but, because it focuses on dyadic relationships, it is of limited use in understanding network or multi-party relationships. It also has a bias towards opportunistic behaviour and does not fully explain cooperative behaviour, particularly in long-standing relationships where emotional decision-making may result from the development of trust. Game theory, the underpinning of core theory, fails to adequately address why firms may cooperate even when it contradicts their self-interest. Population ecology offers an explanation, but arises not from economics but from sociology. Can the strategic management literature provide an alternative view of firm behaviour, the evolution of industry structure and therefore appropriate regulation?

According to Caves (1980), in any firm the top managers' perceptions of market structure and of the particular firm's strengths and weaknesses determine that firm's choice of strategy (its plan to achieve its goals and objectives) and, subsequently, its choice of structure (the internal allocation of tasks and procedures to implement the strategy). A firm's evaluation of its strengths and weaknesses is only meaningful if conducted in the context of those of its rivals.

Chandler (1962) concluded that a multi-divisional organizational structure is discouraged where there are economies of scale in production, and high capital requirements. These conditions also discourage diversification. On the other hand, high levels of risk and cyclic instability promote risk-spreading through diversification. As all of these features are present in liner shipping, it is no surprise that managerial signals about appropriate organizational structure are mixed. The outcomes seen in the market range from parental and multi-divisional financial risk-spreading entities (including Maersk, P&O, Nedlloyd and Hanjin) to traditional single businesses with little unrelated diversification (Cosco, Evergreen and Zim).

Matching strategy to opportunities and structure to strategy increases a firm's profits and "presumably" increases the efficiency with which society's resources are used (Caves, 1980: 79). Strategies and structures have not followed a common path. Innovations by firms trying to make the best use of opportunities have led individual firms to differentiate their strategies and to follow this decision by developing organizational structures aimed at maximizing fit.

Most important are Caves' (1980) two conclusions. First, the structures of the markets have been affected by the organizational options available to firms in the market. The efficient use of society's resources depends on whether or not firms make the best choice of strategy and organizational structure. As noted by Galbraith and Kazanjian (1978), a competitive environment drives firms to make appropriate matches so that structure will follow strategy and a mismatch will not be encouraged (and therefore sub-optimize the use of available resources). Second, superior strategic and structural choices require optimal individual behaviour (as business performance is a result of individual effort). Strategic choices, therefore, are broader than just firm structure, diversification and vertical integration choices.

To the resource-based strategic management theorists, matching the nature of a firm's resources (or addressable resources[21] held by alliance partners) to market opportunities in the environment is a critical step in developing sustainable competitive advantage for the firm. The concept of addressable resources provides a partial explanation for the growth in strategic alliances.

The strategic management literature builds on economic theory; its foundation has a mortar with economic theory ingredients: the importance of market driven forces and the "free will" of firms. However, the strategic management literature also explicitly recognizes the human elements in decision-making and the existence of firm strategy; competition and cooperation as paths of action are not mutually exclusive. If the economic literature is supplemented by the strategic management literature, a holistic understanding is possible.

If we view organizations as biological organisms—they are run by people and therefore subject to human foibles (opportunism, cheating, short-term thinking) as well as the human ideals that allow adaptation for the benefit of the species (altruism, long-term thinking, kinship and trust)—we have a more complete understanding that reconciles both the economic and the strategic management approaches. It then becomes obvious that regulation and managerial decision-making form a continuous loop, each prompting the other to respond. Industry structure is dynamic as a result of the interaction of the two.

The firm makes its strategic choices taking into account both the larger context of the environment and its industry, and the internal evaluation of its resources, capabilities and competencies. A firm's strategy must include its decisions on scope (both breadth—global, regional, multi- or single trade lane—and range of activities). To implement that strategy, structural options will need to be examined, including the alliance and merger alternatives. The balance of the chapter, therefore, will explore the literature on the structural options firms may choose to implement their strategic growth decisions.

---

21  Assets and intangible resources need not be owned by the company but may merely be accessible or addressable through a partnership with a firm possessing the desired resources.

## STRUCTURAL OPTIONS FOR ORGANIZATIONS

In liner shipping, there is significant firm diversity—not all companies have business interests solely within the broader industry context of ocean shipping. In part, this diversity has resulted from firms seeking new growth opportunities beyond those merely possible from developing new services or expanding to new markets. Alternative growth opportunities may materialize (1) in related businesses, such as terminals, ports or ferries, or even offshore oil and gas projects; (2) through vertical integration or development of logistics service businesses, which may integrate the firm more fully into the supply chain of the buyers of its services; or (3) from peripheral businesses which may only be marginally related, such as hotels or management information services. Such diversity may be considered a strength, if the overall organization sees liner shipping as a critical core business and is prepared to bring the talents of the whole business to support the core shipping business through the current and continuing industry restructuring. Diversity may be a weakness if the organization is not structured in such a way as to support the liner business or to benchmark its performance on other than short-term measures.

It is not worthwhile speculating on how some of shipping's diversified firms got that way. Diversification for financial reasons, whether appropriate or not, was more common in the past. Gardner (1985) examined four shipping companies' efforts and concluded that diversification had resulted from each company's financial state and vulnerability to takeover. The more interesting question is: how will today's shipping companies plan to grow in future? For that question, this book will begin with a straightforward examination of the range of structural options available.

As organic growth offers the greatest control without the complexity of meshing organizational cultures, it is the preferred growth alternative for many companies although it is contingent on whether the opportunity and the resources are available. It is considered by most large firms in the liner shipping industry to be too slow a path to follow given the current market dynamics and the scramble for global scope. Therefore, this book makes no attempt to examine organic growth by liner firms.

What other structural options are appropriate? In addition to full internalization of processes through merger (or acquisition), options run a full gamut from joint ventures to alliances of firms for the purpose of coordinating non-core business activities. Each of the options will first be defined and then discussed in more detail.

**Acquisition**, or buying an existing firm, is often seen as an easy way to grow a business as it confers a full set of capabilities and potentially new markets in a short time. In mature markets, market competition may not be as intense as it would be had the firm chosen to enter the desired market with a new operation. A **merger** is a variant of the acquisition. Firms may choose to merge by exchange of shares or capital or both; the new firm is a combination of two or more and who acquired whom may not be clear until well after the merger takes place and the "winning" management team is chosen.

There also remains the issue of the type of acquisition or merger undertaken, generally classed as related or unrelated. The related acquisition is one that seeks to integrate businesses with strategic fit, and provides an alternative to growth via alliance. The purpose of an unrelated acquisition is diversification of systemic risk with a focus on financial gain and economic success through the internalization of benefits; these types of acquisitions were common in the 1960s.[22] As one alternative to an international strategic alliance is a related acquisition, and competition analysts are most concerned about related acquisitions, unrelated acquisitions will not be dealt with in this book.

As alternatives to mergers or acquisitions, companies seeking to collaborate may establish a **joint venture**. Kogut[23] narrowly defines a joint venture as occurring "when two or more firms pool a portion of their resources within a common legal organization." There are two key properties to Kogut's definition of a joint venture: it must involve joint ownership (its source of control) and it must entail a mutual commitment of assets. The formation of a joint venture does not require the participating firms to pool all their resources. This is clearly compatible with the European Commission's definition of a joint venture, which denotes equity participation and permanency as key elements.

Initially the term **strategic alliance** was used to describe a contractual relationship between a firm with a marketable technology and one with the capability to produce the product and/or bring it to market. (Its application to the transport industry has been much later than in other industry sectors.) Early definitions of alliances included joint ventures and some still do.[24] In all cases, alliance partners remain distinctive and separate corporate entities.

Today, the term strategic alliance is used to describe a wide range of organizational structures in which two or more businesses cooperate for mutual benefit and ideally share common goals; the relationship is symbiotic and voluntary. Like the joint venture, the strategic alliance does not require the firm to pool all its resources. Strategic alliances may be both defensive and offensive. Parkhe (1991:581) defined international strategic alliances as

> *relatively enduring interfirm cooperative arrangements, involving cross-border flows and linkages which utilize resources and/or governance structures from*

---

[22]   According to Shleifer and Vishnay (1991), takeovers in the 1960s were often unrelated diversifications driven by companies with large cash flows as an alternative to paying out dividends. They were driven in part by the aggressive anti-trust policies of the day, and followed Williamson's (1975) thinking that the internal market for capital was better than the external market. Because share prices typically rose on the announcement of these types of acquisitions, shareholders reinforced this "mistake." The 1970s was the period many firms used to divest themselves of those acquisitions that failed. Takeovers in the 1980s were often the reverse, financed by cash for stock, often hostile but related as firms sought to specialize. The anti-trust policy in the US was relaxed under the Reagan administration and, accordingly, the acquisition of related firms more acceptable.

[23]   Kogut, B. (1988a:319), "Joint Ventures: Theoretical and Empirical Perspectives," *Strategic Management Journal*, 9, 4, 319-32. © John Wiley & Sons Limited. Reproduced with permission.

[24]   To Lorange *et al.* (1992) the term "alliances" also includes equity joint ventures and the alliances found in the shipping industry are merely *ad hoc* and not strategic.

*autonomous organizations in two or more countries, for the joint accomplish-*
*ment of individual goals linked to the corporate mission of each sponsoring firm.*

Yoshino and Rangan (1995:2) establish three conditions necessary to a strategic alliance: (1) the firms involved pursue a common set of goals but remain independent after the alliance is formed, (2) they share the benefits and control over performance, and (3) alliance firms contribute to the alliance on a continuing basis in one or more strategic areas.

The term alliance has not yet been institutionalized. In Canada, it implies a full range of business relationships, including joint marketing agreements and equipment-sharing agreements, while in the US and Europe the term has different legal and commercial elements. These differences are critical in the treatment of liner consortia; in the US, a consortium (a strategic alliance of liner firms) is a conference for regulatory purposes (thereby exempt from antitrust) and, in Europe, it is not a conference (thereby requiring a separate exemption). Throughout this book, the term strategic alliance is used in a broad sense, and so includes the concept of consortia, but does **not** imply any equity position or permanence and therefore does not include joint venture activity. The reasons for this clear demarcation should become apparent as the reader proceeds through the book.

Even less clear to many is the difference between alliances, and networks and constellations. As with strategic alliances, definitions remain ambiguous.

Williamson (1985) accepted that there were organizational forms between markets and hierarchies; Thorelli (1986) identified these as **networks**. Networks may have internal competition, which is head-on, but still collaborate; cooperation is indispensable but both intra- and inter-network competition is unavoidable (Thorelli, 1986:43). The example he used is the network of a trade association whose members compete with each other but collaborate to set standards of service. The impact of the network can be imagined when a network (such as a buying organization) is introduced to a marketplace and alters the dynamics of its transactions and the power base of its participants. Thorelli argued that his theory of networks is not a substitute for Williamson's (1975) theory of the firm but is a supplement to it.

There is a tendency to use the terms alliance, network and constellation interchangeably. Basing definitions on a metaphor easily understood by this industry, Grabher (1993) used Richardson's (1972:883) island analogy to define networks as "islands of planned co-ordination in a sea of market relations," while Gomes-Casseres (1996) referred to alliances as an archipelago, not entirely land or sea but a sub-unit of each. He then used the term **constellations**[25] to describe the groups of companies which emerge to compete against other groups and what he calls traditional single firms.[26] Dunning (1997) extended the analogy, likening the network to bridges linking the islands in the archipelago. For the purposes of this book,

---

25  See Normann and Ramírez (1993) for illustrations of constellations.

26  Gomes-Casseres (1996:34) defined an alliance as any governance structure involving an incomplete contract between separate firms and in which each partner has limited control. Therefore his definition of alliance includes a constellation.

network and constellation are used interchangeably and considered to be a set of connected and interdependent relationships; an alliance is more narrowly defined. Transport networks are made up of companies that offer a service from origin to destination, a group of firms operating for mutual benefit.

Alliances, networks, constellations and joint ventures differ from mergers in that they live a life separate from their parent firm. They represent to the parent an inferior alternative if control is what is desired. Their intention and purpose may also be different than that desired by the management of the parent. It may be useful to consider these within the context of the human condition—the entity established may be a fully responsible parental form or some type of a child. If the analogy is accepted, some children may be teenagers wishing to make their own decisions with varying degrees of autonomy while others may not be trusted to look after themselves by controlling parents. The degree of autonomy granted by the parent defines the nature of the structural option in business.

## Mergers (and Acquisitions)

There is a significant and substantial stream of strategic management literature on mergers and acquisitions and how they should be managed to secure maximum benefit. The wide variety of motives ascribed to merger activity is categorized by Trautwein (1990). He concluded that three (of eight) theories of why mergers occur have greater plausibility—the valuation theory (bidding firm shareholders acquire gains through private information and managers claim efficiency goals), the empire-building theory (the merger benefits managers) and the process theory (the merger results from a not completely rational process on which managers embark without full information). Brouthers et al. (1998) explored merger motives of the 47 publicly-traded Dutch firms undertaking mergers in 1994 and found that the most important motivations were to pursue market power and increase profitability. Secondary motives were the creation of marketing economies of scale, the creation of shareholder value and to increase sales. The presence of multiple motives for mergers was supported.

Mergers are a relatively fast means of growth, with significant control of the outcome and opportunity to gain economies through streamlined post-acquisition operations. They represent a major commitment on the part of the company and, as such, send a strong signal to the marketplace. However, they may be accompanied by unwelcome businesses or assets, have a high price,[27] and attract the attention of competition regulators if they are seen to remove a competitor from the market.

As will be seen in later chapters, the key issue in contemplating acquisitions is whether they create value for shareholders. Some have argued that takeovers do not (Ravenscraft and Scherer, 1987, 1989; Alberts and Varaiya, 1989) while others maintained the opposite (Easter-

---

[27] The subject of returns to shareholders in acquisitions is well explored in the strategic and financial management literatures. Allen et al. (1995) found that in the 1960s, acquirers earned abnormal returns, in the 1970s returns were not significantly different from zero, and in the 1980s returns to acquiring firms were negative.

brook and Jarrel, 1984; Bradley, Desai and Kim, 1983). Chatterjee (1992), in his review of the issue, noted that Porter (1987) agreed with the IO school when he found that many acquired firms were subsequently divested by the acquiring firm. Ravenscraft and Scherer (1989) concluded that acquiring firms, on average, have not been able to maintain the target firm's pre-merger levels of profitability while Alberts and Varaiya (1989) discovered that post-acquisition gains to the bidding firm were inadequate to cover the premium paid for the acquisition. Chatterjee's study found that the potential for gains in shareholder value lay with the target firm; however, the evidence rejected synergy as the predominant process by which value creation takes place. Restructuring was favoured as the source of shareholder value gain, because capital markets perceive takeovers as motivated by the need for firms in the industry to restructure. Those gains are then achieved as the efficiency of all firms is improved through the adoption of more effective strategies as a result of the restructuring. Datta *et al.* (1992) concluded that it is better to be a seller (target) than a buying firm.

## Joint Ventures

When Kogut (1988a) examined the rationale for the formation of joint ventures, he married three literature streams: transaction cost analysis, strategic management and organizational learning.

Transaction costs analysis led him to argue that the following situation must exist for joint ventures to be the best structure for management of the business: high uncertainty,[28] high asset specificity[29] and frequent transactions.[30] Kogut concluded that joint ventures, a mutual hostage situation, are effective because they have a superior alignment of incentives plus agreement on the division of costs and profits and are, therefore, an efficient structure to deal with economic uncertainty.

On the strategic management front, Kogut noted that Vernon (1983) saw joint ventures as a form of defensive investment enabling firms to hedge against strategic uncertainty, especially in industries characterized by moderate concentration and where collusion is difficult to undertake.[31] The motivations may also be to deter entry or erode competitors' positions.[32] Therefore, he concluded that joint ventures may be used to deal with competitive rivalry and enhance market power through collusion.

---

[28] Uncertainty exists more on the supply side than the demand side for liner shipping.

[29] Asset specificity is the degree to which assets are specialized. Although container ships are desired specifically for some routes and to conduct the business, generic (and non-post-Panamax) vessels may be easily redeployed to a new route. It is not entirely clear whether the asset-specificity test is met; joint ventures were common in liner shipping throughout the 1980s but are not as popular now.

[30] The third condition posited by Kogut is met.

[31] Vernon (1983). The first of these is met but the existence of conferences would argue that collusion is easily undertaken.

[32] Kogut (1988a:322) noted that Vickers (1985) explored research joint ventures as a means of deterring entry through pre-emptive patenting.

As for organizational learning, Kogut also saw an additional advantage accruing to a joint venture: the ability to acquire organizational knowledge from the joint venture partner, providing further motivation for its selection as a suitable organizational structure. Kogut's findings were supported by Harrigan and Newman (1990), who examined a range of equity-based and non-equity (alliance) alternatives for organizational cooperation, identifying the factors behind firms' propensity to choose a joint venture alternative over other options; these were the benefits of cooperation, the resources offered against the costs of such cooperation, the need for the firm to cooperate and the other alternatives available.

Kogut (1988a) noted that joint ventures have greater mutual alignment of incentives that motivates partners to adapt to the changing environment than is the case in merely contractual agreements. To him, there is more at stake in making the relationship work; IJVs are a better means of reducing transaction costs and facilitating internal communication than contractual relationships, including alliances. Harrigan (1988) remarked that joint ventures also offer the firm the ability to engage in incremental divestiture! As will be seen, they share that potential with alliances.

### Alliances, Networks and Constellations

Alliances have been described as mimicking the old adage of 1 + 1 = 3; they offer two players more than the sum of the parts. An alliance may grant a participant, with very little investment, access to new markets or the opportunity to expand its geographic reach or acquire market share. There is also the chance to streamline operations with a new partner, or share and manage risk in expansion. Alliances may combine the complementary strengths of current competitors for mutual gain, or afford access to the expertise of a new partner. Alliances may, for example, narrow the gap between leaders and second-tier firms by enabling groups of smaller firms to challenge the market power of a leader. There is the added advantage of greater flexibility in managing the alliance than is possible via merger, acquisition or joint venture; therefore an alliance is likely to have fewer barriers to exit than exists with the previous options.[33] For some companies, one of the more important benefits bestowed by some alliance structures is the maintenance of a separate marketing identity. For liner shipping firms, the two key factors favouring alliances are the benefits of network configuration (to meet market needs while maintaining a separate identity) and the ability to extract the company from the relationship with minimal effort if benefits are not realized. There is also the speed with which an alliance can be implemented.

Lorange *et al.* (1992) proposed four generic motives for the formation of strategic alliances, dependent on the strategic importance of the activity in the parent's portfolio of activities and the protagonist's position as leader or follower in the market. If the activity is part of the parent's core business, the leader will defend its position through an alliance while a follower will use the alliance to try and catch the leader. On the other hand, if the business is peripheral

---

[33]    Harrigan (1983) explored the benefits of alliances in greater detail while Varadarajan and Cunningham (1995) examined motives for alliance formation and factors influencing a firm to enter into alliances.

to a firm's core activities, the alliance allows the leader to remain active in the business, deriving maximum benefit from its position while follower firms can use the alliance to restructure peripheral activities. This implies that all firms may usefully deploy alliances to secure, defend or acquire market position.

Burgers *et al.* (1993) concluded that alliances are a device to reduce both demand uncertainty and competitive uncertainty. Ciborra (1991) argued that firms engage in alliances to reduce transition costs, costs incurred when companies undergo a drastic restructuring, whether externally or internally instigated. Gomes-Casseres (1996) identified a number of pressures for alliance formation: desire to gain first mover advantages of scale, scope and standards; imitation of rival groups to reduce risk; and efforts to pre-empt rivals from linking up with attractive partners. He also noted that alliance formation may be limited by a scarcity of unattached partners (Gomes-Casseres, 1996).

The key feature of alliances—shared control—also limits the alliance's ability to deal with internal conflict. For this reason, mergers are often seen by firms as a preferable strategy if potential conflict occurs in areas of geographic overlap; a merger rationalizes the conflict away. On the other hand, Lundvall (1993) pointed to two reasons why firms may be reluctant to pursue a strategy of vertical integration: loss of flexibility and the limited scope of inter-active learning. Both of these are offered by alliances. Grabher (1993:13) provided probably the most compelling reason for alliance formation in preference to acquisitions:

> *they [alliances] are a means of pooling complementary assets and competences without abrogating the separate identity and personality of the cooperating partners. ...Whereas acquisitions regularly lead to a 'mashing' of the different corporate cultures...*[34]

According to Gomes-Casseres (1996), the choice of alliance as business structure arises from the firm's examination of three elements—capabilities, control and context. If the firm has sufficient capabilities internally, it can choose to "go-it-alone." If not, it may seek an alliance. The single firm has full control, while in the alliance control is shared. Finally, the context refers to the environment and the opportunities it creates.

This leads to a number of questions about the role of the firm in its transport network; these need to be answered before strategic planning activities can identify appropriate structural options. What does the transport network do? Where does knowledge of customers, routes and systems reside within the network? How does each firm deal with human capital assets within the network? What speed of diffusion of the firm's technical know-how can be expected from its relationships with other firms in the network? (Is the knowledge a commodity?) Therefore, what organizational learning is necessary and can it better be gained through an owned structure or an alliance? For each firm, the answers may result in a different choice of implementing

---

34  Grabher, G. (1993), "Rediscovering the Social in the Economics of Interfirm Relations," *The Embedded Firm: On the Socioeconomics of Industrial Networks*, G. Grabher, ed., New York: Routledge, 1-31. Reproduced with permission.

organizational structure within the range of possible networks in which to participate. This book does not address network choice but only firm growth alternatives within a network.

## THE FAILURE OF ORGANIZATIONAL REDESIGN

The pattern of merger and acquisition activity has changed over time. While in the 1960s and 1970s multinationals tended to pursue conglomerate deals providing the advantages associated with diversifying financial and operating risk, businesses in the 1990s favoured strategic acquisitions, with relatively little debt incurred and friendly agreements combining complementary resources across borders (Morosini, 1998:3-4). During the 1980s, horizontal deals were pursued and it was noted by Brush (1996) that many of these were focused on unwinding the early diversification strategies of conglomerates. His study confirmed that, in evaluating the effects of performance of the acquisition, the researcher should control for industry effects as resources and activities contribute to firm performance in a manner that is unique to the particular industry.

Morosini (1998) noted that numerous studies of post-acquisition performance over the past two decades have found that between 50% and 80% of all mergers and acquisitions fail financially; time does not seem to have improved these statistics.[35] He concluded that the continuing mixed economic results of this activity can be linked to the focus of senior executives on the strategic and financial areas of the business before the merger, and their failure to deal with organizational, cultural and personnel issues until after the deal is concluded.[36] Due diligence on an acquisition is usually financial and not on its corporate culture, its networks or its processes for decision-making.

This conclusion is supported by Chatterjee *et al.* (1992) who found an inverse relationship between perceptions of cultural differences and shareholder gains. They found that capital market perceptions about the earnings impact of mergers are associated with perceptions of cultural differences at the top management level and that management of the buying firm should pay as much attention to cultural fit as to strategic fit.

Joint venture survival rates are not heart-warming either. Contractor and Lorange (1988) pointed to the complexity of parent companies trying to cooperate as partners in international joint ventures. Although they derive benefits, such as sharing costs, reducing risks and acquiring knowledge from their partner (Hamel, 1991), they generally have differing strategic

---

[35] Porter (1987) found that acquisitions have a high failure rate. Mercer Management confirmed that 57% of merged firms lagged behind other firms in their industries in terms of returns to shareholders, as reported by Anonymous (1997).

[36] This view is supported by studies by Kitching (1967), Datta (1991) and Schmidt and Fowler (1990). The first concluded that the keys to a successful merger were the manner in which the transitional process was managed and the quality of the relationship between the merging organizations. The second found a correlation between differences in managerial style and poor merger performance. The last pointed to the challenges of differing personnel policies with respect to executive compensation post-acquisition. A study by McKinsey reported by Anonymous (1997) confirmed this problem with mergers.

objectives (Beamish, 1988). This stresses the stability of the joint venture. Killing (1982) and Kogut (1988b) concluded that joint ventures are very unstable, with Kogut reporting 24% failure rate in the first three years.

Therefore, the type of strategic alliance being seen in the global liner shipping industry is likely less stable than IJVs as the incompleteness of its contracts adds fragility. IJVs tend to have more complete contracts with respect to shareholding, ownership rights and corporate governance than do alliances.

The failure rate for alliances in other industries is considered to be high. Bleeke and Ernst (1993a:9) reported that approximately half of cross-border alliances terminated within seven years. Termination may not equal failure if the termination resulted in one partner acquiring the other; both firms received the benefit the alliance was built to gain or the alliance terminated as planned at the outset. Hamel (1991:101) noted that a long-lived alliance may reflect that partners had failed to learn. Failure cannot be deduced from discontinuation of an alliance as it is in the eye of the participant.

Why do alliances fail? A number of authors have reported reasons such as unrealistic expectations, differing objectives, cultural issues, and so on. The discovery of differing agendas is probably the most disappointing to alliance proponents. Bleeke and Ernst quote colleagues in Japan as saying that nothing is worse than "two partners in the same bed with different dreams."[37]

Most interesting is the research by Bleeke and Ernst (1995) in which they proposed a typology that predicted likely outcomes for each of six types of alliance based on an analysis of more than 200 in a broad range of industry and service sectors. They argued that the future of the alliance will depend on the bargaining power between the alliance partners and its evolution, the competencies of the partners and their ability to garner strength. Based on this typology (Bleeke and Ernst, 1995:103), they predicted that the first four categories of alliances—collisions between competitors, alliances of the weak, disguised sales, and bootstrap alliances—would be short-lived or generally unsuccessful. These would ultimately result in dissolution of the alliance, or acquisition by the alliance partner or a third party. The only alliances predicted as likely to have longevity, i.e. lasting more than seven years, are those that will evolve into a sale or are alliances of complementary equals.

Pilling and Zhang (1992), based on their study of cooperative relationships between buyers and suppliers, argued that the primary threat in any cooperative relationship is the risk of opportunistic behaviour on the part of one of the parties. Any long-term cooperative relationship entails some measure of mutual dependency and vulnerability; therefore, it is incredibly important to the success of the relationship that the rationale for choice of partner is well-understood and that the relationship is monitored for performance on those factors. Likewise,

---

37  Bleeke, J. and D. Ernst (1993a:9), "The Death of the Predator," *Collaborating to Compete: Using Strategic Alliances and Acquisitions in the Global Marketplace*, Bleeke, J. and D. Ernst, eds., New York: John Wiley & Sons Inc., 1-10. © John Wiley & Sons, Inc. Reprinted by permission.

the greater the equity of the relationship, the greater its chances for success. This is in direct contrast to Harrigan (1988) who suggested that partner traits are less important that industry characteristics in determining the outcome of the relationship.

## ALLIANCE OR MERGER—WHAT MAKES A SUCCESSFUL STRATEGY?

What causes a particular strategy to be successful is the critical question for management. Although what defines success will depend on the initial purpose of the alliance or the acquisition, there are a number of factors that have been identified as relevant to the outcome of a structural decision.

If acquisition is the route to growth, Bleeke *et al.* (1993) identified these to be the hallmarks of successful cross-border acquirers:

- Targets are in their core business and are strong local performers.
- The resources of the target's business are focused on a few critical elements, especially those that are global.
- Significant 'skills transfer' to and from the target company takes place post-acquisition.
- Critical systems are integrated by 'patching' them together initially; the urge to spend heavily is resisted by the acquirer.
- Acquisitions are part of a continuing strategy.

However, Ravenscraft and Scherer (1989) found that the profitability of target firms, on average, declines after acquisition, suggesting faulty implementation plans or processes. Bleeke and Ernst (1993a) concluded that companies that take a purely financial and deal-driven approach to acquisitions **and** alliances usually run into difficulty.

What are the hallmarks of a successful alliance? This question is less quickly answered, perhaps because alliances can be so varied in nature. A number of studies have been undertaken, all with quite different foci.

Bleeke and Ernst (1993b) indicated that both cross-border acquisitions and cross-border alliances have similar chances of success (57% and 51%). They maintained that different strategies are suitable under differing circumstances; cross-border acquisitions work best in situations where there are commonalties in the core businesses and there is considerable overlap in the existing geographic areas served by the companies. On the other hand, these conditions do not auger well for a successful cross-border alliance. The success rate of alliances between companies seeking to grow a core business in an overlapping geographic market was only 25%, while the same conditions resulted in a 94% success rate for the acquisition strategy. When both alliance partners have a presence in the geographic market, there is competitive conflict. There is also the likelihood that the alliance will evolve to a sale; of the alliances they studied, 75% terminated with an acquisition by one partner. Therefore, absence of geographic overlap is critical to long-term success of an alliance.

If the alliance is established to share assets or develop economies of scale in operations, its longevity may differ significantly from one established to promote organizational learning. Porter's (1986) conclusion that knowledge acquiring coalitions are more likely to dissolve once access to knowledge is gained conflicts with Kogut's (1989) findings. In Kogut's study of 92 manufacturing firms, he discovered that joint ventures involving R&D-intensive industries tended to dissolve less frequently than those in other industries, explaining that knowledge transfer or creation provided a more potent incentive towards cooperation.

A number of authors (e.g., Bartlett and Ghoshal, 1989; Hamel, 1991) have concluded that the key to success in the global marketplace is the ability to capture and manage learning. Such learning may be "captured" via acquisition but may not be managed most effectively. Such knowledge capture may also take place in alliances. Hamel (1991) noted that corporations that "out-learn" their alliance partners will be competitively vulnerable, particularly if the purpose of the collaboration was internalization of the alliance partner's skills.

Another key to success is flexibility. Bleeke and Ernst (1993a:5-6) argued that successful alliances are those that continually redefine their geographic or product (or service) scope; an alliance that proceeds without such evolution is more likely to fail. They also argued that successful alliances are those that seek to build relationships, conflict-resolution mechanisms and timetables for re-evaluation of the arrangement. This is in direct contrast to the thinking of Håkansson and Johanson (1993) who indicated that analyzing the costs (and benefits) triggers failure because the intangible value of trust is not measurable.

Parkhe (1993a) concluded that structural properties of alliances can be used to differentiate stable, high-performing alliances from unstable poor performers. The structuring of a longer-term relationship, where trust is present due to both a past history of cooperative relationships and perceived lack of opportunistic behaviour on the part of management, goes some way to securing alliance stability. Behavioural transparency and frequent interaction were also found to help build superior performance. Parkhe suggests that structured mechanisms to provide real-time information to partners will enhance behavioural transparency and support successful performance.

One of the dilemmas discussed in the economic literature has been how to separate individuals who have a propensity to act opportunistically from those who do not. Parkhe (1993a) addressed this issue using game theory to analyze strategic alliance outcomes. He found support for the hypothesis that the performance of the alliance will be negatively related to the extent to which those involved perceive the other partner as behaving opportunistically. He also discovered that the perception of opportunistic behaviour will fade with a history of cooperation between the partners.[38]

Overcoming cultural issues is particularly important to the success of globally-oriented strategic alliances. Cultural issues may be seen from two perspectives: the national charac-

---

[38]  This particular finding is tentative, however, given the potential of error due to the limited number of cases assessed on this construct (Parkhe, 1993a:817).

teristics of the home country management and the internal management style of the organization (or its corporate culture). The first is likely to impact most seriously in the areas of decision-making and control. For example, Perlmutter and Heenan (1986) suggested that US managers are by nature less cooperative, believing that power should control cooperative relationships, while their European and Japanese counterparts are more likely to engage in consensus decision-making and secure progress through building shared commitment to goals. Ohmae (1989a) has confirmed the US firm's need for control in strategic alliances and the preference for 51% or more in equity relationships while Thorelli (1986) noted the importance of trust in alliances involving Japanese firms. Parkhe (1993b) explored the linkage between alliance structure and performance, finding that the strength of the linkage was moderated by partner nationality. To promote a successful alliance, Bleeke and Ernst (1993b) recommended equality of participation in the alliance so that it becomes a win-win situation instead of a zero-sum game; that is, neither parent controls the relationship.

Hofstede's work (1980, 1991) on culture has been widely accepted in international management circles. He assumed that the underlying values of culture are stable over time, and that "distance" between national cultures also remains stable. In recent years, it has been argued that cultures are converging and that these assumptions are no longer valid. Barkema and Vermuelen (1997) posited that for some products (e.g., entertainment, jeans, fast food) consumer culture is converging but managerial culture is not. Their research supported Hofstede's original assumptions about culture, but showed that some dimensions of culture are more troublesome than others in the tradeoff between foreign market entry via joint venture or wholly owned subsidiary. They concluded that survival rates for joint ventures are still hurt by cultural distance, primarily by the uncertainty avoidance and long-term orientation dimensions, less so for the masculinity dimensions and not significantly for the power distance and individualism dimensions.[39]

As for mismatches in managerial style (the implementation of business practices reflecting managerial culture), these have paved a road of failure in all types of corporate restructuring. Organizations that are autocratic or have a top-down management style do not integrate well with or relate well to businesses based on grass roots, bottom-up managerial approaches. Datta (1991) found that compatibility of management style is important to superior post-acquisition performance with managerial conflict resulting in poor post-acquisition performance. In 1990s-style mergers, where it is more common for mergers to result from share exchanges, control will accrue to the stronger entity. The personalities of individuals can be as important as personalities of firms. The same is potentially true of alliances; the personality of the firm is a

---

[39] Hofstede (1980) posited culture to be based on a number of value dimensions, with different cultures located in different positions along these dimensions. Uncertainty avoidance (and attitudes towards risk) are quite different in the Japanese than in American managers, for example. Masculinity, as another example, has to do with the importance of family and social norms to the culture, playing a greater role in more feminine societies. Under Hofstede's typology, Latin American firms are more feminine than their North American counterparts. Power distance is an important dimension for organizational structure, measuring the superior-subordinate relationship, while individualism versus collectivism will influence decision-making processes.

factor as much as the personality of its CEO in the success of the implementation of any growth strategies.

Finally, Parkhe (1993a) found that the performance of a strategic alliance was positively related to the expectation of a long time horizon for the alliance; such a conclusion has importance for regulators if time-defined alliance regulations are imposed.

## CONCLUSIONS

As this book seeks to provide food for thought for both firms and regulators within the liner shipping industry, this chapter has laid down some of the economic and strategic management literature used by the two groups to justify the positions they take. As a result, the groundwork has been laid for managers to understand the industrial organization school of thought and the acceptance or rejection of contestability and core theory as a means of explaining the impact of regulation and market structure on liner shipping. The strategic management literature has been presented in an effort to provide understanding to regulators about the strategic managerial decision-making that may take place at the firm level. This chapter has also examined the ways firms grow and the option of collaboration as one path to growth.

In the past century, firms have evolved from entities seen as adversarial in a market of hierarchical capitalism; this model assumed there was little need for cooperation and, when the market failed, the firm chose to exit (replace the market by internal administrative fiat, that is internalization) rather than work to improve it. Today, firms are more cooperative, and "voice" strategies are more common than was previously the case.[40] Dunning (1997) noted that if the voice response is the outcome, the advantages of internalization occur (within an alliance) but without the disadvantages of inflexibility, bureaucracy or risk.

> *The key to achieving the right balance between competition—a "go it alone strategy"— and cooperation—a "do it together strategy"—seems to rest on the perception of managers about the nature and strength of their distinctive or core competitive advantages, relative to those of their competitors...* [41]

The next two chapters will examine the managerial view of competitive advantage in liner shipping. Using Porter's Five Forces Model introduced in this chapter, Chapter 3 will look more closely at industry structure, the firm's competitive positioning and strategic responses, both in terms of strategy elements and in terms of that strategy being a competitive or a collaborative one or a mixture of the two. Chapter 4 will then examine strategy implementation issues and focus on how a firm may successfully implement a strategy for its business, either

---

40  Hirschman (1970) introduced the concept of "Exit" or "Voice" strategies. Exit strategies are methods to circumvent either endemic or structural failure while voice strategies are those whereby firms try to work with buyers or sellers to reduce or eliminate market failure. Helper (1993) studied companies in the US automobile industry using an exit-voice analysis.

41  Dunning, J. (1997), *Alliance Capitalism and Global Business*, New York: Routledge, p. 360. Used with permission.

go-it alone or within an alliance, concluding with a section on making the cooperative relationship a successful one.

Cooperative strategies have evolved but not yet matured. Firms have become more collaborative to extend market reach, share the costs and increase the speed of innovation. Are such new cooperative arrangements anti-competitive or do they improve efficiency within the marketplace? This is the question that regulators need to contemplate. To do so, Chapters 5 to 7 will examine three sets of case studies of firms' decisions to merge or enter into a cooperative arrangement. Having then laid the foundation of managerial decision-making the final two chapters will return to the regulation of the industry. Chapter 8 will take the competition analyst's view of the arrangement and Chapter 9 will explore regulatory response alternatives with a vision of laying a foundation for global harmonization of the regulatory environment.

# 3

# THE STRATEGIES OF LINER COMPANIES

## INTRODUCTION[1]

The purpose of this chapter is to explore the liner shipping industry from a managerial perspective. It begins with a review of the nature of the industry, using Porter's Five Forces Model (briefly discussed in Chapter 2) and examines how these forces influence strategic responses made by firms. This leads to a discussion of the environment in which firms in the industry make strategic decisions. A framework of the strategy development process specific to liner operators is then presented. This framework provides an approach for considering new strategy development, including the alliance or merger (and acquisition) decision made by firms. The chapter concludes with a framework for thinking about growth strategies, be they mergers, acquisitions, joint ventures or alliances in their many forms.

However, before industry structure can be discussed, there is the small matter of understanding the firm's starting point. For the purposes of the discussion, the assumption is that the firm already exists. It has assets it deploys in a network to serve existing customers with a schedule of services, each of which is priced; all of these are variables the firm can control and manage. As will be evident later, the firm's strategic decision process will generate a new strategy in the future which may alter these variables as part of an implementation process. Firms that do not evolve strategically within a dynamic industry structure will eventually run into difficulty. As organisms evolve so do firms; this chapter will provide a framework for exploring managerial thinking. In this chapter, the framework will be tailored to liner firms; in subsequent chapters it will be used to examine managerial thinking in other industries.

## AN ANALYSIS OF INDUSTRY STRUCTURE

In Chapter 2, Porter's Five Forces Model was introduced as a variation on the classic industrial organization paradigm. In order to understand the environment of the liner shipping industry, this chapter examines these five forces as they pertain to the industry. To recap, the five com-

---

1   Some of the material in this chapter is based on work originally published in Brooks (1993) and re-used here with permission. It has been updated to focus on the material relevant to this book and extended further to incorporate new thinking and develop the model presented in Figure 3.2.

petitive forces seen by this model are the entry of new competitors, the threat of substitutes, the bargaining power of buyers, the bargaining power of suppliers, and rivalry among competitors.

## The threat of entry of new competitors[2]

Ever since the formation of the first liner shipping conference, the existence of shipping conferences has served to limit capacity and raise the barriers to entry. Typically, carriers enter the market as non-conference operators using chartered tonnage and then, once established, are co-opted into the conference to stabilize rates, leaving the market susceptible to a new low-priced entrant. In many jurisdictions, rebates and loyalty contracts are deemed anti-competitive and carriers, cautious about jeopardizing their antitrust exemptions, are more likely to seek alternative ways of raising barriers to entry. For example, a line may increase capacity on a particular route to act as a barrier to entry (or as a pre-emptive grasp for market share) or may invest in terminals, inland facilities or agency networks to achieve a similar outcome. Since the promulgation of the US *Shipping Act of 1984,* service contracts and independent action have eroded the ability of conferences to establish the premium rates needed to ensure the continuing long-term profitability of conference operators.

The largest barrier to entry is the requirement for matched or nearly matched ships in order to serve a particular route. To mount a credible service on the longest of the routes, the Europe-Far East trade, nine or ten similar or matched ships are required. The capital cost of providing this injection of capacity is both uneven and massive. Although it is possible to find a few similar ships in the charter market, generally speaking the cost of entry is extremely high. The need for matched ships has led in part to the growth of slot charters over the past decade. In addition, the specialization of the asset (container ship) serves as a barrier to exit. The existence of more tonnage than demanded makes exit difficult as vessel salvage value is often related to the value of the mill's steel as opposed to the value of the asset on the books or in the second-hand market.

Vessel availability in the charter market waxes and wanes throughout the business cycle. There always appears to be a surplus of older, smaller vessels for snipers to employ, although the availability of matched ships may only be possible through new ordering. Some routes have specific requirements, such as ice-class vessels for winter ports, shallower draft vessels for ports with heavy silting or locks, and so on. Deployment is, therefore, an integral part of the asset choice decision.

It is important to remember that the new entrant also needs to have credibility in the market, so that shippers will have confidence that using the carrier will not result in their containers being delayed or, worse, arrested. Such credibility will be more difficult for a new start-up rather

---

2   In addition to this issue being important for understanding industry structure, it is also a critical factor in the analysis undertaken by competition authorities in examining the relevant product market; therefore, this issue is discussed further in Chapter 8.

than an existing firm as it is likely the existing firm already has an experienced sales force and established image, albeit not associated with the new trade lane.

Marine terminals may not be a barrier to entry, depending on the particular trade route. It is customary for port facilities to be over-built. This is driven by the high capital cost of shipping and the ports' desire not to lose the business due to inability to service a carrier without delay. Lack of berth space is not usual if the carrier is prepared to use common use facilities and the port is in the typical situation of excess capacity. Where marine terminals may be a barrier to entry is on routes where dedicated terminals are the norm and common user facilities are unable to meet the schedule demands of a new entrant. It is more likely that marine terminals are a barrier to exit if a carrier has invested significantly in a dedicated terminal it no longer wishes to use.

It has been argued that knowledge is not a barrier to entry. This is not true. A nominal understanding of the container shipping business and the needs of its customers is a competitive necessity. A study of shippers in seven countries (Brooks, 1995) and their requirements of carriers identified the carrier's ability to solve problems as being of paramount importance when choosing which carrier to use. How can a carrier solve its customer's problems if the knowledge needed to do so is not available?

Finally, for many global manufacturing concerns, global coverage is mandatory for a carrier's inclusion on the list of approved suppliers, thereby becoming a necessity for carriers wishing to participate in the high volume end of the business and raising barriers to entry by start-up carriers.

## The threat of substitutes[3]

The practice of splitting business among competitors provides solid evidence of substitutability. Some shippers prefer to arrange service contracts with volume guarantees in return for price concessions and therefore may be emotionally captive due to managerial preferences. Those with a different philosophy will seek to split their business, perhaps to minimize potential risk. Some are quite satisfied to split their business among conference carriers only, while still others want to split their business between conference and non-conference carriers or between container and breakbulk.

The low end of the market is open to competition from **breakbulk** but containerization has gradually eroded the share held by breakbulk. In particular products, such as lumber from Eastern Canada, modal switching is common. Committed breakbulk shippers have become less than enthusiastic about this mode. For most products, breakbulk is not a viable option. It is not a substitute for shippers of hazardous products because of environmental concerns. Breakbulk,

---

[3] This too is a critical factor to competition authorities in examining the relevant product market; therefore, it is discussed further in Chapter 8.

substitution is highly product-specific and often concluded by competition analysts to be marginal.

The top end of the market is open to competition from **air cargo** and air cargo's share has been growing steadily. In the early 1980s, high interest rates and the carrying costs associated with inventory in transit contributed to tremendous growth in the air cargo industry. Air cargo's share of total trade moved in 1985 was 13.7% (Sclar and Blond, 1991). Since 1970, world revenue tonne kilometres (RTKs) have grown at a rate of 8% per annum, 2.5 times the rate of GDP growth and growth is expected to continue at a baseline rate of 6.7% per annum (Boeing, 1997). There has been rapid growth in air cargo moved in the belly of passenger planes, with forecasts of belly cargo share of the total air cargo market expected to move from 48% in 1990 to 59% in 2014 (Boeing, 1996). Furthermore, erosion from sea-air combinations continues to threaten the more profitable portion of the container shipping market. However, this substitute is only available to the shipper of high value products, usually the one for whom a price rise is less of an issue.

**New technologies** also pose a threat; FastShip proponents argue that transit time on the North Atlantic between Sweden and Philadelphia can be reduced to 3.5 days from the current 8 to 10 days and the technology allows for turnaround in 1 to 2 hours (Svensson, 1995). Market analysts predict that 18% of north Atlantic traffic is of a sufficiently high value and time-sensitive that the higher cost of FastShip will not deter switching (Pocock, 1999). In conclusion, substitution is possible at the margins; for most traffic substitutes do not exist in a significant way.

## The bargaining power of buyers

The power of buyers is partly route-dependent. Where significant cargo imbalances exist, buyers on the well-utilized leg have less clout. Where significant excess capacity exists on a particular route, buyers have more power. Some buyers are blessed with a strong position even in an intensely competitive market; they may have so much volume that carriers may price below average cost or give away value-added services to retain their business. Most carriers would prefer to service large shippers and freight forwarders rather than to make the effort necessary to service small buyers; many carriers believe that their margins cannot support servicing this segment of the market, leaving a large number of small buyers with little, if any, clout in their relationships with carriers.

Buyer power is also product-specific as most carriers operate on a commodity-based tariff rating system rather than offering FAK (freight all kinds) rates. Large volume buyers shipping high value goods are better able to protect shipment space while, at the other end of the continuum, small shippers of relatively low value goods can be shut out. For example, Canadian peat moss producers shipping into Europe are often shut out when the Canada–Europe eastbound leg is close to capacity; carriers will make room for a higher revenue product at the expense of the low-rated peat moss. Because traffic westbound into Canada has a lower density per TEU, European shippers of low value goods may have little difficulty finding space westbound into Canada as the ship is less likely to have "weighed out."[4] Buyer power is unlikely to diminish in the near term as manufacturers continue to control the cargo and carriers continue to struggle with excess capacity.

## The bargaining power of suppliers

For the carrier, the power of the suppliers is limited. The continuing sorry state of the shipbuilding industry has often meant vessel prices are depressed. As for labour, the supply of seafarers has been likened to a "Dutch Auction" for those carriers for which price is paramount. However, the carrier seeking quality seafarers to protect its investment in the ship (as is more common in the liner end of the shipping business) is facing a potential shortage of well-trained seafarers (Moreby, 1990). Finally, there is clearly a surplus of flags of convenience from which to choose the fiscal environment most likely to produce a black bottom line.

The provision of land-based elements in the international door-to-door movement of goods is the one area where not all container carriers have equal access to supply inputs. In some cases, ocean carriers have vertically integrated into land-based activities—terminals, trucking services and so on. Where inputs are sought through negotiation, the bargaining power of the trucking and rail transport industries varies widely throughout the world; in some cases, the ocean carrier holds the balance of power, while in others it is the inland transport operator.

## Rivalry among competitors

The conference system is intended to limit rate-based competition. It used to be that if a buyer desired a reliable, high quality service there was little choice but to pay a premium price, the conference price. Now buyers are finding it increasingly difficult to perceive the differences between conference and non-conference carriers; they switch to non-conference operators for price reasons and then often report that the service differences are insufficient to encourage their return. On some routes, container transport services are viewed to be homogeneous.

Some carriers have developed strong customer relationships. In cases where the value of the goods is quite high, shippers have often shown that they prefer to deal with the known operator rather than risk shipping with an unknown one. However, many carriers no longer rely on these relationships as switching costs are low and many shippers, in seeking competitive advantage for themselves, have been willing to try an unknown carrier. In the major trades the presence of non-conference operators on a route raises the level of rivalry. The availability of confidential contracting and independent action intensify that rivalry.

---

4   Vessels can experience a problem where they have space but, because the cargo already stowed is very heavy, they cannot add more containers without exceeding a safe loading limit. This is called "weighing out." "Cubing out" occurs when there is no more space to stow containers but the vessel could still carry more weight. On the North Atlantic, the cargo weight limit on capacity is more restricted than other routes due to weather conditions and the need for greater freeboard.

Once minimum standards, such as acceptable transit times, are met, there is little incentive for buyers to use one carrier over another unless particular service features or standards are desired. Purposely splitting business over a number of carriers is one way in which some shippers diversify their risk, and further evidence of the homogeneity of the container shipping market in the eyes of the buyers. Intense rivalry is the result.

The high barriers to exit give shipowners reasons to delay capacity reduction; unless prices are good for scrap or the second-hand market is buoyant, there is a tendency to hope that a redeployment opportunity will materialize or be created. This results in an industry with an almost perpetual state of capacity oversupply.

### Conclusions about industry structure

Although each firm must assess its own situation within the industry as analyzed above, there are some general conclusions that can be drawn about the stability of the industry. The balance between forces increasing its volatility and those stabilizing the situation is difficult to find. The industry's volatility can be traced to the following facts: (1) demand fluctuates more rapidly than supply (which has a long lead time in terms of new capacity coming on stream), (2) not all vessels available can serve the demand due to some port and route limitations, (3) ships last longer than the financing period, resulting in a significant disparity in the cost bases between owners, (4) the cost of both entry to and exit from the industry are high and, finally, (5) the development of post-Panamax tonnage is likely to further destabilize the market in the short and medium term by increasing capacity in a market already with more capacity than necessary. Although "slow steaming" may moderate the capacity supplied from a fixed asset base, this influence is incompatible with the time-competitive demands of the shipper community and therefore has less of a stabilizing influence in this sector than it does in tanker shipping.

Each carrier must then draw its own conclusions about its prospects for success within this dynamic industry. There exists always the option to exit the industry rather than develop new strategies to improve the profit potential of the firm. The industry structure is not all the firm must contemplate. The next section of this chapter explores the current business environment, which must be factored into the firm's review of its strategic options.

### THE CURRENT BUSINESS ENVIRONMENT

### Customers and requirements

Increasingly competitive pressures are forcing manufacturing companies to look at their operations and their markets as global in nature. In terms of markets, global commonalties facilitate the standardization of products sold to differing markets world-wide. The ability of manufacturing firms to undertake a global strategy has been fostered by both technology and telecommunications advances, while decreases in overall transport costs arising from logistical innovations have encouraged the rise in global sourcing of products, components and services.

The globalization of manufacturing underscores the need for an efficient and cost-effective worldwide distribution system. The result has been downward pressure on transportation rates in general and an increased customer orientation on the part of container lines.

Increased competition on a global scale is also forcing manufacturing firms to consider greater integration of their production processes with suppliers and markets as a means to gain competitive advantage. Just-in-time (JIT) systems, a natural by-product of such integration, are highly dependent on precise international delivery schedules. With a JIT approach to manufacturing, raw materials and goods in transit are considered inventory and the carrier is viewed as a stage in the manufacturing process. Over the past decade, the nature of the buyer-seller relationship in container shipping services has become less transactional and more like a partnership (Brooks, 1995, 1998, 2000; Crum and Allen, 1991; Gibson *et al.*, 1993; Kleinsorge *et al.*, 1991; and Phillips, 1991). Since reliability is critical, the building of trust between parties is essential to the success of a JIT strategy. Strategic alliances between some carriers and manufacturers along the supply chain have resulted (Brooks, 1998). Such logistics alliances commonly have built-in performance standards that are monitored and must be met in order for the relationship to continue (Brooks, 2000).

Many shippers, particularly those with large volumes, just-in-time systems and sophisticated managers, are moving towards supplier reduction strategies, with or without these monitoring programs. The monitoring program enables the transport buyer to negotiate more effectively with the transport seller on issues of service and price as well as develop standards for supplier selection for the next time period (Brooks, 1998).

Not all manufacturers are opting to control the supply chain; logistics is among the most commonly outsourced business support services (LaLonde and Maltz, 1992). The growth of third-party logistics suppliers has strengthened the already strong share held by the traditional freight forwarding industry in negotiating contracts with container lines. *Containerisation International* (1996) as cited by UNCTAD (1998:51-3) found that for 35% of shippers surveyed, freight forwarders selected the ocean carrier used for FCL shipments, with that percentage rising to 40% for LCL shipments. Of those surveyed, 59% required the forwarder to use ocean carriers selected by the shipper for FCL shipments. Forwarders are heavily used for documentation services and their role in the carrier selection decision cannot be ignored. As a result, most lines face three general types of customers—the large volume JIT-oriented manufacturer, the third-party or freight forwarder logistics supplier, and the smaller shipper that opts not to use the services of a third-party supplier. The size of the last group is not clear but its clout in the political process is waning under increasing deregulation and the changing marketplace.

A significant factor in liner shipping managerial decision-making is the customer requirement for regular fixed-day weekly sailing schedules as a minimum. The purpose of fixed date sailing from the customer's viewpoint is predictability. Production and distribution schedules are more easily planned if the interval at which the goods move out the factory door is regular and known. For example, a week's production shipped every Friday at 3 p.m. to meet a Saturday sailing is a known, readily recalled interval appealing to managers. If such fixed interval arrangements are not offered, the shipper will use an alternative carrier that can meet this minimum standard.

Shippers also do not want to be surprised by containers left on the dock when the ship has sailed. The shipper wants to be assured that cargo booked is cargo carried. Unlike airlines, where overbooking may not be welcome but may be recognized as inevitable (and the passenger is delayed slightly), cargo left on the dock may be delayed unacceptably as the next sailing may not be for another week.

Customers with JIT demands and those seeking to reduce the time products are in the logistics pipeline will focus on door-to-door transit time in their assessment of suitable carriers. This emphasis forces carriers to closely scrutinize schedules and network configuration to extract time losses from the system they offer the customer.

Manufacturers expect the carrier to deliver what it has promised in terms of any special equipment, services and delivery time at an agreed time and price. Many container shippers are port-blind, leaving the choice of port and routing to the carrier they have chosen. Once the carrier has booked the cargo, it is a matter of ensuring that its choice of route to destination delivers what has been promised the customer. It is up to the carrier to ensure that the quoted price delivers profit. This results in the carrier choosing a terminal that will minimize labour costs, an inland transport service that is cost-effective and time-competitive, and a route with the least amount of regulatory interference. The carrier's schedule must work to attract the shipper's booking and still earn the carrier an acceptable profit when all of these factors have been considered. So the primary drivers of changing trading patterns are the carrier's ability to deliver a desired service package at a competitive price mindful of the regulatory climate imposed on the route.

Just how important is price in the set of benefits sought by a carrier's customers? For those shipping low value goods, it may be the difference between a sale and no sale. The answer varies widely and is customer-dependent. (For this reason, differential pricing has developed in the industry through conference tariff-setting.) A series of studies conducted by Brooks (1985, 1990, 1995) concluded that price is not the primary determinant of carrier choice, although it is one of the factors considered. Significant differences in carrier quotes were not perceived to exist. The salient service attributes sought in 1982 were frequency of sailings and cost of service, as all carriers were viewed to provide similar transit times because of similar routing structures (Brooks, 1985). By 1989, carriers had improved their performance significantly but transit time, the door-to-door elapsed time, had become the sole deterministic criterion on which carrier selection decisions were made. Performance on other criteria had improved but significant differences between carriers were not perceived by shippers (Brooks, 1990). Brooks (1995) concluded that the market is definitely not homogeneous in its requirements of carriers; different elements surfaced as important both in distinct geographical markets and customer groups and some customers clearly bought a package of attributes for the rate paid while others evaluated individual attributes separately. Each carrier's understanding of the requirements of its customers, and its competitor's customers, is critical to the formation of a successful strategy.

In general, however, it can be said that one of the more important features of the system that customers desire is predictability of rates. Many manufacturers seek to offer delivered prices to their customers with price lists that change infrequently. The ability to establish a fixed price list with a foreign agent or a distributor imposes upon the manufacturer the obligation to mitigate two risks: the one inherent in pricing in foreign currencies and the other in predicting future transport costs. The former may be addressed by hedging the currency based on the projected sales or existing sales contracts but the latter demands the use of time-volume rates, service contracts or the knowledge that rates will be predictable or stable for the planning horizon.[5] The passage of the *Shipping Act of 1984* encouraged the first two. The original purpose of antitrust protection for conference carriers was to advance the last.

Many of today's container operators depend on brand awareness for consideration by shippers. An easily recognized logo may remind shippers of their options. But, if the carrier participates in an alliance or joint venture, does the buyer believe the carrier that sold the service is the one producing it? The need to maintain a market identity for long-term success is one of the reasons why slot charters have been a popular means of market entry and reducing costs; the vessel actually used is not obvious but the identities of the sales representative and the booking agent are. The problem with slot charters is that they blur the identity of those carriers participating, and the carrier with the differentiated service may find that it has negotiated the advantage away to its competitors. This differs very little from the dilemma faced by air carriers involved in code share arrangements; customers can be lost if service does not measure up to the expectations of the buyer.

More than anything else, the buyer's perception that one carrier's offering differs very little from the next is a major competitive disadvantage for many firms. Many shippers do not distinguish the performance of one carrier from another except on a few dimensions, which may lead a tendency to engage in discount pricing—an option not available to members of a shipping conference except through independent action or service contracts. It is extremely tempting for conference carriers to respond to non-conference price-cutting by reducing inland charges "passed on" to the customer in order to bypass conference rules. It is perhaps this reason that inland pricing has become such an issue of divergence between the US and Europe.[6]

In sum, supply chain management and outsourcing of logistics expertise can be expected to drive customer requirements for the foreseeable future. Today's logistical systems are being

---

5    There are some shippers who try and engage in market-timing; that is, they are prepared to run the risk inherent in trying to predict the direction of the market. These shippers will seek to use time-volume rates or service contracts in rising markets but switch to the tariff rate when they believe the market will fall. This same type of company is one that thinks it can also manage its foreign exchange risk by only hedging some of the time. As the manufacturing business matures, management becomes more professional and fewer of these risk-taking firms survive.

6    This issue is discussed in detail in Appendix D and Chapter 9.

streamlined to optimize the services desired by the company controlling the distribution and, to the chagrin of shipowners, carrier rationalization. Where manufacturers once spread the business over a number of carriers, they are becoming more sophisticated and choose only a few who can meet all their needs. This encourages carriers to examine competitors and identify potential partners or acquisition targets in order to enhance service offerings and market coverage, in other words, to become more global.

## Changing trading patterns

The globalization of manufacturing is not the only driver of changing trade patterns. The Asian crisis of late 1997 and early 1998 presents the most obvious illustration of the importance of economic health and trade to continuing container service demand. In the aftermath of economic failures in Thailand, Indonesia and Korea, for example, local demand for finished consumer goods dropped dramatically, thereby reducing the demand for raw materials inbound. Many companies were simply unable to pay for inbound components short-term. As the materials produced were cheaper to market, space on the outbound leg became tight, and the already imbalanced trade was further destabilized. Very little container traffic was moving into Asia but significant volumes of low-priced goods were moving out; on the transpacific, empty boxes for repositioning were the highest volume of business into Asia while the pressure for slots eastbound grew throughout the fall of 1998. To illustrate, eastbound cargo was up 22.4% in the second quarter of 1998 while westbound was down 17.1%, over the same quarter the year previous.[7]

Figure 3.1 charts the directional imbalances existing in the transpacific before the crisis; at the time the market was already unstable. Throughout 1998, there were numerous attempts by both east- and westbound conferences to raise rates under a rate restoration program in order to better finance the two-way service. Westbound, the lines argued that volumes were low and therefore rates had to go up, while eastbound demand was up so rates could be restored as the end market could accept the increase. Rate restoration proved to be difficult and some firms decided that wholesale restructuring of the trade or even temporary withdrawal of capacity was inevitable.[8] As a result, new or streamlined service connections were not just imposed on the transpacific. The lines used the changing market conditions to engage in wholesale network reconfiguration system-wide. Changes in one part of the network are usually felt on other lanes, as equipment and vessel cycle times adjust through the system.

---

7    http://www.schednet.com, 8 September 1998.

8    Meanwhile, the topic became a significant one for the Stabilization of Trade Committee of the Asian Ship-owners Forum in March of 1998, with the result that capacity management was a tactical decision by some of the lines. Maersk and Sea-Land, for example, cut a vessel string from their transpacific service (about 5% of capacity), while increasing service in China and Southeast Asia. The company expected that would enable a 10% increase in freight rates to stick (Mongelluzzo, 1998). By withdrawing capacity, rate restoration might have some chance of succeeding. It was not long before the FMC announced its investigation of shipowners' responses to the dilemma they faced. (The FMC initiated a Section 15 investigation on 10 carriers in the transpacific trade on 29 May 1998, believing that the Stabilization of Trade Committee of the Asian Ship-owners Forum might be serving as an unmonitored forum for collective rate and/or capacity management discussions.)

## Figure 3.1: The Changing Trade Dynamics

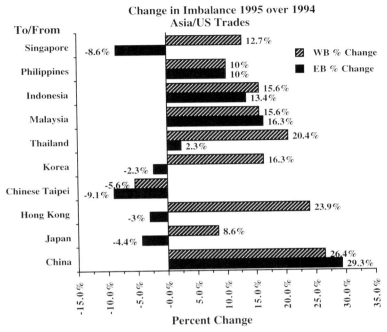

**Change in Imbalance 1995 over 1994 Asia/US Trades**

Source:   OECD (1997), *Maritime Transport 1995*:96, Table 7, © OECD, 1997. This data was not tracked in later years.

Technological developments may also drive container lines to alter network configurations, with knock-on effects on the trading patterns. Railroads can gain the volume necessary to make doublestack rail cars and unit trains cost-effective for long-haul container moves by feedering overseas container lines. Significant cost savings are possible and, as a result, carriers may redirect containers over new routings. Likewise, regulatory changes or fiscal policies may influence the configuration of the network; the imposition and subsequent removal of the Harbor Maintenance Tax resulted in some diversions in traffic from and then to US gateways.

The global trading environment is changing rapidly and the future patterns of trade are less easy to predict than two decades ago when growth in liner shipping came from additional penetration of containerization into general cargo transport; the resulting benefits accrued to manufacturers. Today, geographic concentrations of interconnected businesses and supporting institutions, called clusters (Porter, 1998), are making trading patterns even more dynamic but also unpredictable. As trade liberalizes further and the World Trade Organization dispute resolution grants greater access, the rate of change will accelerate.

Trading patterns are also influenced by the increasing modularization of manufacturing. This is most apparent in the global automotive industry where modular consortia of suppliers have formed, and become co-investors; the relationships in production processes have become more dependent and, most important for shipping, so demanding that competition ceases to be on price but on time and quality. If other industries move in this direction to the same extent, the strategic responses of liner firms will need to meet this trading reality and price will diminish even further in importance as a factor in carrier competition.

## Competitors

No examination of the current business environment undertaken by a liner company is complete without looking at its competitors, both on a trade lane operational basis as well as at the strategic level. The process of conducting and analyzing a competitor's strengths, weaknesses, opportunities and threats, and its competitive position in the marketplace, will provide the company with some predictive capability about that competitor's likely future strategic responses. Competitor analysis is a well-developed marketing science and, as it is firm-specific, will not be dealt with here. Suffice it to say that in the process of conducting a competitor analysis, a particular liner firm should also explore the competitor's potential as a target for acquisition or a partner for merger or alliance.

### COMPETITIVE POSITIONING: THE FIRM'S EXISTING STRATEGY

Liner shipping companies, like all businesses, seek firm-specific competitive advantages by examining their particular strengths in context with the industry and the trading environment already discussed. Each carrier must also explore its weaknesses and the threats it faces to ascertain the specific competitive disadvantages which must be overcome. Some of these disadvantages are temporary and may be readily overcome while others may result in the eventual demise of the firm, as in the case of insufficient access to capital or the deterioration of route-related volume for reasons the firm fails to comprehend.

Porter (1985:3) concluded that competitive advantage results from the value a firm is able to create for its buyers in excess of the cost of creating that value. Some carriers choose to cater to the demands of JIT-oriented customers with an integrated door-to-door service backed up by EDI container tracing and documentation systems. For others, the existing strategy might focus on low prices and acceptable service delivery in a niche market. What is the firm's existing strategy and how well does it perform when examined in the context of competitor performance? The customers, the competitors and the changing trading environment, coupled with the regulatory environment, all influence the liner company's perspective of its existing strategy.

The final element in the puzzle that is a firm's strategy is managerial preference, as expressed by the actions of the company's senior management. Individual personalities of board members and senior management, as well as the governance and ownership structure of the organization all play a role in the drama that unfolds as a company decides on its strategy and implements it. Managerial preference in government-owned entities is quite different than in entities with strong single financial backers or families. Family-dominated enterprises impose their preferences on the organization or may abdicate responsibility to strong senior management. In the end, managerial preference guides organizational decision-making by putting a human face on it.

Shareholder-driven organizations may lack that human face; the widely-held, publicly-traded company may find its shareholders possessing different agendas than the vision held by its Board or management. Senior management may seek to grow organically while shareholders, looking to maximize their profits, may be more willing to see the firm as a takeover target. Conversely, senior managers holding share options as part of a performance incentive package may make decisions more in the shorter term financial interests of themselves than in the longer-term best interests of all stakeholders.[9]

Finally, managerial preference may be limited or constrained by the regulatory climate and the rules governing corporations operating in specific jurisdictions. Over the course of Chapters 5 to 7, the constraints the regulatory environment imposes on managerial preference will become more clear.

The relationship of these elements to the formulation of new strategy is presented in Figure 3.2. These dynamic influences may work towards the company's realization that its existing strategy is not as successful as hoped, or may convince the carrier that the strategy is not likely to be successful when, in fact, not enough time has elapsed for its successful implementation. Reinforcement of beliefs about the existing strategy come from the internal data a firm has garnered on its own or with the help of outside consultants. The outcome may be the development of a new strategy or reaffirmation of the existing strategy.

## FORMULATING A NEW STRATEGY

As noted in Chapter 2, Porter (1985) proposed in his Three Generics model that firms make a strategic choice between cost leadership or differentiation, each offering a further choice of a broad or narrow scope. A differentiation strategy with a geographic or equipment focus is commonly called a niche strategy. Some carriers are seeking global status, and this broad geographic focus scope may be accompanied by a strategic approach which is either a cost leadership or differentiation one. The firm in trouble is the one that is unable to articulate a clear vision of its choice and scope.

To illustrate the importance of the decision about scope of operations, Brennan (1989) explored the strategies of the carriers of the world, categorizing them into four groups as illustrated in Figure 3.3. Brennan identified eight companies well on the way to being global firms, with another 25 in position to challenge the eight. Even then, Maersk (one of the eight) was

---

9     The impact of share options is well explained by Anonymous (1999). Share options should not be seen as a distortionary factor in managerial preference, but as one which can potentially distort the outcome.

obviously ón a path of global focus while Zim, a large but second tier carrier, was not so inclined.[10] Strong regional carriers like ACL, Australia National Line (ANL) and United Arab Shipping (UASC) were clearly taking a different approach (geographic niche). For these lines, the decision to maintain high market share in a regional market was a successful one. As geographic scope is only one aspect of the scope decision, the discussion of scope will continue in the section on differentiation strategies.

### Figure 3.2: A Model of Strategy Formulation in Liner Companies

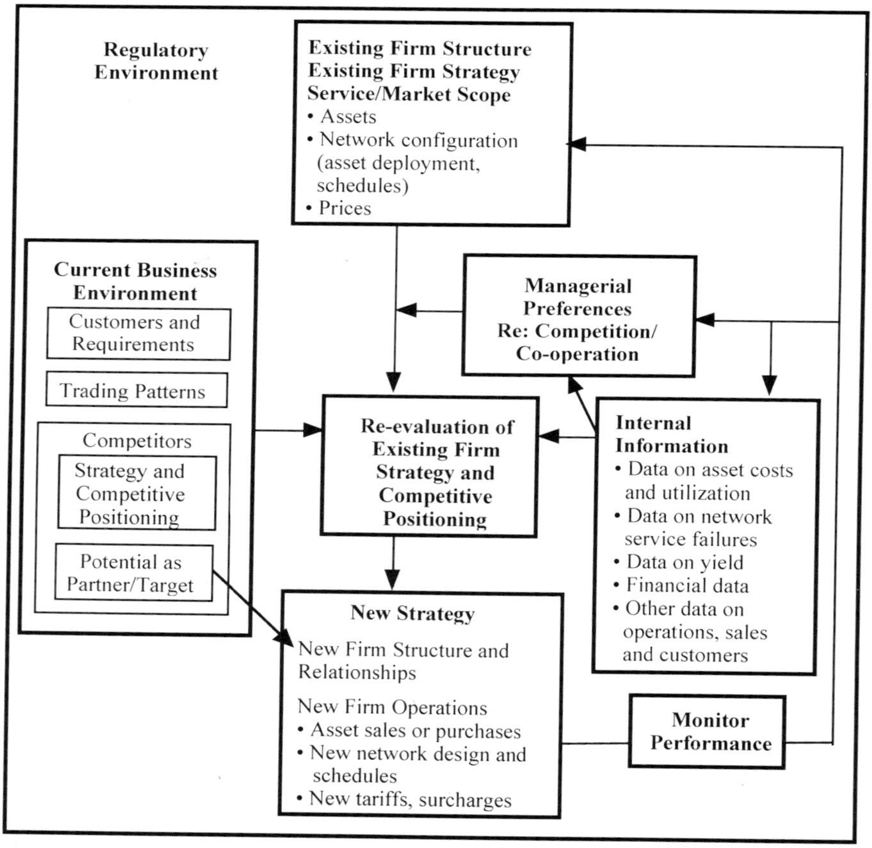

---

[10]  The Global Eight were APL, Evergreen, Hapag Lloyd, Maersk, NYK, P&O, Sea-Land, and Yang Ming. A number of the 25 contenders (Second Tier Global companies) he proposed have since moved up in market share while First Tier Yangming has subsequently dropped out of the top grouping.

**Figure 3.3: Market Shares and Strategies 1989**

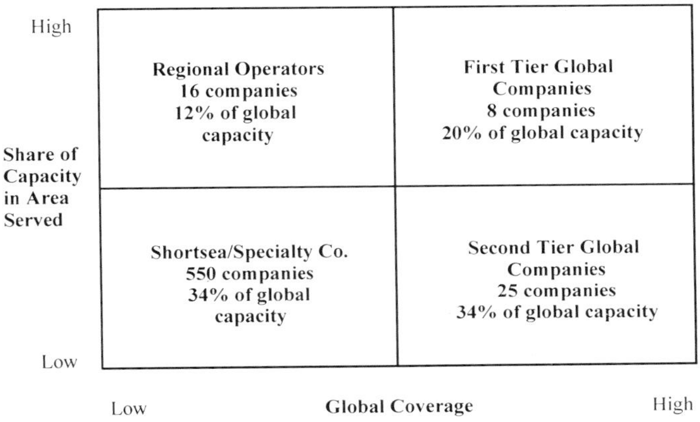

| | Low ◄ Global Coverage ► High |
|---|---|

| | | |
|---|---|---|
| High | **Regional Operators**<br>16 companies<br>12% of global capacity | **First Tier Global Companies**<br>8 companies<br>20% of global capacity |
| Share of Capacity in Area Served | **Shortsea/Specialty Co.**<br>550 companies<br>34% of global capacity | **Second Tier Global Companies**<br>25 companies<br>34% of global capacity |
| Low | Low     **Global Coverage**     High | |

Source:   Based on a more detailed figure by J. Brennan (1989).

## Cost leadership

Costs have been dropping in this industry over the last 15 years and, in spite of phenomenal productivity growth, revenues have failed to deliver solid profitability. While facilities, ships, labour, equipment and flag of registry all offer the potential for some cost savings, their potential to position a carrier as a cost leader is doubtful. Economies of scale, competitive interest rates or charter prices from parent companies can all offer **short-term** cost leadership. However, **sustainable** competitive advantage is unlikely as most sources of cost leadership have been fully exploited.

To reduce costs, some carriers have opted to supply a limited selection of equipment types. The narrower the selection, the cheaper the container supply element becomes in the total cost profile of the company. Others have tried to secure cost advantages through investment in value-added cost-reducing activities, such as e-commerce. Carriers who seek to integrate into intermodal services for cost leadership have been disappointed by the fact that this move does not necessarily bring higher freight rates (Bangsberg, 1991); many shippers are simply unwilling to pay for any improvements (Broadwater, 1992).

Most prevalent among carriers is the belief that the carrier with the lowest slot cost[11] will have the long-term edge. As can be seen in Table 3.4, each of the companies dramatically reduced their cost per TEU per day at sea with the purchase of newer vessels. Technological advances

---

11   The calculation of slot cost is illustrated in Table 3.5.

plus rising fuel and maintenance costs inherent in older vessels makes a significant difference to the cost profile of the carrier.

**Table 3.4: New Vessel Efficiencies Over Old**

| Cost Element | Operator | Vessel | Year Built | Cost |
|---|---|---|---|---|
| Fuel ($/TEU/sea day) | APL | C-8 | 71 | 6.57 |
| | APL | C-10 | 88 | 2.66 |
| | Hanjin | Kobe | 86 | 3.42 |
| | Hanjin | Osaka | 93 | 2.71 |
| | P&O | Liverpool Bay | 72 | 4.53 |
| | P&O | Colombo Bay | 95 | 2.47 |
| Manning ($/TEU/year) | APL | C-8 | 71 | 822 |
| | APL | C-10 | 88 | 240 |
| | Hanjin | Kobe | 86 | 319 |
| | Hanjin | Osaka | 93 | 298 |
| | P&O | Liverpool Bay | 72 | 376 |
| | P&O | Colombo Bay | 95 | 244 |

Notes:   (1) Manning data assume $50,000 annual/crew member not adjusted for flag or nationality
(2) Fuel data assume average fuel cost of $94/tonne HFO and $98/tonne IFO.

Source:  Drewry Shipping Consultants (1996:124, Table 7.2).

Participation in a slot charter and coordinated sailing arrangement can also reduce costs. This approach is implemented by many carriers in the belief that it will lead to a successful cost leadership strategy. Table 3.5 illustrates the principle theoretically. (The financial relationships are approximately correct.) In Strategy A, the carrier's existing strategy, the carrier has only six ships in its fleet and operates only on one route (with a 25% market share). All vessels are older and, therefore, have higher fuel consumption costs and lower capital costs. These vessels are deployed on a North-South route and offer a single weekly multi-port (42-day round trip) service to customers on the route. There are two competitors, one in a similar situation (with 25% share) and one with 50% of the market (and two sailings a week but different port rotations). The carrier is concerned about high operating costs and yet cannot finance a new vessel acquisition program that will replace all six ships. One strategy which may replace Strategy A is Strategy B. Strategy B requires the carrier to reject its go-it-alone approach in favour of an alliance with the smaller competitor (competitor 1, also with six older ships). Each would purchase three new vessels (selling or redeploying the old ones) to reduce the slot costs while maintaining the capacity on offer on the route.

However, as may be obvious to some, the resulting situation may not be the bed of roses it first appears to be based on slot costs. (There is always significant variance fleet to fleet and vessel to vessel.) First, both the alliance partner and the large competitor may have even lower slot costs because choice of flag or the existence of subsidies have meant lower total system costs.

Second, although the capacity on offer may not have changed, the large competitor may have the better marketing team, or additional services which makes his service perceived to be better by the customer. The ability on the part of Competitor 2 to offer two strings a week may be desired by the buyers. Our strategist may have retained the same capacity to offer the market but now must slot charter space on its former competitor's sailings every second week.

**Table 3.5: Slot Cost Comparison—Two Theoretical Alternatives**

|  | *Strategy A* | *Strategy B* |
|---|---|---|
| Carrier's Fleet | 6 X 500 TEU | 3 X 1,000 TEU |
| Annual Vessel Capital and Operating Costs | $26,900,000 | $16,800,000 |
| Annual Port Charges | $7,800,000 | $3,800,000 |
| Annual Fuel Consumption | $10,700,000 | $3,700,000 |
| Annual Total System Costs | $45,400,000 | $24,300,000 |
|  |  |  |
| Total Capacity Offered (round trip on route) |  |  |
| Carrier | 52,000 TEU | 52,000 TEU |
| Competitor 1 (Potential alliance partner) | 52,000 TEU | 52,000 TEU |
| Competitor 2 (Larger competitor 12 X 500 TEU) | 104,000 TEU | 104,000 TEU |
|  |  |  |
| Number of Sailings per Year (one-way) |  |  |
| Carrier | 52 | 26 |
| Competitor 1 | 52 | 26 |
| Competitor 2 (No change) | 104 | 104 |
|  |  |  |
| Carrier's Slot Cost |  |  |
| at 100% Utilization | $873 | $467 |
| at 75% Utilization | $1,164 | $623 |

Note:  The network schedule remains a 6-ship 42-day cycle for the two smaller companies. Instead of two sailings a week by the larger competing line, the alliance results in one sailing per week using a larger vessel (1,000 TEU vessel).

The quest for the lowest slot cost through new orders from subsidized yards has led to a massive infusion of new ships which carry more TEU and use less fuel but do not confer sustainable advantage. Cost advantages gained by new asset investment are but a single arrow in the strategist's quiver. There must be other sources of cost leadership.

The problem with cost leadership as a strategy is that only one firm can lead. In the short term that is not a problem. Sustaining the advantage is. The cost leader is able to discount prices to achieve acceptable market share, but the discounting should not fully offset the leader's cost advantage so that the leader maintains above-average returns. Finding the capital to both invest and price discount in the face of intense competition is extremely difficult. Cost leadership is only suitable for non-conference carriers, as cost advantages otherwise cannot be passed on to the buyer except through independent action or confidential service contracts. Cost leadership has not been truly sustainable, except perhaps for Evergreen.

## Differentiation strategies

Differentiation strategies may be broad or narrow in scope. The latter, niche strategies, concentrate the firm's activities in its choice of geographic market or core service offering. Most niches tend to be geographic—developing a route that has insufficient volume to attract carriers looking for global domination on the main trades. The geographic niche-seeking firm pursues domination of the route and the strategy can be profitable as long as the route is well-served. The greatest fear of the geographic niche player is that the profitability of the segment will attract attention leading to new entrants who might segment the market further.

The success of containerization as a concept stemmed in part from the dramatic improvement in ship turnaround times and in part from the economies of scale possible by handling a standard unit using more than one mode. This standardization makes it hard to develop a niche strategy globally by means other than equipment choice. Even so, most carriers seeking to service the specialty equipment niche do so regionally rather than globally. For example, ACL offers its North Atlantic customers a wide range of equipment and ro-ro service in addition to the standard container service available from its competitors. For shippers with an unusual product to be shipped or with a mix of cargo requiring a diverse range of equipment types, ACL is the natural choice. This strategy has worked well for ACL when its stock market performance is examined. Australia New Zealand Direct Line, well-known for its refrigerated container service serving the Australasian market, provides another example. Once the strategy has become established, buyer loyalty is generally stronger than found in the standard container market, raising barriers to entrants who might consider segmenting the market further.

In contrast to cost leadership as a strategy, there can be many differentiators, each with a unique base of service offering. There is room for more than one service leader if different segments of the market value different attributes and, in seeing a difference, shippers are willing to pay a premium for it. With little room for individual price competition, each conference line must somehow distinguish itself or lose market share to those who can. In the case of conference carriers, differentiation must be the strategy of choice, as the conference rate tends to be the highest rate on the route rather than the floor. The service considered for differentiation must provide a unique advantage, not easily imitated, in order to ensure that the advantage created is not eroded in the short and medium term. The fundamental element in service differentiation is knowing what customers want and what meets that expectation. Once these are known, the shape of the carrier's particular service strategy can be defined.

The key aspect of any strategy is that it must be sustainable. In the airline industry, both computer reservation systems and frequent flyer programs were innovations that initially promised sustainable competitive advantage, paving the way for air carriers to manage demand and therefore minimize the need to alter capacity (Armistead, 1985). The benefit of both innovations was that, once the competitive advantage was eroded, they continued to be competitive necessities and thereby served as barriers to entry.

Sustainability of competitive advantage for the conference carrier requires it to identify a service element that is both unique and difficult to imitate. Ghemawat (1986) identifies three categories of sustainable advantage—(1) size in the targeted market, (2) superior access to resources or customers, and (3) restrictions on competitors' options. Dominating a market niche is the most easily sustainable strategy of all. In shipping, economies of scale in a geographic niche can be easier to establish as a sustainable advantage than economies on a global basis.

The majority of conference carriers contemplate one or both of two major initiatives to secure superior access to resources or customers: (1) vertical integration or alliances to secure participation in inland transport (and the expected although not necessarily realized goal of complete control of the door-to-door move) and (2) EDI systems to link themselves with their major customers. The attraction of EDI is powerful. It offers the carrier the opportunity to build an integrated system, including production, marketing and competitor intelligence components, which will enable the firm to forecast trends and develop pre-emptive strategies in the future (MacMillan, 1984). The investment in EDI is substantial but, once in place and effective, like computer reservation systems, it will raise entry barriers and restrict competitors' options. It enhances the firm's capability to differentiate service efforts, particularly if keyed to customer requirements and its information potential is exploited. Finally, if the system is placed in the hands of empowered and well-trained front-line staff, the service enhancement potential is very high.

## STRATEGIC RESPONSE—ALLIANCE, OWNERSHIP OR ORGANIC GROWTH?

As a result of each carrier's attempts to differentiate its services, a wide variety of new firm structures have developed. For example, some carriers have equity interests in stevedoring companies, port terminals, inland trucking or rail connections and even in forwarding, warehousing and third party logistics businesses. Many carriers now have "third party" logistics supply subsidiaries.[12] Others have opted to stick closer to their core business of ocean shipping with a strategy that aims to service the global customer. For still others, the strategy has been to diversify the firm's activities away from the shipping business. Whatever the choices made at the time of re-evaluation (the centre box of Figure 3.2), a decision is made to reaffirm the existing strategy or a new firm strategy is developed, and the firm structure will adapt accordingly if not distorted by the regulatory climate.

---

12  The use of the term "third party" implies an external and arm's length relationship between the buyer and the seller of the transport service. However, a carrier may be listed in a directory as a third party service provider even when it is not at arm's length in its relationship with the carrier. A July 1996 listing of the top 50 third-party logistics suppliers in the United States by *Inbound Logistics* noted that 28 of the 50 were asset-based.

The firm that seeks to grow can do so organically through asset purchase and business development (go-it-alone), strategic alliances with other carriers, or by purchasing growth via an acquisition of or merger with another business. It is also possible to grow through a diversification strategy involving any of these options, but this will not be explored further in this book. Suffice it to say, many carriers have diversified; a 1998 examination of profitable shipping companies noted that diversified companies of the Malaysian International Shipping Corporation and the Wilh. Wilhelmsen Group were the second and fourth most profitable shipping companies in 1997 (Damas, 1998). The development of strategic alliances was discussed in Chapter 1 while Appendix B presents those choosing the acquisition or merger route in the 1995-98 period. All options are being used in liner shipping, but why?

Integrated door-to-door systems are costly both in financial and time terms. In the time it takes a firm to develop its own door-to-door capabilities, others may build defensive market positions in those very markets by speedier means. Acquisition may be a much speedier way to develop an integrated door-to-door capability but suitable candidates are not always available or the buyer may be forced to pay a substantial premium to acquire a suitable firm. As noted in Chapter 2, acquisitions are not guaranteed successes in any event. The difficulties of integrating acquiring and acquired firms are legendary and, on routes where there are only two primary carriers—the premium operator and the discount one, not only is this extremely difficult but subject to allegations of anti-competitive behaviour.

Strategic alliances offer another vehicle for growth. Their use is premised on the belief that seamless service does not require ownership of all the assets and results from managerial values that accept cooperative behaviour. Today's charter market can turn assets into mere financial instruments with management decisions about their deployment firmly held in the hands of the charterer. There is also evidence of well-coordinated alliances where successful service delivery is not contingent on ownership.

There is another reason for engaging in an alliance, an anti-competitive one. In this example, one liner company is able to dominate an alliance of unequal firms, and thereby increase its market power. The hypothetical scenario: the company is in the reefer business and one of many firms participating in a pooling arrangement. As the largest firm in the pool and the one with the greatest financial depth, the company controls the marketing of the pooled service. Although the company has the capability of "going-it-alone," participation in the pool results in the company being the prime contact point for a larger part of the market. As the strongest partner in the pool, and as the controller of market information, the company has effectively split the operators/managers of the other vessels in the pool from the source of power in the business: knowledge of the customer. The carrier best able to gain sustainable competitive advantage is the one with the best ability to understand the customer's problems and provide the optimum solution for that customer. (This situation opens the door for abuse of dominant position.)

The current situation of alliances among the Top 20 is driven in part by the tremendous capital demands of constructing post-Panamax vessels; few firms can do it alone. For smaller companies, strategic alliances may be the only way for a firm with limited financial resources to compete with others developing integrated transportation systems. Alliances may also be the fastest way for firms to take advantage of present opportunities and develop defensible competitive advantage.

If there is to be some form of cooperative relationship, will it be a simple slot charter arrangement or equipment-sharing deal for inland services, or a more detailed alliance involving marine terminal facilities investment? Will the company seek to segment the service with each leg viewed as a profit centre or will a philosophy of cross-subsidization prevail? In part, this will have to do with the company's choice of alliance based on its competition-cooperation preferences. (The competition-cooperation continuum is discussed in the last section of this chapter.)

Looking to the future, the availability of adequate capital and the managerial capability to ensure long-term market presence are critical factors in the further evolution of the carriers seeking global scope. This does not, however, mean that the trend has slowed. Further concentration in the industry is still underway as strategic alliances between global carriers supplement service expansion and vertical integration activities in the search for global dominance of the industry.

## THE CONTINUA OF ALLIANCES

All strategic alliances are cooperative arrangements between firms. In some cases they are between firms that are in direct competition and are designed to lessen the level of competitive rivalry and/or improve capacity utilization and service levels. In other cases they are between firms whose service capabilities complement each other and jointly make a complete, integrated service possible, providing a way for participating firms to grow cooperatively.

In spite of the belief that strategic alliances are a relatively recent phenomenon, **conferences** were the earliest strategic alliances in this industry and they have existed for more than a century. Through pre-determined prices and, sometimes, cargo volume ceilings, the industry should be able to use conferences to restore profitability and control predatory pricing and cut-throat competition. There is almost no organizational interdependence between conference members and cooperation is civil but members remain competitors seeking to serve the same customer.

There are a number of other forms alliances may take. Simple **slot charter** agreements, like airline codeshare agreements, are alliances which expand market scope. In a slot charter, a carrier on a route may offer to another carrier (which may be a competitor), a fixed number of spaces, or slots, per sailing for a fixed period of time at an agreed price. Although both firms may still be competitors, the firm offering the slots secures revenue for those slots it may not be able to sell otherwise, thereby financing the investment in the ship. In this case, the shipper may have contracted with one carrier to move his goods, when in fact they are carried on another's vessels in the chartered slots without the shipper's knowledge. When a carrier's sailing schedule is not compatible with a particular shipper's needs, a slot charter agreement is one way to continue serving the customer.

Slot charter agreements are commonly found in conjunction with **coordinated services**, where two firms co-ordinate sailing schedules so as to jointly offer regular fixed-date sailing schedules. Although similar from a competitive point of view, coordinated services feature greater interdependence between lines. In the combination arrangement, not only are slots bought, sold or traded, but service patterns jointly provided. For example, two unrelated carriers may agree on a joint schedule which will provide two sailings a week, say Wednesdays and Saturdays; each company will retain its separate identity and marketing organization but the slot charter and coordinated sailing combination allows each to market the more frequent sailing to potential clients.

Carriers may also form alliances in the non-core, e.g. not vessel-owning or -operating, part of the business. For example, through **equipment sharing agreements**, partners share the costs and utilization of land-side chassis or containers. Highly competitive firms often view this to be a neutral ground where the savings from better asset management can be substantial and risks to the core business minimal.

The mounting capital cost of ships in the 1970s drove many Western operators to rethink their strategies and respond by participating in a **vessel-pooling consortium**. In this alliance, which may or may not have been structured as a **joint venture**, shipping companies contributed ships and other resources to create a new brand, offering more frequent service than each could provide alone. In the 1980s, multinational consortia included the United Arab Shipping Company, Scandutch, ACL and Gearbulk. However, the loss of market identity and the need for consensus between the partners limited the success of some early consortia.[13] Both of these structures imply far greater cooperation and the inter-organizational dependence is only marginally less than if a merger had taken place. It is the joint but common face to the customer that moves them closer to a merger in effect. Brooks *et al.* (1993) illustrated the range of the strategic alliance vehicles common in the transport industry along a competition-cooperation continuum (Figure 3.6). This framework is a simplification of one proposed by Denham (1991).

According to Brooks *et al.* (1993), one of the reasons why the slot charter is viewed as an acceptable strategic alliance alternative by both regulators and carriers is its position on the competition–cooperation continuum—very close to the competition end. It enables carriers to retain their individual marketing identities and compete vigorously in the marketplace while they gain the advantages of sharing costs. Such competition allays the regulators' fears of a collusive environment. While competitive, it is quite difficult for such competitive entities to cheat on the cooperative part of the agreement without jeopardizing the total arrangement.

---

13   ACL encountered considerable financial difficulty in the 1980s, was restructured, sold to Bilspedition by the members of the consortium, and eventually floated on the Swedish Stock Exchange; the company is successful today but would not have likely survived in its original structure.

Brooks *et al.* (1993) also concluded that this competition–cooperation continuum provided insufficient explanation for firm strategic behaviour and that more was required. They noted that the work of Contractor and Lorange (1988) provided another dimension on which to evaluate the strategic behaviour of firms—inter-organizational dependence. The degree of inter-organizational dependence experienced by partners in a coordinated service or slot charter agreement is greater than that in a conference but less than takes place between two companies establishing a common marketing entity, even though they may be similarly positioned on a cooperation–competitive continuum. They illustrated the relative position of each form of alliance in terms of its inter-organizational dependence in Figure 3.7, and proposed that the combination of the two continua would provide a simple framework for exploring competitive behaviour.

**Figure 3.6: A Cooperation Continuum of Alliances in Container Transport**

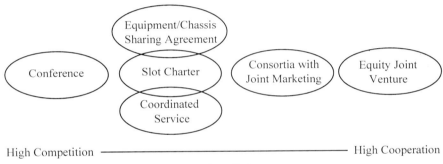

High Competition ———————————————— High Cooperation

Source: Brooks, Blunden and Bidgood (1993:226, Figure 10.1).

All alliances noted in Figures 3.6 and 3.7 are not necessarily mutually exclusive of other inter-firm arrangements. They all imply an agreed commitment made between firms to complement and support each other's activities for as long as it serves a mutually beneficial purpose. While it has been argued by some (e.g., Lado *et al.*, 1997) that the use of a continuum implies a hier-archy, that is not necessarily the way these continua should be interpreted. Each alliance will be somewhat unique, depending on its terms and conditions, and so the "distance" between alliance forms may vary widely. A company may engage in different options with different partners or even with the same partner.

If a company engages in more than one alliance form with the same partner, what happens? Of course, any combination of these alliance alternatives is possible, but each time a combination agreement is established, the firm becomes more dependent on its competitor partner and so moves along the continuum of inter-organizational dependence towards the right. The effect is similar on the competition-cooperation continuum.

**Figure 3.7: A Dependency Continuum of Alliances in Container Transport**

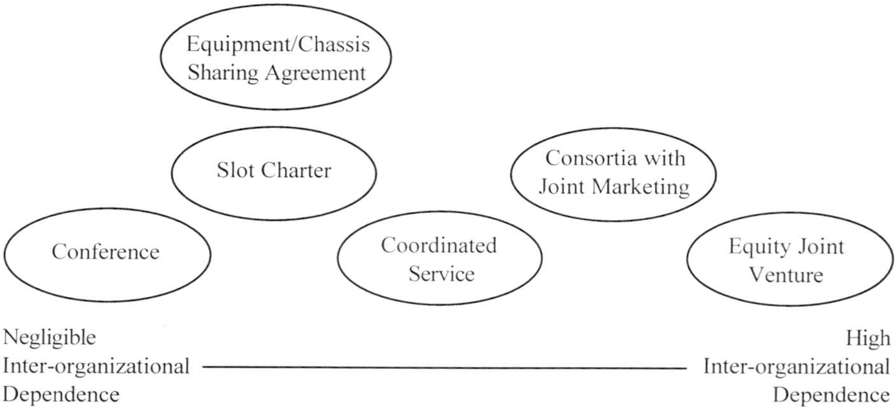

Source:  Brooks, Blunden and Bidgood (1993:227, Figure 10.2).

In sum, strategic alliances as a means of achieving global presence quickly offer an important alternative. Conferences are the least cooperative (and most competitive) of strategic alliances, and afford significant independence of the other members of a conference. Slot charters and other forms of asset sharing require greater cooperation but also hold the potential for increased benefits as equipment utilization is maximized. However, firms engaged in these are often in head-to-head competition on the same trade route and, although inter-organizational dependence has increased, it has not yet passed the threshold where regulators need to be concerned about anti-competitive behaviour. Vessel sharing consortia are also cooperative and more dependent but not yet "crossing the line." Once consortia begin to secure joint marketing agreements and management committees, they become more like equity joint ventures, and require even more cooperation. They also become more dependent, more like virtual mergers. At some point, the eggs are scrambled and the two firms become like one. Should these alliances be examined as if they were mergers? This is a question to be addressed in Chapter 9.

# APPENDIX B

# PRINCIPAL MERGERS, ACQUISITIONS AND TAKEOVERS

| Date of Deal | Companies involved | Price (1) | Details |
|---|---|---|---|
| **Mergers and Acquisitions 1996-97** | | | |
| January 96 | Safmarine (51%) and CMB-T | NR | New company called Safmarine and CMB-T Lines established. Given that Safmarine owns 49% of CMB-T, the South Africa group controls 75% of SCL. CMB NV owns the remaining 25% |
| May 96 | Frota Amazonica and Frota Oceanica Brasileira | NR | Consolidation of management functions into a single entity |
| January 97 | P&O Containers and Nedlloyd Lines | US$175 (2) | Creation of P&O Nedlloyd Container Line. The new venture has a combined revenue of US$4 billion, a shipping armada of 112 ships (224,000 TEU) and box inventory of more than 540,000 TEU (owned and leased). |
| January 97 | Australia-New Zealand Direct Line and Union Shipping of New Zealand | US$33.5 | A cross-shareholding deal in which Bollore (owner of ANZDL) acquired 50% in Union Shipping and Brierley Investments (owner of Union) purchased 50% of ANZDL. The joint venture is known as ANZDL Management Services |
| July 97 | Shanghai Haizing Shipping Co., Guangzhou Shipping, China Marine and Services Corp., Dalian Shipping and Zhong Jiao Marine Industrial Corp. | NR | Creation of China Shipping Group. The new entity focuses on China's cabotage and feeder trades |
| August 97 | Safmarine and Deutsche Africa Linien | NR | Creation of SAFDAL to represent Safmarine and DAL's interest in Saecs |
| **Principal Takeovers 1995-98** | | | |
| March 95 | CP Ships and Cast | CAN$150 | Rationalization of operating costs, but maintenance of individual sales and marketing teams |
| April 95 | Pyramid Ventures and Navieras de Puerto Rico | US$140 | Sale of government controlled line, subsequently renamed NPR Inc. The Puerto Rican Government absorbed US$310 million in accumulated debt. |
| January 96 | P&O Containers and ANL | NR | Acquisition of ANL's Europe/Australia trade. Previously, the two carriers had had a joint management agreement on the trade. |

| Date of Deal | Companies involved | Price (1) | Details |
|---|---|---|---|
| April 96 | Contship Containerlines and Pro Line | NR | Purchase of Pro Line's northern Europe/east coast S. America. Transaction involved the carrier's two charter vessels container pool and South American-based agents. |
| April 96 | Seawheel and BET | NR | BET sold its shortsea shipping operation, which traded as United Transport Container Holdings, prior to its own takeover by Rentokil. |
| November 96 | CMA and CGM | US$3.8 | CMA acquired the container asset and services of the former state-run-company. |
| December 96 | TMM and FMG | US$20 (3) | Establishment of Transportacion Maritima Grancolombiana in which TMM has 60% shareholding and FMG 40%. In return TMM secured all of FMG's charter tonnage and 25% shareholding in Contecar (box terminal in Cartagena) |
| February 97 | Hanjin Shipping Co. and DSR-Senator Linie | Approx. US$75 | Hanjin subscribed substantially to recapitalization of DSR-Senator and now controls between 75% and 80% of the company. A complete revamp of the German carrier's east/west liner network is underway. |
| April 97 | Transportacion Maritima Mexicana and Compania Transatlantica Espanola | US$3 | Memorandum of Understanding signed by TMM to acquire 99.9% of equity in the Spanish liner company. |
| July 97 | CP Ships and Lykes Lines | US$34 | Lykes was undergoing a financial restructuring following its filing for Chapter 11 bankruptcy protection in October 1995. The eventual sale to CP Ships involved all operating assets (ships and containers), service brand, route network, vendor contracts, plus assumption of liabilities. Approximately US$200 million committed for investment over the next two years. |
| August 97 | Petronas and MISC | US$700/ US$750 | Petronas, Malaysia's state-controlled oil and gas company, acquired a controlling interest in MISC by purchasing Kumpulan Wang Amanah Pencen's 29.35% shareholding. |
| August 97 | Preussag and Hapag-Lloyd AG | US$1,500 | Preussag, the Hannover-based industrial and services conglomerate, acquired the stock owned by Agfa-Gevaert (18%), Veba (18%), Lufthansa Commercial Holding AG (18%), Kaufhof (15%), Deutsche Bank (10%), Dresdner Bank (10%) and Veritas Vermoegen (10%) |
| October 97 | CP Ships and Contship Containerlines | NR | Purchase of Contship's brand name, services, agency organization, ships (19 chartered units of 1,500/2,700 TEU) and container pool. |

| Date of Deal | Companies involved | Price (1) | Details |
|---|---|---|---|
| October 97 | Mediterranean Shipping Co. and Kenya National Shipping Line | NR | MSC has purchased 45% of shares previously owned by Kenya Ports Authority (KPA). KPA remains a major shareholder with a similar 45% equity interest. |
| November 97 | NOL and APL | US$825 | Purchase by Singapore national flag carrier of the US's second largest liner company's international liner and intermodal businesses. Creation of a group generating annual revenues of US$4.5 billion and controlling containership fleet of over 75 vessels (approximately 200,000 TEU) |

Notes: (1) All prices in US$ million; for takeovers, includes cost of acquisition and subsequent reorganization;
(2) Nedlloyd's payment to P&O in order to balance the shareholding structure in the new venture. This case is discussed in Chapter 7.
(3) Involved payment of US$10 million to FMG and injection of US$10 million in new equity.
NR = not reported.

Source: Companies and *Containerisation International* as cited by Fossey (1998:37, Table 2 and 38, Table 3.)

# 4

# KEYS TO SUCCESSFUL LINER STRATEGY IMPLEMENTATION

## INTRODUCTION

Once the decisions about overall strategy (cost leadership or differentiation) and the scope of the firm's endeavours (global versus regional, broad or limited range of equipment) have been taken, and the strategy is conceptually developed in the context of a cooperative or competitive implementation, there remains the development of an implementation plan. Such a plan should be made with eyes focused on the customer's requirements.

In this industry, successful implementation has been elusive. The profitability of the industry is poor and totally inadequate given the asset intensity of the industry, the capital involved and the volatility of the market. In 1997, *Containerisation International* studied 21 carriers' financial results and found average ROI (return on investment) to be 6.2%, and five of those companies had return on total assets employed of less than 1% (Boyes, 1998). This confirmed *American Shipper*'s annual survey (Damas, 1998) which found that while operating profit accounted for an average of 5.8% of revenues of nine major carriers, net profit was a mere 0.1% of revenues. These two studies reinforced the results of an earlier study by Drewry Shipping Consultants (1996a) into the profitability of selected larger carriers (Table 4.1). Furthermore, when this industry is compared with the rail industry (discussed in Chapter 5), the truth emerges. Poor profitability has nothing to do with the fact that both are asset intensive. The rail industry works hard to secure an operating ratio below 80%. (The operating ratio is operating expenses as a percentage of operating revenue.) The liner shipping industry's track record in these terms has been and is dismal, not even as good as the poorer performing railroads. (Compare Table 4.1 with Table 5.6.)

Profitability is a double-edged sword: expenses must be controlled and revenue enhanced. Asset utilization and network scheduling can work towards cost containment while a revenue management strategy focuses on the second. Appropriate network configuration can do both.

Broadwater (1992) has argued that most shippers would prefer improvement in the execution of the core services rather than new services they may neither want nor need. This chapter focuses on the key elements of a successful operating strategy for liner companies including

marketing the service and monitoring its performance. It concludes with a survey of the literature on making the cooperative relationship work.

### Table 4.1: The Profitability Record of Selected Carriers

| | *Operating Profits (in US$ millions)* | | | *Operating Ratio (1)* | | |
|---|---|---|---|---|---|---|
| *Carrier (2)* | *1991* | *1993* | *1995* | *1991* | *1993* | *1995* |
| Sea-Land | 166 | 193 | 238 | 94.9 | 94.1 | 94.2 |
| Evergreen | 124 | 169 | 124 | 89.9 | 85.8 | 89.2 |
| NYK | 207 | 322 | 369 | 96.5 | 95.8 | 96.2 |
| Nedlloyd (3) | 47 | 31 | 70 | 98.8 | 99.1 | 98.3 |
| Mitsui-OSK | 104 | 202 | 210 | 97.2 | 96.5 | 97.0 |
| P&O | -4 | 63 | 65 | 100.0 | 96.3 | 97.2 |
| Hanjin | NA | 138 | 146 | NA | 91.0 | 94.1 |
| AP Companies | 143 | 133 | 68 | 94.2 | 94.9 | 97.7 |
| Zim | 52 | 84 | 54 | 95.2 | 93.2 | 97.2 |

Notes: (1)   The operating ratio is the percentage of revenue used to pay operating expenses. The difference
             between the operating ratio and 100% is the operating profit.
       (2)   In order of 1995 rank as per Table 1.4 in Chapter 1.
       (3)   Group result.

Source:   Operating profits are as presented by Drewry Shipping Consultants (1996a:144, Table 8.1, selected
          elements). The operating ratio is directly calculated from the data provided in the same table.

## ASSET MANAGEMENT—CHOICE AND UTILIZATION

The importance of asset management is underscored by a study undertaken by Drewry Shipping Consultants (1996a). In addition to the poor profitability noted above, one of its findings
was shocking given the asset-intensive nature of the business—the very poor level of return on
assets (Table 4.2). Other industries are certainly able to secure far greater revenue from the
assets in which they invest.

Asset choice, to some extent, begins with the customer and requirements. If, for example, the
carrier has opted for a wide-ranging equipment choice to meet the needs of vegetable exporters
and their desires for reefer equipment, the vessel will need to be well-equipped with sufficient
reefer outlets. Asset choice will also be dictated to some extent by the route of deployment
(e.g., water depth, special conditions), availability of second-hand tonnage for charter or
purchase, and so on.

As many shipowners have long known, timing in the sale and purchase market is a key success
factor and probably only a little more scientific than the random walk theory in the stock
market. Needless to say, some have the skill, or perhaps it is luck, to time the market well.
Generally it may be said that those who would rather make their money in the sale and
purchase of ships have found that the tanker market is more amenable to this type of capitalist

endeavour than the liner market because, in the liner market, the majority of expenses are now landside (Drewry Shipping Consultants, 1996a:154, Table 8.7). The liner industry has ceased to be merely a shipping business.

### Table 4.2: Asset Turnover in Container Shipping (1)

| 1995 Rank (2) | Carrier | 1991 | 1993 | 1995 |
|---|---|---|---|---|
| 1 | Sea-Land | 1.6 | 1.6 | 1.7 |
| 3 | Evergreen | 0.8 | 0.7 | 0.7 |
| 5 | NYK | 0.7 | 0.7 | 0.6 |
| 6 | Nedlloyd | 1.2 | 1.4 | 1.5 |
| 7 | Mitsui-OSK Line | 0.7 | 0.7 | 0.6 |
| 8 | P&O | 0.8 | 1.1 | 1.9 |
| 9 | Hanjin | N/A | N/A | 0.9 |
| 11 | AP Companies | 1.6 | 1.8 | 1.5 |
| 12 | Zim | 1.4 | 1.6 | 1.6 |
| | Drewry Average (3) | 0.9 | 0.9 | 0.9 |

Notes: (1) Asset turnover equals total revenue: total assets.
(2) Cosco (4th) and MSC (10th) not included in Table. The rank is the 1995 rank as per Table 1.4 in Chapter 1.
(3) Based on the 16 carriers selected by Drewry for its table.

Source: Drewry Shipping Consultants (1996a:131, Table 7.11, selected elements).

It appears that the key driver for carriers to choose larger vessels is their promise of cost savings, in terms of the capital cost of each slot or the fuel savings promised from a more technologically advanced propulsion system.[1] The choice of new post-Panamax vessels for the main trades by the Top 20 carriers also reflects an optimism about their ability to garner market share. It would be foolhardy to base the entire investment on cost savings.[2] Which carriers are the rash ones will be judged by the trade press soon enough as not all will succeed. As noted in Chapter 1, the injection of the substantial post-Panamax capacity currently on order will not be absorbed by the existing rate of growth in trade in either the short or medium term unless scrapping levels rise significantly. In addition, it has been shown that the slot cost advantages realized by ordering post-Panamax tonnage become a disadvantage if utilization levels fall below 79% (Drewry Shipping Consultants, 1996b:45).

The dilemma of trade imbalances has already been noted in Figure 3.1. Where serious trade imbalances exist, asset utilization problems arise. Figure 4.3 illustrates that the utilization

---

1  According to McLellan (1997), it is theoretically possible with today's existing technology to put a vessel of 15,000 TEU into service.
2  Drewry Shipping Consultants (1996a:131) concluded that post-Panamax construction is not aimed at reducing capital costs per slot as construction costs per TEU have flattened and there are no further construction economies to be had. The impetus is strictly from reduced operating costs.

problem may be worse on some trade lanes than on others. Firms must decide whether to deal with this problem through alternative asset choice or whether the network needs to be reconfigured so that the asset is deployed differently than is the existing case. The alternative of network reconfiguration is dealt with in the next section.

**Figure 4.3: Asset Utilization by Route (1991, 1993 and 1995)**

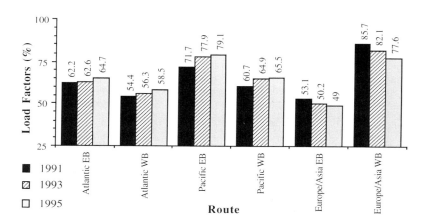

Source:    Created from data in OECD (1997:126); *OECD Maritime Transport 1995*, Table 13. © OECD, 1997.

The key question for those scrutinizing asset utilization is: what is the appropriate reserve capacity the shipowner should include in the strategy implementation plan? The answer must reflect two principles to be successful: (1) key customers are always served, and (2) capacity provided should not be so great that it will ultimately be dumped on the market. This should lead to a discussion of who are the company's key customers, and is the customer mix appropriate. These questions will be addressed later in the section on marketing the service.

Early gains in asset utilization were made when carriers switched from mixing containers and general cargo to fully cellular vessels, reducing port turnaround times. Improvements also came from efforts to manage the equipment fleet, bringing down the equipment investment needed to support each slot in service. Today, the largest single commodity carried by container is air; the transport of empties for purposes of repositioning them to the next user accounted for almost one-fifth of all traffic in 1994 (Drewry Shipping Consultants, 1996a:2, Table 1.1). This reinforces the conclusion that there is still room for improvement.

## NETWORK CONFIGURATION AND SCHEDULES

There is also the question of routing, ports of call and equipment, as these define the service offered. If a service is to be expanded or new vessels introduced, the current schedule and possible future alternatives need to be examined as part of the strategy implementation plan. Shippers like service offerings to be regular and stable; they do not appreciate carriers tinkering with the service characteristics too frequently as export/import contracts with regular customers are often negotiated a year or more in advance.

One of the network structures being considered by container lines today is the hub and spoke system. One of the reasons that growth in container moves is occurring at a faster rate than growth in trade is that an increasing share of moves is attributable to transhipment; by 1994, transhipment was 22% of port handling (Drewry Shipping Consultants, 1996a:2, Table 1.1). Although many ports, since the beginning of containerization, have had ambitions to become hub or load centre ports, few are chosen. Where are hub and spoke networks successful?

The quick answer is in the airline industry. Air carriers have documented the ability to generate economies of traffic density from hub and spoke networks. That is where the analogy appears to end. At a hub, the passenger can transport himself or herself to the next carrier; freight cannot. Passengers see the routing and care to some extent about their comfort in the process; they also see the benefits of greater frequency to smaller locations.[3] Freight, on the other hand, is blind to the route so long as the service and price needs of the company paying the freight bill are met. Why is transhipment occurring at all?

A key explanation is the ability of the carrier to match traffic volumes to assets on each stage or leg of the trip. In doing so, the carrier's fixed costs to service the market may be reduced. (However, they may also increase if the resulting network is less efficient or requires a broader mix of vessel types to be serviced and maintained.) There is also the straight operational economics that may convince operators to adopt the strategy. For example, Bendall and Stent (1998) have demonstrated the cost savings possible from long-haul fast feeder ships as an alternative to larger vessels with normal hull designs and propulsion systems. Such vessels may offer cost savings through innovative network configuration.

An important factor in examining the appropriateness of hubbing as a strategy is the identification of who will bear the hubbing costs. At the moment, shippers bear the transhipment costs. If a container is grounded and then reloaded, there are the additional terminal charges not incurred in direct service. While these charges are not evident on the carrier's financial statements, they are usually not insignificant in the total delivered price, accounting for 10% or more of the total door-to-door cost. The carrier gets savings in fleet productivity but the shipper trades off whatever savings are passed on against the additional terminal handling charges. Such costs seen by the shipper may render a hub and spoke configuration uncompetitive. Hub and spoke networks do not work in markets where the shipper is unwilling to risk the time

---

3    Landing charges for smaller planes are generally less and spoke service frequency supporting long-haul trunk activities pulls short-haul passengers out of their cars and onto planes.

delay or pay the extra charges and there is a competing carrier willing to provide direct services. As a result, hub and spoke networks in shipping are highly vulnerable to snipers offering niche services.

Part of controlling the hubbing costs for a carrier lies in control of the terminal, and particularly its work force. The development of a greenfield terminal site[4] for container shipping may bring with it lower labour costs (as a result of it being non-unionized) and, if labour is paid by salary rather than by the hour, costs to the line may be more a matter of volume throughput and less a product of the number of times the container is handled. For carriers like Maersk and Sea-Land, transhipment costs provide a partial explanation for their strategy of diversification into terminals on a worldwide basis.

Some liner companies are enthusiastic about the hub and spoke configuration. One is Maersk. Its 1997 hubs and frequencies are presented in Table 4.4. Tommy Thomsen, President, Maersk Inc., explained the company's philosophy (Damas and Gillis, 1997:54): "We believe in having global reach with a local touch. ... A customer from the Midwest would rather talk to a sales representative from the same region." The Maersk strategy of owned sales offices and local sales staff runs contrary to the current practice by many lines of agents and lower-cost centralized sales staff. This strategy has been very successful for Maersk but, as a more costly approach, it requires Maersk to secure a large share on many routes. It cannot fail on strategy execution.

**Table 4.4: Maersk's 1997 Network Configuration**

| Route | Frequencies | Hubs | |
|-------|-------------|------|---|
| **Intercontinental** | 17 sailings/week | Singapore | Gioia Tauro |
| 10 services | | Kaohsiung | Algeciras |
| | | Dubai | Miami |
| **Regional Feeder** | | | |
| 5 Asian services | 4 weekly | Singapore | Kaohsiung |
| | 1 biweekly | Dubai | Hong Kong |
| 7 European | 6 weekly | Gioia Tauro | Rotterdam |
| | 1 biweekly | Algeciras | Hamburg |
| 4 North American | 2 weekly | Miami | |
| | 2 biweekly | Long Beach | |

Source:   Damas and Gillis (1997:52).

Hub and spoke is not the only network configuration available in the vessel scheduling and utilization challenge. Pendulum and round-the-world networks work extremely well when

---

4   A greenfield development is one that takes place in a whole new location as opposed to one which may be an incremental development of an existing facility.

carriers find trade imbalances difficult to reconcile with prices customers are willing to pay for a particular leg. They also add the ability for medium-sized carriers to target the best-paying cargo on a high volume route while potentially avoiding the legs with lower contribution margins. A further variant is the two-string X-pattern where two service strings, each a trunk-haul between hubs and with their own spokes, cross at a mega-hub enabling the transfer of cargo between strings and effectively servicing more origin-destination combinations.

Network reconfiguration within a newly formed alliance also provides companies with the opportunity to reduce capacity in markets that have low load factors and are not profitable. For example, on a north-south route that is over-tonnaged but has no carriers wishing to exit the market, two could form an alliance, using the alliance to extract the extra capacity for mutual benefit. Carrier A (with six 2,100 TEU vessel offering a 12-day departure schedule) forms an alliance with Carrier B (with five 1,000 TEU vessels and an equally unusual departure schedule). The two are able to reorganize the way they service the route. Using slot charters and coordinated sailings, their new network offers two strings with different port calls, while saving the deployment of one vessel. To reach the agreement, the total system cost savings are shared. Next they engage in joint planning to adjust assets owned so that a fleet of seven 2,100 TEU vessels is deployed and weekly fixed-day sailings offered to major ports and biweekly service to minor ports in a 49-day cycle. The result is one where all the cargo is still carried but load factors have improved significantly and so have profits for both partners. The shipper gains service benefits in the form of the desired fixed-day weekly sailings not offered previously. Had the capacity not been extracted, it was likely that the market would have experienced the bankruptcy of one or more carriers and none would have been profitable enough to invest for long-term survival.

Cost and coverage are not the only drivers of the network configuration decision. A carrier's optimal port call structure is not just a function of voyage distance, steaming time, or port time (as mathematical models often imply), but a complicated interplay of these operational factors with shippers' needs for transit time, service frequency, special equipment, or other service elements. Each carrier has a different company-specific set of variables influencing its network decisions and will try to build a service pattern that will provide it with a competitive advantage.

**Figure 4.5: 1990 Network for SLCS**

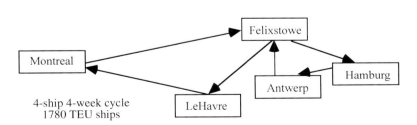

To illustrate, the St. Lawrence Coordinated Service restructured its network in 1991 to build a service pattern that would better service customers currently facing long transit times (Brooks, 1992). The company had the network illustrated in Figure 4.5. Shippers in Canada with cargo bound for France faced interminably long transit times, as the ship called Felixstowe twice, Hamburg and Antwerp before arriving in LeHavre to drop the container. Likewise, containers coming from Hamburg sailed via Felixstowe, Antwerp and LeHavre en route to Canada.

By changing from the 4-ship 28-day cycle network to the 2-string 6-ship 21-day cycle configuration, illustrated in Figure 4.6, the company injected a heart-stopping 50% additional capacity into its north European service. The reconfiguration also enabled the company to offer its customers in Canada, France and Germany faster transit times on legs where the company had low share. With service faster than the options available from any of its competitors, the company was able to grow its share through better service times. It was a very successful strategy at a time when conventional wisdom would have argued that the anticipated recession should force a withdrawal of capacity. The competitors paid the price.

**Figure 4.6: 1991 Network for SLCS**

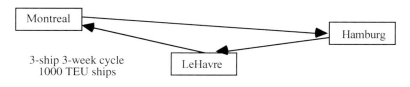

**Route A**

Montreal — Felixstowe — Antwerp

3-ship 3-week cycle
1780 TEU ships

**Route B**

Montreal — Hamburg — LeHavre

3-ship 3-week cycle
1000 TEU ships

This suggests that the implementation of a successful operating strategy includes the requirement to study the needs of shippers in close detail. Do they want the weekly (or twice-weekly) service and fixed day sailings demanded by shippers on other trade routes, or is existing service adequate and priced to their needs? Would they be willing to pay more for a better service? (This question, if asked directly, always runs into the problem that trade-offs (service to price) need to be reflected in the market research program.) What time frame is planned for introduction or expansion of just-in-time systems by manufacturers and their suppliers/buyers in the market(s) served? What economic development initiatives are underway in the market(s) to be served to convert raw material shippers to more value-added and time-sensitive businesses?

Carriers can only confirm that the market is not static and attempt to explore all the ways it may change. While asset choice, utilization and network configuration are usually considered to be the domain of the operations (production) side of the business, managing the network and the revenue generated from it should be seen as marketing functions, as is clear from the illustration of SLCS's 1990 reconfiguration. Once the carrier has made the decision to buy, sell or redeploy its vessels and has a plan for their deployment in a well-designed network, inside or outside a set of alliance relationships, the new strategy implementation plan must address the management of revenues and costs, the topic of the next section.

### REVENUE MANAGEMENT (INSIDE AND OUTSIDE THE CONFERENCE SYSTEM)

Asset choice, network schedules and resultant asset utilization dictate carrier costs to a great extent. Therefore, one approach to enhancing profitability is to focus on cost containment. The efficiencies of new vessels over old has already been clearly noted and cost leadership, as a strategy, has been broadly discussed in the previous chapter. Its likelihood of success as a strategy in this industry was concluded in Chapter 3 to be limited. Most cost advantages can be easily replicated. Managers must keep their eyes on the costs of operating the business but the long run winners will be those who grow the business with revenue management firmly entrenched in their implementation strategies.

That said, understanding the cost structure of the business is the necessary foundation for exploring new approaches to revenue management and new ways to examining the activities of the company. For purposes of this discussion, Figure 4.7 presents a simple schematic, a two-dimensional one where a three-dimensional one would provide a better illustration of the cargo-related variable costs.

Before Figure 4.7 can be explained, the differing cost categories must be discussed. In the typical business, planners have divided costs into two categories, fixed and variable. By knowing the unit costs of production along with fixed charges which must be covered, any entrepreneur can identify the sales level at which the business will begin to make a profit. This is too simplistic, however, for any business selling a perishable service, and more so for those businesses which are asset-intensive services. A clearer picture emerges if, at minimum, three categories of costs are considered:

- **Fixed costs**—Those incurred whether the transport asset is in storage or in service. (These costs are called "common costs" by Davies (1990) and other economists and "unattributable fixed costs" by industry.)
- **Trip-related variable costs**—Those incurred whether the transport asset moves empty or full.
- **Cargo-related variable costs**—Those directly related to the volume of business carried.

**Figure 4.7: Cost Structure in Shipping**

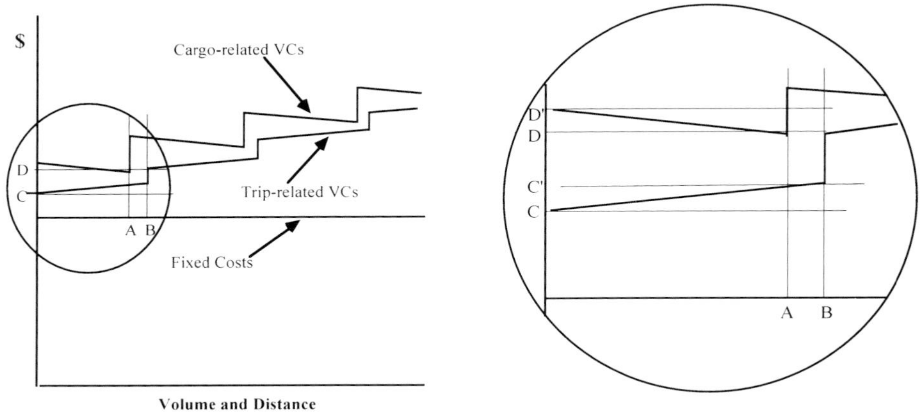

These are more precisely detailed for the liner shipping industry in Table 4.8.

**Table 4.8: Cost Elements in Shipping**

| Fixed Costs | Voyage-Related Variable Costs | Cargo-Related Variable Costs |
|---|---|---|
| Capital costs—vessels (in service and in lay-up) | Manning costs | Port charges (wharfage) |
| General overheads<br>  Administration and management<br>  Marketing and research<br>  Fixed agency expenses | Fuel costs<br><br>Maintenance and repairs<br><br>Insurance | Terminal handling charges*<br>Stevedoring charges*<br>Inland transport charges* |
| Vessel operating expenses<br>  Surveys<br>  Manning costs<br>  Maintenance and repairs | Port charges (harbour dues, berthage, pilotage, towage)<br><br>Agency commissions | |

Note:  * These charges may be passed on to the customer as a straight flow-through or they may be built into a door-to-door price depending on the regulatory environment.

One of the dilemmas of cost analysis is determining the method by which costs should be allocated. The fixed costs are allocated by some companies on a distance basis, while others may allocate them by unit sold. The airline industry usually allocates them on a per departure basis so that they can be merged with trip-related variable costs to understand the cost of each plane repositioning as well as each plane leg in service. Trip-related variable costs vary by distance while cargo-related variable costs vary by slot sold (volume). Putting all analysis on a per ocean leg basis is the first step in a simple cost analysis system. Once the simple system is mastered, carriers may increase the complexity of the analysis in order to maximize box usage and explore repositioning issues. That additional complexity will not be explored here.

Now return to Figure 4.7. Assume that the fleet characteristics have been determined and the fixed costs found to be the solid flat line indicated. The variable costs have a step function. Trip-related variable costs step up each time a new trip is added to handle additional volume and tend to vary with the distance of the trip. In the airline industry this would be equivalent to the costs incurred with each departure and in shipping with each sailing. Even if there are no seats or slots filled, the costs for the first trip taken would total between C and C' for the departure or sailing, dependent on the distance. Then the cargo-related variable costs are added to the determination. In the airline industry these would be the costs per seat sold, and they **may** decline as the distance increases or they may increase as the number of seats or slots are sold. The illustration reflects the former but not the latter, as it is two-dimensional, not three. In shipping, these variable costs may approach zero if all, or almost all, charges in the cargo-related cost category are passed on in the invoice sent to the customer.

The interesting feature of the schematic is the spoilage factor. It is often assumed that adding the last customer or box (to the last seat or the last slot prior to departure) comes without a cost increase. The difference between Volume A and Volume B in terms of the total cost incurred by the carrier is spoilage—the cost of having turned away a customer that might have been served and was not (while looking for the higher paying one that failed to materialize), or of having service deterioration due to asset utilization exceeding the level that is possible to manage without a service deterioration. There is a price tag to the carrier of not adding an additional departure (sailing) in favour of trying to secure perfect asset utilization. This spoilage, or service failure cost, is extremely difficult to quantify but necessary to evaluate.

Once a carrier has undertaken the complex task of allocating costs to the appropriate category, the tasks of revenue management and cost containment become possible. Trade-offs between costs and service levels become more obvious.

Revenue management is a difficult and complex task at the best of times, when growth is solid and capacity is squeezed. If load factors have deteriorated and excess capacity exists, implementing a strategy featuring revenue enhancement looks to be a wasted effort. However, revenue management is the complement to cost containment; it can move operating ratios into the desirable range while at the same time providing the service the customer expects. To choose this path, it is necessary to ignore the existence of the conference system temporarily.

Revenue management is more than just pricing. An assessment of load factors by departure is a good first step. The transpacific has been a difficult trade even at the best of times. As illustrated in Figure 4.3, asset utilization westbound, even before the Asian meltdown, often ran between 60% and 70%, while eastbound fared better with load factors above 70%. In Table 4.9, the revenue eastbound reflects the better load factor situation. Improvement in load factors either east- or westbound would enhance the operating margin and move it into the black. As management seeks to improve load factors, conditions change. The situation is always dynamic.

### Table 4.9: 1996 Service Profitability Transpacific

| Revenue | | $000 per voyage | % |
|---|---|---|---|
| | Eastbound | 3,917 | 59.5 |
| | Westbound | 2,671 | 40.5 |
| | | 6,589 | 100% |
| **Expenses** | | | |
| Fixed | Bunkers | 297 | 4.4 |
| | Ports | 193 | 2.9 |
| | Capital | 754 | 11.2 |
| | Operating | 330 | 4.9 |
| | Administration | 576 | 8.5 |
| | | 2,150 | 31.9% |
| Direct | Terminals | 1,084 | 16.1 |
| | Transport | 2,209 | 32.7 |
| | Depots | 29 | 0.4 |
| | Refrigeration | 30 | 0.5 |
| | | 3,352 | 49.7% |
| Indirect | Equipment | 329 | 4.9 |
| | Empty Containers | 532 | 7.9 |
| | Maintenance & Repair | 288 | 4.3 |
| | Claims & Insurance | 96 | 1.4 |
| | | 1,245 | 18.5% |
| Full Service Costs | | 6,747 | |
| Voyage Result | | -158 | |
| Margin | | | -2.4% |

Source:   Drewry Shipping Consultants (1996a:154, Table 8.7).

Variance in freight rates over time reflects the changing dynamics of each particular market (Figure 4.10).[5] In the case of the transpacific, the steady deterioration eastbound has not yet reached the average rate charged on the weaker but more unstable westbound leg. The figure demonstrates that both directions do not move in tandem, signaling that revenue management tactics will likely be implemented differently in each trade lane by astute revenue managers. If the trade lane forms part of a multi-leg long-haul move, the revenue management problem will be more complex than that explored in this chapter.[6]

---

[5]   Given that the transatlantic is the shortest of the three main trades in Figure 4.10, and its rates, particularly eastbound, are strong, it is not surprising that a number of alliances chose to enter this route in 1998, further driving rates down.

[6]   While per departure costing (and voyage accounting) enables carriers to fully understand their costs in a simplified manner, some carriers have returned to periodic accounting believing that a focus on per departure costing encourages fully informed sales personnel to become deal-makers on a single leg ignoring the multi-

Good revenue management establishes a pricing philosophy for a fixed volume of capacity and the tariff schedule reflects differentiation by commodity and directional demand.[7] It may also build in other differentiating factors as determined by the company's revenue management team. Brooks and Button (1996) identified a preliminary set of determinants that explain pricing differentials for one leg of one trade route (the transatlantic) and these determinants may be extended to explain some of the variance in evidence in Figure 4.10 between trade lanes.

**Figure 4.10: Freight Rates on the Major Trade Lanes (US$ per TEU)**

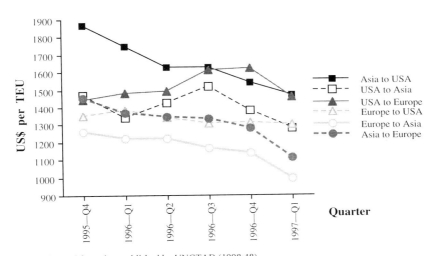

Source:  Created from data published by UNCTAD (1998:48).

The solution more than a century ago was the development of a conference system with its tariff structure based on charging differentiated prices at "what the market will bear" levels, a crude revenue management system. Jansson and Schneerson (1987:217) used the terms archaic and obsolete to describe the practice. They concluded that, while buyers would not accept the frequencies of sailings that would result from capacity appropriately matched to profits, the existence of the conference pricing approach results in low cost-consciousness. Innovative pricing is not encouraged.

In today's excess capacity market, any liner company will always find shippers willing to buy slots at below cost prices. One only has to look at the variation in price charged by commodity,

---

leg factors. At the end of the day, no carrier wants to invest in new capacity to service a network driven by low value business on a single leg.

7    Demand differentiated pricing (Ramsey pricing to economists) allocates costs on the basis of the value of the service to the consumer, mathematically expressed as its elasticity of demand. Ramsey pricing maximizes the opportunity to achieve adequate return while being rewarded for innovation and efficiencies which deliver cost reductions. This has been illustrated in the liner shipping industry by Zerby and Conlon (1978).

illustrated in Figure 4.11, to understand the carrier's profitability dilemma with an excessively differentiated conference tariff.

Does revenue management offer an alternative for the future? Vessel profitability per departure depends both on how well each carrier's marketing team manages to maximize the revenue and how good the operations team is at controlling the expense side of the ledger. The two must work hand-in-glove and the glove must fit. The purpose in maintaining a balanced view between revenue management and cost containment is to widen the gap between revenue and expenses, thereby enhancing the operating ratio and the subsequent profitability of the strategy. The remainder of this section will focus on the process and techniques of good revenue management, building on lessons from the airline industry.

**Figure 4.11: North Atlantic Eastbound Conference Tariffs**

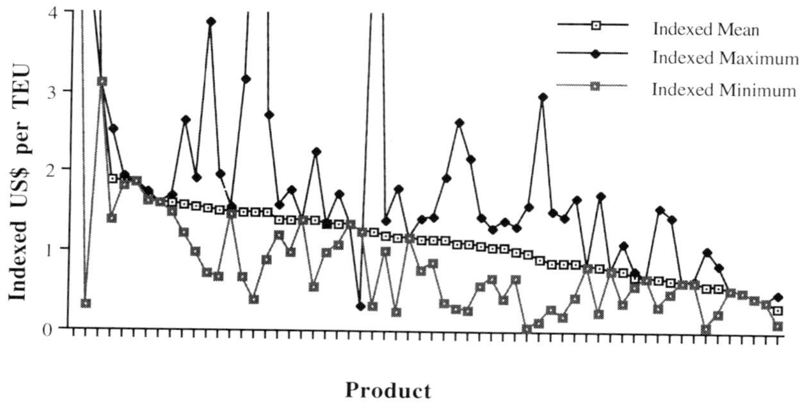

Source:    Brooks and Button (1994:189, Exhibit 5).

The following is a modification of the process used for revenue management in the airline industry. It begins with a good management information system which can provide demand data from past sailings and is coupled with real-time booking information. In order to work, the carrier must have reasonably good information on the demand elasticities of its prospective customers. The yield analyst tracks both and adjusts "price" accordingly, something not possible without cheating in a conference system. The following discussion is based on the process as explained by Tretheway and Oum (1992) for the airline industry, and Figures 4.12 to 4.15 were adapted from their figures with permission. The process begins by identifying the probable demand curve (Figure 4.12) for the **particular** sailing based on past data from the management information system. This will vary by season, for example.

The demand curve for this illustrative sailing is a normal probability distribution. Swan (1998) noted that a gamma distribution is more likely in the airline industry for premium service buyers (business class) than for those who are more price conscious. The coefficient of variance will need to be calculated for time of day, day of week and week of year. It is quite clear that each company will need to do its own assessment of its management data in order to identify the appropriate nature of demand probabilities, and to secure the managerial confidence in the data to make the forecasts a useful tool.

The next step is to examine historical records to define the likely or expected booking curve, setting it into a time frame before the sailing closes. Once the expected booking curve is defined, the analyst sets probable limits, or exception thresholds, on the variance of that curve (Figure 4.13) using statistical analysis. Carriers may not set the upper threshold with as tight a tolerance as the lower threshold, if the purpose is to limit downside risk in the price determination. The sailing may close for bookings 24–36 hours before the vessel actually sales. While there remains time for last minute exceptions, Figures 4.13 and 4.14 set the activities as completed when the sailing closes.

**Figure 4.12: Demand for Slots Above a Predetermined Price of $750**

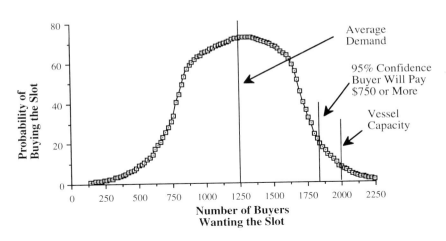

In the airline industry, the sheer number of plane departures in any given week necessitates that a large airline will manage by exception. The computer identifies exceptions and triggers an alarm when a threshold is violated. The analyst will then decide if incentives for last minute bookings are warranted. In the shipping industry, with fewer sailings per week, the analyst may examine all sailings or may rely on computerized exception reporting at critical pre-departure times. The system is ideally linked to a company sales tracking report that looks for under-booking by key customers. The sales staff would then be mandated to follow predetermined sales plans developed for underbooking scenarios.

If Figure 4.13 is superimposed on Figure 4.14, which plots the actual booking experience for a particular sailing, it becomes obvious that the exception thresholds were exceeded in this particular case. The response will depend on the carrier's revenue management policies for dealing with exceptions. To explain Figure 4.14, sales tracked as close to "expected" in the beginning of the sales period, and even exceeded expectations a few days before the sailing. However, last minute shipments did not materialize as planned; as these are often made by consolidators, inducements may work to bring these customers "on board." Seldom do manufacturers have such last minute sales to take advantage of these inducements and so a sales push with this segment of the market would be less likely to bear fruit. However, inducements to consolidators are a double-edged sword and savvy consolidators may begin to play booking games if a pattern in a carrier's operations becomes readily discernible.[8] The data developed can also be fed into fleet planning models so that asset choice and network configuration decision become more dynamic.

### Figure 4.13: Expected Booking Curve

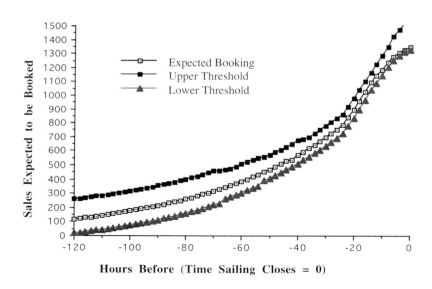

**Hours Before (Time Sailing Closes = 0)**

While Figure 4.14 illustrates an actual booking curve without any cancellations, this is seldom the case. The booking curve with cancellations would peak in the days immediately before sailing and then drop as bookings cancel. Therefore, an astute carrier will plot actual bookings

---

8    Airlines with exception reporting triggers set three days prior to departure have become known to frequent discretionary travellers, who wait for the opportunity to use inducements when they would have paid more.

against cargo deliveries and develop scenarios to calculate cancellation probabilities. In this manner, an overbooking estimate can be developed and incorporated into the company's planning activities.

**Figure 4.14: Actual Booking Curve**

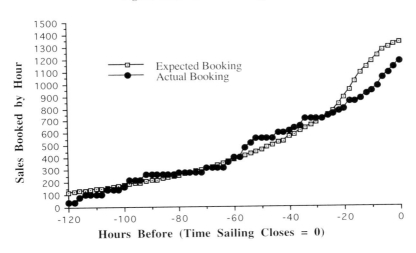

Finally, there is the matter of setting an appropriate price with restrictions; in the airline industry, these restrictions are called fences. A fence serves to restrict a customer prepared to pay more from using a discounted price; that is, it prevents "spillage." Common fences in the airline business are a better quality of service (business or first class), Saturday night stayovers, advanced booking requirements, and cancellation or change penalties. An airline passenger is then able to make the decision whether a Saturday night stayover is undesirable or return flexibility is worth the additional premium, making fences relatively simple for the airline to impose.

From Figure 4.12, it was determined that, with a 95% confidence level, customers for the sailing would be prepared to pay $750 (or more). Figure 4.15 translates the demand data for each price level into possible price scenarios and calculates resulting revenue. A non-conference carrier could opt for a FAK pricing approach and set the price at the known acceptable price of $750. This price, given the demand curve in Figure 4.15, would result in total revenue of $1.56 million gained by selling 1250 slots (which just happens to be the average demand) at $1250. The carrier could opt for poorer asset utilization and only a marginally lower total revenue with a higher FAK price of $1750. This strategy opens the carrier to sniping and does not maximize the total revenue as would be possible from using a differentiated pricing strategy. The carrier could garner $2.59 million in total revenue for the sailing from a differentiated pricing strategy with four price levels and an appropriate set of fences to prevent spillage. If more intermediate fences are able to be set and implemented effectively, the carrier may be able to secure even more total revenue as some customers are still not paying the last cents they may be prepared to pay. The logic of multiple prices is difficult to resist, but the carrier is advised to limit enthusiasm or the result will look little different than Figure 4.11.

**Figure 4.15: Fares and Fences**

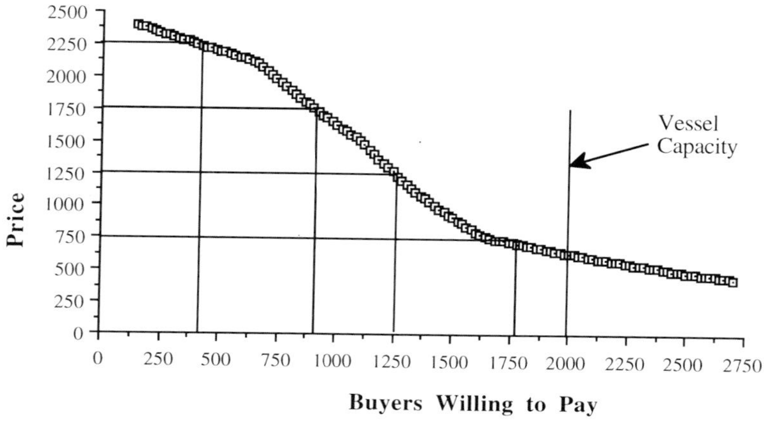

Resulting Revenue Scenarios:

| Price | Quantity | Incremental Quantity | FAK Revenue | Incremental Revenue |
|-------|----------|----------------------|-------------|---------------------|
| $2,250 | 400 | | $900,000 | $900,000 |
| $1,750 | 890 | 490 | $1,557,500 | $857,500 |
| $1,250 | 1250 | 360 | $1,562,500 | $450,000 |
| $750 | 1760 | 510 | $1,320,000 | $382,500 |
| | | | total | $2,590,000 |

In conclusion, Brooks and Button (1994) identified a number of preconditions necessary in order for price differentiation to occur:
- the service involves a fixed commitment
- the supplier has information on the charges the user "will bear"
- the supplier enjoys a relatively high degree of monopoly power
- it is possible (in the eyes of potential customers) to product differentiate
- customers have less information on options than the supplier has on available capacity and
- the supplier is able to respond quickly.

The first three are features of this industry. The last does not exist within a conference system and the fourth will be discussed shortly. The fifth of these will be more likely under the *Ocean Shipping Reform Act of 1998*; the ability to enter into confidential, global service contracts will provide less information to potential buyers than existed under the filing requirements of previous legislation. Thus, changing regulation has partially paved the way for more sophisticated revenue management practices in liner shipping. As growth in service contracts results from the implementation of the Act, and from greater incorporation of supply chain management principles by buyers, the ability to employ revenue management principles will grow.

However, it is the fourth of these conditions that poses the greatest challenge. Freight cannot distinguish its location on the ship (or any benefits that might accrue from that location); the trip is one-way. Early booking discounts, like late booking premiums, may secure more stable business if the carrier is working outside the conference system where such practices are possible. The conference system has attempted to impose fences such as commodity classification, trade direction and special container supply to ameliorate the dilemma that fences are difficult to identify and impose. To most conference carriers, revenue management is more about asset utilization and less seen in its full potential. It is the dilemma of fences, more than any other, that limits the applicability of revenue management as developed by the airlines from being applied in more than a crude way in the liner shipping industry. As long as conference membership exists, conference carriers will only be able to see revenue management as an exercise in cost containment.

## MARKETING THE LINER SERVICE AND MONITORING ITS PERFORMANCE

Returning to Figure 3.2, the implementation strategy is shown as an operations strategy. This is not fully explanatory as it is the marketing team that will interface with the customer in the execution of the strategy. The marketing team will also be on the front line to monitor the carrier's performance, as they are particularly well-positioned to note any service failures that occur. While many liner sales agents or sales staff will see their role as providing price quotations, implementation of revenue management is only part of marketing the service. Sales personnel must also solve the customer's logistical problems and provide feedback to the management team about the carrier's performance. This section of the chapter will focus on these roles but will not address another key element of the strategy, whether the marketing function is outsourced to agents or managed in-house.[9]

Of primary importance in marketing the liner service is identifying any customer segments with special requirements and the attributes customers in those segments are seeking. Brooks

---

9   Leaving out this element of marketing strategy is a matter of expediency. While the marketing literature has plenty to say about the agent or company sales office decision as a sales management issue, there has been very little research to determine whether this industry has features so unique that findings in the general literature would not be applicable. Ahlander and Spanholtz (1998) agree about the dearth of research on this issue. The sales structure decision is of importance particularly if the carrier opts out of the conference system and implements a full revenue management system. Outsourcing sales would logically be difficult in this scenario. The topic provides a critical area for future management research.

(1985, 1990, 1995) detailed this process for the liner industry, identifying a number of key purchase determinants for a liner company's services. The research series illustrated that different criteria can be identified for different customer segments but that these criteria are a moving target over time. As industry has evolved, emphasis on price has diminished and other factors like transit time have grown in importance. She also concluded that shippers, consignees and freight forwarders all have significantly different decision criteria and that these are used to evaluate carrier performance. Therefore, implementing the carrier's operating strategy will require extensive market research activity to thoroughly understand customer requirements, and that activity will need to be repeated at consistent intervals to provide insight into the evolving dynamic of their needs. Verma *et al.* (1999) provide some of the requisite tools in their assessment of discrete choice analysis to understand preferences. This information, coupled with the Aaker and Day model first proposed for this industry by Brooks (1985) for defining determinants of behaviour, result in relevant market research for effective operating and marketing decisions available to the carrier prepared to make the investment.

Tailoring the service to the customer is only the beginning. Preparing to discriminate the service comes next. One key to successful execution of revenue management is knowing which customers the carrier wants to serve. Here the old purchasing classification ABC system is useful; A and B customers are those you always want to serve, C customers are those you serve with any excess capacity. Spoilage occurs when a C customer is served and an A customer's cargo is left on the dock.

The final element in understanding the customer is one of performance that meets or exceeds the customer's expectations. A more recent body of work by Brooks (1998, 1999a, b, 2000) has examined the issue of carrier performance monitoring and concluded that carriers have some distance to go in implementing performance programs that focus on the criteria by which they are chosen, and whether the service is both efficient and effective. She noted that many carriers focus only on measuring customer satisfaction (on a scale of 1 to 5, for example) without fully understanding the way customers may measure their performance. Performance and satisfaction may not track similarly at all, in spite of being related. In Figure 4.16, the company has captured operating performance data in terms of the number of deliveries per month missing a specified customer delivery time window, and plotted that data against monthly customer satisfaction surveys; the result paints a more complete picture of whether or not a service failure has existed in the mind of the customer. It is the juxtaposition of service actually delivered with customer's perception of service received that provides for fuller comprehension. Also, as can be seen from Figure 4.16, customer satisfaction may drop further after a service failure if the customer has experienced a sought for and now expected outcome. The second part of the performance measurement process must therefore be a plan for addressing service failures.

In addition, Brooks discovered that customers are more likely to measure a carriers' perform-ance on key service elements than is the carrier. Relying on one's customers to indicate unsatisfactory performance is like walking down the street past an unprotected construction site. Responding after being hit on the head by a falling brick is too late. It is better to plan a strategy for passing the construction site when you are fully aware of its dangers. This requires proactive performance monitoring as a continuing element of strategy implementation.

**Figure 4.16: Impact of Carrier Performance on Customers**

As carrier/shipper relations move from transaction-based ones to negotiated supply chain alliances, and shippers increasingly outsource their logistics activities, successful carriers will be those who monitor performance by measuring it and proactively address service failures as defined by the customer. In some cases, carriers will be the recipients of outsourced logistics activities; this does not imply that carriers all have the skills to take on these activities and do them well. Monitoring performance will become even more important for those carriers straying from a solid focus on managing vessel operations. Whether logistics subsidiaries are established or not, it is simply insufficient to choose appropriate assets, configure networks to provide a desired service and develop a revenue management system if the entire operation fails to be appropriately monitored. Information learned must be fed back to the management team deciding on the appropriate long-term strategy for the company.

Monitoring is not just a financial or operations activity. Each carrier will, therefore, have to develop its own performance measurement system. It must be done on a company-wide basis. In the process of designing a performance evaluation system, there are pitfalls to be avoided. Performance metrics should be determined as an integral part of the implementation plan for the company's overall strategy.[10] Kaplan and Norton (1996) introduced the Balanced Score-

---

10   In particular, Hauser and Katz (1998:524) develop a paradigm to ensure that all the correlations between the elements of relationships between customers and employees, outcomes, company priorities and work processes are fully understood.

card as an approach by which managers can evaluate existing company performance and set objectives for future improvement and growth. Virtually all organizations use financial measures to evaluate performance and most companies use non-financial measures to improve performance in targeted areas such as front office[11] operations which interface with customers. The Balanced Scorecard approach, however, is an integrated one which takes all areas and assesses their performance in a cohesive manner. There are four areas which implement strategy and vision in a top-down manner: financial, customer, internal business processes, and learning and growth; each translates the philosophy of the organization into a set of objectives, measures, targets and initiatives. The company is then set on a cycle which clarifies its strategy, links it to the objectives and measures, supports the plan with targets and strategic initiatives, and then enhances performance through feedback and organizational learning.[12]

The implementation of a marketing plan and a performance monitoring system is a prerequisite to sustained success whether the growth strategy favours merger or alliance. In a merger, the merged company would have the sole leadership to encourage the necessary organizational acceptance to achieve the maximum benefits of the process. Such a process, however, would be more difficult to implement in an alliance because it requires all parties in the alliance to adopt the common vision, and the information processes to support that vision, as well as have the political will to embark operationally on the chosen course. Agreement with performance monitoring principles thus favours growth via merger or acquisition in the face of divergence of alliance partners' opinions on the matter.

## MAKING THE RELATIONSHIP WORK

Slot charters have grown out of shippers' demands for both transit speed and frequent service while they also try to engage in carrier reduction strategies. As vessels grow in size, carriers have experienced a lower cost per slot from an operating point of view. However, because of poor profitability, ship owners have been less able financially to order new vessels and maintain a "go-it-alone" strategy. To provide weekly service, or twice weekly service as is required on the US–Japan/north Asia route, the capital cost of ships necessitates joint services or strategic alliances in some form to meet shipper demands. Few carriers have the wherewithal to go-it-alone. This chapter will therefore close with a discussion of the broader implementation issue of making the relationship work if alliance is the strategy of choice.

Despite the significant volume of research on alliances, little is known about what makes them successful (or why they fail). Some of the most common conclusions are that a successful alliance must have commitment from senior management, compatible participants that view alliances from a network perspective, trust each other and learn from the relationship. Saxton (1997) determined that if alliance partners are reputable, share decision-making responsi-

---

[11]  The term "front office" implies those corporate activities undertaken by a company in front of its customers, while "back office" activities are out of the sight of the buyer.

[12]  G. Fraser (1999), personal interview, 8 November, noted that Australia New Zealand Direct Line is an example of a company successfully using the Balanced Scorecard approach.

bilities, and possess strategic similarities, the alliance should be successful. However, he also contradicted reports that "culture clash" negatively influenced alliances by finding that partners with similar organizational characteristics were less successful.

Cooper and Gardner (1993) studied the relationship between a third party supplier and its core customer to develop a list of characteristics that make partnerships successful. They concluded that planning, sharing benefits and burdens, demonstrating trust, the systematic exchange of information, allowing the partner to monitor or control some of the operations, and undertaking activities to bridge corporate cultures were all found to lead to successful business relationships.

According to Devlin and Bleackley (1988) and Main (1990), an alliance has a better chance of being successful if senior management is committed to the partnership and it is not merely seen as a "quick-fix." Management must be involved in every aspect of forming the alliance, but especially active in the actual decision to form the alliance, in choosing the partner, and in planning for the management of the partnership. Devlin and Bleackley (1988) provided a checklist of criteria to aid firms in their pursuit of successful alliances; the checklist focuses on two key elements: choice of the partner and managing the alliance. Roland Smith, chairman of British Aerospace in 1990, went even further, stressing that management cannot simply give instructions and expect the partnership to be successful (Main, 1990).

According to Main (1990), a firm's ability to learn from its partner(s) will improve the alliance's chance of success. Although entering an alliance will potentially expose all partners to an increased amount of knowledge, not all will have the absorptive capacity or the willingness to share information (Kumar and Nti, 1998; Feldman, 1998). Those companies already possessing a good knowledge base, management systems, and employees predisposed towards cooperative behaviour will be in a much better position to engage in organizational learning (Kumar and Nti, 1998). Inkpen and Dinur (1998) believe that successful alliances have the ability to create new knowledge at all levels of the organization.

One of the most frequent problems with alliances is attributed to firms selecting incompatible partners (Vollman and Cordon, 1998) and Harvey and Lusch (1995) provided a framework for partner evaluation that included quantitatively assessing the macro environment, industry structure and organization structure in conjunction with other qualitative factors.

On the other hand, Brouthers *et al.* (1995) believed that alliances should be avoided unless absolutely necessary due to a lack of resources; they asserted that partnerships can be effective if those entering the relationship use the Four Cs—complementary skills, cooperative cultures, compatible goals, and commensurate levels of risk in the undertaking—as the criteria for selecting an appropriate alliance partner.

Given the wide availability of advice for entering alliances, Medcof (1997) felt that more should be successful and participants should have greater confidence in partner selection. However, in a survey of 750 US CEOs with alliance experience, he found that firms felt themselves weakest in assessing potential partners. As an aid, he too provided a framework for evaluating partners in the context of a firm's business strategy. He concluded that most of the advice, while valid, only considered alliances involving two participants and that, in much of the literature, long term strategic alliances[13] were not discussed. Multi-partner alliances are certainly common in today's environment of networks and constellations. Therefore, to encourage successful alliances, firms should assess their strategic fit with potential partners and ensure that Brouthers *et al.*'s Four Cs are employed, without losing sight of their long-term strategies.

When considering potential alliances, a company has to consider its self-interest as well as its interest in the network. Duysters *et al.* (1999: 184) concluded it is necessary to use a network perspective because it has a mix of competitive and cooperative aspects and cannot be properly managed with a model designed for only two members. They explained their point of view by considering the profitable relationship between Disney, Coke and McDonald's: formal alliances exist between Disney and McDonald's as well as between Disney and Coke, but there is no official connection between McDonald's and Coke. A decision by Disney to ally with Pepsi instead would strain its current relationship with McDonald's and perhaps destroy a very profitable relationship. Therefore, to prevent mismanagement of complicated networks, they recommended managing networks as a portfolio. This entails selecting a partner that fits both bilaterally and within the network, leveraging knowledge, and managing a set of competencies, not contracts, because "combining competencies in a network to satisfy a client's needs lies at the core of portfolio thinking."[14]

Kanter (1994) described a company's ability to be a good alliance partner as a "collaborative advantage." The importance of compatibility among partners is emphasized by the fact that not all alliances are long lasting and, in order to extract immediate benefits from the pairing, the partners' legacies, philosophies and desires should match. As the partnership progresses, a successful alliance will be one in which collaboration continues and five levels of integration (strategic, tactical, operational, interpersonal, and cultural) are achieved.

As noted in Chapter 2, the majority of mergers and alliances fail. Three phenomena may contribute to this for mergers—a great deal of attention being paid to the deal but little to the integration, rushing the deal, and using the merger as a strategy in its own right (Anonymous, 1999). The same may be argued as appropriate explanations of alliance failure. Many companies rush their deals to merge or ally themselves, thinking that most aspects of their businesses will naturally fit together. This is not the case, as Feldman (1998) and Anonymous (1998) document for the Star Alliance.[15]

---

[13]    These strategies enable alliance firms to improve their positions for participation in future alliances .

[14]    Reprinted from Duysters, G., A. P. de Man, L. Wildeman (1999), "A Network Approach to Alliance Management," *European Management Journal*, 17, 2, 182-7. © 1999, with permission from Elsevier Science.

[15]    Within the Star Alliance there were at least 24 committees handling everything from customer relations and purchasing to network connectivity. Chairmanships of these committees tended to be allocated not for efficiency but to maintain good relations between alliance members (Anonymous, 1998). In addition, alliance staff from several of the airlines complained of the time commitment required from them. Interestingly, once a commitment from top management became apparent to Austrian Airlines employees, the problems they had

Håkansson and Johanson (1993) postulated that partners in networks gradually build mutual trust through a process of social exchange. But, once partners begin to calculate the costs and benefits of continuing cooperation, the relationship becomes fragile. Falkenberg's (1992) study of 16 Norwegian shipping companies and their alliances concluded that trust was an important ingredient, without which the relationship would break down. On the other hand, if the relationship is based on trust, even when serious problems occur with one firm's equity, the alliance may still be successfully renegotiated (Ariño and de la Torre, 1998). In conclusion, commitment and confidence, necessary ingredients for building trust, are key intangible features of a stable alliance relationship.

Both Cauley de la Sierra (1995) and Doz and Hamel (1998) provide useful guidebooks on alliances. The former contains strategies and tips for planning and negotiating the deal and principles for making global alliances work, while the latter provides important insights into their strategic role. Cauley de la Sierra's basic premise is that mutual respect, senior management commitment and equitable treatment go a long way to making the alliance successful. She concludes that businesses need to collaborate to compete but they must achieve balance between collaboration and competition. This sounds like a good recipe for any successful relationship.

---

with being required to spend time (in addition to their normal jobs) on alliance issues greatly diminished (Feldman, 1998).

# 5

# LESSONS FROM OTHER INDUSTRIES: RAILROADS[1]

## INTRODUCTION

In the last four chapters, the groundwork was laid for understanding the liner shipping industry. The first chapter described the events leading to the state of the industry today. Chapter 2 presented the theoretical bases for its analysis in both the economic and strategic management literature. Chapter 3 used some of the simpler models in the strategic management literature to draw conclusions about the industry and the reasons why firms make the strategic choices they do. Chapter 4 examined the operating elements of successful implementation of the carrier's strategy so that the link between strategy, structural options, operations and regulation can be made in the concluding chapters of this book.

This chapter is the first of three on other asset- or infrastructure-intensive networked service industries. In these three middle chapters, events and the managerial decisions taken will be explored through the use of illustrative "case studies."[2] Each of the industries chosen for this middle part of the book have much in common: the strategy formulation process (outlined in Chapter 3) and the operating strategies which prove successful for the business (detailed in Chapter 4) are similar as the industries share many features. However, firms in these industries differ substantially in their choice of merger, acquisition or alliance approaches to growth. They also have regulatory peculiarities which influence the direction of managerial preferences.

It may appear that the rail industry is not, and cannot be, a global industry with global reach. Unlike both the air and marine transport industries, its assets are less mobile. It is, however, a networked, asset-intensive service industry and understanding how companies in this industry

---

1   I would like to thank very heartily Jim Blaze of Zeta-Tech Associates for his review of this chapter and for his suggestions for its improvement. The content remains my responsibility.

2   A true case study presents the reader with a protagonist and a decision point in time, and is based on in-depth analysis by the case writer of all the facts at the time. It is used for teaching managerial problem solving. The studies presented in this book are really narratives about a company as they were presented by the trade press. They have neither the depth nor the insight normally found in a true case study, but are intended to challeng the reader to explore further. The case studies in this chapter were developed with the research assistance of Naomi Andjelic and Annette Johnson, Dalhousie MBA/LLB '99 students.

have chosen to expand their geographic scope of operations will have lessons for the liner industry. The chapter concludes that for this industry, merger is a preferable strategy to the formation of some type of cooperative relationship. Railroads do appear in the roster of the world's largest corporations, the Fortune *Global 500*; rail's growth options are limited by regulation, imagination and, in some cases, public ownership.

After presentation of the case studies, there will be brief discussion on the management issues along with the competition issues, concluding with a short section on the possible lessons for liner companies. The case studies provide some insight into regulatory differences and food for thought as we proceed to the closing chapters of the book and its discussion of competition issues as they relate to liner shipping. This chapter does not devote much of its content to the economic literature on the rail industry as this has been well-developed by those with greater expertise in this particular industry.[3] It begins with an extremely brief overview of deregulation in the US rail industry, introducing the major players—the Class I railroads.

Deregulation of the US rail industry began with the *Railroad Revitalization and Regulatory Reform Act of 1976*[4] and *Staggers Rail Act of 1980*, hereinafter referred to as the *Staggers Act*. The first of these identified guidelines for regulators to determine revenue adequacy of the rail system and contained the statutory changes to implement revised procedures for merger approval. The second gave carriers greater flexibility in managing their rail operations and enabled them to explore strategic approaches to regaining market share lost to the trucking industry. The centrepiece of the *Staggers Act* was rate reform: railroads were free from Interstate Commerce Commission (ICC) regulation to set rates (as long as they did not possess "market dominance"), they were permitted to enter into long-term service contracts with shippers, and the role of rate bureaus was reduced. Abandonment processes were also expedited. These changes freed carriers to develop intermodal strategies and abandon unprofitable track, preparing the way for more productive rail companies.

In recent years, much has been made of the consolidation of the rail industry in the post-deregulation era. The statistics reported in the trade press have varied widely. Both consolidation and a change in the definition of a Class I railroad were intertwined; Class I railroads at the time were those with a three-year average operating revenue of at least US$50 million. There were 40 Class I railroads operating in the US in 1980;[5] of these, 27 would meet the definition of a Class I railroad by 1996 (operating revenue of US$255 million).[6] (See Table 5.1.)

---

3    If more coverage of the rail economics literature is desirable, the reader is recommended to read the following: Caves *et al.* (1981, 1985); Kessides and Willig (1998); Keeler (1983); and Waters (1985).

4    Also known as the *4-R Act*.

5    As listed in the Interstate Commerce Commission *Transport Statistics of the United States* for the year ending 31 December 1980. (The list was provided by the Association of American Railroads.)

6    These 27 assume that 1980 revenues are converted to 1996 dollars using the chain-weighted GDP deflator. (S. Dennis (1999), Association of American Railroads, personal interview, 11 January.)

## Table 5.1: Rail Mergers in the US

| *Class I Railroad (1)* | *Event Since 1980* |
|---|---|
| **Atchison, Topeka & Santa Fe** (SF) | merged with Burlington Northern 1995 |
| Baltimore & Ohio | merged into CSX in 1980 |
| **Burlington Northern** (BN) | renamed Burlington Northern Santa Fe in 1995 |
| Central of Georgia Railway | part of the Southern Railway in 1980 (reported separately) |
| Chesapeake & Ohio | merged into CSX in 1980 |
| **Chicago & Northwestern** (CNW) | fully acquired by UP 1994 |
| Chicago, Milw., St. Paul & Pacific | split between the **CP Rail** and other railroads; some abandoned |
| Cincinnati, New Orleans & Texas Pacific | part of the Southern Railway in 1980 (reported separately) |
| **Consolidated Rail Corp.** (Conrail) | acquisition by **CSX** and **Norfolk Southern (NS)** 1998 |
| Delaware & Hudson | lost Class I status; acquired by CP Rail 1991 |
| Denver, Rio Grande & Western | merged into the SP 1988 |
| Grand Trunk & Western | part of **Canadian National** (reported separately) |
| **Illinois Central Gulf** | acquisition by Canadian National in 1999 |
| **Kansas City Southern** (KCS) | |
| Long Island Railroad | passenger only service today |
| Louisville & Nashville Railroad | merged into CSX |
| Missouri–Kansas–Texas | merged into UP 1988 |
| Missouri Pacific | merged into UP 1982 |
| Norfolk & Western | merged with SRS to form NS 1982 |
| Saint Louis–San Francisco | merged with Burlington Northern in 1980 |
| Saint Louis, Southwestern | part of SP |
| Seaboard Coast Line | merged to form CSX 1985 |
| Soo Line Railroad Co. | acquired by CP Rail 1990 (reported separately) |
| **Southern Pacific** (SP) | merged with UP 1996 |
| Southern Railway System | merged with Norfolk & Western to form NS 1982 |
| **Union Pacific** (UP) | |
| Western Pacific | merged into UP 1986 |

Notes:   Those in bold are the Class I railroads existing by 1994.
   (1) Those which would meet the Class I threshold in 1996 (US$255 million in operating revenue). The ones which were Class I in 1980 but did not meet the 1996 threshold and were not absorbed into one of the Class I systems were the Boston & Maine (lost Class I status 1989); the Florida East Coast (lost status 1992); and those now owned by Transtar—the Bessemer & Lake Erie (lost status 1985), the Duluth, Missabe, & Iron Range (lost status 1985), and the Elgin Joliet & Eastern (lost status 1985). The remainder were either unable to meet the Class I criteria or were already part of another Class I rail system, but reporting separately. The Chicago, Rock Island & Pacific went bankrupt in 1980 and parts were purchased by various railroads.

Source:   Created with information from the Association of American Railroads.

By 1994, the beginning of the current wave of consolidation, these 27 had become 12. At the time of writing, Class I railways comprised four large railways and three smaller ones.[7] This chapter will discuss the recent wave of consolidation in the US rail industry beyond that already encouraged by deregulation in the early 1980s.

## THE BURLINGTON NORTHERN AND SANTA FE MERGER

The latest wave of rail mergers began in July 1994, when Burlington Northern Inc. (parent company of Burlington Northern Railroad, BN) and Santa Fe Pacific Corp. (parent company of the Atchison, Topeka, and Santa Fe Railway, SF) announced they had signed a merger agreement. At the time of the merger, the consolidated company would be the largest railroad in the US, covering the midwestern and western two-thirds of the US with more than 31,000 route miles reaching across 27 states and two Canadian provinces (Minahan, 1995).

BN, based in Fort Worth, Texas, was created on 2 March 1970 by the merger of four railroads: the Chicago, Burlington and Quincy Railroad, the Northern Pacific Railway, the Great Northern Railway, and the Spokane, Portland and Seattle Railway. Predecessor railroads numbered more than 330 (http://www.bnsf.com). The 1980s were not without their difficulties as BN restructured its business. The parent company was diversifying away from rail into energy, and the railroad was used as a cash cow to finance the diversification. Capital expenditures in support of rail operations were limited to about half of what should have been spent to keep up with rapidly changing technology. In 1988, when its parent sold its energy business, the railroad was US$2.8 billion in debt, more than three times equity. Furthermore, in 1992, BN had the worst operating ratio among the large publicly traded US railroads at 87% (Berman and Khalaf, 1993).

Chartered in 1859, the Atchison, Topeka and Santa Fe Railway, based in Schaumburg, Illinois, had a long history in the railroad industry but, unlike most other US railroads, saw little merger activity. It initially developed a legendary passenger service which continued until 1971, when Amtrak took over passenger service from most railroads. In the 1980s it gained industry recognition for its advances in intermodal traffic and its dedicated Houston to Barstow, CA, chemical service (Morris, 1994). SF played a key role in bringing innovation and creativity to the transportation industry with such developments as the first land-bridge container train, the first articulated rail car, and industry-wide improvements to other types of railcars as well, including the development of the Super Hopper and the articulated autoveyer. More recently, SF was the first railroad to develop an intermodal partnership, the one it negotiated with trucking giant, J. B. Hunt (http://www.bnsf.com). Its double-tracked service between Los Angeles and Chicago was among the fastest. SF has long been noted as a railroad with a strong commitment to research and development, a factor that helped place SF among the top Class I railroads in the US. However, SF was not without its warts. A merger with the Southern

---

7    The large ones are Burlington Northern Santa Fe, CSX, Norfolk Southern, and the Union Pacific. The smaller ones are Canadian National, Canadian Pacific and the Kansas City Southern.

Pacific had been announced in 1983 and denied in 1987, costing the company several years of focus on its existing business and by the late 1980s the company had financial problems.

The proposed merger between BN and SF was announced 30 June 1994. SF shareholders would receive 0.27 of a BN share for every SF share, a deal worth approximately US$2.7 billion (Morris, 1994). It was anticipated that it would not be a simple merger, due mainly to Santa Fe's ownership of the gold company, the Santa Fe Pacific Gold Corporation, and the financial complications that this ownership might entail (Welty, 1994). Ultimately, Santa Fe did spin off its gold company. However, the merger became considerably more complicated when, on 5 October 1994, Union Pacific (UP) made an unexpected offer of US$3.4 billion to acquire the SF.

The UP proposal amounted to nearly 38% more than was involved by the exchange of shares proposed in the deal with BN (Anonymous, 1994b). SF rejected the UP offer citing its commitment to BN and its view that the UP offer was little more than an attempt to derail the merger with BN (Anonymous, 1994a). In response, UP filed suit in Delaware Chancery Court against SF, BN, and the members of the SF board, seeking a judgment to force SF to negotiate with UP.

Shortly thereafter, BN and SF filed their formal merger application with the Interstate Commerce Commission on 13 October 1994. The application included letters of support from more than 450 shippers such as General Motors, Ford, ConAgra, and Nestlé (Anonymous, 1994a). BN countered UP's offer with another bid of US$3.2 billion for SF on 27 October 1994. Raising the stakes, UP increased its offer on 30 October to US$3.8 billion, and on 2 November, SF rejected this latest bid (Weber and Chandler, 1994). The higher price meant that SF shareholders would be better off but customers were worried that it would result in rate hikes. The decision for shareholders was one of weighing more money from UP (for shares in a proposition many analysts felt was less likely to receive merger approval) against an offer with a lower price in a merger more likely to be approved.

In January 1995, BN increased its offer again to US$20.40 per share, substantially better than the bid from UP. Under this new proposal, BN and SF would together buy 33% of SF's stock for cash. SF would buy 3.8 million shares, or 20% of SF's outstanding shares at US$20 per share and BN would buy 13% at the same price. The cash outlay was US$760 million for SF and US$500 million for BN (Anonymous, 1995c). At this juncture, there was a new wrinkle. SF agreed to a "poison pill;"[8] SF would pay BN US$50 million if another suitor (such as UP) were to acquire SF. UP terminated its tender offer on 31 January 1995, following the Delaware Chancery Court's ruling against UP's efforts to block the merger (Welty, 1995a). BN was successful but at a higher price than it had intended to pay (Anonymous, 1995d).

---

8   The "poison pill" strategy is a long-standing one. Publicly traded companies put in place provisions to prevent an unwanted suitor (hostile takeover) and the provisions may be made to encourage a particular "white knight" to complete the deal thereby rescuing the "damsel in distress." In this case, as with any other companies contemplating merger, the rationale for the provisions may not always be obvious to those outside the boardroom. Managerial preferences for one merger suitor over another may have as much to do with personalities as with the economic benefits of merger or what is in the best short-term interests of shareholders.

BN shareholders voted the morning of 7 February 1995 to approve the merger with SF. SF shareholders voted in the afternoon of the same day (Morris, 1995a). At the BN special meeting, 78% of outstanding shares were voted in favour of a merger between BN and SF. At SF, the vote was better than 70% (Welty, 1995a).

What was the thinking behind the merger? According to Nowicki (1997), the two CEOs wanted to

(1) strengthen their rail franchises by reducing rail costs, increasing efficiencies and consolidating facilities,

(2) increase the volume of business, and

(3) increase the mix of businesses.

The merger was seeking three outcomes: revenue growth, operating cost savings and the ideal traffic mix. To get the desired revenue growth, 40% would have to come from diverting traffic from the highway, possible with intermodal service improvements. To illustrate, the SF started measuring service in 1991 and found only 66% of service was delivered on-time, however that was defined.[9] Post-merger, the company was pleased with the improvement in service quality (Nowicki, 1997). Operating cost savings were expected to accrue from the consolidation of facilities and the use of more efficient routes. Nowicki (1997) noted that shipping rates have declined 51% in real terms since the implementation of the *Staggers Act*. He also reported that McKinsey & Company studied BN in 1995, concluding that 80 cents of every dollar of productivity improvements gained was competed away and returned to customer. As for traffic mix, SF was too dependent on intermodal, while BN was too dependent on bulk. The post-merger mix is one-third commodity, one-third general merchandise, and one-third inter-modal, and is now seen by the company as a perfect mix.

The merger was approved 20 July 1995 by the ICC subject to the employee protective measures normally imposed plus several specific conditions to alleviate competitive harm. Included in these were trackage and interswitching rights to provide competitive access. In September 1995, the deal was completed with SF shareholders receiving 0.27 of a share of BN common stock for each SF share. The railroad became Burlington Northern and Santa Fe Railway Co. (BNSF).

It was argued at the time that shippers and regulators went easy on the BN–SF deal because of the end-to-end nature of the two systems and their proactive negotiations with competing railroads (Morris, 1995c). Normally expected opposition to the merger from other railroads was reduced when BN and SF reached agreements for trackage rights with several potential protesters, including UP, the Southern Pacific (SP), and Kansas City Southern (Anonymous, 1995b).

---

9   Ideally, on-time service is defined by the customer and varies by customer tolerance. Every company measures this differently.

The trade press also was easy on the merger. It was noted that the two railroads had pursued different and defined strategies which were complementary in the eyes of the parties. SF was reported to know and understand intermodal. BN, on the other hand, with much more of its business focused on serving coal, lumber, and grain markets, concentrated on efficiency rather than speed (Morris, 1995b). The merger had the potential to enhance the skill set of management; SF had a more stable management team track record while BN's management was seen to be in need of a succession plan.[10] The two were strategically complementary as well; BN sought a strategic plan for intermodal business, while SF was successful with its intermodal operations. The merger would combine BN's strengths in bulk commodities with SF's strength in intermodal. It promised cheaper, more convenient, "single line" service for shippers, and was anticipated to result in substantial cost savings through operational improvements, increased traffic densities, and reduced administrative costs and duplication (Welty, 1994). For BN there would be access to southern California and the Southeast and indirect access to Mexico via the El Paso border crossing, while for SF there would be access to the upper midwest and across the Northern Tier to the Pacific northwest (Welty, 1995a). The fit of management culture was not particularly compatible but, for the most part, the deal looked good to the trade press.

In October 1995, Burlington Northern Santa Fe announced third quarter earnings of US$1.95 per share, well above the estimate of US$1.62 (LaMonica, 1995). The operating ratio in the first quarter of 1996 was 81%, down from 84.3% in the first quarter of 1995,[11] although still not close to that of UP. Krebs and Grinstein were voted "Railroaders of the Year" by Gus Welty of *Railway Age* (Welty, 1996). BNSF achieved the gains identified as possible from the merger, and ahead of schedule. The bidding up of the tender offer did not appear to have severe long-term repercussions on the company.

## THE UNION PACIFIC–SOUTHERN PACIFIC MERGER

In 1869, the UP connected with the Central Pacific railroad at Promontory, Utah, to form the first transcontinental rail line in the US. By 1994, UP had become the third largest railroad in the US, with 17,500 route miles linking the Pacific coast and Gulf coast ports with the midwest, and serving the western two-thirds of the country. Its growth pattern was not unusual; it was by merger. Throughout its expansion, UP maintained agreements with other carriers for the handling of freight to and from the Atlantic coast, the Pacific coast, the southeast, the southwest, Canada and Mexico and so had a normal history of cooperative agreements as well. In 1998, UP's largest single customer was APL Land Transport Services, with General Motors in second place (http://www.uprr.com).

The story of the SP acquisition began with Union Pacific's failed bid to acquire the Atchison, Topeka and Santa Fe Railway. UP pursued the acquisition for several months, making a num-

---

10  Welty (1994). This was implied by the author. Grinstein of BN was 62 at the time and its management had recently brought in new blood from outside the industry. Krebs of SF was young and considered capable.

11  By the end of 1998, BNSF's operating ratio was running at 75.9% (http://www.bnsf.com).

ber of revised bids, each of which was rejected. These rejections, coupled with the poison pill adopted by SF, caused Union Pacific to withdraw its offer to acquire SF on 31 January 1995.

Prior to its withdrawal of the SF bid, UP chose to play another strategic card: in December 1994, the ICC approved UP's application to control the Chicago and Northwestern (CNW). UP agreed to purchase the 70% of CNW that it did not already own for approximately US$1.1 billion (Anonymous, 1995e). This merger produced a 23,000-mile western railway system, and better positioned UP to compete head-on with the newly created BNSF. Unfortunately, the CNW acquisition was not easily digested; UP reported in the trade press that there were no problems but unfortunately shippers did not agree. Many customers began experiencing unprecedented difficulties with service (Welty, 1995c). Eventually, UP's President Ronald Burns sent an apologetic letter to customers (Palmeri and Marsh, 1995). This, with hindsight, may have been a sign of things to come.

For its part, San Francisco–based Southern Pacific was once considered the best railroad in the country, but had fallen on hard times. In 1994, SP's debt-to-equity ratio was 58%, down from 80% in 1992, but still 20% above the industry average (Byrnes, 1994). This poor financial situation was the result of an ill-fated attempt to merge with the SF in the mid-1980s; the ICC ruled that merger to be anti-competitive in 1987. Also according to Byrnes (1994), the ruling triggered the 1988 US$1 billion leveraged buyout of SP by Denver billionaire Philip Anschutz. The value of the company did not reflect the value of its real estate holdings[12] and, shortly after the leveraged buyout, SP began selling off its real estate, as it was still unable to generate sufficient operating income to cover its interest expense. The real estate market softened and five years later SP was still unable to generate an operating profit.[13] The network was deteriorating. Service reliability was already a sore point with SP customers, and SP lost one of its United Parcel Service contracts in 1993. With the BN acquisition of SF, financially-troubled SP became the smallest of the big Class I railroads in the west, and one with an uncertain future except as a takeover target.

Given the efficiencies gained by the BNSF merger, UP's Chairman Drew Lewis believed that a UP–SP combination could accomplish similar objectives. UP turned to its second choice of partner, proposed marriage and was accepted. The Union Pacific and Southern Pacific initially planned to merge by September 1996, just 12 months after the merger between BN and SF (Lewis, 1996). The goal was to forge a new rail system in the west capable of competing with BNSF (Miller, 1995).

The UP acquisition of SP was formally announced on 3 August 1995, just 13 days after the ICC approved the acquisition of SF by BN. Subject to regulatory approval of the merger, Union Pacific agreed to acquire Southern Pacific for the equivalent of US$25 per share in cash and stock, about US$3.9 billion. Under the terms of the acquisition agreement, UP would buy 25% of SP's shares for cash at US$25 per share in an initial tender offer; these shares were to

---

12   Berman and Khalaf (1990:39). In 1987, the real estate held by SP was estimated at a value of $1.6 billion by Goldman Sachs, higher by Anschutz.
13   Feder (1996:D4) noted that SP had operating losses in 14 of the previous 17 years.

be held in a voting trust until after receipt of regulatory approval. After receiving approval, SP's remaining shares would be purchased. UP put the total value of the deal at US$5.4 billion, including the assumption of SP's debt load (Anonymous, 1995f). For a comparison of the two companies, see Table 5.2.

**Table 5.2: Selected 1994 Financial Data on UP and SP**

|  | *Union Pacific* | *Southern Pacific* |
|---|---|---|
| Operating Revenues ($b) | 6.44 | 3.1 |
| Employees | 36,756 | 19,014 |
| Track | 22,896 | 16,492 |
| Freight Trains Operated Daily | 1,200 | 750 |

Source:   Union Pacific, as reported by Morton (1996).

Beyond cost savings, there were several other reasons for UP to consider SP as a suitable merger target. SP had extremely good NAFTA prospects: its six gateways to Mexico reportedly added US$200 million to its 1993 revenue, its intermodal presence at Long Beach was solid, and it had a sizable rail network (Byrnes, 1994). A UP/SP combination could dominate US–Mexico rail traffic.

There were also good reasons for SP to agree to a merger with UP. SP clearly needed financial support; its debt burden was crushing at a time when re-investment in infrastructure was sorely needed and other railroads were seeking the ICC's blessing for their growth through merger. UP was generating considerable cash flow, and possessed a route structure that complemented SP's in several key markets (Byrnes, 1994). A merger would also go a long way toward solving SP's problems with customer dissatisfaction. UP had been, in spite of its difficulties digesting the CNW acquisition, a candidate (although not a winner) for a Malcolm Baldridge Quality Award (Welty, 1995b). The UP was highly regarded for its customer focus. SP expected the merger to bring new market opportunities, and improved service to and from Mexico. Finally, the marketplace had changed and a combined BNSF had more than double SP's 15,000 route miles.

UP and SP believed that, without the merger, they would not be competitive in the California–Chicago corridor against BNSF in terms of service time and reliability (Lewis, 1996:63). They also planned to expand the network of single-line operations to and from Mexican border points; it would also be possible to combine the shorter of their routes and, consequently, to adopt more efficient train routings, with lower crew and fuel costs, passing savings on to shippers.

While the BNSF merger affected 20 market areas where the combined carriers' revenue was US$165 million, the UP–SP merger would reduce the rail options for shippers from two carriers to one on routes connecting a total of 164 market areas (Anonymous, 1995a). The scope of the merger was of concern to many shippers. Union Pacific's Chairman Lewis was determined that the planned acquisition of SP would succeed. Between them, BNSF and the UP–SP combination would control more than 90% of all car loadings west of the Mississippi, and nearly 60% of all railroad revenue in the US (Palmeri and Marsh, 1995).

On 30 November 1995, the UP–SP merger application was formally filed with the ICC; the merger applicants hoped to receive the go-ahead from the Surface Transportation Board (STB), the successor to the ICC, by August 1996. The merger proposal promised improved service levels, enhanced information systems, and streamlined transfer of equipment (Moore, 1996). It would also encompass more than 31,000 miles of track in 25 states, Mexico, and Canada. UP officials stated this would allow them to compete more effectively with BNSF and produce US$750 million in annual savings—US$100 million of which would be passed on to shippers in the form of price reductions. The STB eventually predicted big savings from the merger, although it expected savings to be closer to US$633 million a year (Minahan, 1996).

Unlike the BN and SF combined network, which was seen as an end-to-end merger, many UP and SP tracks run parallel: more than 4,000 miles, 11% of the combined system. In addition, a merged UP–SP would control as much as 70% of the petrochemical shipments from the Gulf coast in Texas and 90% of train traffic with Mexico (Palmeri and Marsh, 1995). UP and SP expected to introduce new single-line services in the following corridors: southern California–Chicago; northern California–Chicago; Seattle to/from California and Arizona (the so-called I-5 corridor); southern California to Memphis. In addition, by merging with SP, UP would gain access to SP's much shorter Los Angeles to Dallas route. Trucking would provide the competitive counterbalance to rail.

This largest proposed rail consolidation in US history generated enormous interest from shippers, carriers, and public officials. Figure 5.3 provides an illustration of the sheer size of the deal. Complicating the issue was the demise of the Interstate Commerce Commission, slated for 31 December 1995. What regulatory agency would oversee the merger? Would it make the decision according to the provisions of the *Staggers Act*? The National Industrial Transportation League (NITL), a vocal shipper organization, argued that the merger should be subject to antitrust laws and more closely involve the Department of Justice (DoJ). Its view was that the rail provisions had been developed when there were 40 Class I railroads and mergers were a desirable way of dealing with bankrupt rail lines. The NITL wanted rail-to-rail competition and pro-competitive agreements, such as trackage agreements, as part of the public record (Miller, 1995). It looked like BNSF's timing was better than UP's.

The public debate about the UP–SP merger pitted UP, SP, and their supporters against Kansas City Southern (KCS), Conrail, and a number of shipper groups. The debate mostly focused on issues of competition and the reduction in choice of railroad service vendors. The merger was expected to effectively remove rail options for shippers who spent US$1.65 billion in 1993 in freight shipments (Miller, 1995); opponents claimed a negative impact and were vocal in their rejection of the proposition. The Coalition for Competitive Rail Transportation (one of the shipper groups) argued that the scope of the UP–SP merger was 79% larger than the 1986 SP–SF merger the ICC had previously ruled as anti-competitive (Miller, 1995).

## Figure 5.3: 1994 Freight Traffic

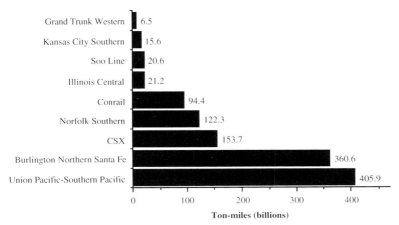

Note:     Union Pacific includes CNW.

Source:   Created from the data provided by the Association of American Railroads.

Other voices against the merger included the DoJ, the Chemical Manufacturers Association, the Society of the Plastics Industry (SPI), many farm groups and Senator Byron Dorgan (Democrat–North Dakota). DoJ's Anne Bingaman, assistant attorney general, was quoted:

> *The department is concerned that this transaction will create monopolies or duo-polies for crucial transportation services that industries and consumers depend upon throughout the U.S.*[14]

The DoJ predicted price increases of US$800 million and US$6 billion in commerce affected. They argued that trackage rights would neither prevent rate increases in single line markets nor provide an adequate remedy in markets moving from three service providers to two. They concluded that the compensation rates paid for trackage rights would be excessive. They also argued that SP would survive as a viable competitor (Anonymous, 1996a; Feder, 1996:D4), an argument many in the know did not buy given SP's need for a positive cash flow and capital.

SPI's concerns focused primarily on the control the merged company would have over some commodity shipments; in particular it was concerned about UP's control of 88% of Gulf coast resin shipments as transport costs account for about 20% of total resin costs. In addition, UP would control 86% of all Gulf area storage capacity and 92% of the region's switching yards (Fairley and Morris, 1996). SPI also noted that 92% of US polyethylene and polypropylene shipments originate in Texas and Louisiana, and that most polymer producers are captive shippers (Morris, 1996a).

---

14    Anonymous, 1996a. © 1996 Cahners Business Information. Used by permission.

Senator Dorgan's amendment to the bill transferring rail merger authority to the new regulatory board within the Department of Transportation sought to make rail mergers (including pending ones) subject to antitrust legislation (and therefore DoJ criteria) but failed to get the required support in the Senate (Calderwood, 1996). The STB was created and its first task was to rule on the merger and define the conditions under which it could proceed. The decision: the criteria to be used were those of the old ICC rather than the DoJ. Rail continued to be seen as a special industry warranting its own competition rules.

In the months that followed, the public debate continued heatedly. NITL's formal submission argued that trackage agreements do not go far enough to resolve shippers' concerns. They sought divestiture of specific lines (Bradley, 1996b). UP and SP publicly maintained that divestiture of these lines would be a deal-breaker. Trackage rights were discussed at length with the outcome that the UP and BNSF concluded the largest trackage rights agreement in US history (Palmeri and Marsh, 1995). The Illinois Central agreed not to oppose the merger in exchange for preferential treatment on future track sales and access agreements (Anonymous, 1996b). However, Kansas City Southern and Conrail were not so quickly quieted; they also sought divestiture of specific lines, believing that trackage rights were insufficient as a substitute for right-of-way ownership (Anonymous, 1996c). Conrail bid US$1.9 billion for SP track from Texas to Chicago and was rebuffed by UP. As the STB hearings continued, the Chemical Manufacturers Association eventually withdrew its opposition as it was satisfied with the trackage agreement BNSF made with the UP (Morris, 1996a).

UP and SP waged an active public campaign. They had sound political connections, Drew Lewis having been Secretary of Transportation under Ronald Reagan, and Philip Anschutz being a Dole fund-raiser (Palmeri and Marsh, 1995). They lined up more than 1700 shippers, railroads and lawmakers in support (Anonymous, 1996e). One of these was the parent company of their largest customer, American President Land Transport Services (Lewis, 1996):

> *American President Companies strongly supports the proposed merger.... We believe that the merger will benefit APC, its subsidiaries and its many customers through a more efficient rail transportation service than currently exists. At the same time, the proposed merged railroad will create a healthy competitive balance within the western United States.*

On 12 August 1996, a decision by the STB approved the mammoth rail merger. The 35 conditions imposed included extensive trackage rights for BNSF but did not require UP to divest itself of track as called for by opponents of the merger. It also imposed common carrier obligations on BNSF. Of particular importance in the decision was the oversight provision; the STB would monitor the merger for five years for anti-competitive behaviour and reserved the right to order track divestiture (or other remedies) if trackage agreements failed to protect shippers.

The written decision was not unequivocal. Some of the conditions attached to the approval were vague. For example, the ruling on competitive bidding for captive shippers was problematic; by not defining what was meant by a 50% volume requirement—tons, carloads, dollar-value, contracts, and so on—the merged company was off to a rocky start (Watson, 1996;

Morris, 1996b). The STB was required to later define contentious features in an interpretation ruling (Morris, 1997).

Problems with the UPSP merger surfaced in the summer of 1997. On-time delivery, misrouting of shipments and equipment shortages became a nightmare for the company. Shippers had hoped that the strong management systems and capital position of UP would bring up the service standards so languishing at SP. Instead, the previous service levels deteriorated. An NITL survey reported by *Industry Week* noted that NITL members on UP lines or connected to UP lines by another carrier had incurred additional costs up to US$349,000 a month with an increase in transit times ranging from 7% to 100%. Some customers, like Occidental Chemical, were reporting to the STB negative impacts in the millions of dollars (Harrington, 1998b). By August 1998, Dow Chemical, Union Carbide and DuPont claims were settled and UP had already paid almost US$500 million in claims for lost business and alternate transport costs (Morris, 1998b).

There were certainly disappointed shippers. Throughout 1997 and the first half of 1998 UP's severe indigestion and service problems became the focus of numerous media stories.[15] The STB stepped in and required UP to temporarily open access to competing rail lines to alleviate congestion, among other measures.[16] The trucking industry, which did not appear overly concerned with a merger that supposedly had truck traffic as its primary target, was not expecting the competition to be too stiff (Moore, 1996):

> For the immediate future, trucking shouldn't lose too much sleep. Mergers don't solve service problems. The merger of two railroads, neither of which understands customer service, does not create one that does.

The focus for competition analysts in the future will be one of questioning whether there is sufficient capability on the part of the trucking industry to provide effective competition to rail providers in the absence of competitive access provisions and single line service.[17]

## THE CSX AND NORFOLK SOUTHERN ACQUISITION OF CONRAIL

The CSX announcement of its intention to acquire Philadelphia-based Conrail in mid-October of 1996 came as a surprise to most observers. Although Conrail was viewed by many to be a possible takeover target, it had long been anticipated that Norfolk Southern (NS) would be the suitor. This proposed acquisition was merely the latest chapter in the on-going saga of US railroad consolidation (Table 5.1).

---

15  Minahan (1996); Bradley (1996a). In particular, the story carried by *Fortune* (Anonymous, 1998c), in its "Mismanagement" section was widely discussed outside industry circles.

16  The STB monitored service levels by route and there were numerous filings to renew or remove these access provisions as 1998 progressed.

17  For some commodities, trucking will be an effective competitor where rail does not adequately understand or service its customers. However, there will always be customers for whom truck or intermodal are not substitutes for rail. In this sense, rail is closer to liner shipping. It has only substitutes at the margin. Shipping at least does not face a fixed route infrastructure investment.

CSX was formed in 1980 by the merger of the Chessie System Railway ("C") and the Seaboard Coast Line Railroad ("S"), each having non-transport subsidiaries ("X").[18] However, the merger was not fully completed until 1985. In April of 1986, CSX announced its proposal to acquire Sea-Land Service Inc., and completed its divestiture of its mineral companies, becoming a *Fortune 500* transportation company with a unique combination of rail, container-shipping, barging, intermodal and logistics services. By 1996, CSX holdings included: CSX Transportation Inc., a major eastern railroad; Sea-Land Service Inc., a US-based ocean carrier; CSX Intermodal Inc., providing transcontinental intermodal transportation services; and Customized Transportation Inc., a third-party logistics provider. CSX continued to hold a number of non-transportation businesses in the resort and real estate industries (http://www.csx.com).

For its part, Conrail began operations in April 1976, rising from the ashes of several railroads. The federal government intervened in a troubled market, combining the bankrupt Penn Central Transportation Co. with five other failed railroads in late 1976 and providing a net US$6 billion in taxpayer subsidies in the 1970s and the early 1980s. By 1981 Conrail began to turn around, no longer requiring federal support after June of that year. Full implementation was completed by 1986 and the predecessor companies ceased to file reports to the ICC separately. After what many believe to be the most tortuous privatization process to take place in the US in the 1980s, the federal government sold its 85% ownership interest in Conrail on 26 March 1987 in what was at the time the largest initial public stock offering (IPO) in US history. Many believed the company's continuing prosperity was due largely to its market power in the New York market.

By 1994, the company was paying a good dividend and was expected to earn approximately US$340 million on revenues of US$3.7 billion. Conrail had improved its operating efficiencies and was hauling about the same traffic as it was two decades previous but with a third of the railcars, substantially less track and one-fourth the workers (Norman, 1994). Its share price had grown to four times its IPO price. CEO Jim Hagen was vocal in quoting his Board's endorsement of a continuing "go-it-alone" strategy. When pressed by the media to comment on the potential for merger, he noted the 31 months before the Interstate Commerce Commission was a deterrent against the merger alternative; lengthy proceedings are costly in terms of managerial focus on the business (Miller and Vantuono, 1994).

Unfortunately, not all was rosy for the company. Much of the traffic flowing from the Mississippi to the Ohio and Indiana markets had other rail options. Conrail's asset utilization was reported by some sources as the poorest in the industry[19] while others believed it to be within acceptable limits. Conrail was also said to be having difficulty in financing its capital program with its cost of capital at 11% and return on capital at 9%.[20] Whether Conrail was in

---

18  "CSX Chronology," http://www.csx.com/med/csxchronology.html

19  Gilbert (1995) reported that locomotives spent only 37% of their time in revenue generating activity while the industry average in 1995 was 50%. Each railroad provided its own calculations and there was not a standard approach to benchmark performance.

20  Norman (1994). J. Blaze, personal communication, 4 January 1999, reports that this was simply not true and that the company had internally imposed stringent guidelines for the financing of its capital program.

difficulty or not, it needed to grow its network to give it more long-haul traffic or its role would gradually diminish to being a short haul operation as it failed to extract the additional economies of scale. (See Figure 5.3.) In addition, the merger of the BN and the SF changed the dynamics of the industry, highlighting to Conrail management the tenuous nature of its situation relative to that of its competitors. Both east coast competitors, CSX and Norfolk Southern (NS) were growing in operating revenue while Conrail's revenue growth appeared stalled.

In addition, many of the problems that sank Conrail's predecessor railroads still existed. Operating costs and taxes were high in the northeast and the competition from trucks was intense. Conrail was forced to reinvest more than US$500 million a year just to maintain its track as well as its aging locomotive fleet. Its operating cash flow barely covered this and the dividends expected by shareholders. The winter of 1993–94 was harsh and the soaring traffic volumes that followed left Conrail short of both locomotive power and crews. The trade press reported that customers were dissatisfied with Conrail's service (Anonymous, 1996f). In May of 1995, Conrail began to look at ways to improve profit margins; it focused spending on its more successful lines, identified track for sale, and announced a job reduction program in response to its poor first quarter results (Laabs, 1996). It also realized it needed to grow the business or it would not survive. Its "go-it-alone" approach had become perilous.

Conrail realized that the length of haul had to be extended to get the necessary economies of scale. The means to accomplish this growth was not readily apparent as there were no large end-to-end merger targets available. It had failed to acquire part of Southern Pacific's network and thereby expand southwest to Texas. It could acquire regional railroads; a possible target was one or more of CP Rail's regional properties, given its re-focus on western Canadian operations and the move of headquarters to Calgary. There was also the possibility of trading track for trackage or haulage rights with another railroad. The dilemma was that neither of these strategies would necessarily grant the benefits of a larger merger; the cash flow could not be grown quickly enough. Mere network extension was not sufficient.[21]

When the STB announced in June of 1996 its approval of the Union Pacific acquisition of Southern Pacific, a merger with significant parallel track, Conrail management could contemplate a change in its strategic direction. The approval "made a mega-merger institutionally thinkable."[22] Conrail had three new strategic options not thought possible before: CSX and Conrail could get together and buy Norfolk Southern; Conrail could accept a friendly acquisition by CSX and Norfolk Southern, or Conrail and CSX could merge and compete against Norfolk Southern. The last would not have been possible to consider prior to the UP acquisition of SP and was now the one favoured by Conrail management. A mega-merger gave Conrail the economies of scale it desired.

---

21  J. Blaze, Zeta-Tech Associates, personal communication, 5 January 1999.
22  J. Blaze, Zeta-Tech Associates, personal communication, 5 January 1999.

On 15 October 1996 the CEO of CSX, John Snow, and David LeVan of Conrail jointly announced plans to merge their railroads to create the largest railroad in the US. Seen as a compatible match, this was a friendly deal between the two companies.

Motivation behind the merger was simple: economies of scale and operational efficiencies would result in very large cost savings. The new company would be more competitive against the trucking industry and the dominance of trucking in the northeast was of concern to the rail industry. It would also dovetail with the trend in liner shipping to ever larger consortia or alliances of globally-focused carriers. Snow's vision was to build CSX into a "total solution" company, taking care of all the transport needs of large customers, like the auto manufacturers (Martin, 1996). To head off antitrust concerns, CSX indicated it would be willing to grant some trackage rights to competitors (Anonymous, 1996i).

What were the key selling points of the merger? The US$8.4 billion deal would result in the country's largest freight company with annual revenues in excess of US$14 billion, including the earnings of CSX subsidiaries Sea-Land and CSX Intermodal. Estimated annual savings for the merged entity were US$550 million: US$350 million from savings on equipment, service rationalization and other efficiencies, and US$200 million from a more efficient operation grabbing business from truckers (Griffiths, 1996). CSX and Conrail said customers could look forward to better single-line service, faster transit times and greater market reach.

The shipping public was very concerned about the merger. This merger would reduce the number of very large railroads to just four, two in the east and two in the west. But unlike the two in the west, the existing three in the east would become one larger and one smaller, as is evident from Figure 5.3 and Table 5.4. Port access under the merger was of concern to those shipping containers overseas. According to Robert Banks of R. L. Banks and Associates, a Washington DC based rail consulting firm, the acquisition had the potential for substantial reduction in competition in the steel producing areas between West Virginia and Lake Erie (Anonymous, 1996j). Steel suppliers expected a bottom line squeeze.

The happy merger of CSX and Conrail was not the story which unfolded. Norfolk Southern's role as a suitor for Conrail went back to the days before Conrail's IPO in 1987. In fact, Norfolk Southern had even worked covertly with CSX to develop an "NS acquisition of Conrail" scenario including divestiture of trackage to CSX for not blocking the sale (Miller, 1996). Publicly, NS published a position paper, *Principles of Balanced Competition*,[23] to explain its philosophy to shippers and public agencies and departments. But the two companies failed to agree. NS was reported to have agreed with CSX on geography and price but not on either labour or dealing with Pennsylvania legislative requirements (Miller, 1996). Analysts speculated that NS

---

23  The principles are: competition requires rail systems of comparable size and scope; the largest markets must be served by at least two large railroads; owned routes are essential to competition; competition depends on effective terminal access (not just routes); and competition is not free. (As summarized by Hanscom, 1996:29.)

was not prepared to pay the premium price that Conrail shareholders would demand. Some estimated the required price for Conrail at US$70 a share and too high for NS.[24]

**Table 5.4: American Class I Railroad Operating Revenue 1995**

| *Railroad* | *US$ billion* | *%* |
|---|---|---|
| Union Pacific (1) | 9.54 | 29.6 |
| Burlington Northern Santa Fe | 8.17 | 25.3 |
| CSX Transportation | 4.82 | 14.9 |
| Norfolk Southern | 4.01 | 12.4 |
| Conrail | 3.59 | 11.1 |
| Soo Line (2) | 0.68 | 2.1 |
| Illinois Central | 0.64 | 2.0 |
| Kansas City Southern | 0.50 | 1.6 |
| Grand Trunk Western (3) | 0.32 | 1.0 |
| Total | 32.27 | 100.0 |

Note:  (1) Including CNW and Southern Pacific
(2) Subsidiary of Canadian Pacific
(3) Subsidiary of Canadian National

Source: Association of American Railroads as cited by Anonymous (1996k:71), "Steaming," *The Economist*, 19 October, 341, 7988, 66-71. © The Economist, London, 14 Oct 1996.

When CSX and Conrail announced their merger, NS was both surprised and upset. David Goode, CEO of NS, said,

*A Conrail–CSX combination posed a serious threat to Norfolk Southern. It promised to change the dynamics east of the Mississippi, where there had long been three carriers.... The deal would make us a much smaller force in terms of overall market share. I was concerned about being excluded from important markets in the Northeast.*[25]

The deal became a takeover battle.

Like many other US Class I railways, Norfolk Southern Corporation was formed through consolidation, in its case the merger of the Norfolk and Western Railway and the Southern Railway on 1 June 1982. Both of these companies were the products of more than 150 predecessor lines that had been combined, reorganized and recombined since the 1830s. NS had

---

24  Gilbert (1995). According to Jim Blaze (Zeta-Tech Associates, personal communication, 5 January 1999), the value of Conrail had been steadily growing in the eyes of its management team. Management believed that, even though Conrail was trading in the low to mid US$50's a share, the strategic plan in place in 1994 was worth about US$80 a share over a 3 year time horizon. NS made an undisclosed offer which the Conrail Board did not accept.

25  Martin (1997), *Fortune*. © 1997 Time Inc. All rights reserved.

a reputation for sound, conservative management and a tradition of quality and reliability (http://www.nscorp.com).

After a long, difficult period, the rail industry by 1994 was seeing quite dramatic growth (Miller, 1994). NS was no exception. Carloads were growing at record levels. The company increased shipments of low-sulphur coal 13% in 1994. Moreover, they had made investments to improve the utilization of freight cars and planned to spend US$708 million on capital improvements in 1996 (Anonymous, 1996g). Norfolk Southern boasted strong management and a high dividend yield (Edgerton, 1995). The analysts respected NS for its solid balance sheet, debt-to-total-capitalization of 26%, earnings per share growth of 10–13% and plenty of leverage capacity. Its operating ratio in 1994 was an industry-leading 71%.

Like CSX, NS saw significant savings potential in the merger—$145 million in 1998 rising to US$515 million in 2000—resulting from the elimination of common overheads and more efficient rolling stock and maintenance facilities (Griffiths, 1996). One of the principal motivations for NS to take on CSX was the potential for access to markets in the northeast (Anonymous, 1997i). These two rivals desired Conrail due to its access to the Port of New York and its "Big X" services from the east coast into the US midwest. While intermodal was a relatively small part of the three railroads' business, it had growth potential. As the industry leader in intermodal growth, Conrail made it an attractive buy. Tables 5.5 and 5.6 compare the three.

**Table 5.5: Selected 1995 Equipment Data**

|            | *Conrail* | *CSX*   | *Norfolk Southern* |
|------------|-----------|---------|--------------------|
| Trailers   | 706,000   | 381,000 | 700,000            |
| Containers | 792,000   | 477,000 | 561,000            |
| Total      | 1,498,000 | 858,000 | 1,261,000          |

Source:   Data from Griffiths (1996:42).

Furthermore, NS's market motivation was extremely strong. If CSX was successful in merging with Conrail, what strategic options would NS have for growth? It could examine a western railroad to build greater east-west network opportunities, but the two previous mergers had severely limited its options. The company could also contemplate re-sizing its network to concentrate on those niches it already dominated (but this is not a growth strategy to capture scale economies). These options had less promise than a bid for Conrail. In addition, the company was financially strong and capable of a bid that, at minimum, could force CSX to pay an unpleasant premium.

On 23 October 1996 NS launched a US$9.1 billion all-cash hostile bid for Conrail. The deal was complex as NS faced two obstacles. First, CSX and Conrail had added a poison pill to their agreement—$600 million in break-up penalties. Second, Pennsylvania had strong shareholders' rights legislation in the *Pennsylvania Control Transaction Law of 1990*; intended to make hostile takeovers extremely difficult. It invested boards of directors with the power to consider more than just the dollar value of the buyout offer and select the offer best for customers, employees and the local community. In addition, because a company cannot buy more than 20% of shares without shareholder approval, shareholders would ultimately have to approve any buyer of Conrail.

**Table 5.6: Selected 1996 Financial Data**

|                                     | *Conrail* | *CSX*  | *Norfolk Southern* |
|-------------------------------------|-----------|--------|--------------------|
| Gross Rail Revenue (US$m)           | 3,597     | 10,536 | 4,101              |
| Rail Expenses (US$m)                | 3,010     | 9,014  | 2,936              |
| Income from Rail Operations (US$m)  | 587       | 1,522  | 1,165              |
| Net Income (US$m)                   | 427       | 855    | 770                |
| Earnings Per Share (US$)            | NA        | 3.96   | 2.01               |
| Employees (rail)                    | 23,510    | 28,559 | 23,361             |

Source: Norfolk Southern Corporation, *Annual Report 1997*; CSX, *Annual Report 1997*. Conrail data taken from the Annual report Form R-1 filed with the STB and reported at the STB web site at www.stb.dot.gov.

Norfolk Southern's initial offer for Conrail represented US$100 a share in cash for Conrail's common and convertible preferred stock. This was higher than the CSX bid of US$92.50 per share in cash for 40% of Conrail's shares and 1.85619 CSX shares for each of the remaining 60% of the shares. On 5 November 1996, CSX raised its bid for Conrail, increasing the cash element from US$92.50 to US$110 per share, while maintaining the conversion ratio for the remaining 60% of the stock (equivalent to US$82.14). NS countered on 8 November by increasing its offer to US$110 per share, offering Conrail shareholders a premium by its calculation of US$17 a share over the CSX offer (Anonymous, 1996h). On 21 November, CSX proceeded to purchase 19.9% of Conrail's shares at US$110 a share, leaving the balance until shareholder approval of the remainder of the 40% was secured. Many investors were reported to be angry that the all-cash bid by NS was not accepted by the Board (Anonymous, 1996d). The battle escalated with CSX and Conrail announcing, 5 December 1996, that they were suing NS for tortious interference; its actions were malicious and intended to disrupt and cripple a merger of equals (Conrail, 1996). On 19 December the price offered by NS rose to US$115.

By January 1997, the bidding war had stalemated. NS had lost the judicial ruling and appeal on its efforts to block CSX's first tender of its two-tier offer. However, on 17 January, a Conrail shareholder revolt began; at least 53% of the shareholders of the outstanding shares voted against the motion to exempt CSX from paying all cash for the shares of Conrail. CSX and Conrail both indicated that they were committed to the merger in spite of this setback (Anonymous, 1997j). On 4 February, NS bought 9.9% of Conrail stock at US$115 a share, the maximum it could purchase without triggering Conrail's poison pill. The NS offer was over-subscribed; more than 90% of the Conrail shares not owned by CSX were tendered (Anonymous, 1997b). With these indications of shareholder support, NS announced on 10 February that it intended to conduct a proxy contest to replace the Conrail Board of Directors (Norfolk

Southern Corporation, *Annual Report 1997*). On 12 February, NS began a tender offer for the 90.1% of shares it did not already own. (Actual purchase would be delayed until poison pill provisions were removed (Anonymous, 1997f). CSX raised its offer to match NS's on 3 March. The offer price was now 60% more than Conrail's share price when bidding began. Conrail's Chairman and CEO David LeVan was reported to have been disappointed that CSX chose not to fight NS, and therefore the company had no option but to agree to be split in two (Anonymous, 1997c).

Eventually CSX and NS agreed to form a jointly-owned entity to acquire all the outstanding shares of Conrail for US$115 in cash per share. NS would contribute US$5.9 billion for its 58% share and CSX US$4.3 billion for its 42% of the acquisition. The agreement meant that CSX and NS would dominate freight rail activity in the eastern part of the US. NS and CSX agreed in principle that Conrail would be first bought by CSX for US$115 per share and then subsequently half would be sold to NS (Anonymous, 1997e). Under the plan, NS and CSX divided all of Conrail's principal routes. According to the agreement, CSX would operate the portions of the "Big X" between Boston and Cleveland through Albany and Buffalo, with connecting lines to Montreal, New York and New Jersey and between Cleveland and St. Louis (Anonymous, 1997d). For its part, NS would operate the legs between Chicago and Cleveland, Cleveland and northern New Jersey via Pittsburgh and Harrisburg, as well as the Conrail line serving the metropolitan New York area between northern New Jersey and Buffalo, and between Buffalo and Harrisburg. In addition, NS would gain some form of access to Baltimore and Philadelphia. Both CSX and NS continued to serve the Port of Hampton Roads over their existing track structures.

For CSX, which earned US$10.5 billion of revenue and US$727 million of after-tax net profit in 1995, this move would have a dramatic effect on its bottom line and working structure. The operating plan detailed US$410 million in acquisition-related benefits including US$146 million in new business. CSX planned to acquire 51% of the eastern US market. A 58% ownership level for NS would give the company US$2.04 billion of current Conrail revenue. After adding its 1996 revenue of US$4.1 billion to its Conrail purchase, NS would have 49% of the revenue, on a pro forma basis, of the eastern US Class I rail market (Watson, 1997a).

The CSX–NS agreement looked to be a good deal for most parties interested in or affected by it, including shippers and the railroads and their shareholders. Under the proposed arrangement, CSX and NS created a shared assets area. Chemical producers saw an end to Conrail's near monopoly on rail traffic into New York (Morris, 1996c). Other immediate beneficiaries appeared to be shippers on the north-south routes who were able to improve transit time to their northeast customers (Griffiths, 1996). However, some customers were concerned about the high price paid to Conrail shareholders and worried that the resulting debt service costs would ultimately be passed on to them in the form of higher rates.

Those initially unhappy with the plan proposed by CSX and NS included Canadian National (CN) and CP Rail (CP). They believed that competitive access to New York would be limited on the northern and western boundaries and pushed the STB to consider this issue in its review of the merger.

Because of the structure of the agreement, both CSX and NS would have access to New York, previously only serviced by Conrail. They argued this would lead to new competition on New York corridors and drive down the current high rates for shippers (Anonymous, 1997a). On the other hand, it is possible that the competition will also drive down profit margins for these routes; if so, this could force each company to examine other trade corridors to extract the return needed to pay for the acquisition. As each railway based its long-term ability to recover the premium paid on its expectations of growth, this raises the question of whether these expectations were realistic in a mature industry. Possibly they were too optimistic about the extent of modal switching by shippers or the potential for productivity improvements as a result of the merger.

CSX and NS filed a 15,000-page joint application with the STB on 23 June 1997 and the STB's final decision was released on 8 June 1998. As part of the application both companies committed to spend a combined US$1.2 billion in capital improvements over three years, over and above the existing expenditure plans (Watson, 1997a). This would result, they argued, in two evenly matched rail systems offering single-line service between New York and Chicago, New York and St. Louis, and New York and the south and southwest. The Conrail plan, presenting nearly US$1 billion in public benefits, was easily promoted because it promised shippers that time-consuming hand-offs and drayage would be removed through truck-competitive single-line service reducing transit time for many shippers.

Prior to the STB decision, there were a number of agreements made between CSX, NS and those disgruntled with the proposed acquisition of Conrail. NITL came to an agreement with the railroads over the terms for their acceptance of the shared assets area. The agreement included the creation of a shipper advisory council, terms on how shippers' Conrail contracts would be served, commitment on reciprocal switching points, and clarification of service parameters within the shared assets area (Harrington, 1998a). These conditions were then forwarded by the NITL to the STB, with a request that they be imposed on the deal. Because of the potential for the merger costs to be passed on to customers in the form of higher rates, the NITL also asked the STB to impose post-merger conditions which would limit rate increases (Harrington, 1998b).

The STB's favourable decision was verbally issued 8 June, but the written decision was not published until 23 July 1998. After some last-minute maneuvering by opponents to secure better conditions (Anonymous, 1998b), there was finally widespread support found for the decision among shippers, federal departments and unions (Wilner, 1998a). There were only 12 petitions opposing Conrail's division; of these, the most critical for ensuring continuing competition fairness was the petition by APL seeking STB support for increased commercial protection from CSX. (APL was concerned that sensitive information about its operations would be leaked to CSX-owned Sea-Land.[26]) The approval contained some interesting provisions, including a reduced reciprocal switching fee for competitive access in the Buffalo NY area and better access arrangements for CP Rail.

CSX and NS were painfully aware of the pitfalls of a poorly executed merger strategy and moved cautiously to ensure that they did not suffer the same fate. The implementation plan was not a speedy one. They retained key staff and agreed to joint track ownership, head-to-head competition in the shared assets area and third-party operations in the Philadelphia–New York corridor (Morris, 1998a). It took almost a year from approval to completion of the division of Conrail.

## MANAGEMENT ISSUES IN RAIL MERGERS

The UP problems also did not dissuade CN from making an offer to acquire the Illinois Central for US$3 billion, or from entering into a marketing alliance with IC and KCS in April 1998. Both deals are essentially end-to-end deals and extend CN's network to a promising three-coast configuration (Atlantic to Pacific to Gulf of Mexico). The STB approved the CN–IC merger application 25 March 1999.

Why did CN choose to merge with IC and enter into an alliance with KCS? The motivations for CN's acquisition of IC have not been reported as fact. It has been speculated that IC may have moved first rather than wait and find itself without options, while CN may have targeted IC hoping not to arouse the larger competitors in the US east or west (Watson, 1997b). The merger is built on a history of cooperation as the two had shared investment in facilities in Chicago's Harvey Yard to take advantage of the growing intermodal trade and had long cooperated on interlining agreements over the Chicago gateway. As for the answer to the KCS alliance question, there is only speculation as well:. It may be financial (how much would it cost?), availability (was KCS at a point where it was a suitable target?) or regulatory (as there was significant overlap between the IC and the KCS network, would it have problems with the STB?).

Looking back to the model developed in Chapter 3, what were the drivers of the wave of mergers recounted in this chapter? First and foremost was the interaction between the regulatory environment and each railway's competitors and their strategies. The Burlington Northern Santa Fe merger, primarily an end-to-end merger, received regulatory approval and had first mover advantages in the western US. UP, although interested in SF, was the unsuccessful suitor and the SP was the only east-west Class I merger target west of the Mississippi. Of course, UP could have looked east for another merger target to create the first US transcontinental network.[27] However, the US industry appears to have a common managerial preference for more geographically concentrated network structures. While other merger targets

---

26  Wilner (1998b). Given that CSX had introduced a one-stop shopping approach for customers of its subsidiaries, this concern was likely a valid one.
27  Both Canadian Class I railroads are transcontinental, water-to-water.

may not have met UP's preference in this respect, the indigestion of this choice, with hindsight, could hardly have been worse.

The UP–SP merger would likely never have been contemplated if there had not been some willingness on the part of UP to test the regulatory waters. The ICC's well known preference for end-to-end mergers over parallel mergers[28] had been tested by SP in the mid-1980s; its failure to merge with SF (because of the ICC's ruling against the merger) was partly responsible for SP's dire financial state. In speculation, perhaps UP assumed that SP's financial state would mean that competition authorities would not see this as, to use Canadian regulatory language, "removal of a vigorous and effective competitor."

The BNSF merger announcement also caught the attention of the three major rail companies east of the Mississippi. It tested Conrail's stated managerial preference for a go-it-alone growth strategy. Conrail's focus on cost containment (and managing its operating ratio) was not generating the results desired by shareholders and there was no growth strategy to keep pace with its larger eastern competitors. Cost containment can only be part of an equation for organic growth; the revenue generation part of the equation was not working at Conrail (Table 5.7). In short, it had become a takeover target.

The role of managerial preference in growth strategy development in railroads cannot be under-stated. As should be clear by now, US railroads do not appreciate cooperative approaches to growth. Trackage rights, haulage rights and alliances do not deliver the desired control of assets and leave potential merger and acquisition targets in play. In this way, and examining all three merger case studies reported in this chapter, it is reasonable and understandable that CN chose, in spite of a long-standing cooperative relationship with IC, to merge with IC rather than leave the company as a potential target for a larger railroad to acquire in future.

More problematic in these mergers is making the merger's operating strategy successful; thorough planning of its implementation is paramount. As noted in Chapter 4, the key features to operating success are understanding the customer and competitive environments and then matching them with a strategy that maximizes asset utilization, optimizes network configura-tion for those assets and manages the revenue stream to maximize the yield. The first two colour the strategy chosen for implementation, while the following three secure its success. The strategy formulation and implementation process is not linear but iterative.

**Asset utilization** improvements in the rail industry require getting the volume of business per asset to rise without suffering deterioration in service quality. The means to this end is through improvements in service reliability. A focus on improving asset utilization as if it were an operations research problem can have debilitating and disastrous results. Asset utilization improvements must be made with service quality and customer requirements in mind.[29] Only if

---

28  Most recently recounted by Grimm and Plaistow (1998).
29  On-time performance data is not collected by the Association of American Railroads nor is there a standard method for its calculation. Until such data exists, broadly in the public domain, the pressure on rail companies to improve their performance will be less.

the two perspectives are contemplated concurrently can both asset utilization and service to customers improve simultaneously. As with liner shipping, the elasticity of demand does not necessarily generate sufficient additional returns. Carl Martland of the Massachusetts Institute of Technology noted that prices have dropped 50% in this industry to generate roughly 33% more traffic.[30] Managing the relationship between asset utilization and service relationship is like walking a tightrope: you get better with practice but a lack of focus can be fatal.

**Table 5.7: N. American Railways Financial Performance 1996**

| Railroad | 1996 turnover US$ million | 1996 net profit US$ million | % Return on turnover |
|---|---|---|---|
| Burlington Northern Santa Fe | 8,150 | 889 | 10.9 |
| Canadian National | 3,995 | 310 | 7.8 |
| Canadian Pacific | 3,379 | 604 | 17.9 |
| Consolidated Rail Corp. | 3,714 | 342 | 9.2 |
| CSX Transportation | 1,248 | 302 | 24.2 |
| Illinois Central | 658 | 136.6 | 20.8 |
| Kansas City Southern | 518 | 86.5 | 16.7 |
| Norfolk Southern | 1,020 | 200 | 19.6 |
| Union Pacific | 11,219 | 664 | 5.9 |
| Wisconsin Central | 759 | 232 | 30.6 |

Source:    Adapted from Bascombe (1998:49). Return is calculated as profit/turnover.

In the rail industry, the **network configuration** element is not as flexible as it is for ocean carriers. Given the high cost of new track construction, and the extensive networks already in place, growth is more suitably planned through growing the market coverage of the network, giving rise to network acquisition by merger, alliance or joint venture. Given the fixed infrastructure issue, the choice of these is a decision of managerial preference, the specific facts of the opportunity, and the creation of the opportunity. There are severe limitations imposed by managerial culture and past infrastructure investment on the options available for consideration.

**Revenue management** demands that rail lines invest heavily in information systems. Like airlines, the investment in systems hardware has been made; whether they are fully utilized in managing revenue is, of course, a judgment to be made at the operational level. It is likely that the full benefits of revenue management have yet to be extracted from the rail system, but this will not happen until service standards match those desired by the buyer and are superior to those delivered by competitors, be they trucking or other rail companies.

---

30    C. Martland (1998), MIT, personal communication, 30 October.

The ability to get the strategy right is felt on the bottom line. The rail industry is superior in terms of its profitability and return on assets than is liner shipping.[31] Yet there is significant room for improvement. In concluding this section on rail management, it is appropriate to compare the financial and operating performance (Table 5.8) of these railroads.

**Table 5.8: N. American Railways Financial and Operating Performance 1997**

| *Class I Railroad* | *1997 turnover US$million* | *1997 net profit US$ million* | *% change 1996–97 net profit* | *On time performance (Parameters)* |
|---|---|---|---|---|
| Burlington Northern Santa Fe | 8,400 | 942 | 6.0 | 80% (30 min.) |
| Canadian National | 4,352 | 403 | 21.5 | 90% (1 hr) |
| Canadian Pacific | 3,428 | 802 | 32.6 | 92% (30 min.) |
| Consolidated Rail Corp. | NA* | NA | NA | 95% (30 min.) |
| CSX Transportation | 1,274 | 325 | 7.6 | 90% (30 min.) |
| Illinois Central | 700 | 150 | 9.9 | 90% (1 hr) |
| Kansas City Southern | 573 | 134 | 54.0 | 95% (1 hr) |
| Norfolk Southern | 1,062 | 224 | 12.0 | 90% (30 min.) |
| Union Pacific | 11,079 | 432 | –35.0 | 90% (6 hours) |
| Wisconsin Central | 805 | 253 | 9.0 | 90% (30 min.) |

Note: NA = not available due to acquisition by CSX and Norfolk Southern.

Source: Adapted from Bascombe (1998:49).

Further examination is worth undertaking. When reviewing BNSF's financial statements, it is clear that BNSF has remained profitable; by 1998, its long-term debt to stockholders' equity ratio has dropped from 81.3% prior to merger (1994) to 70.2%, and its operating ratio has fallen from 82.6% in 1994 to 75.9% in 1998.[32] On the other hand, the Union Pacific continues to struggle, with an operating ratio in 1998 above 100% reflecting the continuing losses it has absorbed in trying to digest its acquisition of SP. The UP's 1998 Statement of Consolidated Cash Flow exclude the impact of SP's assets and liabilities acquired in 1996![33] Meanwhile, it is too soon to uncover the full eventual impact of the division of Conrail, a process whose implementation was only finalized in June of 1999. All that remains is to speculate on their possible next moves.

---

31 Comparing the data in this chapter with Tables 4.1 and 4.2 of Chapter 4.
32 http://www.bnsf.com/media/html/annual_report_98.html.
33 http://www.up.com/investor/98annual/cashflow.htm.

## COMPETITION ISSUES IN RAIL MERGERS

On 21 April 1998 the STB began proceedings to determine if changes should be made to the way it determines rail revenue adequacy and its competitive access rules. Although the process gave shippers a forum to voice their concerns about rail service and mergers, the rail industry was not enthusiastic and no agreement was reached.[34] This process could have begun the re-regulation of rail, an outcome that is undesirable according to the Association of American Railroads (Burke, 1998). The industry recognized that, to date, mergers have been good for the industry; those that have taken place since deregulation have had greater benefits than pitfalls (Nowicki, 1997).

Rail companies share the asset-intensity of liner companies and, in fact, have an even larger investment in that they must literally "pay their way." Generally speaking, ocean and air "ways" are not an investment demanded of airlines and shipping companies but are provided relatively freely. As we will see in the next chapter, although this generalization is not entirely accurate, the rail company must make a significant investment in its infrastructure—building and maintaining track and the support infrastructure that makes that track both usable and safe. The key driver of non-organic growth (merger or alliance strategy) is the acquisition of network.

To those who have argued that joint operating agreements might have the same benefits as mergers, NS's VP of Strategic Planning, James W. McClellan, has said (Wilner, 1998a)

> *major railroads seem unable to work together on a consistent basis. They each have their own strategic, commercial and operating agendas and those agendas are seldom in agreement.*

Do trackage and haulage rights work? As interlining drags down the performance figures, interlining shipments is not as desirable an activity as is a single-line service. According to BNSF's VP of UP/SP Lines, Peter Rickershauser, the company has vigorously competed against UP on the 4000 miles of rights it acquired in the UP–SP merger decision; the outcome is that volume has increased sufficiently so as to make good use of the haulage rights as well as the trackage rights. Shippers do have two-carrier competitive access. However, access problems remain; the company believes that it has not been able to secure all the access the STB decision intended to grant (Anonymous, 1997g). This is a clear indication that railroads see trackage and haulage rights as inferior to ownership of the way, but that the rights system is one possible method of securing acceptable competitive access.

As noted previously, alliances leave the network assets of the weaker partner in an alliance in play for a competitor's takeover strategy. If the network configuration of an industry player is relatively fixed, as in the case of railroads, mergers present, for this very reason, a stronger growth strategy than is available from alliances or other cooperative relationships. Paul Tellier, CEO of CN, viewed the Conrail acquisition as not healthy for CN's long-term future because it

---

34  Surface Transportation Board (1998), Decision Case Docket EP 575 0, 24 July (http://www.stb.dot.gov/decisions).

threatened existing north-south business, and limited CN's ability to compete against trucking for trade within the NAFTA region (Anonymous, 1997h). These concerns led CN to contemplate its acquisition of IC, a company that until recently had strictly a cooperative relationship with CN.

The key question about mergers from a regulatory point of view then becomes one of how to ensure the system remains pro-competitive without resorting to re-regulation to prevent abuse of dominant position. There are a number of alternatives.

One way of altering the competitive playing field is by implementing the standard model for road transport in the rail sector—namely a separation of track and fixed infrastructure from operations. (See Brooks and Button, 1995, for a review of the international thinking on this approach and a taxonomy of options available, and Kessides and Willig (1998) for an economic evaluation of them.[35]) Traditionally, it has been assumed that there are economies of scale in railroads; Brooks and Button (1995:241) argued that it only applies to the operation of the rail bed. The key economic argument in their thinking follows:

> *The more recent econometric evidence brought about through improved model-ing and estimation procedures, though, indicates that ... there are limited scale economies overall except for very small rail roads. What does exist, however, are very significant economies of density [Keeler, 1983]. In short, what this effectively means is that the economies of scale that are to be found are associated with the rail infrastructure (track and signaling) and not the operations making use of this infrastructure. Further, some of these studies (for example, Friedlaender et al 1993) have found that these operational economies are increased when the capital stock is optimised. In such circumstances, the logic suggests that to obtain high levels of dynamic and X-efficiency there should be competition for the provi-sion of these services, since there is little tendency toward natural monopoly in providing rail services. The economies of scale argument (at least up to a certain network size) still seems to apply to the track, however, and the associated problems of natural monopoly, therefore, remain in infrastructure provision. The argument, however, for vertical integration of operations and track is broken.*

When there is public ownership of the track it is possible to limit abuse of market power by imposing rate of return regulation.[36] However, they did not recommend that approach (Brooks and Button, 1995:255):

> *While price-capping regulation has the well known advantage of a closer principal-agent relationship, if for no other reason than that the costs of gaining*

---

35  The idea is not new; seminal papers on the subject appeared in the UK over half a century ago (such as Mance, 1940) and the issue has been raised in transport policy debates in countries such as Canada (Gratwick and Heaver, 1985), Britain (Else, 1993) and Sweden (Jansson and Cardebring, 1989).

36  One of the problems with the rail sector in many countries, however, is existing excess capacity. It is well above that likely under a rate-of-return regulatory regime. The issue of time frame is also important; the industry also features extremely long waits for returns to be made when investment is undertaken. Defining appropriate institutional frameworks to stimulate investment in the short term is particularly difficult (Helm and Thompson, 1991).

*information is lower, it is more effective in industries experiencing rapid technical progress and, consequently, continually changing cost structures. Rail track does not seem to fall into such a category.*

Conceptually speaking, there are other means of separating operations of track and other fixed infrastructure (such as signaling) from ownership: trackage and haulage rights, competitive line rates, and so on.

Those arguing against the concept note that the interface between the operation of the track and the rolling stock is sufficiently complex to make the concept unworkable. There is the tradeoff made between equipment chosen and track specifications that could be suboptimal; furthermore, the allocation of liability in the case of an accident would be difficult, each party arguing that the other had failed mechanically.[37] Kessides and Willig (1998) conclude that the concept is likely to be most attractive where a dense and extensive rail network permits many operators to function and where a mature infrastructure exists, so that new infrastructure incentive problems are not present.

The shared assets area resulting from the division of Conrail by CSX and NS provides an interesting variant on the shared infrastructure concept. In this model the shared assets area remains a joint venture controlled by the two investing and competing railroads. It reintroduces competition to the New York area and serves as an alternative model for the industry to either an imposed, publicly-managed corporation or a regulated, private, not-for-profit entity. It is incumbent upon US regulators to put in place a plan to monitor this concept and determine if it will succeed as a pro-competitive option to re-regulation of the industry in regions where shippers are captive.

By dividing Conrail, the industry was also brought into balance with two dominant carriers in the west (UP and BNSF) and two in the east (CSX and NS). The progress to four dominant carriers was also accompanied by significant productivity improvements[38] and the US rail system can be declared by all economists to be more efficient than it was 20 years ago.

In Canada, the debate about rail regulation was significant in both the deregulation of transport leading to the *National Transportation Act, 1987* and its five-year review in 1992 (NTARC, 1993). Through these two review processes and subsequent legislation, the Canadian government laid the guiding principles for pro-competitive industry regulation that would ensure rail-to-rail competition. This process introduced a regime, finalized in the *Canada Transportation Act, 1995*, with features such as final offer arbitration in case of disputes, competitive lines rates and joint running rights options for captive shippers, and removed the barriers to abandonment and sale of track to short-lines that had hampered the development of a more efficient rail system. In spite of its failure to define an "essential rail network," the regulation

---

37  For further discussion, see Keeler (1983:130-1) and Starkie (1993).

38  In rough figures, route miles are down by 33%, employment by almost two-thirds, and ton-miles carried is up by 50% over those 20 years (Wilner, 1998a).

has experienced little criticism from either shippers or railways since and provides an alternative approach for regulators to contemplate.

Looking forward, the STB has now eliminated the geographic and product competition test for purposes of determining market dominance,[39] and adopted rules for obtaining alternative rail service during periods of poor service.[40] Ensuring competitive access, encouraging the development of shared assets areas and proposing other forms of vertical disintegration are all options to be examined more fully.

### LESSONS FOR LINER SHIPPING?

This string of mergers should work to the benefit of liner companies; a more seamless single-line inland network should reduce transit times (if implementation is better than that achieved by UP) and assist shipping lines in developing new origin-destination markets via alternative routings. Of course this ability to grow intermodal business will be limited if rates increase significantly to pay for the mergers. In the New York corridor, the creation of competition through the shared assets area also bodes well for liner companies calling New York.

What lessons were learned from the case studies?

One particularly interesting lesson for liner companies is found in the financial outcome in the case of the division of Conrail. In the high stakes acquisition business, bidding often mirrors an auction of rare memorabilia: bidding up the price gets out of control when the assets have significant intangible potential. In the case of Conrail, that intangible potential was the opportunity for delivering growth, and its value was obvious from the responses of both CSX and NS. The loser stood to become too small to provide effective competition; it was the downside risk of the deal that caused the bid price to escalate. The "share-the-spoils" approach has been seen as a possible paradigm for settling takeover disputes involving three or more firms; in particular, it is suitable in industries where the target is a key player in an industry with few firms and occupies a unique position of geographic or product-line power (Anonymous, 1998a). The industries cited as illustrative of this situation were telecommunications, railroads and banking.

Why not liner shipping? Perhaps the answer resides in the proportion of geographically fixed assets in which there is an investment. The greater the percentage of assets which are not mobile, the more likely merger and acquisition are preferable approaches to growth over cooperative relationships. The answer may also reflect the constraint due to the lack of public trading of liner companies. Good targets are small but numerous in the shipping industry; however, many are privately-held and therefore may not be driven by shareholders looking solely at maximizing the return on their capital invested.

---

39  Surface Transportation Board Decision, *Market Dominance Determinations—Product and Geographic Competition*, Docket EP 627 0, 10 December 1998.

40  Surface Transportation Board Decision, *Expedited Relief for Service Inadequacies*, Docket EP 628 0, 21 December 1998.

Managerial preference was a strong factor in the Conrail division; the extraction of value was clearly shareholder driven. Lesson two: governance structure is an important influence on managerial preference. Although Conrail management may have preferred the deal for its acquisition by "white knight" CSX, shareholders held out for the financially superior hostile bid from NS to the point of revolt; they took advantage of the regulatory constraint imposed on directors under Pennsylvania law. After all, shareholders look for return and if a shareholder had bought Conrail for US$28 in 1987, she was able to sell the share eight years later for US$230,[41] a shareholder's dream. As another example, SP's poor financial state can be traced to the asset-stripping strategy of its owner, Philip Anschutz.[42] For him, the primary purpose of the rail holdings were their asset value to him as a shareholder not as an operating business. His view of the business solely as a financial asset drove its strategy.

Regulatory constraint on managerial preference is also apparent for the smaller Class I's. For example, CN will not likely be bought by another railroad due to a poison pill in its Articles of Continuance; under the *CN Commercialization Act*, these articles were required to ensure that CN's headquarters remain in Montreal and its ownership be widely distributed (so that no one shareholder can control managerial decision-making.) This works both for and against CN's strategic options. It may never be acquired so it must therefore become the bidder, and bidders often are not the financial winners, as noted in Chapter 2. Meanwhile IC's managerial preference was not to be left as a wallflower at a dance surrounded by those larger and more powerful; if not CN, then who?

Lesson three: managerial culture is critical to the success of the merger or alliance. UP suffered more than just indigestion. SP was known as a company that operated on a shoestring; its equipment was safe but "held together with baling wire and gum," and it had managers who knew its flaws. UP was known for its efficiency, operations on a grand scale, and a CEO who disliked bad news (Anonymous, 1998c). These were two cultures destined to collide. As noted in Chapter 2 and the discussion of Morosini (1998), culture and cultural compatibility play a significant role in merger success.

There is a fourth lesson as well. A merger (or alliance) strategy may conceptually make sense at the top management level, but grand designs do not necessarily work on implementation. Integrating top management is only part of the implementation of a new strategy. The formulation of the strategy must include implementing plans which reach down into the grass roots of the organization. It is insufficient to assume that train operations and information systems can somehow be mashed together and all will be well. This applies equally well in liner shipping. The acquisition of the assets, the people and the terminals does not naturally lead to successful implementation. The strategy must detail a consistent and streamlined approach to the utilization of those assets, their network deployment and revenue management details to be

---

41  Blaze (1998). There was a stock split during these years, accounting for the equivalent price of US$230 instead of the acquisition price of US$115.

42  The sale of non-core assets after a leveraged buyout is the prerogative of the buyer. If not coupled with reinvestment, it can hardly be considered a growth strategy.

successful. If cultural incompatibility is likely, an alliance may provide an intermediate step and, if successful, the dance partners may eventually marry.

Looking forward, has the premium paid for Conrail imposed adverse conditions on its acquirers? According to Chatterjee (1992), target companies are more likely to gain than bidders in any merger scenario. Conrail shareholders certainly benefited as did many shareholders on the management team. NS appears to have fared better than CSX; NS has sold its interest in North American Van Lines while CSX, in spite of assurances to the contrary,[43] has sold its barge subsidiary. Will Sea-Land be next? Will CSX, in head-to-head competition with NS in the shared asset area, be able to withstand a potential price war if the two compete on price? If not, then will we still see a case built by shippers on other trade lanes for re-regulation of the industry? It is likely that CSX will need to restructure its business to make the best use of its large, some would say, over-priced acquisition.

## Postscript

As this book was being prepared for printing CSX did indeed first restructure its shipping companies, making a divestiture easier. Then, in July 1999, announced the sale of Sea-Land's international liner operations to A. P. Møller, parent of alliance partner Maersk.

---

43  John Snow was reported in Isidore (1997) as having no interest in selling either Sea-Land or CSX's barge business to focus attention on rail.

# 6

# LESSONS FROM OTHER INDUSTRIES: AIRLINES

## INTRODUCTION

Traditionally, the regulation of domestic and international air services has differed. Domestically, in many markets, entry is often restricted, rates are subject to approval and service levels (e.g. frequency of flights) are determined by regulatory authorities. Over the past two decades, domestic industry liberalization has reduced regulatory intervention significantly so that today we could conclude that the internal air markets of OECD countries operate freely.

Internationally, air transport has been regulated on the basis of the *Convention on International Civil Aviation of 7 December 1944*, otherwise known as the Chicago Convention. The countries active in civil aviation had failed to establish a multilateral agreement on aviation and therefore adopted a framework that promoted industry regulation through bilateral air services agreements. These agreements set the terms and conditions of business activity for companies of the contracting states and fixed barriers to entry against air carriers of other states. The first air services agreement was between the US and the UK and established a template for those that followed. Typical air services agreements include market access, routes, "freedoms" granted,[1] size of aircraft, frequency of flights and defined rules about how prices would be determined. Subsequent discussions have failed to alter this regulatory situation or secure a multilateral agreement, except within the European Union.

In the 1980s and 1990s, a number of bilateral aviation agreements were signed liberalizing the conditions of operating on certain international routes. On these routes, airlines have been allowed to compete on price and service frequencies, with the equipment of their choice. However, many airlines continue to face severe restrictions on their ability to make commercial decisions.

In order to promote greater competition, many countries have deregulated their airline industries. Within the OECD, deregulation of the industry began in the US with the *Airline Deregulation Act of 1978*. UK liberalization took place over the 1980s and since 1991 several liberalization packages have enhanced competition with the EU. Completion of the Single European Market by 1 April 1997 permitted any airline licensed in any EU country to service EU routes outside its own domestic boundaries.

---

1   Freedoms are rights respecting overflight, technical stops, carriage of traffic and cabotage.

Was deregulation successful in producing a more competitive market? The US experience is detailed by Morrison and Winston (1995). In the US, prices fell by one-third from 1976 to 1993, with 60% of the decline attributed to deregulation, while labour productivity grew by 120% over the period 1975-1993. Capital productivity increased as load factors improved. Passenger miles grew by a phenomenal 200% (probably due to the restructuring to hub and spoke networks) and passenger revenues by 93% in constant dollars. Employment grew from 300,000 in 1976 to almost 540,000 in 1993. A recent US commission found evidence confirming that deregulation has been beneficial to consumers in the 1990s (Transportation Research Board, 1999). The Australian experience reported by Grimm and Milloy (1993) was remarkably similar in effect.

The UK experience with deregulation was also positive, and with a similar pattern. Fares on British Airways, both domestic and international, fell 24% over the period 1985–1990. Average productivity grew 3% annually in 1985–1991 and 11% annually in 1991–1994. Passenger load factors illustrated productivity improvements, growing from 60% in 1985 to 70% in 1994. Capacity grew, with available tonne kilometres (ATKs) doubling in 1985–1994 (Yarrow, 1995). In Europe, on scheduled services, prices dropped and leisure passenger traffic grew along with service frequencies (Abbott and Thompson, 1991).

High price elasticity in the demand for passenger air services makes cost a key determinant of airline success.[2] In spite of deregulation, however, prices and costs in the sector continue to vary widely, with differences related to stage length[3] and also efficiency (Table 6.1). Prices and costs are lower in the competitive markets of the US and UK when compared with other, more regulated OECD countries. Some cost differences have to do with service characteristics; for example, US airlines operate with fewer cabin crew. The net result is that the large European carriers British Airways and KLM are significantly less efficient than their US confrères (Blöndal and Pilat, 1997).

Regulatory reform plus productivity improvements have lowered real prices, as shown in Table 6.2. Høj *et al.* (1995) concluded that strong competitive pressure in the US resulted in similar prices and low cost variances between carriers, whereas in Europe and the rest of the OECD, competitive pressures were less even and prices varied much more. Deregulation in Australia, Canada and New Zealand led to competitive pricing, but Japan continued to have difficulty.

Blöndal and Pilat (1997) noted that regulatory reform might not result in increased competition if incumbents control take-off and landing slots[4] at airports; this has become a critical issue for competition regulators, as will be seen later.

---

2    Price elasticity is much less for business travel.

3    Long flights have lower revenue per passenger kilometre (RPK).

4    The use of the term slot in the airline business is quite different from its use in shipping. A slot is a pre-defined take-off or arrival time the airline has been granted by or purchased from the airport. An airline must acquire both a take-off slot at one airport and a landing slot at another to be able to offer a service. The

**Table 6.1: Potential Impacts of Regulatory Reform in Airlines**

| | *Actual* | *Potential* | | | |
|---|---|---|---|---|---|
| *Impacts in 1993* | *US* [1] | *Japan* | *Germany* | *France* | *UK* |
| **Costs and Prices (in US$)** | | | | | |
| Average Cost per ASK | 0.06 | 0.12 | 0.13 | 0.16 | 0.07 |
| Average Price per RPK | 0.09 | 0.18 | 0.21 | 0.23 | 0.10 |
| Operating Expense per ATK | 0.45 | 0.84 | 0.71 | 0.88 | 0.54 |
| **Product & Service Quality** | | | | | |
| RPK per Employee | 1,808 | NA | 1,444 | 998 | 1,810 |
| Average Stage Length (in km) | 1,204 | 1,274 | 1,155 | 1,193 | 1,361 |
| Cabin Crew to Flight Crew | 1.8 | 2.2 | 2.6 | 2.2 | NA |
| Load factor passengers | 0.64 | 0.64 | 0.61 | 0.67 | 0.73 |

Note:    (1) The actual impacts for the US are 1978–1993 while the potential impacts are for 1993.
Source: Blöndal and Pilat (1997), "The Economic Benefits of Regulatory Reform," *OECD Economic Studies*, Paris: OECD, 28, 1, 7-48. © OECD, 1997.

**Table 6.2: Average Airline Prices and Costs**

| | *1980* | *1985* | *1990* | *1993* |
|---|---|---|---|---|
| **Prices (US cents per RPK)** | | | | |
| US | 7.74 | 8.11 | 8.39 | 9.08 |
| OECD Europe (flag carriers) | 12.02 | 10.73 | 15.37 | 14.96 |
| Australia, Canada, Japan, New Zealand | 9.05 | 9.94 | 13.13 | 14.55 |
| **Costs (US cents per ATK)** | | | | |
| US | 36.99 | 40.68 | 46.50 | 45.72 |
| OECD–Europe (flag carriers) | 59.16 | 53.55 | 83.82 | 84.01 |
| Australia, Canada, New Zealand | 49.00 | 42.33 | 45.07 | 39.61 |
| Japan | 39.99 | 45.98 | 74.66 | 82.42 |

Source: Høj, Kato and Pilat (1995), "Deregulation and Privatisation in the Service Sector," *OECD Economic Studies*, Paris: OECD, 25, 2, 37-74. © OECD, 1995.

The economics of the airline industry provide some understanding of the growth decision that carriers make. Tretheway (1984, 1991) and Caves *et al.* (1986) have found that, when the amount of traffic on a route is held constant, the addition of new routes or destinations to the

---

offering of a service may also be foreclosed by the absence of gate infrastructure. The terms and conditions surrounding both slots and gates determine airport access.

network does not generate lower costs per passenger. Australia's Bureau of Transport and Communications Economics (1994:11) concluded that unit costs fall modestly as both the size of the aircraft and the stage length increase. Economies of scale may be found in groundside activities like aircraft maintenance.[5] Economies of traffic density do exist, however, until the maximum efficient traffic density level is reached. This encourages the addition of flights and seats on a given route. Both economies of scope and traffic density promote the development of hub and spoke networks.[6] There are also economies of standardization; carrier management has long known about the benefits of minimizing the number of aircraft models as well as suppliers within the asset base to reduce fleet maintenance training costs and parts inventory carrying costs.

Although there may be limited economies of scale in the airline industry, there are significant characteristics which may create entry barriers:

- control of feeder operations by a trunk carrier may limit the ability of a start-up carrier to begin life as a feeder operation
- control of the ticket distribution channel by large carriers offers the potential for abuse of agent commission overrides[7]
- computer reservation system (CRS) control by the carrier can offer the controlling carrier a competitive advantage
- code-sharing to the destination moves the code-share alternative further up the screen from the two-carrier option,[8] and
- access to airport infrastructure—take-off and landing slots and gates—may be difficult if not impossible at congested facilities.

The final feature of this industry that has relevance to the growth alternatives of a carrier is ownership. Public ownership is pervasive, tying commercial interests to national politics. While there has been significant private sector participation in the US, it is only the last decade that has seen privatization of the participants in many other countries. Høj *et al.* (1995) concluded that privatization has not been a sufficient condition to increase competition in this industry.[9]

---

[5]  Caves *et al.* (1984) found that economies of scale exist only for very small carriers and that, in fact, there may be diseconomies of scale for the very large because of network complexity.

[6]  While hub and spoke operations may bring airlines the benefits of economies of traffic density, there are diseconomies in the groundside support operations between the peak operating periods.

[7]  US Department of Transportation (1990:28). This study found that travel agents tend to prefer a small override commission from a large carrier to a larger commission from a smaller carrier.

[8]  This becomes extremely important as sales are usually made from the first screen on the travel agent's terminal.

[9]  On the other hand, Eckel *et al.* (1997) studied airline stock prices at the time of BA's privatization, concluding that privatization improves economic efficiency.

## AIR TRANSPORT LIBERALIZATION IN THE EU

Ortiz Blanco and van Houtte (1996) noted that in the 30 years after the promulgation of the *Treaty of Rome*, interstate air transport within the European Community was organized not on free market principles but on the basis of public regulation of the conditions of competition.[10] Governments, either unilaterally or bilaterally, controlled the conditions of business—network routes, capacity and price—resulting in markets dominated by virtual monopolies charging high prices (Ortiz Blanco and van Houtte, 1996). Europe had not experienced the advantages seen by consumers in the US air market post-deregulation. Liberalization of the market was required if Europe was to achieve its ambition of a Single European Market.

It is interesting that the regulatory authorities in Europe, unlike those in the US, did not liberalize the market in a single move, but opted to stage its liberalization agenda; three packages of legislative instruments were introduced in 1987, 1990 and 1992. The 'First Package' began the process of liberalization of the internal market. In particular, Council Regulation 3975/87 paved the way for the application of competition rules just as the adoption of Council Regulation 4056/86 had in the maritime transport sector, while Council Regulation 3976/87 defined the conditions of cooperation that would be considered acceptable. The 'Second Package,' adopted in June of 1990, comprised measures that would alter these provisions, providing a transition to the liberalizing measures of the 'Third Package,' adopted in July 1992. All three packages are outlined in Appendix C at the end of this chapter. While they did not address extra-Community air transport regulation, Ortiz Blanco and van Houtte argued that the packages established a European stance on competition policy for the industry. The regulations determined the rules applicable, set the Commission's powers of investigation and defined the exemption criteria for agreements and practices.[11] This belief is not held by DG VII, the Transport Directorate.[12]

Although the process of putting a competition policy in place in the air transport sector was relatively smooth, the application of the policy to intra-Community flights remained a serious problem from the DG IV's perspective (Ortiz Blanco and van Houtte, 1996:259-61). While some routes were characterized by intense competition, market-sharing and price-fixing continued on others. While the three packages of liberalizing measures moved intra-Community air transport towards greater efficiency, DG IV believed there was still room for improvement in the sector.

Examples of practices of cooperation between companies in the market which are deemed to be acceptable are detailed in the Annex to Regulation 3975/87. Activities that may be deemed to be anti-competitive by DG IV are joint operations, revenue pooling agreements, schedule coordination, airport scheduling and slot allocation, tariff coordination agreements, tariff

---

10  Development of the air common transport policy is described by Ortiz Blanco and van Houtte (1996:21-6). Additional detail is provided by Argyris (1989), Button and Swann (1989), and Van de Voorde (1992).

11  It was noted by Ortiz Blanco and van Houtte (1996:168) that it would serve little purpose if opportunities created by liberalization were then countered by restrictive agreements on the part of the airlines.

12  K. Button (1999), personal communication, 3 November.

construction rules, ground handling agreements, computer reservation systems and strategic alliances.[13] While in Chapter 3 it was noted that any of these might constitute a variant of the strategic alliance, the use of the term is more specifically contemplated by the Commission to be an arrangement that falls short of merger as it preserves the **participants' identities** and **individual autonomy**, although it may allow them to mimic a single airline.

In its assessment of equity-based relationships, the Commission has examined these in terms of the benefits created and the market power which results; if the benefits of coordination are considerable, the agreement is approved by the Commission unless significant market power results. If the agreement eliminates competition on the route, or if the companies control access to essential facilities, the Commission seeks ways of either stimulating competition or protecting the interests of third parties. For example, when Swissair, a non-EU firm, acquired a 49% stake in Sabena in 1995, the Commission ruled that while there would not be creation of a dominant position on intercontinental extra-Community routes, there would be a monopoly position created on certain routes between Belgium and Switzerland. Approval of this acquisition required the two airlines to give up slots at Brussels, Geneva and Zurich airports if requested by another airline, to limit increases in frequencies, to enter into interlining agreements with new entrants, to offer frequent flyer program participation to new entrants without one, and for Swissair to terminate its alliance with SAS and Austrian Airlines.[14] A similar set of undertakings was required when the strategic alliance agreement between two EU companies, Lufthansa and SAS, was examined; both were required to give up slots at Frankfurt, Dusseldorf, Stockholm and Oslo; Lufthansa was required to terminate its alliances with Transmede and Finnair in the German and Scandinavian markets; and SAS was required to terminate its alliance with Swissair and Austrian Airlines.[15]

As for the regulation of mergers within the EU, the Commission has taken the stance that Articles 85 and 86 of the *Treaty of Rome* apply to the air sector as they do to other industries and therefore mergers will be examined on the principle of preventing restriction of competition, abuse of dominant position and restraint of trade. The airline industry receives no special treatment in the case of mergers. It will determine if the merger meets the threshold of a Community dimension[16] and then, if it does surpass the threshold, examine whether it leads to an overall reduction in competition, as was illustrated in the alliance cases noted previously.

---

[13]  Each of these is detailed in Ortiz Blanco and van Houtte (1996:177-90) with explanations as to past decisions on those terms and conditions that have been deemed to be restrictive by the Commission.

[14]  Commission Decision of 10 July 1995 in the case of Swissair/Sabena (M.616) under Article 6(1)(b) of Council Regulation 4064/89.

[15]  Commission Decision of 16 January 1996 in the case of Lufthansa/SAS (35.545) under Article 85 of the *Treaty of Rome*.

[16]  As already defined in Chapter 1 on page 21.

## THE BA–AA CASE[17]

Before the formal plans were announced on 11 June 1996, American Airlines' CEO Robert Crandall and Sir Colin Marshall, CEO of British Airways, had been preparing for a broad-based alliance between their companies for years. Both believed that the alliance, to commence April 1997, would satisfy their common goals of increasing profits with minimal associated costs (Wines, 1996). The arrangement would allow each carrier access to new markets without a loss of existing brand equity. It would entail both passenger and cargo cooperation and feature extensive code-sharing arrangements and full reciprocity between each partner's frequent flyer program. The case was not a merger or a joint venture under Commission rules because no equity would be exchanged. Each would retain its brand identity and nationality and operate its own fleet. Unlike alliances of the joint marketing variety, this alliance would allow cost savings from sharing aircraft and ground facilities to flow to the alliance partners.

Conditions precedent on the agreement were antitrust immunity for the deal in both the US and the UK and changes to the air services agreement governing US–UK traffic. The antitrust immunity would be necessary to allow the two to coordinate schedules and pool revenue. This was not a precedent-setting request of government, as the US had previously granted antitrust immunity to the Northwest–KLM alliance and to the United–Lufthansa alliance, both upon completion of new air services agreements between the US and, respectively, the Netherlands and Germany. Furthermore, the Delta–Swissair–Austrian–Sabena alliance and the American–Canadian alliance had also been blessed. In all cases there were strings attached to the immunity and exceptions included.[18]

What was the managerial thinking behind the alliance? American desired growth, but the US market was already mature. Since the European and Latin American markets had room for growth, expanding into these areas appeared to be the profitable alternative. In Europe specifically, BA's main hub—London's Heathrow Airport—was the primary target. At the time of the proposed alliance, AA and United were the only US airlines with direct access to Heathrow, and because it is among the busiest and most constrained airports in the world, new access was extremely difficult to obtain. Through an alliance with British Airways, American expected increased access to Heathrow and subsequently to destinations in Africa, the Middle East, and other parts of Europe not currently being served by AA (Wines, 1996). By allying themselves, both airlines hoped to use BA's position at Heathrow to direct US passengers on to other destinations (Dwyer, 1998).

Sir Colin Marshall, then Chairman of BA, had been an advocate of alliances in general for several years. He predicted in 1995 that deregulation would lead to consolidation and, to be a competitive force in the industry, BA should look to form global alliances (Prokesch, 1995). Under Marshall's leadership, the first code-sharing link was established between BA and

---

17  The two case studies in this chapter were developed with the assistance of Roberta Morrison (Dalhousie MBA '00 student).

18  Button (1997:36, Table 7) identified a list of these exceptions for three of the four alliances.

United Air Lines in 1987 and, although since terminated, it set the stage for all such alliances to follow (Feldman, 1996). Marshall believed that alliances would result in decreased costs, shared resources, more efficient use of aircraft and employees, increased world market share for alliance partners and increased business for all involved (Prokesch, 1995). BA's commitment to alliances meant the company held equity stakes, code-sharing or franchise agreements with 14 other airlines by 1996 including US Air, Qantas, TAT European Airlines, Deutsche BA, Canadian Airlines International, and Maersk Air UK.[19]

For British Airways' part in the proposed agreement with AA, it found the access to the US market very attractive. It would contribute to the company's global strategy and Bob Ayling, the most recent CEO of BA, felt the alliance would create an "incomparable network" in the industry and aid the company in achieving its goal of becoming "the undisputed leader in world travel" (http://www.britishairways.com). Even with the low growth potential of the US market, US passengers account for 40% of the world's air traffic; BA had been disappointed with its entry into the US market via US Air and hoped the new relationship with AA would result in increased revenues to BA.

The UK Office of Fair Trading responded in December 1996; its approval was contingent on the alliance relinquishing 168 take-off and landing slots at Heathrow (and UK authorities would allow some of the slots to revert to the carriers after other carriers entered the market). The US Department of Transportation was reported to be seeking 420 slots as the price of approval, while the European Commission presented a compromise between the two (Kayal, 1997b). In addition, the Commission would prohibit cooperation on the Dallas–London route (the combined market share was 100%), and would require a reduction in the frequencies on a number of others.[20] The two would also be prevented from combining their frequent flyer programs.

The UK approvals would allow the partners to sell the slots relinquished, but the Commission replied by noting that slot sales are illegal under EU law, and that the reduction in slots proposed was insufficient.[21] This position was reinforced in the Commission's subsequent ruling; on 8 July 1998, the Commission issued the preliminary conditions for its approval: the alliance would have to release up to 267 slots at Heathrow if a rival airline wished to expand an existing service or launch a new one.[22] The release of slots would have to be accompanied by the airport infrastructure necessary for the effective use of the slots. Similar conditions were attached to a reduction in frequencies on the London–Dallas, London–Miami, and London–Chicago routes. There were further conditions related to frequent flyer programs, computer reservation systems, travel agency and customer relations, and interlining.

---

[19]  http://www.britishairways.com/inside/media/archive/archive97.shtml#1966, "How the Alliance Partners Compare."

[20]  The routes where reductions were required were London to/from New York, Los Angeles, Chicago, Miami, Boston and Philadelphia.

[21]  Kayal (1997a). In the US, airlines have anti-trust immunity to form scheduling committees and allocate landing and take-off slots through their sale and purchase (Morrison and Winston, 1987:61).

[22]  http://europa.eu.int/en/comm/dg04/dg04home.html, accessed 8 July 1998, Document: IP/98/641. It is worth contemplating the implementation of an odd number of slots when a pair is needed for a service.

The main concern of the General Accounting Office (US) was that the two airlines accounted for nearly 58% of the seats on scheduled US and UK airlines between the US and London, and more than 70% of all available seats between London Heathrow and several major US cities (GAO, 1998). The General Accounting Office's concern is not surprising given the long series of studies it has undertaken on air fares at hub airports.[23] The principal concern of the European Commission was that entry barriers would be created which could limit market access for existing competitors and prevent new entrants. Furthermore, the dominance of the companies at their respective hubs made the availability of take-off and landing slots an illusion. Control of a large number of frequencies at peak operating hours would mean that a new competitor might be unable to start a viable service.

As for the new air services agreement necessary for the alliance to be fully executed, progress was extremely slow; there was clearly little consensus on what constituted "open skies." The US Department of Transportation cancelled hearings into the air services agreement scheduled for October 1998. BA then decided, given the Commission's preliminary conditions, that a more relaxed approach to its relationship with AA was in order. The outcome was a new marketing alliance including BA, AA, Canadian Airlines, Cathay Pacific, Japan Air Lines and Qantas, with the name of Oneworld (Table 6.3). Finnair, Iberia and Lan Chile joined in 1999. When BA announced its results for the year ending 31 March 1999, it noted that it would continue to follow its strategy of focusing on serving the premium end of the market and reducing its exposure to the discount sector.[24] The relationship with AA as originally envisioned has disappeared from the press release file.

## THE STAR ALLIANCE

The Star Alliance began as a partnership between Lufthansa of Germany and America's United Air Lines in 1994. In May 1997, the alliance grew to be a global force with the addition of Air Canada, SAS, Thai and Varig. Air New Zealand, All Nippon and Ansett joined in 1999. The purpose of establishing the alliance was a "global" airline partnership offering seamless travel to 578 cities in 106 countries (as noted by the original six). The Star Alliance proposed sharing groundside facilities and reservation systems, offering customers access to partners' lounges and crediting frequent flyer programs with points earned on partners' flights (Kayal, 1997c). The grouping accounted for 27.6% of 1997 worldwide revenue passenger kilometres (Anonymous, 1998).

The multi-partner alliance was a natural progression for Lufthansa, a company with a global strategy and a belief that an airline (of its size) required more than one partner in order to be successful. Lufthansa was positive about the gains it achieved through the expanded alliance, as

---

23  The GAO has consistently and continuously found that while many consumers have benefited from reduced airfares, communities with airports dominated by one or two airlines have faced substantial increases in fares since deregulation (e.g. GAO 1990, 1993, 1996).

24  http://www.britishairways.com, 25 May 1999, "Preliminary Results on Target."

arrangements with SAS and United were judged to have saved the company DM200 million. Jurgen Weber, Chairman and later CEO of the company, felt that the global alliance was necessary as it would result in increased revenue and access to other markets—welcomed benefits after a 63% decrease in net profits was reported for 1996 over 1995 (Anonymous, 1997a). Traffic increases of 20–30% on the transatlantic were also a factor; they surpassed those of all other European airlines as well as that of AA in 1997 (Upbin, 1997).

### Table 6.3: Star versus Oneworld 1998

| *Star* | *Oneworld* |
|---|---|
| Air Canada | American Airlines |
| Lufthansa | British Airways |
| SAS Scandinavian Airlines System | Canadian Airlines |
| Thai Airways International | Cathay Pacific |
| United Air Lines | Qantas |
| VARIG | |
| *Associated* | *Associated* |
| Air New Zealand | Air Niugini |
| All Nippon Airways | Air Pacific |
| Ansett Airlines | Ansett New Zealand |
| China Airlines | Asiana Airlines |
| China Southern Airlines | China Eastern Airlines |
| Korean Air | EVA Airways |
| Mandarin Airlines | Finnair |
| Mexicana | Japan Airlines |
| Singapore Airlines | Pakistan International Airlines |
| | Philippine Airlines |

Chairman Gerald Greenwald of United Air Lines believed the global alliance was vital for maintaining the company's high profit margins; in his mind, the alliance was a key to success in a highly cyclical industry where how well the company does in a depressed market is as important as how well it does in the boom (Upbin, 1997). Greenwald felt that the alliance enhanced United's staying power by extending its reach beyond its strong Atlantic and Pacific routes.

Air New Zealand, with its equity partner Ansett, became a member of the alliance for a number of reasons. The airline, which originally resisted following the alliance trend, saw the Star Alliance as its opportunity to compete with the pairing of its regional rival Qantas with British Airways. Also, due to the Asian recession, Jim McCrea, Managing Director of the company, saw the alliance as its means of survival. By allying with larger global partners, Air New Zealand could extend its reach outside of the mature domestic market and thereby replace some of the losses it was incurring on its Asian routes. In order for alliances to remain beneficial, all parties must profit from the pairing; despite the fact that New Zealand and Australia account for only about 2% of the world's passenger traffic, having a partner in the South Pacific opened an entirely new market for the alliance (Hill, 1999).

It appears that Air Canada, SAS, Varig and All Nippon were interested in the alliance for the obvious global access provided and perhaps also out of necessity. With alliances among larger airlines such as Lufthansa and United taking place, the smaller carriers' choices seemed limited to two—face the financial stress likely to accompany continued independent operation or survive through alliances with successful companies. Air Canada, once strongly opposed to US open skies and third-country code-sharing agreements, reversed its traditional position hoping to generate new passenger traffic (Feldman, 1998), perhaps also hoping to shore up its increasingly troubled financial situation. Shareholders were growing restless with its long run stock performance.

Initially, this alliance did not encounter the regulatory opposition experienced by the BA–AA agreement. It took the US Department of Transportation only three months to approve the alliance between Lufthansa and United (Jebb, 1998).[25] However, after reviewing the BA–AA agreement, regulators re-examined the Star Alliance and imposed conditions on it. On the same day as its announcement on the BA–AA proposal, the European Commission also released its preliminary conditions for approval of the Lufthansa–SAS–United alliance and these were similar.[26] The conditions focused on the Frankfurt–Chicago and Frankfurt–Washington city-pairs with release of up to 108 slots at Frankfurt and Copenhagen airports established as the requirement for approval.

In terms of the regulations necessary for approval and the motives behind the alliance, the Star Alliance was no different from the rail or other airline alliances discussed thus far, except in one important aspect: branding. The Star Alliance decided to create a single brand as an umbrella for all of its members. Each of its members retained its own name, but each also carried the easily identified Star logo, enabling the group to convey to consumers the common values held by all participants, including an emphasis on safety and reliability (Killgren, 1998). The chairperson of Star's communication and brand management group, Louise McKenven, stressed that creating awareness for the group and leveraging the brand in the minds of consumers were priorities for the alliance (Beirne, 1999). The plan was to create a synergy of all participants in the alliance and not have United's or Lufthansa's strengths alone transferred to smaller members. Interestingly, BA–AA had originally avoided being associated under one name, calling Star a "brand nightmare" (Jebb, 1998); recently there has been a change of heart and the Oneworld brand was created. Oneworld has countered Star's branding campaign of US$6.5 million with its own of US$15 million in 90 countries worldwide. To offset any marketing progress Oneworld would make with its larger budget, Star has retaliated in its advertisements with the message that its single-brand alliance was the first of its kind. Competition between Star and

---

25  K. Button (1999), personal communication, 3 November. Button believes that the speedy regulatory approval was *quid pro quo* for the Government of Germany's acceptance of an "Open Skies" air services agreement with the US. The German market had been tightly regulated but Lufthansa was in financial difficulty. There was also new airport capacity in Germany. On the other hand, the BA–AA proposal required an "Open Skies" agreement with the UK, one much less likely to occur, and Heathrow was considerably congested.

26  http://europa.eu.int/en/comm/dg04/dg04home.html, accessed 8 July 1998, Document: IP/98/640.

Oneworld is becoming intense as the global airline market looks to be heading for difficult times.[27]

## MANAGEMENT ISSUES IN AIRLINE STRUCTURAL OPTIONS

Analyzing these two alliances in the air industry can only be highly speculative. Unlike the rail industry mergers discussed in Chapter 5, there was very little public commentary made by the involved airline executives that was not sanitized by each airline's legal and public relations advisors.[28] Any discussion of managerial preference for structural options is therefore constrained. There are, however, the unavoidable facts and that, for this industry, it is clear that regulation has limited managerial choices.

National ownership is a desirable state incorporated into the Chicago Convention; Article 7, Part VIII allows each state

> *to withhold or revoke a certificate or permit to an airline of another state in any case where it is not satisfied that substantial ownership and effective control are vested in nationals ...*

These regulations effectively limit mergers and acquisitions as options for growth to those firms within the boundaries of one country, such as the merger of British Airways and British Caledonia and the merger of Air France with Air Inter.[29]

Airlines are generally prevented by national law from following the merger path. In the US, the *Federal Aviation Act of 1958*, section 101, limits foreign ownership to no more than 25% of the voting interest in a US airline.[30] In Canada, the same 25% limit on foreign ownership applies through the *Canada Transportation Act*,[31] with further restrictions on ownership by one entity to no more than 4% of Canadian Airlines through the *PWA Act* of the Province of Alberta.[32] The *Air Canada Public Participation Act* sets an individual limit of 10% on the ownership of shares in Air Canada that may be used to elect directors.[33] In Europe the limit on foreign

---

[27] There appears to be a new twist on the horizon. At the time of writing, the Star Alliance was putting together a plan to invest in 23% of the privatizing Thai Airways (Anonymous, 1999). The members of the alliance planned to create a holding company to buy stakes in the airline, and if successful, it would be the first time Star participants (as a group) have held equity in other members.

[28] Perhaps the new alliances have learned from the poor press KLM's relationship with Northwest received (e.g., Tulley, 1996).

[29] Approval of these intra-country mergers gained approval only after the airline relinquished routes or slots (Button, 1997).

[30] Transportation Research Board (1999) recommended this be changed.

[31] *Canada Transportation Act*, Section 55 establishes ownership requirements.

[32] This did not prevent American Airlines from purchasing a one-third ownership of the economic interests and 25% of the voting shares of Canadian Airlines in 1993 as the Province of Alberta waived the *PWA Act* rules.

[33] Section 6 (1) (a). Furthermore, section 6 (1) (e) requires that the corporation's head office shall be maintained in Montreal, a "poison pill" against takeover not unlike that noted in Chapter 5 as applying to Canadian National.

ownership is less restrictive at 49%. Ownership restrictions are reinforced by the terms of the myriad of air services agreements signed by each government.

There is a second problem with the merger alternative for growth. As there are few economies of scale in airline operations, and the generalization that mergers involving overlapping networks tend to bring less to the table than those with an end-to-end nature, mergers in the airline industry are likely to be successful only if they can put the company in a position that allows it to exploit its dominant position or remove a vigorous competitor. In either case, they will be unlikely to pass scrutiny by competition authorities without the imposition of some strategically unacceptable conditions as the regulators examine impact on a route-by-route basis. In the interim, the company may have lost its business focus and valuable time that could have been devoted to building the existing business.

The individual ownership restrictions also severely curtail the ability of airlines with such limits to attract minority equity investments from partner airlines, also restricting airline consideration of the joint venture or cross equity investment. American Airlines' acquisition of Canadian Airlines was technically acceptable to the Canadian authorities because its acquisition of 33% of the economic interests of the company included only 25% of the voting shares! This illustrates a more serious outcome of such restrictions for equity holders: that the governance structure for the business may not reflect the level of investment (Button, 1997). Such a situation strains the nature of the relationship and may distort managerial preferences when key partners do not agree on the direction the business should take strategically. Nowhere has the strain been more obvious than in the KLM–Northwest alliance. Gary Wilson and Al Checchi purchased 44% of Northwest for US$40 million in a leveraged buyout and then less than a year later convinced KLM to put in US$400 million for a 20% stake. The clash between the two managerial philosophies is detailed in Tulley (1996).

There are demand conditions in the industry that favour large carriers over small ones and therefore encourage efforts to grow faster than possible through organic growth. These include customers' preferences for airlines with a wider choice of destinations and frequent flyer programs as well as the belief that larger airlines will likely travel to the desired destination, thereby reducing the customer's information costs (Tretheway, 1990). Therefore, in the absence of a merger option, and limited by cross-equity restrictions, it is possible to conclude that alliances are the only viable option given the restrictions imposed by bilateral air service agreements. Alliances can bring the marketing benefit of new routes and destinations, without the associated expenditures of growing firm size organically, while simultaneously adding passengers to improve load factors[34] and hence asset utilization by attracting new passengers to existing routes.

---

[34] Load factors in the airline industry show considerable variability, ranging from, in 1993, a low of 59% to a high of 71%, the former belonging to US Air and the latter to BA and Singapore Airlines (Oum and Yu, 1998a:413, Table 1). By 1995, the marketplace had shifted and the range showed general improvement overall, with a low of 63% and a high of 76%, the former being experienced by Air Canada and the latter by KLM (Oum and Yu, 1998b:231, Table 1). (US Air had improved to 69% in just 2 years!) If alliances improve load factors, the result correspondingly improves both the participating airline's operating ratio and profitability.

Having concluded that outright development of a global carrier through merger is not possible given the legal and political impediments to mergers of airlines of differing nationalities,[35] Tretheway (1990) argued that global carrier systems could take two forms: simple carrier alliances or stronger alliances featuring equity positions. He reasoned that cost advantages are not strong enough to promote consolidation, but that demand side forces such as the premium passengers place on same carrier service, the information cost savings and benefits of frequent flyer programs could encourage such developments. He believed that the simple alliance is not favoured because it is too volatile, and too easy to cancel, to justify the investment necessary for global reach.

Tretheway's view was supported by Button (1997) whose research summarized data on the instability of airline alliances of the simpler type and the strength of alliances involving cross equity holdings. However, the number of cross equity alliances is on the decline and accounted for less than 16% by 1996 (Button, 1997:19). In particular, Button noted that those with equity investments have a better track record in this matter.[36] Many successful alliances have been those between a commuter and a trunk airline rather than those between trunk operators. The reasons for failure do not appear to vary much from those found in other industries and reported in Chapter 2.

What are the benefits of airline alliances? They bring the participating airline increased volumes on trunk routes to and from its hubs, thereby gaining additional economies of traffic density, and they also enable airlines to achieve geographic market reach not quickly obtainable through organic growth. Nyathi (1996) found that airline managers ranked network expansion and/or reconfiguration as the most important strategic motive for entering into collaborative arrangements; cost reduction came second.[37] Cost cutting was not a driver of the Star Alliance's formation; seamless customer service and savings from elimination of overlap were not expected to be accompanied by staff layoffs, but rather by revenue growth (Anonymous, 1997b). Park and Zhang (1998) found that, following an alliance, the allying airline sees an increase in gateway-to-gateway traffic and its partner's profit also likely increases as a result of the adverse effect on non-aligned carriers, thereby driving non-aligned carriers to contemplate alliances in order to defend market share.

Alliances are seen by some as a cost-effective means of achieving both a company's marketing and production efficiencies and its strategic objectives. However, they do have their detractors. Alliances are also viewed to have high transaction costs in negotiation and implementation, draining managerial resources from existing business activities. The leakage of managerial innovations is considered by some as a price too high for the benefits gained.

---

[35]    This is not entirely true as SAS, Air Afrique and Gulf Air are three examples where transnational airlines with ownership in multiple countries has been allowed.

[36]    Button (1997:47). See also: Anonymous (1995). This article reports a Boston Consulting Group study which concluded that fewer than 40% of regional alliances and 30% of international alliances have been successful. Partial equity alliances between SAS and Continental, and BA and US Air provide illustrations of the fact that equity participation does not ensure success.

[37]    Furthermore, partner choice was driven by that motive in terms of expected network outcomes.

How do successful airline alliances extract the benefits of alliances? In their study of three transatlantic alliances up to 1989, Dresner *et al.* (1995) concluded that the KLM–Northwest alliance generated the greatest advantages through increased load factors and improved market share; to do this, the carriers realigned their route networks to exploit partners' hubs. Furthermore, it has been reported that the alliance was able to increase its transatlantic market share from 7% to 11%, enabling Northwest to report a US$830 million operating profit in 1994, up from a US$60 million loss in 1991 (Anonymous, 1995). Youssef and Hansen (1994) documented the impacts of the Swissair–SAS alliance and concluded that the immediate effect was a significant growth in traffic; traffic between hubs rose by 54% and transfer traffic by 86%. They concluded that alliances involve tradeoffs and that there will be redistribution of benefits between types of customers, routes and airports. While alliances may not be seen by some as being as acceptable as mergers, there are benefits to be extracted if the economies of traffic density are fully exploited by cooperative partners, although they are likely to be extracted at the expense of other carriers in the market.

By January 1998, there were more than 500 airline alliances around the world (Anonymous, 1998), up from 389 in 1996 and 280 in 1994 (Button, 1997:16). Some of these alliances are global in orientation, while others are point-specific with airlines purchasing and reselling blocks of space on each other's aircraft, not unlike slot charter agreements in shipping. Such blocked space arrangements are on the Commission's list of agreements that do not normally restrict competition.[38] *The Economist* identified, in September of 1998, that the big four global alliances (Oneworld, Star, Northwest–Continental–KLM–Alitalia and Delta–Swissair–Sabena–Austrian) accounted for all but 19.3% of the 1997 total RPKs (Anonymous, 1998). It is looking increasingly like airline alliances are acting as virtual mergers because the merger option is severely restricted by the ownership regulations. However, it remains debatable whether mergers would result if foreign ownership restrictions were removed as a result of a multilateral agreement.

In conclusion, the choice of alliance or merger in the airline industry, even though it is a severely constrained one, still remains influenced by managerial preferences. Colin Marshall, Chairman of BA, was quoted in 1996 as predicting that a few large players would operate in all the major markets, either directly or through partnerships, while the Singapore Airlines CEO, Cheong Choong Kong, was forecasting organic growth (Leung, 1996). With hindsight, it appears that although organic growth may be preferred, no one seeking traffic densities takes it seriously as an option in this industry.

### COMPETITION ISSUES IN AIRLINE RESTRUCTURING

The greater freedom accorded by deregulation resulted in efforts by airlines to erect barriers to entry, through computer reservation systems, loyalty programs, and influencing the slot allocation decisions at key airports. Post-deregulation, numerous studies of the impacts of these

---

38    Ortiz Blanco and van Houtte (1996:176-7) noted that these agreements will be considered to restrict competition when they prevent the buying airline from concluding similar agreements with other airlines.

activities and their anti-competitive nature were undertaken. Høj *et al.* (1995) concluded that effective competition policy for this sector must address the following five areas: take-off and landing slots, predatory pricing, predatory timing,[39] frequent flyer programs,[40] and computer reservation systems.[41] However, this list does not include two further elements: dominant carrier control of key inputs (ground handling services, catering, and so on)[42] and the hub airport issue with its potential for abuse of dominant position, a key concern of the competition authorities.

Morrison and Winston (1990), in their study of post-regulation air fares, concluded that fares fall with increased competition but the effect is restrained on routes involving a carrier hub. They proposed that competition could be enhanced by eliminating slot control and replacing it with congestion-based pricing for take-off and landing fees. They also noted (Morrison and Winston, 1990:392) that entry and exit behaviour is significantly influenced by a carrier's network but not by that of its competitors, suggesting that "one of the most important effects of a well-developed airline network is that it preserves competition on routes that are served." Carriers should be allowed to engage in hub and spoke network configuration as the higher fares initially associated with hub formation eventually are eroded by network expansion and hubs do result in better service frequencies to smaller communities. Any narrowing of margins in the long-haul business may be accompanied by a lessening of competition in feeder markets. The trade-off becomes the question of balance for the regulatory authority.

Dressner and Windle (1998) found little or no evidence to suggest that major incumbent carriers engage in predatory practices against new entrants. In a second study (Windle and Dressner, 1999), they argued strongly for the promotion of competition through regulatory encouragement of the entry of low-cost carriers; they found that established carriers already engage in profit maximizing on a route-by-route basis and so do not tend to put up prices on alternative routes to compensate for increased competition from the low-cost entrant. The net result is greater consumer surplus.

Airline alliances do not just bring benefits to cooperating companies; Park (1997) has found that complementary alliances improve economic welfare, particularly in larger markets.[43] Alliances deliver improvements to passengers through network coordination. Berry (1990) and Brueckner and Spiller (1994) argued that hubs allow carriers to operate in more markets, at a lower cost, and that these savings are passed on to consumers. Merged firms can develop hub

---

[39] Examples of predatory timing include scheduling departures to coincide with a new entrant's timing and scheduling departures so that connections with new entrants are poor. Defining what constitutes predatory timing is difficult and determining its existence even more so.

[40] This is because they impose switching costs and may act as a barrier to entry, segmenting the market between incumbents.

[41] Owners of CRS may promote their own flights through flight ordering or through agent commission overrides. Codes of conduct to prevent abuse have been developed. This area of competition policy has been well explored and will not be discussed further here as its application to liner shipping is extremely limited. Sales systems in liner shipping tend to be proprietary.

[42] This can restrict the ability of competitors to reduce costs.

[43] He also concluded that parallel alliances diminish economic welfare.

and spoke systems to gain economies of route integration. Furthermore, hub development can act as a powerful incentive in mergers and strategic alliances.

However, control of the hub can be anti-competitive; the competitive dilemma arises when hub airports are congested and airport slot access becomes limited. Saunders and Shepherd (1993) suggest policy options, from making frequent flyer rebates taxable (or marketable) to reducing travel agent commission overrides, when market shares rise above 30-40% and hub dominance becomes problematic. It has also been suggested that airport slots at congested airports be auctioned, although this is considered an unacceptable practice by the European Commission.

As for ensuring that airport slot use is pro-competitive, there must be a system for ensuring slot access to new entrants. Grandfathered rights favour incumbents, yet the value of the slot strategically to the company should be reflected in regulation. Auctions are not always effective as a matching take-off and landing pair of slots is required. Relinquishing slots without compensation, as required under the Commission decision in the BA–AA, case does not reflect the fact that slots have a strategic value as well a historical cost. Findlay *et al.* (1996) have proposed that slot access provisions be phased in; during the transition, new slots would be auctioned and existing slots sold by incumbents to meet targets established by common competition regulations. It is a concept worth considering.

Strassman (1990) concluded that in the airline industry actual competition in the form of substitutes provides a more potent check on market power than potential competition, while Reiss and Spiller (1989) concluded that direct and indirect flights are substitutes, although not perfect substitutes. The former recommended that a strong and effective merger policy is needed while the latter noted that, given considerable variation in competitive conduct within and across routes, route-specific conditions should be taken into account in public policy with respect to airline mergers. The question that remains is whether or not the virtual mergers now seen between airlines are internally competitive or should be treated as mergers.[44]

Airline regulation in the global industry environment should, like liner shipping, seek a harmonized regulatory climate.[45] The way to get such harmonization is not to follow the course which the European Commission has proposed; on three separate occasions before the end of 1997, the Commission applied to the European Council of Ministers for the authority to apply European rules on air transport to air transport between Europe and third countries (ICAO, 1998:15). Seeking extraterritorial jurisdiction is neither conciliatory nor viewed positively in a time when competition authorities should be pulling in the same direction, not

---

44  It must also be remembered that airline alliances can be highly unstable. At the time of finalizing this chapter, Swissair announced a new code-sharing agreement with American Airlines on the heels of its alliance partner Delta entering into an agreement with Air France. The alliance game is a dating game; if there is no hope of marriage, relationships will be inevitably unstable and therefore it is not necessary to treat code-shares with the heavy hand fully integrated alliances might attract. As a result, Delta eventually withdrew from its alliance with Swissair.

45  There are those who would argue that divergent regulation encourages business to be creative and to innovate while others believe that harmonized regulation encourages more efficient industry. It is the view of this author that divergent regulation is undesirable. This position is developed further in Chapter 9.

staking claims. Although the existence of bilaterals ensures that a particular route has a common set of operating principles with respect to pricing and permitted activities, their inflexibility and duration are not suited to this era of rapid global change. The Chicago Convention, while it established the International Civil Aviation Organization and standards for the industry, has outlived its usefulness.[46]

The implementation of the *General Agreement on Trade in Services* (GATS) failed to deliver the airline industry from its present situation; the Annex on Air Transport Services exempts civil aviation from the purview of the WTO (although it has become a player as it acquired soft rights in minor areas under the GATS). Air transport, like shipping, suffers from the want of a widely-accepted, consistent multilateral policy on competition. Findlay *et al.* (1996) argued that the industry needs the benefits of GATT–type oversight to curtail anti-competitive practices. Perhaps this is an area where both shipping and air transport services could seek regulatory harmony in concert.

## LESSONS FOR LINER SHIPPING?

Lessons from the air transport industry are more limited than those from the rail industry; passenger activity drives the business decisions made by the first, while both rail and shipping managers focus on serving the freight market primarily. The markets also show very different types of buyers; cargo buyers tend to be more sophisticated than leisure travellers, the largest growing segment of the air business. That said, there are three areas where conclusions may be drawn.

First, unlike shipping and rail, airline management faces a much more restrictive regulatory environment which affects its consideration of growth options. Moreover, the rail and shipping industries have the full range of structural options to consider as paths for growth. In all three, the organic growth option does not appear to be the first choice for firms seeking greater market reach. The merger option enables back office savings where economies of scale exist, while alliances can be beneficial where economies of traffic density are evident and mergers are prohibited or not financially executable.

Second, airline alliances are driven by the potential for revenue maximization through seat management. Two key factors in seat management are price elasticity and capacity limits. There are also differing demand elasticities for segments of the market, with leisure travel being more elastic than business travel. Therefore price reductions in the leisure segment can result in substantial traffic increases. For example, the OECD estimated price elasticity in France for airline tickets to be 1.5 (Blöndal and Pilat, 1997). This means that a 1% drop in the price of a French plane ticket, for example, would be accompanied by a 1.5% increase in traffic. The same cannot be said of liner cargoes, except that some very low value commodities may uncover temporary new buyers for the duration of the price reduction. Without such price concessions

---

[46]  Bureau of Transport and Communications Economics (1994:146-51) explored this issue further by examining efforts to alter the regulatory environment for the air industry.

permanently available, the international sales of these commodities would not result in long-term sales arrangements and hence provide core demand for liner service.

Both rail and shipping feature low demand elasticity in the short term, suggesting that reduced prices may result in lower total revenue at the end of the day. The gains from revenue management activities in shipping therefore appear to be less, providing little incentive to alter the commodity-based conference tariff systems to a sophisticated revenue management system. Revenue management is more effective when excess capacity is small. Currently, excess capacity in shipping slots occurs on many routes and empty box management is the resulting challenge. When capacity becomes constrained and there are few barriers to entry, the route becomes attractive for fleet redeployment and network reconfiguration. On the air side, capacity is constrained by ownership rules, take-off and landing slot availability, gate availability and air service agreements. It is unlikely the shipping industry will face similar capacity conditions to those that permit airlines to engage in extensive and technology-intensive revenue management.

Third, airline alliances may mimic mergers and, if they do, should be treated like mergers. This means that if the alliance exceeds structural limits and is in a position to abuse its dominant position, remedies should be forthcoming and the entity subject to monitoring. That is, if the alliance mimics a merger, it should be entitled to engage in activities as if it were merged; this implies internal price-fixing, schedule coordination and the full range of activities taken to implement the alliance's strategy. It should also be subject to merger scrutiny. However, if it wishes to compete with its alliance partner, then it is not attempting to mimic a merger and should face a different set of rules. The dilemma regulation authorities face is where to draw the line between the two. The extent of branding and production systems integration may offer some guidance.

## Postscript

As the book was being readied for printing, Canadian Airlines sought and received from Canada's Competition Bureau a 90-day suspension of Section 47(1) of the *Canada Transportation Act*. This section says:

*Extraordinary Disruptions*

*47. (1) Where the Governor in Council is of the opinion that*

*(a) an extraordinary disruption to the effective continued operation of the national transportation system exists or is imminent, other than a labour disruption,*

*(b) failure to act under this section would be contrary to the interests of users and operators of the national transportation system, and*

*(c) there are no other provisions in this Act or in any other Act of Parliament that are sufficient and appropriate to remedy the situation and counter the actual or anticipated damage caused by the disruption,*

> *the Governor in Council may, on the recommendation of the Minister and the minister responsible for the Bureau of Competition Policy, by order, take any steps, or direct the Agency to take any steps, that the Governor in Council considers essential to stabilize the national transportation system, including the imposition of capacity and pricing restraints.*

The suspension not only enabled financially troubled Canadian to seek buyers with minimal government interference, but also put Air Canada ownership in play. Onex, the white knight endorsed by Canadian, had begun buying shares in Air Canada mid-July, raising questions about insider trading on the part of Onex (Reguly, 1999). As American Airlines and Oneworld stand to gain control of the back office activities (e.g., CRS, management systems) of the Canadian international airline business, there is a strong sense in Canada that the Canadian government was careless in agreeing to the 90-day suspension. Furthermore, doubts were raised about why the suspension was necessary at all. The fight over Air Canada reinforces the lesson that airline alliances should be treated more like mergers and that regulation should not favour one business structure over another, as it so obviously does in the airline industry. The airline industry, more than the liner shipping industry, is in need of a global harmonized system without the rigid bilateral structure it features today. As events in Canada unfold, the Competition Bureau's interest in ownership issues butts against the politicians' view and underscores the need for multilateral renegotiation of air policy.

# APPENDIX C

# EU REGULATORY REFORM IN AIR TRANSPORT

## FIRST PACKAGE MEASURES

- Council Regulation 3975/87[1] established the procedures to be followed for the implementation of competition rules in air transport.

- Council Regulation 3976/87[2] empowered the Commission to grant block exemptions to the air sector. (Subsequently three block exemptions were granted in 1988: one enabling joint planning of capacity, revenue sharing, tariff consultation and airport slot sharing,[3] a second on computer reservations systems,[4] and a third respecting airport ground handling services.[5])

- Council Directive 87/601/EEC[6] put in place a new system for tariff approvals on intra-Community international scheduled services.

---

1   Council Regulation (EEC) 3975/87 of 14 December 1987 laying down the procedure for the application of the rules on competition to undertakings in the air transport sector, *Official Journal of the European Communities*, 1987 L 374, 1.

2   Council Regulation (EEC) 3976/87 of 14 December 1987 on the application of Article 85(3) of the Treaty to certain categories of agreements and concerted practices in the air transport sector, *Official Journal of the European Communities*, 1987 L 374, 9.

3   Commission Regulation (EEC) 2671/88 of 26 July 1988 on the application of Article 85(3) of the Treaty to certain categories of agreements between undertakings and concerted practices concerning joint planning and coordination of capacity, sharing of revenue and consultations on tariffs on scheduled air services and slot allocation at airports, *Official Journal of the European Communities*, 1988 L 239, 9.

4   Commission Regulation (EEC) 2672/88 of 26 July 1988 on the application of Article 85(3) of the Treaty to certain categories of agreements between undertakings relating to computer reservation systems for air transport services, *Official Journal of the European Communities*, 1988 L 239, 13.

5   Commission Regulation (EEC) 2673/88, of 26 July 1988 on the application of Article 85(3) of the Treaty to certain categories of agreements between undertakings decisions of associations of undertakings and concerned practices concerning ground handling services, *Official Journal of the European Communities*, 1988 L 239, 17.

6   Council Directive 87/601/EEC of 14 December 1987 on fares for scheduled air services between Member States, *Official Journal of the European Communities*, 1987 L 374, 12.

- Council Decision 87/602/EEC[7] put in place a new system for sharing capacity on a route by route basis on intra-Community international scheduled services. The system also enabled multiple designation of national carrier in place of the traditional single carrier designation system.

## SECOND PACKAGE MEASURES

- Council Regulation 2342/90[8] on tariff setting altered the workings of Council Directive 87/601/EEC with respect to condition of tariff approval refusals.
- Council Regulation 2343/90[9] on carrier access further liberalized the system put in place by Council Decision 87/602/EEC.
- Council Regulation 2344/90[10] amended Council Regulation 3976/87 on block exemptions to grant new exemptions to the three agreements established in 1988. (These were deregulated further the following year.[11])

## THIRD PACKAGE MEASURES

- Council Regulation 2407/92[12] established new criteria and methods for awarding operating licences.
- Council Regulation 2408/92[13] established without restriction the ability of Community air carriers to provide intra-Community international air service, essentially liberalizing the restrictions imposed by Council Regulation 2343/90 and the earlier Council Decision 87/602/EEC on carrier access.
- Council Regulation 2409/92[14] established carriers' freedom to set tariffs.

---

7   Council Decision 87/602/EEC of 14 December 1987 on the sharing of passenger capacity between air carriers on scheduled air services between Member States and on access for air carriers to scheduled air-service routes between Member States, *Official Journal of the European Communities*, 1987 L 374, 19.

8   Council Regulation (EEC) 2342/90 of 24 July 1990 on fares for scheduled air services, *Official Journal of the European Communities*, 1990 L 217, 1.

9   Council Regulation (EEC) 2343/90 of 24 July 1990 on access for air carriers to scheduled intra-community air service routes and on the sharing of passenger capacity between air carriers on scheduled air services between member states, *Official Journal of the European Communities*, 1990 L 217, 8.

10   Council Regulation (EEC) 2344/90 of 24 July 1990 amending Regulation (EEC) No 3976/87 on the application of Article 85(3) of the Treaty to certain categories of agreements and concerted practices in the air transport sector, *Official Journal of the European Communities*, 1990 L 217, 15.

11   Commission Regulation (EEC) 82/91, *Official Journal of the European Communities*, 1991 L 10, 7 (ground handling); Commission Regulation (EEC) 83/91, *Official Journal of the European Communities*, 1991 L 10, 9 (computer reservation systems); Commission Regulation (EEC) 84/91, *Official Journal of the European Communities*, 1991 L 10, 14 (joint planning, tariff consultation and slot allocation).

12   Council Regulation (EEC) 2407/92 of 23 July 1992 on licensing of air carriers, *Official Journal of the European Communities*, 1992 L 240, 1.

13   Council Regulation (EEC) 2408/92 of 23 July 1992 on access for community air carriers to intra-community air routes, *Official Journal of the European Communities*, 1992 L 240, 8.

14   Council Regulation (EEC) 2409/92 of 23 July 1992 on fares and rates for air services, *Official Journal of the European Communities*, 1992 L 240, 15.

# 7

# CASE STUDIES FROM THE LINER SHIPPING INDUSTRY

## INTRODUCTION

Now that the previous two chapters have explored mergers, acquisitions and alliances in two other networked, asset-intensive, service industries, this chapter will return to the industry of focus for the book. It will examine, in greater detail, some of the alliances and mergers noted in Chapter 1. Before presenting these "case studies," this section will briefly review the points to be considered resulting from the earlier chapters.

What are the drivers of change in the liner shipping industry? First, change is being customer-driven. Technological innovations enable carriers to meet these demands through the provision of fully-integrated logistical services or superior delivery of shipping services. The regulatory environment is not seen by the industry to be supportive of innovation but neither has the industry shown itself as willing to forgo the advantages it extracts from the regulatory environment. (Pro-innovation regulation will be explored further in the final two chapters of the book.) Second, carriers that move decisively in meeting customer requirements may be able to create sustainable competitive advantage in their markets. Finally, carriers that are slow to respond to their customers may be forced to follow innovative carriers as the bar is raised on minimum acceptable practices; failure to follow will hasten their elimination from the market.

Many carriers have concluded that they can no longer attempt to grow solely through organic growth. The past ten years have witnessed a dramatic shift in the strategies of ocean carriers as they have engaged in mergers, acquisitions and strategic alliances, seeking to develop integrated door-to-door capabilities in response to a rapidly changing environment and the requirements of increasingly demanding customers. How will carriers in the future attempt to develop the capabilities they need to service a complex, and increasingly global, trading environment? It seems less likely that they will go it alone, developing the required capabilities through internal growth or acquisition, and more likely that they will seek to fill the missing links in their networks through strategic alliances. While there are clear advantages to each of these paths, perhaps it is appropriate to examine the decisions taken in a few, higher profile cases.

## THE SEA-LAND/MAERSK ALLIANCE[1]

Sea-Land Services Inc. shocked the industry in early March of 1991 with its announcement about joining forces in a "global" alliance with Maersk, a subsidiary of Denmark's A. P. Møller. Although such cooperation on the inland side had been anticipated for years by industry observers (Bowman, 1995), the arrangement came as quite a surprise to many shipping executives, particularly as Sea-Land had spent several months prior to this agreement conducting joint service talks with American President Lines (APL) (Wastler, 1991). These talks ended abruptly after changes in the marketplace caused both sides to rethink their original proposals. As the oldest of the new consortia, the Sea-Land/Maersk alliance warrants closer examination.

### About Sea-Land Service Inc.

Sea-Land's founder, trucker Malcolm McLean, was best known as the originator of the containership concept when, in 1956, frustrated with the interface between ocean shipping and trucking, he transferred the first "containers" directly to a converted tanker (the *Ideal X*) and sailed them from New Jersey to Texas. Using the rights of the Pan Atlantic Steamship Company, he took delivery in 1957 of the first container ships, later changing the name of the company to Sea-Land.

When Sea-Land was acquired in 1969 from Malcolm McLean for US$160 million by R. J. Reynolds, it was the leading container line in the world (Magnier, 1981). By 1983, Reynolds, a key player in the tobacco, food and beverage sectors, had decided to spin off Sea-Land; the container business needed a substantial infusion of cash to maintain its leadership in the industry. Reynolds believed that the divestiture would enable Sea-Land to raise capital on its own, without diluting Reynolds' ability to raise the capital it needed for planned expansion in its more profitable and stable businesses.[2] Also, Sea-Land's activities had very little to do with Reynolds' other business activities and it was believed that divestiture would encourage further development of the company. The date of record for the divestiture was 21 May 1984 with Reynolds' shareholders receiving stock in Sea-Land.

It was not long before Sea-Land stock attracted the unwelcome attention of well-known corporate raider, Harold Simmons. It was believed that Simmons was drawn to the large amount of capital in Sea-Land's Capital Construction Fund (Hardwicke, 1985). In May 1986, CSX moved to gain control of Sea-Land. The purchase enabled CSX to move into the international intermodal transport business from its strong US domestic position.

---

[1]  This section was written with the research assistance of Annette Johnson (MBA/LLB '99) and Sarah Sexton (MBA '99), Dalhousie University students.

[2]  Anonymous (1983). Sea-Land and its parent Reynolds had attracted the unwelcome attentions of corporate raiders and it would only be a matter of time before the company would be separated from its conglomerate parent. Reynolds went on to acquire Nabisco Brands before becoming the subject of a leveraged buyout and a best-selling business book *Barbarians at the Gate* (Burroughs and Helyar, 1990.)

By September 1987, both Sea-Land and CSX began to reap the benefits of the acquisition; operating profits for Sea-Land were expected to hit near US$80 million by the end of the year and CSX reported that Sea-Land was a positive and contributing member of the CSX family (Beargie, 1987). The completion of acquisition approvals cleared the way for Sea-Land to undertake a large capital expansion program, upgrading the fleet though the acquisition of 26 second-hand vessels from the creditors of bankrupt United States Lines (Anonymous, 1989).

Sea-Land had a long history of going-it-alone but began to experiment with cooperative relationships in 1985, beginning with a venture with the French and Italian flag companies in the "Trident" service between Western Europe and the Middle East. This arrangement gave Sea-Land more frequent calls to the Middle East and added Kuwait and Bahrain to the route. At this time the company also initiated relations with the Italian containership operation, Merzario, which was well established in Mediterranean/Middle East routes. The strategic decision was to enter into relationships with national lines having a significant marketing presence regionally and a proven track record (Anonymous, 1985).

By 1988, Sea-Land had lost its leadership position, ranking third in containership tonnage after Evergreen and Maersk. In February 1988, Sea-Land opted to take greater advantage of the *Shipping Act of 1984* and its provisions for cooperative working agreements. With the recently-acquired 12 USL Econships (the world's largest container ships), Sea-Land chartered three of the Econships to P&O Containers Ltd. (P&OCL) and two to Nedlloyd. This arrangement was accompanied by a vessel sharing agreement[3] (VSA) on the transatlantic, aimed at improving asset utilization and reducing costs. The agreement had Sea-Land take 58% of the capacity while Trans Freight Line (a P&O subsidiary) took 25% and Nedlloyd 17% on trade between US east and Gulf coasts and some of the largest European markets (Vail, 1988). Of particular interest are the limits found in the agreement; the three agreed to limit the vessels to 3,400 TEUs (even though they were built to carry 4,482 TEUs) in an effort to achieve speed improvements as the ships were otherwise too slow.[4] Capacity management was being practiced within the alliance.

In addition to its relationship with P&OCL and Nedlloyd, Sea-Land broadened its global reach in 1989 when it entered into a vessel sharing agreement with Swiss carrier Norasia Shipping on the Europe/Far East route, terminating its existing slot charter agreements with United Arab Shipping Company and Joint Container Service. The resulting service capability of the carriers was upgraded to weekly, fixed day sailings. It did not compete directly with the Far East Freight Conference Service because it called many intermediary ports and was therefore not time-competitive (Canna, 1989).

This was not the only alliance Sea-Land maintained with Norasia. On Norasia's Asia–Middle East–Europe service, Sea-Land provided the terminal facilities and EDI systems while Norasia provided a fleet of ten state-of-the-art vessels (Middleton, 1990). (This alliance was formed for

---

3    FMC Agreement Number 203-011171, filed 28 March 1988.
4    Vail (1988). These limits disappeared with subsequent amendments to the agreement.

the express purpose of improving asset utilization and reducing costs.) Increased penetration of the Asian market was anticipated as it had become the second fastest growing market in the world.

These strategic responses were early evidence of a marked departure from its traditional philosophy; Sea-Land had been described as "private, competitive and committed to a go-it-alone philosophy" (Middleton, 1990). The company, however, became a strong advocate of strategic alliances and planned to use the full range of alliance options to meet its needs. Its adopted strategy was soon vocalized.

In 1990, Sea-Land announced that it had changed its emphasis from "being a liner company— that circles the globe—to a full service transportation company offering global logistics packages that can be competitive with firms providing contract logistics" (Middleton, 1990). It expressly included a proactive strategy of vessel sharing arrangements with other lines, pooling ships and equipment with other lines to cut costs and improve asset utilization. Slot exchange programs were intended to increase access to ports not on their schedule and alliances for equipment interchange and joint inland management were meant to further reduce costs and improve asset utilization (Middleton, 1990). Sea-Land offered customers, through its many subsidiaries and joint venture partners, complete logistics packages, which could include assembly, packaging and consolidation (Armbruster, 1990).

In late August 1990, Sea-Land and P&OCL expanded their alliance to include Maersk Line for vessel sharing on the route between Europe and the US west coast. Sea-Land reported that, prior to vessel sharing agreements, the cost of operating the Sea-Land fleet accounted for 27% of its total costs; by 1990, that had dropped to 12.9% (Middleton, 1990). Encouraged by these results, Sea-Land and Maersk began joint operations in the transpacific in 1991; this closer relationship paved the way for the eventual global alliance announced in 1995.

## About Maersk Line

Maersk Line is a subsidiary of the two largest companies on the Copenhagen Stock Exchange —Steamship Co. of Svendborg and Steamship Company of 1912, holding companies known collectively as the A. P. Møller Group. In 1990, through its companies in Denmark, the UK, the US, Canada and Singapore, Maersk reported owning about 175 container ships, supertankers, dry cargo carriers and tugs, as well as 25 offshore drilling rigs (Reier, 1990). Since then, it purchased the assets of Copenhagen-based competitor, EacBen, terminating the EacBen brand. By 1995, Maersk was the second largest container line in the world after Sea-Land. What was the history leading to the announcement in 1995?

In 1987, Maersk was already well-established on Europe–Far East and transpacific trades, and ran a US east and Gulf coast to Middle East service, but had not yet attempted to serve the north Atlantic. The company decided to aggressively expand its operations into the transatlantic container trade and begin the final stage of its transformation into a global carrier. It did so by extending its Far East/US east coast service to Europe. Although the company captured more than 10% of the transatlantic market in the first three years on the route, profit-ability eluded it. As a result, in 1990 the line announced a rationalization of its transatlantic operations; this rationalization included negotiations with CSX for the possible purchase of Sea-Land. While these negotiations did not result in an acquisition, they produced a vessel sharing agreement. Under this VSA, Maersk provided space on its ships, serving the US west coast from Europe, to Sea-Land and P&OCL. In exchange, Maersk received space on Sea-Land and P&OCL vessels calling on east and Gulf coast ports.

Maersk has been a financially stable company. During the period 1992–1996, it more than doubled its capacity from 120,000 to 260,000 TEUs and invested significantly in post-Panamax tonnage, all without serious financial damage. A fundamental plank of Maersk's global strategy has been to search out areas of the market where they may not have a con-nection and make one. The company divided the world into several blocs, establishing regional headquarters. It also advocated a hub and spoke approach to network configuration as noted in Chapter 4. The company recently acquired Safmarine to consolidate its operations in develop-ing markets. Today, there are very few routes Maersk does not serve.

**The Quintessential Dance Partners**

Throughout the early 1990s, rumours of the Sea-Land Maersk relationship being a slow dance to merger circulated in the industry. By 1995, CSX chairman and CEO, John Snow, felt he needed to address the rumours of Sea-Land's impending sale to A. P. Møller publicly (Glass, 1995):

> *Sea-Land is not for sale. We are very satisfied with Sea-Land. This is an alliance that holds tremendous promise as we pool with Møller to share costs, but it is not contemplated that we buy them or they buy us. ... Alliances are the way the industry is going. After all, just three alliances now control 70% of the industry.*

Shortly after, Sea-Land and Maersk announced their global alliance with operating details released in early 1996 in joint press releases. It was not just the rumours that sparked the announcements. The alliance was precipitated by P&OCL's withdrawal from its partnership with Maersk in favour of the Grand Alliance.[5] According to Ib Kruse, CEO of Maersk, it was time to take the company's operating alliance another step further. From May 1996, Maersk cooperated with Sea-Land operationally in most of its trades. Today, the alliance is one of the more complete ones, with only Africa and Australia outside the agreement as Sea-Land did not serve those areas at the time of the announcement (Fossey, 1996).

To form the alliance, Maersk reviewed the whole of its service network and the assets deployed, met with a number of its customers, established future requirements of customers,

---

5   The hasty departure of P&OCL and the speed with which Sea-Land's new arrangement with Maersk developed posed problems for Sea-Land; its capacity through the alliance with Maersk suddenly doubled on the Europe-Asia trade, a route it had serviced with its former alliance partner Norasia. Sea-Land was suddenly head-to-head with Norasia, and with significant additional business to acquire.

analyzed the trade flows and then sat down with Sea-Land to design schedules. The alliance between Sea-Land and Maersk is geared toward three specific goals: providing reliable multi-week sailings in the principal Asia/Europe and North American/Asia routes, achieving faster transit times, and extending the global network to include direct calls at specific outlying (regional) ports (Fossey, 1996). (The direct call element conflicts with Maersk's stated preference for hub and spoke network noted in Chapter 4.)

One critical attraction of the alliance for Maersk was Sea-Land's ownership by CSX, and the accompanying cooperation this brought on US mini-bridging and land-bridging operations. Sea-Land also had strong market share in the northern US while Maersk was considerably stronger in the south; the complementarity of service routes was yet another reason the alliance was mutually beneficial (Anonymous, 1991d). The two companies were a good strategic fit: each had substantial assets, a global perspective, managerial talent, commitment to quality, and a high level of customer service (Anonymous, 1991c).

Neither Sea-Land nor Maersk have any obvious reasons to extinguish their relationship. When developing the master plans, both companies were interested in developing a package that would "meet and exceed the very demands of the shippers/consignees that will be using the product." (Fossey, 1996) They both agreed not just to ocean-side cooperation but terminal and equipment sharing as well. Wall Street predicted the relationship would not result in a merger, noting that Maersk's Tommy Thomsen has taken "pains to emphasize that the team-up is not a consolidation. 'It is an operational alliance, not a structural merger' " (Cauthen, 1996:27).

Together, the companies have expanded their operations and profits. More important, their efforts have created one of the more successful alliances in the industry. They have built services with enviable geographic coverage. Maersk believed that its alliance with Sea-Land provided an effective tool to reduce costs and rationalize asset use. Maersk's 1996 profits rose 23% to US$349 million (Damas and Gillis, 1997). In 1996, the Danish carrier reported slot utilization in the high 80s (at a time when the industry average was 62%) and that it was able to emphasize a program of "selective cargo mix" to maximize profits (Anonymous, 1996d). In 1997 the company boasted nearly 10,000 employees in 250 offices in more than 70 countries serving over 80,000 customers worldwide (Damas and Gillis, 1997). Maersk's strategy has been successful in delivering global coverage and leadership through alliances, and 1998 was another profitable year for the company.

According to the trade press, Sea-Land viewed its alliance with Maersk as a centrepiece of its strategy. The last few years have been rewarding for Sea-Land; in 1996, for example, against a situation of declining market rates, their operating income increased by US$80 million to US$318 million (Anonymous, 1997a). Through its alliance with Maersk, Sea-Land was reported to have expected savings of US$100 million per annum within three years and US$125–$150 million by the year 2000 (Machalaba, 1995). Sea-Land's 1998 annual revenues exceeded US$3.9 billion.[6] However, the potential for merger remains. While Sea-Land has reported its continuing satisfaction with its relationship with Maersk, CSX has admitted that, like all large conglomerates, sales are always possible if the price is right (Bascombe, 1998c: 89). In March of 1999, Sea-Land announced a restructuring that would separate its international container operating company from its terminal and domestic shipping businesses,[7] a move often seen by the financial world as the first step in either a spin-off or isolation of a subsidiary as a target for a friendly takeover. It would not be long before a strategic decision would be made.

## THE P&O NEDLLOYD MERGER[8]

The 8 September 1996 merger announcement between P&OCL and Nedlloyd Lines came as a complete surprise. After almost five years of quiet talks, negotiations began more seriously in the fall of 1995; the merger created the largest containership fleet in the world in terms of TEUs operated (Table 1.4). With an annual throughput of 2.5 million TEUs, P&O Nedlloyd ranked slightly behind Maersk and Evergreen for loaded containers carried (Anonymous, 1996e). Operating 112 owned or chartered vessels and 540,000 TEUs of owned or leased containers, the new entity was named P&O Nedlloyd Container Line Ltd. and its combined revenue was reported at nearly US$4 billion on net assets valued at US$1.5 billion (Anonymous, 1996c). Savings expected from the merger were more than US$200 million within the first 18 months (Anonymous, 1996b). Were the anticipated savings the only driver of the merger decision?

### Nedlloyd (pre-merger)

By May 1996, Nedlloyd Lines was one of eight divisions of the Rotterdam-based Royal Nedlloyd Group NV. It had grown to become a reliable global carrier with 65 highly advanced owned and chartered vessels with 240,000 TEU capacity, operating 38 fixed liner services to more than 190 ports in 80 countries.[9]

Prior to 1986, the company participated on a wide variety of routes, both independently and as part of consortia, such as Scandutch. It co-owned vessels with Overseas Container Limited.[10] However, those routes did not include either the transpacific (although it did include the Far

---

6   http://www.sealand.com. Approximately 12% of Sea-Land's revenue is derived from terminal services and other operations.

7   http://www.schednet.com, 18 March 1999.

8   This section was written with the research assistance of Dalhousie University students Annette Johnson (MBA/LLB '99) and Sarah Sexton (MBA '99).

9   Royal Nedlloyd NV company brochure (1996).

10  According to *Containerisation International Yearbook 1985*:285. Overseas Container Limited was itself a British consortium of Ocean Transport and Trading (32.8%), British & Commonwealth (19.83%) and P&O (47.37%). In 1986, Overseas Container Limited became a fully owned subsidiary of P&O when it acquired the equity interests of the others.

East to west coast South America route) or the transatlantic. Nedlloyd's transformation to its pre-merger character effectively began in 1986 with its entry into the north Atlantic trade.

It did not take the company long to conclude that its organizational structure was not suited to the US market. Following a report in 1987 by consultant Booz-Allen & Hamilton, the company made large-scale changes to its North American operations in hopes of laying the groundwork for successful operations well into the 1990s. These included decentralization of North American operations, formation of a new geographic organizational structure, development of dedicated agencies and full inter-modal services, and a new focus on logistics and automatic data processing (Canna, 1987). The restructuring in North America was only a piece of Nedlloyd Chairman Henk Rootliep's plan to create the first integrated intermodal operation, and to secure a place in the top ranks of the world's logistics companies.

The strategy in Europe was kick-started with the purchase of the money-losing Van Gend & Loos trucking operation (with 6,000 employees) from Nederlandse Spoorwegen. Despite the criticism, Royal Nedlloyd insisted at the time that this was the right decision; it would fill a key niche in the company's plan to offer a complete intermodal package (Barnard, 1988a, 1988b).

There was widespread criticism of the firm when, in 1989, it sought to increase its capacity on a significant scale. At the time Nedlloyd had 12 container vessels offering a total capacity of 25,257 TEU and requested tenders for five 3,000 TEU capacity ships with options for an additional 10 (5 at 3,800 TEU and 5 at 4,600 TEU) on top of the five (White, 1989)! The market was showing signs of excess capacity and the trade press was not positive in its assessment of the move. Coupled with similar bids from other companies such as Evergreen, the orders were reported to add nearly 420,000 TEUs to the world's containership fleet. Nedlloyd's rebuttal to the trade press was to be vague in their plans for the use of the vessels (White, 1989). The company eventually ordered five 3,000 TEU ships and two 3,950 TEU vessels, adding NLG 1 billion of debt to their financial statements (Anonymous, 1991a).

Like many other transportation companies, Nedlloyd's financial woes began during the Gulf War. Although the company had benefited from military contracts through its space-sharing agreement with P&OCL and Sea-Land on the north Atlantic (Porter, 1991a), the loss of nearly $49 million for the liner division added to the Royal Nedlloyd Group's net losses of nearly US$79 million in the first half of 1990 (Barnard, 1990b). Attempts to reduce costs and reorganize the company (again) resulted. In August 1990, Nedlloyd Lines moved to a hub and spoke system, both reducing fixed costs and providing larger ships in the north-south markets (Magnier, 1990). In addition, as a cost-cutting measure, the company's container buying strategy was put on hold for 1991 (Anonymous, 1991b). Nedlloyd's problems were explained by analysts as bad timing on its entry into the north Atlantic market and its new ship orders as well as its failure to negotiate the best terms in many of its joint venture projects (Porter, 1991a; Anonymous, 1991b).

It was not just the vessel orders, the North American restructuring and the losses that put Nedlloyd into the headlights of the trade press. Royal Nedlloyd traded on the Amsterdam Stock Exchange, and it was the undesirable publicity about its corporate governance that attracted serious attention. In addition to strong market growth and solid returns (1989 returns exceeded the 12% achieved in 1988) (Barnard, 1990a), shares were being consistently bid up by takeover rumours. In 1989, the share price doubled. Norwegian shipping executive Torstein Hagen had, for several years, attempted to gain a seat on the board of the company; by 1991, he had increased his shareholding to 23% and claimed to represent an additional 22% of Nedlloyd's shareholders (Barnard, 1991b). His views on the company's strategic direction did not match those of Chairman Henk Rootliep. Hagen urged the company to move away from its non-core businesses and focus on its ocean liner shipping and European trucking divisions (Barnard, 1991a), while Rootliep believed that the non-related businesses balanced the Royal Nedlloyd portfolio (Anonymous, 1991a). It was the classic struggle of competing visions about the type of company Royal Nedlloyd should be.

The Board did not give Hagen the seat he sought and a high profile struggle ensued. The darkest moment was when the shareholders refused to accept the company's annual financial statements at the Annual General Meeting in May 1991. (This was only the second time such an event had happened in Dutch history, according to Porter (1991b).) After the meeting Hagen boosted his stake in the company to 27%. In January 1992, he finally gained his seat on the board in return for reducing his company holdings to below 15% (Barnard, 1993). This marked the beginning of another colourful year.

Nedlloyd Lines expanded its operations by returning to the US west coast–Europe trade and entered into a number of joint ventures with other carriers, strengthening Royal Nedlloyd's core businesses. Royal Nedlloyd also sold a number of its assets, including its stakes in bulk shipping, energy and airlines, in order to cut back on costs and reduce its non-core areas. The sale of assets revived the company and put it on a more solid financial footing. Particularly interesting, the company split its liner division into two parts, one to manage shipping and another for container logistics services; as a result, the costs of each were more clearly defined (Porter, 1992a).

Of particular note during this period was the forced resignation of Hagen on the grounds that he violated the conditions under which he was elected to the board; he had sought changes to Nedlloyd's by-laws which would have made the company an easier takeover target (Porter, 1992b). Shortly after this resignation, the Chairman announced his retirement and a new Chairman, L. J. M. Berndsen, was recruited. By now, the company was in very bad financial shape, having suffered significant losses in 1992 (NLG 58 million or approximately US$33 million); the balance sheet featured US$430 million in equity and US$1 billion in debt (Roberts, 1993a).

Under Chairman Berndsen, staff were cut 10%, the company's management structure was adjusted and the company strengthened its existing positions in ocean shipping and inland transport (Roberts, 1993b; Porter, 1993c). However, the company continued to be plagued by rumours, this time that Sea-Land was looking to take over the company (Abrams, 1993). The new strategy did not take effect quickly; first-half results for 1993 were double 1992's losses, but the company achieved a US$31 million profit in the second half of 1993 (Porter, 1993b).

The year's results overall were worse than those of 1992, but it appeared that the company had turned around.

The following year proved difficult. Nedlloyd's ocean activities showed marked improvement while inland transport suffered significant losses (Anonymous, 1994a). Although the trade press reported on the company's struggles throughout 1994, the year-end results were commendable.

Then Nedlloyd embarked on its alliance strategy; involved in the Global Alliance with Nedlloyd were American President Lines, Mitsui O.S.K. Lines and Orient Overseas Containers Line. The Global Alliance consisted of vessel sharing, coordinated sailings and cooperative terminal exchanges in the transpacific and Asia/Europe shipping markets, hardly living up to its name. Unfortunately, the decision to work within a strategic alliance did not end all of Royal Nedlloyd's troubles. The 1995-96 period was a difficult time. The deteriorating exchange rate with the US dollar, lower volumes of traffic on new services, and an in-house investigation into financial irregularities in its Nedlloyd Road Cargo branch in Austria all played a role in its distress (Anonymous, 1996a). An October 1995 report of lower earnings than anticipated for 1995 sent share prices down 28% in two days (Porter, 1995c). At year end, Nedlloyd's 1995 profit of US$16.4 million compared poorly with its 1994 profit of US$69.1 million (Anonymous, 1996e). The US$30 per container operating economies the company attributed to its participation in the Grand Alliance (Drewry Shipping Consultants, 1996:5) were clearly not enough. The need for improved financial performance was pressing.

## P&OCL (pre-merger)

Formed by the acquisition of its partners' equity in OCL, Britain's largest container shipping line, P&OCL, was created in 1986, under the parent corporation of Peninsular and Oriental Steam Navigation Company (P&O).[11] P&O traces its history to 1837, long before the days of liner conferences. From its early beginning as a line offering service between the UK and the Iberian peninsula, the company grew to be a highly diversified conglomerate, owning cruise ships, ferries and port management interests as well as significant investments in construction and property development.

During the summer of 1991, P&O initiated talks to buy Cunard Ellerman, the container shipping division of Trafalgar House PLC (Porter, 1991c). In the four years after Trafalgar House formed Cunard Ellerman by adding its acquisition of Ellerman in 1987 to its Cunard holdings, it had never gained the economies of scale it had anticipated (Porter, 1991d). In addition, its partners in Associated Container Transport showed little interest in presenting themselves to the market under one brand name (Crichton, 1991). A frustrated Trafalgar House lost interest and focused on its engineering, construction, hotel and cruise businesses; it was only a matter of time before a buyer would show interest in the liner end of its businesses.

---

11  Porter (1996b). For earlier partners see footnote 10.

P&O's purchase of Cunard Ellerman, Britain's second largest container shipping line behind P&OCL, signaled a major rationalization in the UK liner shipping industry. It combined the assets of long-established UK liner operations, including Cunard Ellerman's shares of Associated Container Transportation (Australia) Ltd. (ACTA), Ellerman Harrison Container Line and Ben Line Containers Limited as well as a side deal for Blue Star Lines' interest in ACTA (giving P&OCL full control). However, it excluded some non-liner activities; for example, Trafalgar House retained Cunard Line, a passenger and cruise operation (Crichton, 1991; Porter, 1991e). The complicated deal was finalized in early November and a number of plans were made to resell some of the newly acquired operations to others as well as to restructure some of Cunard Ellerman's subsidiaries. This consolidation created a powerful new UK container shipping line participating in 30 liner services linking the world's major trades except the transpacific (Porter, 1991d). At a cost of GBP 42.5 million (US$70 million) in cash and GBP 20 million (US$33 million) in debt absorption, P&O gained stronger presence in the trades between Europe, Australia, and New Zealand (Porter, 1991e). P&OCL rose to rank sixth in TEU owned. Particularly interesting is the fact that competition authorities viewed this merger differently than had been the case in the 1984 hearings into P&OCL's formation. This merger which gave P&OCL so much control (85% of UK–Australia trade) was not hobbled.[12]

It was not smooth sailing for the new company. P&OCL reported a 45% drop in its pre-tax profit from US$223.2 million in the first half of 1990, to US$123.5 million, for the first six months of 1991 (Toll, 1991). Faced with declining profits, increasing costs and changes in the European market, the company reviewed its core business activities, set targets for returns for shareholders and forged new agreements. By January of 1993 P&OCL undertook a complete reorganization of its European operations to focus on developing through transport capability and fend off rivals Nedlloyd and Hapag Lloyd for second place (after Maersk) in the continental European market (Porter, 1993a).

However, the company was still not a global player but too large for a niche player and viewed this as a dangerous position in the marketplace (Canna, 1995b). It had not consolidated its relationships yet, as partners differed significantly by trade lane. Its absence from the transpacific was noticeable and this was corrected in 1993 when it began, in cooperation with Sea-Land and Maersk, a direct service between the US and India (Anonymous, 1993a). The situation changed once again in the spring of 1995, when P&OCL announced it would be severing its Europe–Asia alliance with Maersk Line in 1996, an alliance which had been in operation since 1991. Essentially, P&OCL wanted to enter the Pacific trades, but Maersk was already involved in a transpacific venture with Sea-Land (Porter, 1995a). Consequently, with alliance moves by other carriers, P&OCL formed the Grand Alliance with NYK of Japan, Hapag Lloyd of Germany and Singapore's Neptune Orient Line (NOL).

*The intention of the new alliance is to establish a comprehensive network of services in the Europe-Asia, Asia–East Coast North America and transpacific*

---

12    The merger was considered to be inspired for tax reasons, and the two entities were seen as largely competing in different markets.

*trade lanes. There is also a declared intention to extend cooperation to the transatlantic trades as soon as is practical.* (Anonymous, 1995)

The new alliance did not ameliorate P&OCL's financial problems. There was a negligible profit impact in the first half of 1995 for the parent company; improved profits for cruise ships and bulk carriers offset declines in both the liner and ferry subsidiaries (Barnard, 1995). It was widely reported that P&O shareholders were not pleased with P&OCL's performance (Porter, 1996b). The parent's performance on the London Stock Exchange was one of its worst; P&OCL's return on capital employed (ROCE) was only slightly more than 5% in 1995 after the parent company had set a target for the subsidiary of 15% ROCE (Porter, 1996a). The company was handling almost three times as many boxes as it had in 1989 with very little change in staff but was still not able to meet shareholder expectations of profit (Crichton, 1996). It was not clear that the new alliance would solve P&OCL's continuing financial difficulties.

**Unfolding Events**

While P&OCL and Nedlloyd were no strangers, there was little evidence of a serious negotiating relationship between the two companies. From 1988, they had a space-sharing agreement on the north Atlantic with Sea-Land which gradually grew to include a large-scale chassis-sharing pool (involving 50,000 truck chassis) for inland operations (Armbruster, 1991). However, both companies were concerned about the situation in Europe; with the Single European Market in 1992, they faced stiffer competition. As both had serious problems with financial stability since 1990, consolidation seemed appropriate, yet industry analysts were surprised by the joint venture announcement. Part of the shock of the announcement was its timing, coming little more than a year after the announcement of the Grand Alliance and after P&OCL's announced departure from its alliance with Maersk (May 1995).

A new company, P&O Nedlloyd Container Line, owned equally by P&O and Royal Nedlloyd, was created by P&O transferring the assets of P&OCL to the new entity, and Royal Nedlloyd transferring the assets of Nedlloyd Lines BV alone. A balancing payment of US$175 million to P&O was required to equalize the shareholdings.[13]

The approval of the deal by the European Commission was not long in being granted. The initial announcement was made 8 September with Commission notification occurring on 19 November 1996. The decision, dated 19 December 1996, concluded that the merger constituted a concentration within the meaning of Article 3 (1) (b) of the Merger Regulation, and one which has a Community dimension under Article 1 (1). The merger was examined by looking at market shares in the relevant markets, actual competition in those markets,[14] and the potential for creation or strengthening of a dominant position in those markets. It was concluded that

---

[13]  Porter (1996b). Nedlloyd's investment was financed by the proceeds of its sale of Neddrill.

[14]  In some, these were deemed to already be restricted by existing alliance agreements.

"the establishment of the joint venture would not appear to create or strengthen a position of dominance."[15]

Headquarters for the joint venture was established in London and a eight-member board, chaired jointly by Lord Sterling and Leo Berndsen, was formed. Tim Harris was appointed chief executive officer.

> *Nedlloyd and P&O may turn out to be a good match. Both have experienced little growth in recent years and need ways to expand without huge capital expenditures. Both also offer containerized service on all major trade lanes and are conference members.*[16]

Both companies seemed to be a good cultural fit. Britain and the Netherlands have a long history of commercial cooperation (both Royal Dutch/Shell and Unilever grew out of Anglo-Dutch relationships) and much in common. Cultural fit is also one of managerial style. Both P&OCL and Nedlloyd stood apart from the other lines when, in 1993, they proposed to implement significant improvements in customer service policies. P&OCL was promising customers a "zero-defect" service with more customer follow-up after booking (a strategy which had won it Lloyd's Shipping Line of the Year award in 1995). Nedlloyd was in favour of empowerment of sales personnel (Roberts, 1993c), even though numbers had been cut back as part of its cost-cutting activities. In spite of cultural fit, merger implementation still had to face the usual transborder hurdles: Dutch taxes were much higher, the UK cost of living was higher, salary bases differed, and so on.[17]

The fact that both P&OCL and Nedlloyd belonged to two rival alliances became a major source of contention for the industry. In the beginning, both P&OCL and Nedlloyd insisted that they would honor their commitments to their consortia; it was inevitable that one contract would have to be broken.[18] Participants in both the Global and Grand alliances feared that the P&O Nedlloyd merger would cause their consortia to collapse.

After detailed analysis of both alliance groups, P&O Nedlloyd opted to join the Grand Alliance in June of 1997, ending months of speculation in the liner shipping industry. The choice was reported to be based on four questions (Crichton, 1997):

1. Concerning the east-west trade, which alliance would enable P&O Nedlloyd to:
   a) retain its market lead in Asia/north Europe trade,
   b) keep a prominent position in transatlantic trade, and
   c) raise its share in transpacific trade?

---

15  Commission of the European Communities (1996), *Merger Procedure Article 6(1)(b) Decision: Case No IV/M.831 - P&O/Nedlloyd*, 19.12.1996.

16  Anonymous (1996c), "Nedlloyd-P&O Merger Will Create Mega-Carrier," *Logistics Management*, October, 22. © 1996 Cahners Business Information. Used by permission.

17  D. E. Sikkens (1997), P&O Nedlloyd, personal communication, Rotterdam, 16 May.

18  Porter (1996d). The Grand Alliance agreement filed with the FMC had provisions requiring one year notice of withdrawal and that notice could not be given before 30 April 2005. The Global Alliance agreement was to remain in effect until 31 December 2001.

2. Which alliance would provide a better return on assets, including its ships on order?

3. Which alliance would provide a lower cost base?

4. Which alliance would provide a stronger set of partners?

P&O Nedlloyd concluded that the Grand Alliance was better suited to the company's needs for the following reasons (Crichton, 1997):

- The Grand Alliance offered more weekly strings on the Asia/north Europe route than the Global Alliance.

- The Grand Alliance had its own Atlantic and Gulf services which could be used to supplement P&O Nedlloyd's own services

- P&O Nedlloyd's 6,600 TEU newbuilds were compatible with the five ships that NYK Line had on order.

- The Grand Alliance's terminals offered a better overall cost package than those used by the Global Alliance.

- The Grand Alliance participants were all considered to be strong companies.

**Concluding Remarks**

Given the dynamics of the European Single Market and growing competition, it was inevitable that companies would begin to search out strategic consolidation within the industry as a means of achieving greater economies of scale. The formation of P&O Nedlloyd was almost a natural response to each company's quest for survival. It was made less painful by the ownership structure of each company; both were publicly traded and this reduced the need for capital to execute the merger. A balancing payment and asset contribution arrangement was possible.

The P&O Nedlloyd joint venture was constructed out of necessity. It was cost-driven and there was very little discussion of revenue enhancement potential by the parties. Publicly, little note was taken of the market reach benefits that were inherent in the deal or any of the non-monetary synergies which might be sought. It was positioned as a survival strategy in relatively well-matched shareholder-driven companies.

Managerial preference in the P&O Nedlloyd case was strongly in favour of the path chosen. CEO Tim Harris, at a *Containerisation International* conference, noted that the most effective means of streamlining costs is clearly merger, particularly given the European Commission's imposed time limit on consortia agreements. Harris reported that merger costs of US$100 million had already resulted in annualized savings of US$200 million by 1997 (Fossey, 1998). Throughout the first half of 1998, in spite of rising volumes, the company experienced continuing losses; revenue was down due to the Asian crisis and the company was forced to absorb a loss over its acquisition of Blue Star Line (Crichton, 1998). By the third quarter, a small net profit was reported and the company ended the year up on its 1997 performance.[19]

## CP SHIPS—GROWTH BY ACQUISITION

CP Ships, a subsidiary of Canadian Pacific Limited,[20] has long been active in the liner shipping business, and has provided liner services on the north Atlantic for more than a century. Container operations on the St. Lawrence were established in the 1960s and, by 1981, CP was a participant in an early alliance, the St. Lawrence Co-ordinated Service (SLCS). The SLCS was initially a cargo and net revenue-pooling agreement between Dart (owned by Compagnie Maritime Belge NV, CMB[21]), CP Ships and Manchester Liners, acquired by Tung in 1980. Each partner contributed one vessel, with the fourth being jointly owned. In 1983, after a protracted rate war incurring substantial losses for both Manchester Liners and Dart, CMB and CP Ships decided to withdraw from Dart Containerline Limited and sold their interest to Tung. The two then reformulated their interests in a joint venture, Canada Maritime Limited. The Bermuda-registered company was founded in January 1984, with parents Canadian Pacific Limited holding 57% and CMB holding 43% of the shares. A new SLCS agreement was negotiated; it was a pure slot charter with OOCL (not Tung's Manchester Liners) and the revenue and cargo pooling elements were dropped. This alliance between Canada Maritime and OOCL continues today.

Until recently, CP Ships was not considered by many in the industry to be a global contender. The company's reputation as a niche player and its long-standing strategic alliance with OOCL were well known. The first step in turning CP Ships into a global company by broadening its scope began in 1993 when CP Ships purchased CMB's interest in Canada Maritime to take control of the company. In 1994, CP Ships (mostly Canada Maritime) contributed US$61 million in operating income to parent Canadian Pacific (Canna, 1995a). Industry players expected the niche strategy to continue and were surprised when CP went on a buying spree.

### The Cast Acquisition

In 1983, Montreal-based Cast was salvaged from bankruptcy by a leveraged buyout. The resultant debt burden was significant and the company remained vulnerable throughout the 1980s. By 1993, there were serious rumours about its ability to meet its debt service obligations to the Royal Bank of Canada. Its continuing reliance on debt financing made it a takeover target.

---

19  http:\\www.schednet.com, 7 April 1999.

20  Since the early 1990s, Canadian Pacific has transformed itself from a highly diversified conglomerate to a narrowly focused company in the energy, transport and hotel businesses. It trades on several stock markets and has a market capitalization of C$14 billion (http://www.cp.ca).

21  In the 1980s, CMB was part of the industrial and financial conglomerate, Société Générale de Belgique SA, one of the largest companies in Belgium. Safmarine, a South African carrier, acquired an interest in CMB in the early 1990s and CMB merged with Safmarine in January 1996.

In June 1994, CP Ships made an offer to the Royal Bank for the shares and assets of Cast (1983) Limited. It subsequently told the trade press that it was saving Cast from certain bankruptcy. In the preceding fiscal years, Cast had lost US$10 million (as of 31 March 1994), US$50 million (1993), and US$70 million (1992) (Canna, 1995a). The offer by CP Ships was to be consummated in the fall of 1994. The plan was to have separate brand names, sales organizations and customer service operations.

Canada's National Transportation Agency held hearings into whether the merger could proceed. It ruled in January 1995 that the acquisition could go ahead and the motion for leave to appeal the decision by Canadian National was denied 2 March 1995. In January 1995, the Competition Bureau commenced an inquiry. The pressure on the Bureau was stepped up when, on 21 February 1995, the Royal Bank recalled its loans and announced its intention to enforce its security through an asset sale agreement. The sale agreement with CP included containers, goodwill, intellectual property, marketing information, receivables, computer systems, contracts and the brand name. The price was set at US$55 million with closing on 31 March 1995.[22]

Although it had until 31 March 1995 to begin proceedings to prevent the merger, the Bureau opted not to do so as the Director of Investigation and Research advised the parties he did not have sufficient grounds. Under Canadian competition policy, the Bureau could challenge the acquisition any time in the next three years, that is until 31 March 1998, and it notified the parties it would reserve that option. Canadian Pacific immediately injected about US$36 million to assist Cast with cash flow (Canna, 1995a).

The three-year time frame proved to be problematic. On 20 December 1996, the Competition Bureau initiated proceedings to force CP Ships to either dissolve the merger or, in the alternative, dispose of assets or shares as directed by the Competition Tribunal, taking any other actions the Tribunal deemed advisable. The Tribunal considered that the Cast acquisition would likely lead to a lessening of competition for non-refrigerated cargoes moving between the provinces of Ontario and Quebec and northern Europe through the Port of Montreal. It was their view that the merger co-opted Cast into the SLCS and thereby removed the only competitor which could constrain a non-transitory price increase in the market. It argued that the SLCS was a consortium that could be treated as a single entity, and that the market concentration would rise to unacceptable levels.

At a second level, the Tribunal's Notice of Application noted that the Royal Bank preferred CP as the buyer and therefore did not undertake an adequate search for alternative buyers, although there were four other groups interested in the acquisition. Perhaps key was the Tribunal's contention that foreign sources of competition would not likely constrain the ability of the merged parties to sustain a significant price increase. It was the August 1997 announcement of a new non-conference service ex-Montreal being offered by Sea-Land, Maersk and

---

22    Competition Tribunal, Notice of Application, 20 December 1996.

P&O Nedlloyd which resulted in the Bureau asking the Tribunal for a stay of proceedings. The Cast acquisition cleared the 31 March 1998 hurdle without further intervention.

## The Lykes Acquisition[23]

Beginning operations in 1900, Frederick and Howell Lykes shipped cattle to Cuba on their own account and established the Lykes Bros. Steamship Company in 1922 in New Orleans. By the mid-1930s, the company owned more than 52 ships and in 1958 was listed on the New York Stock Exchange (Fabey, 1995). By the beginning of 1995, the company operated 34 ships, of which only 15 were larger than 1000 TEU. The company chartered four of these out, while seven were chartered-in; they served routes between the US and northern Europe, the Mediterranean and Africa on a go-it-alone basis and a US Gulf coast-west coast South America service jointly with a Chilean shipping company. It was by no means a healthy company.

The company had struggled in the two decades prior to 1995, cutting its labour force and seeking alliances as containerization and intermodal shipping eroded its traditional breakbulk base. Its key problem was that, in the 1930s, it traded away its ability to configure its network to meet the market in return for government subsidies (Fabey, 1995:6A). It did not move into container shipping until the early 1980s and then with disastrous results on the transpacific, which left the company with a large, unhedged debt in yen. Potential partners balked at the size of Lykes' debt. Its dependency on government subsidies meant its hands were tied on most strategic decisions. Although the company gained concessions on flagging and reorganized its business in 1993 (Bonney, 1993; Fossey, 1994), it seemed unable to deal with the debt burden imposed by the error of its 1984 decision to enter the transpacific. In the early 1990s, money coming in from operations was used for its restructuring rather than reinvested in shipping. A potential partner, Forum Maritime, insisted the company file for court protection.

When Lykes sought Chapter 11 protection in October of 1995,[24] the company owed US$201.7 million to its creditors and listed US$229.7 million in assets. The deal with Forum Maritime failed shortly after. In seeking another investor, the company indicated it was willing to sell up to 100% of the business (Baldwin, 1996a). It had no cash and was facing arrest of its ships (Bascombe, 1998a).

In December of 1996, while it was still embroiled in Canadian Competition Bureau investigations over its acquisition of Cast, CP Ships signed a letter of intent to acquire Lykes Lines, the Lykes Bros.' container line subsidiary. The proposition was to retain Lykes as a self-sustaining operating unit of CP, not unlike the structure proposed for Cast. In addition to its approval by the bankruptcy court in Tampa, the deal was subject to review by the Federal Trade Commission (FTC) and by the Maritime Administration (Marad). CP's offer was reported to be

---

23  The author is grateful for the research assistance of Javier Bru, Steven Kempton and Joachim Petzilikoglou, Masters in Marine Management ('98) students at Dalhousie University, on the Lykes acquisition.

24  Chapter 11 provides a bankrupt company with protection from its creditors while it reorganizes under court supervision.

approximately US$30 million, insufficient to cover Lykes' debts but more than adequate to pay the banks forcing the liquidation. One of the conditions (established by CP) precedent to the acquisition was the continuation of Marad's subsidies to Lykes' US-owned and -flagged ships under the Maritime Security Program (MSP). CP also proposed that an additional US$170 million would be spent restructuring the company (Baldwin, 1996b, 1997; Anonymous, 1997b).

On 8 January 1997 the approval of the letter of intent was granted by the bankruptcy court, with a deadline of 14 February 1997 set for matching offers. None materialized. What followed was a debate about the MSP condition. CP argued that the MSP subsidies of approximately US$2.1 million per ship annually should still be paid as the ships would remain US-controlled. (The CP plan called for Lykes Bros. to retain ownership and charter the vessels to CP-controlled Lykes Lines.) Both Sea-Land and International Shipholding Corporation (the parent of Waterman Steamship Corp. and Central Gulf Lines Inc.) opposed the deal, arguing against payment of the subsidies. American President Lines opposed the continuation of Marad support, even though it was itself in the process of being purchased by Neptune Orient Lines of Singapore.[25]

On 5 June 1997, Marad provided Lykes with an additional US$2 million in support of operations. However, on 20 June 1997, Marad announced its intention to deny MSP support to Sea Crews II, as Lykes Bros. was to be called under the restructuring plan. Despite the denial of the subsidies and an appeal of the decision in progress, CP decided to withdraw the condition precedent and completed the deal. CP acquired the brand name, the Lykes organization, its container fleet, main vendor contracts, and the outstanding trade payables and receivables as well as charter contracts for six container ships and two conventional ships. Lykes Lines became a CP subsidiary in August of 1997 at a price of US$34 million.

The salvage of Lykes was, according to Frank Halliwell, Lykes' new CEO, much harder than the turnaround he performed at Cast (Bascombe, 1998a). He was able to project the CP image of strength with the flexibility of an independent regional carrier. There were revised network schedules and new relationships put in place. The company turned around and by June of 1998, Lykes was reporting an undisclosed profit in comparison with its losses of US$4 million a month at the time of acquisition (Brennan, 1998).

### Subsequent Purchases and CP Ships' Strategy

In August 1997, CP Ships entered into an agreement in principle to acquire Contship Containerlines Limited. As with previous acquisitions, CP acquired the brand name, services

---

25  When APL announced their intention to merge with NOL in March of 1997, the contract was carefully worded so as to present the deal as a merger rather than an acquisition, thereby making APL eligible for continuing subsidy support. This should be seen as little more than semantics as NOL acquired APL's stock; keeping the name APL makes it no less of an acquisition. The Marad decision apparently was in favour of APL on the grounds that it would retain its Oakland, CA, base for managing fleet operations. CP's operation, although based in Tampa, FL, was not deemed acceptable.

and container fleet. This acquisition also featured a chartered-in fleet of ships, 19 in all, and so was substantially larger than the previous purchases. The acquisition did not include Contship's investments in terminal and inland operations in Italy. Unlike the previous acquisitions, Contship was a profitable operation and had the added advantage of a management philosophy similar to that of CP Ships.

Next came the Ivaran Lines acquisition on 20 May 1998. This acquisition extended the geographic reach of CP yet again and the acquisition included brand name, services, organization, container fleet and nine chartered ships, three of which remain owned by Ivarans Rederi AS of Oslo, Norway.

The Ivaran acquisition was quickly followed by Australia New Zealand Direct Line (ANZDL). Not unlike the others, the acquisition included brand name, services, organization, container fleet, and nine chartered ships (7 container ships and 2 ro-ro vessels). The fleet of containers totaled 20,344 TEU and included 15% refrigerated containers as ANZDL's reputation had been built on excellent reefer service. All of these acquisitions are summarized in Table 7.1.

### Table 7.1: CP Ships' Brands

| Service | Year Acquired (Est.) | Capacity (TEUs) | Trade Lane(s) |
|---------|---------------------|-----------------|---------------|
| Australia–New Zealand Direct Line | 1998 | 7,780 | USWC/Australia & New Zealand, Trans-Tasman |
| Canada Maritime | 1984 | 13,600 | N. Europe/Canada and Med./Canada |
| Cast | 1995 | 8,676 | N. Europe/Canada and Med./Canada |
| Contship | 1997 | 39,858 | Australia/S. E. Asia, Europe/Australia, Europe/S. Pacific, Europe/ USEC, Europe/ S. E. Asia, Europe/Med/eastern Med., Europe/Med/Mid-East, Europe/Med/ Indian subcontinent, Europe/EC S. America, Med./US gulf/Mexico, S. E. Asia/Europe |
| Ivaran Lines | 1998 | 11,570 | USEC & Gulf/Central & S. America |
| Lykes Lines | 1997 | 23,016 | Europe/USEC & Gulf; Europe/Mexico; Med./USEC & Gulf; Med./Mexico; USEC & Gulf/S. Africa |

Source:  Capacity and route data from *Containerisation International Yearbook 1998* and company press releases at the time of acquisition.

Each acquisition brought new markets and new experience to the company. Both Cast and Lykes were essentially bankrupt. The former solidified the company's dominant position Canada/Europe. Then Lykes expanded the company's market base to include the US east coast and Gulf coast ports with further strengthening in the adjacent Mediterranean to that area already served. Lykes' service into Africa broadened the company's horizons beyond the transatlantic. The addition of Contship further broadened the company's geographic reach with an around-the-world (RTW) service and a number of new niche markets. It also added experience on another major trade lane—Asia/Europe—through the line's Asia/Australia service (Fossey, 1997a). Ivaran strengthened Lykes' ex-Gulf offerings while ANZDL supported Contship's position in Australasia. The CP acquisition program followed a strategy quite different from that found in other Top 20 carriers. The company has grown via merger to lead in three geographic niches—the north Atlantic, the Latin American and the Australasian (Canada Newswire, 1998)—with a multi-brand strategy in contrast with other carriers that have all opted for growth under the parent name.

Ray Miles of CP Ships did not merge brands but extracted savings from rationalizing the container equipment system and overhead expenses (Boyes, 1998). There has been a consistent managerial style. He also enhanced revenue through improvements in service reliability. The brands have been maintained but each made more effective following extensive market research; the approach has been one of letting the acquired company get on with running its own business while seeking synergies in land-side operations and equipment management through CP Ships Logistics. Rationalization of terminals, agencies and head offices in any significant way did not happen initially but evolved as synergies between sister brands could be exploited. The company clearly opted for the merger route over alliances, in spite of a long-standing alliance with OOCL in the transatlantic.

Ray Miles has particularly focused on the dilemma of post-merger market share. He is quoted as having said that $1 + 1 = 1.7$ in market share post-merger while maintenance of brand separation resulted in $1 + 1 = 2.2$ for the Cast acquisition as the Canada Maritime and Cast brands were differentiated (Anonymous, 1997c). Frank Halliwell, Executive Vice President of CP Ships, has described the process as brand repositioning after extensive market research (Bascombe, 1998c). Even in the case of its most recent announcement of a joint venture with the Mexican line Transportacion Maritima Mexicana (TMM), the company has sought to continue its philosophy of separate branding. The new venture, Americana Ships, offers the TMM and Lykes brands to the marketplace, with separate sales forces.[26] Miles did not dismiss the idea that this joint venture might eventually be a sale in disguise (Freudmann, 1998), although the next day it was confirmed in the press that this was not its intention (Hall, 1998). Bleeke and Ernst's (1995) typology suggests it will eventually result in an acquisition.

This case underscores the importance of extracting back office savings through streamlined management and technology, an outcome only possible from a merger or acquisition strategy or one which forms a permanent joint venture. CP Ships may not technically be a global carrier as defined by this research[27] but in its *Annual Report 1998*, the company boasted it was one of the ten largest shipping companies in the world. Its short-term future will depend on its ability

---

[26] In early 1999, Americana Ships announced it was dropping the Ivaran name; the brand was found to have inadequate returns for the cost of maintaining the brand. Ivaran routes were taken over by the Lykes brand.

[27] The company is not a global carrier because it does not participate in the transpacific main trade lane and has only limited Europe-Asia participation. It does have a niche strategy that may make it a global carrier if its geographic focus eventually broadens to a sufficient number of niches.

to extract improvements from Americana Ships, repeating the performance results of its other acquisitions.

## THE NEPTUNE ORIENT LINES' ACQUISITION OF APL

Few were surprised when the acquisition of APL was announced on 13 April 1997; APL had been seen as an acquisition target for some time as its financial results continued below forecast. What was surprising, however, was its buyer—Neptune Orient Lines. The two companies had no history of cooperation. Furthermore, many in the industry believed that the US government would not accept a foreign buyer and would deny such a buyer the right to use one of APL's key assets—its access to Maritime Security Program subsidies. (This belief has been strengthened when Marad objected to CP Ships' acquisition of failing Lykes.) The APL acquisition was couched in merger terms to protect against that eventuality, but there was no doubt in the minds of industry analysts it was an acquisition. APL ceased to be publicly traded and became a wholly-owned subsidiary of one of Singapore's leading corporations. How did the acquisition unfold? Why did Marad retain the MSP subsidy? Are there any lessons to be learned?

## About APL

APL had a long history. It began its life as the Pacific Mail Steamship Company in 1848, with a paddle wheel operation on the west coast of the US servicing the California Gold Rush. Transpacific service began in 1867. Throughout its history, the company had various owners including the Southern Pacific Railroad. American President Lines was created in 1938 by the US government with assets of the bankrupt Dollar Line, its previous owner. The government sold the APL in 1952 and it entered the container shipping business in 1973. It acquired significant respect within the global transportation industry when it introduced its revolutionary doublestack rail service between the US west coast and Chicago in 1984.

At the time of the merger announcement, APL ranked 15th in the world in TEU operated. It was involved in a number of related businesses, including marine terminals, the largest stack train service in the US and an integrated freight logistics company. However, the liner and stack train businesses accounted for most of its revenues (Fossey, 1997b).

The company had a simple strategy: "to be one of the best container companies in the world." "Best" was defined as meeting these requirements: shareholder return at about 15% on equity, satisfied customers and, internally, a company with integrity (Boyes, 1997). APL had been challenged to do better throughout the 1990s; its financial results disappointed shareholders. The operating income in 1992 through 1995 was well below forecast; in 1992 the error was 55% and, although it had improved to 23% below forecast by 1994, 1995 results were 40% below forecast (Tirschwell, 1997a). The company responded in 1994 and 1995 by reorganizing internally and cutting 950 positions. It also bought back stock to support its share price. Like many other firms reviewed in this book, these efforts were not sufficient. Shareholder pressure for better financial results was mounting but all the savings the company was able to extract were passed on to customers as APL's markets softened and rates continued to fall, particularly on the transpacific.

By the fall of 1996, the directors of APL began to consider a range of strategic alternatives— asset sales, re-focusing the business on logistics and intermodal operations rather than ocean shipping, spinning off businesses, and restructuring. They concluded that there were limits to cost-cutting and the efficiency gains these offered (Cauthen, 1997). The company began its search for a merger partner.[28]

The *Annual Report 1996* reported APL's pleasure at being able, through its alliances, to book cargo on 66 ships rather than 23 and offer eight rather than three weekly transpacific sailings. It was close to reaching its target of 15% return for shareholders (at 14.3% up from 11.6% in 1992), but long-term debt was rising out of proportion with the total asset base and the longer term future of the company was uncertain. On 4 April 1997, its stock price hit a five-year low (Tirschwell, 1997b). The company had become an acquisition target.

## About NOL

NOL was a strong operator and had been an early entrant into container shipping. The largest shipping company listed on the Singapore Stock Exchange, NOL was diversified, with businesses such as marine terminals, warehousing, ship management services and property management. The NOL group of companies comprised more than 50 subsidiaries in both transportation and non-transportation service businesses.[29] NOL boasted a fleet of 45 vessels including 36 container ships at the time of the announcement (Anonymous, 1997d). Liner business accounted for the largest share of its revenues (Fossey, 1997b). Although 50% of the size of APL, in terms of total revenues, and 73% in terms of number of TEUs carried,[30] it was ranked only two places behind APL in *Containerisation International*'s ranking of container lines.

NOL too had the dilemma of responding to shareholder concerns. Profits had been declining since 1993. It responded to its market difficulties with internal business process restructuring and alliance participation. The Group's performance was not as stellar as shareholders hoped. For the year ending 21 December 1996, turnover was up 3% over the previous year but profit attributable to shareholders fell 54%.[31] It was said that the company lacked focus (Bangsberg, 1997). Merger rumours were in the air with NOL reported to be a takeover target for the new

---

28  It has been suggested that the P&O Nedlloyd announcement in September of 1996 likely hastened management's acceptance of this structural option.

29  According to the company's web site, it is also in the Top 5 of carriers operating Aframax tanker tonnage.

30  NOL had total revenues of US$1.36 billion while APL had total revenues of US$2.74 billion. They carried 746,000 TEU compared with 1,016,000 TEUs for APL (Anonymous, 1997d).

31  http://www.nol.com. *Annual Report 1996.*

P&O Nedlloyd; NOL's management was on record as prepared to consider merger with a like-minded company.[32]

## The Deal

On 13 April 1997, NOL offered US$825 million for the 24.6 million outstanding shares of APL; at US$33.50 a share, this offer represented a 56% premium over the trading price of US$21.50. The financing package for the acquisition was bank loans and cash, raising NOL's debt to equity ratio to 4 times. According to NOL, there were three reasons behind the offer to make APL a wholly-owned subsidiary: global trade and carrier reductions meant shippers wanted carriers able to service the globe, the use of vessel sharing agreements enabled greater market reach, and cost efficiencies were offered by the merger option (Dow, 1998).

Tim Rhein, APL's CEO, was quoted as noting that APL was neither a global player nor a niche player; the company had decided on a strategy to become a global player and NOL's offer provided an attractive way to do so faster. At the time of closing, APL admitted that it had four serious suitors and one offer in excess of the NOL offer;[33] the NOL offer was, however, in cash in US dollars. It also offered the opportunity for the combined company to try and match the revenues of another US company, Sea-Land.

The fit was a complementary one. APL was strong in intermodal service and on the trans-pacific and intra-Asia trades, with a smaller interest in Asia/Europe and Asia/Latin America while NOL was stronger in Asia/Europe and Asia/East Coast via Suez. However, the combined company was still not the global player it sought to be; APL had no transatlantic service and NOL was a small player through its participation in the Grand Alliance and its US west coast/US east coast/Europe service. Broader market scope was still required. Even before the merger was finalized, APL announced its entry into the transatlantic trades. By early June 1998, there was discussion of expansion by NOL possibly through an acquisition of a smaller company (Anonymous, 1998).

Annual merger savings were projected to be in the order of US$130 million. This was not seen by some as adequate given the incredible increase in debt that the combined company was accepting. Shortly after the announcement of the merger, APL was placed on Standard & Poors Credit Watch List due in part to the proposed debt financing. Although the merger made strategic sense, the combined company was seen to be weaker than APL as a stand-alone enterprise (Tirschwell, 1997a). Sale of stock was suggested by analysts who felt that earnings in APL did not warrant the premium price proposed, particularly when the price climbed above US$30 a share in the period immediately following the announcement.

---

32  Anonymous (1997d:10). APL was also in preliminary discussions with P&O Nedlloyd at this time (Anonymous, 1997e).

33  Mottley (1997). It was rumoured that one of these suitors was P&O Nedlloyd with an offer of US$30 a share (Tirschwell, 1997a). Hapag Lloyd was reported as interested with a price in the range of US$24.40 to US$36.50 a share while OOCL and Evergreen were also rumoured to be suitors (Schultz, 1997).

The acquisition was structured so that the APL name would remain in markets where it had strong brand recognition. However, there were also markets where the NOL brand recognition was strong and some markets, like India, where both brands had strong recognition. The "branding" issue was unclear.

APL shareholders were pleased with the offer; fewer than 1% voted against it (Anonymous, 1997f). The takeover was completed on 12 November 1997, creating the 5th largest containership operator. The merger also, like the P&O Nedlloyd merger, combined two companies from different alliances; NOL was in the Grand Alliance while APL was in the Global Alliance. As P&O Nedlloyd eventually chose to participate in the Grand Alliance, the decision on a suitable alliance for the "new" APL was thought to be more predictable; as second mover it only made sense to those in the industry that NOL/APL would rebalance the playing field by choosing the Global Alliance. However, the new company also had the option of trying to go-it-alone. Their combined container vessels numbered 76, more than the 66 in the Global Alliance. However, that is not what followed. NOL/APL entered into a new alliance with Mitsui O.S.K. Lines and Hyundai, participating with OOCL on the transpacific and Asia–Europe trades.

The Maritime Security Program subsidies were to be maintained through a complicated legal entity not unlike the one CP Ships' tried to use. The US flag ships would be transferred to an APL-owned grantor trust, which would bareboat charter the ships to a US-citizen entity, American Ship Management, not owned by APL; this entity would collect the subsidies and operate the ships which would then be time-chartered to APL. More interesting, Marad pre-approved the arrangement, in the sense that it gave APL a letter allowing it to transfer its subsidy rights (if APL proposed such a plan) prior to APL enrolling its ships in the program. Why CP Ships failed to secure a similar situation in its Lykes acquisition was that it was seen to have undue control over the US-citizen intermediary established for the purposes of subsidy collection. One attorney noted (Roberts, 1997) that it was simply "political" while another called it "fiction."

At the time of the merger announcement, there was considerable discussion in the trade press about NOL's acquisition of APL's stack train business as being a very worthwhile part of the deal. It was not long, however, before NOL announced it was that APL's stack train services might be available for sale[34] thereby raising questions about the ability of NOL to extract the value in the merger for shareholders. In early 1999, the stack train operations were sold, pending approvals, to Apollo Management, a New York investment firm.[35]

At the time of the merger, problems were expected in the areas of culture, training and systems integration.[36] Culture does not appear to have played its usual devilish role, perhaps because of

---

34  http://www.nol.com.sg/nol/nolnews, press release "APL Outlines Strategy for Future," 30 October 1998.

35  The divestiture was part of NOL's strategy to spin off non-core businesses and focus on its global container transport and logistics businesses. The deal included a 20-year commitment to service APL (Anonymous, 1999). NOL also announced a US$500 million share offering, of which two-thirds would be used to reduce debt (http://www.schednet.com, 15 July 1999).

36  According to Tim Rhein, CEO of APL, in an interview with Bascombe (1998b).

the complementarity of operations and the skill sets of each firm—NOL with its terminals and warehousing expertise and APL with its intermodal and stack train skills. APL brought quality and an excellent service orientation to the merger to be combined with NOL's discipline, focus and integrity; NOL acquired imagination and creativity while APL acquired discipline. The merger of the two cultures was presented as very successful (Tirschwell, 1998b). It may have also been because both companies shared a vision and an urgency encouraged by shareholder expectations.

However, NOL did not report a profit in 1998.[37] The financial burden proved quite difficult to manage, with NOL selling tankers, residential property in the US, and seeking a buyer for its corporate headquarters in Singapore. This did not stop the firm from announcing its interests in future acquisitions, albeit smaller ones than APL.

## Lessons

The APL/NOL merger seems to have suffered slightly from the usual merger problem of 1+1 not equaling 2. The combined traffic carried into the US in the first quarter of 1998 was only 95% of the sum of that carried by each in the first quarter of 1997 (Bascombe, 1998b:41). In other words, combined traffic only reached a target of 1.9 not 2. Although there were good explanations for this drop in traffic, including the cancellation of its US east coast/Asia service (via Suez) and softening markets, the drop is not as severe as the 1.7 result which followed the P&O Nedlloyd merger, but certainly not the 2.2 CP Ships' boasted about following its acquisitions. The 1.9 outcome may in part have resulted from the decision to brand the container operations under the better-known APL brand,[38] reserving the NOL brand for non-container activities.

The disposition of a brand is a key consideration in the future ability of a company to secure continued sales to its customers post-merger.[39] Branding reflects the corporate culture of the company; customers relate the brand to the attributes they buy and the customer service they expect. Building on a brand's strengths ensures continued value for a company. This is particularly important where specific products or services are difficult to differentiate. Successful mergers ensure that brand structures and marketing goals and consistent with long-term growth plans (Haigh, 1999); discarding an established brand removes the intangible value it represents and is recognized in its share price. There is a price to pay for poor branding decisions made post-merger.

Support for the APL/NOL deal was broad-based, unlike the Lykes situation. It may have been that Lykes paved the way for acceptance of the APL/NOL deal or it may have been that APL,

---

[37]  http://www.nolweb.com, 7 May 1999.

[38]  Fossey (1997c). This was the conclusion of a worldwide marketing study.

[39]  It is certainly cheaper to acquire a product with an established brand name than launch a new brand (Reiss, 1985). Rebranding is also expensive; in the Mobil/Exxon deal, it was suggested that BP buy out the Mobil-owned BP outlets rather than incur rebranding costs post-merger (Buxton, 1998).

realizing there were no potential US partners, paved the way for US acceptance of NOL. This should have been difficult, given the Singapore government's ownership stake in NOL and the long US history of "controlled carrier" legislation and policy.

It is also interesting to note that the Federal Trade Commission had no concerns about the merger, not all that different than the European Commission's take on the P&O Nedlloyd merger.

To Rhein, alliance membership allowed APL to improve vessel utilization and engage in direct calls at ports in Asia which used to be served via hub and spoke systems; this offered the advantage of eliminating double handling. He viewed the downside of alliances as a loss of flexibility and a longer decision-making process (Boyes, 1997). On the other hand, customers do not care about the vessel used only the service they get. Owning the asset used is not necessary.

## DISCUSSION

The entry of Sea-Land and Maersk jointly into the transpacific in 1991 marked the beginning of a new wave of cooperative business arrangements. Prior to this, carriers might cooperate in slot charters to provide more destinations to existing customers or they might add a vessel to a consortia because they were unable to provide a desired service alone. With this alliance, Maersk's with P&O in the Europe/Asia trade and the three in the VSA on the transatlantic, the idea of strong companies cooperating with strong companies to multiply sailings was born. These were the earliest alliances of complementary equals, to use Bleek and Ernst's (1995) alliance terminology.

Brooks *et al.* (1993) examined the issue of types of business structures likely to evolve in the industry based on anecdotal evidence to 1990. At the time, the competition–cooperation and interdependency continua presented in Figures 3.6 and 3.7 were proposed and the following conclusions drawn. The question now is: are those conclusions still relevant?

Conclusion (Brooks *et al.*, 1993:246):

> *Other than traditional conferences, strategic alliances between shipping companies often take the form of slot-chartering agreements, such as that which existed between ACL and Hapag-Lloyd on the North Atlantic since 1986, or vessel-sharing agreements, like the ACL consortium, which lasted two decades. But vessel-sharing agreements have proven to be less flexible in highly competitive environments and, if the restructuring of ACL and the demise of the Scandutch and Trio consortia are merely the more prominent indicators of the growing disenchantment with consortia, it is likely that future strategic alliances will take the form of slot charters and equipment-sharing agreements rather than consortia. Such alliances permit firms to retain their flexibility and marketing identity, while realizing the benefits of sharing ships or equipment.*

The flexibility that VSAs and slot charters provided, along with their lack of long-term commitment, enhanced the ability of participants to transfer knowledge, a highly desirable side benefit for some companies. However, at the time the conclusion was drawn, none of the consortia or alliances, with the exception of the Sea-Land/Maersk alliance, were showing any signs of global consistency. The other players were "trying on" different partners in different lanes and acting more like aggressive boys at a high school dance than earnest young men seeking a serious dating relationship or perhaps marriage. The willingness to behave cooperatively for mutual benefit has matured and the dating become more sedate in the intervening years.

Conclusion (Brooks *et al.*, 1993:246):

> *Judging from the strong preference by market leaders for strategic alliances which focus on the middle range of options—equipment alliances or slot charters—strategic alliances are key to developing that "seamless" distribution service. ... The cost-savings are clear.*

It appears that the industry has moved further along the competition–cooperation continuum. Equipment sharing and slot charters no longer appear to be sufficient to gain the operational efficiencies needed to survive in the industry. The alternatives of merger and joint venture have risen in usage and coordinated services and vessel sharing agreements are more common.

Conclusion (Brooks *et al.*, 1993:246):

> *Although strategic alliances are often not the preferred route of companies, they are often the only affordable option. Maersk wanted ownership of Sea-Land, its closest competitor, but when it could not dominate the market through ownership, the option of a strategic alliance was preferable to the continuation of the existing competition. Clearly, strategic alliances will remain an important option for ocean container carriers and, given the advantages of the middle range of options, it seems likely that they will play an ever-increasing role in the global container transport industry.*

The growth in alliances has continued and they remain an affordable option. Even in the rapidly changing market dynamics, organic growth will be a favourite choice for some companies because managers prefer that pace and the extent of control. Managerial preferences will likely mean that neither Evergreen nor Zim, with their "go-it-alone" attitude, will indulge in the alliances at the more cooperative and more interdependent ends of the continua. The price to be paid for lost independence is judged to be simply too great.

Are alliances a preferred option? Little has changed since Brooks *et al.* (1993) drew their conclusions. Hapag Lloyd has reported that participation in the Grand Alliance resulted in savings of US$40 million annually since 1996 and that alliances should result in savings in the order of US$100 per TEU (Lim, 1998:366). More savings in the area of container logistics are possible. APL's President and CEO, Tim Rhein, admitted in an interview in 1996 that it was difficult to quantify the cost savings that resulted from APL's membership in the Global Alliance (Boyes, 1998). On the other hand, two years later he reported unequivocally that the

APL–NOL merger would result in annual savings in the order of US$160 million.[40] Mergers offer significant benefits over alliances for liner companies, but such savings must be weighed against any acquisition premium in the merger pricetag. The back office scale economics appear to be a primary motivator to be weighed against managerial preference for continued independence.

The administrative burden of a liner company has been estimated as 20–25% of sales (Porter, 1996e); reduction in these costs can only be achieved through a rationalized back office, integrated information technology systems and streamlined sales structure. Ray Miles has noted that greater savings are likely to be achieved through mergers than alliances (Anonymous, 1997c). As consortia members still compete in the same markets, these savings are unavailable to them. Although some might conclude that P&O Nedlloyd, through its merger, became large enough to initiate a "go-it-alone" approach, the company still did not believe it had attained sufficient size to offer the global reach and frequency desired by customers; it chose to continue to participate in alliances as well (Porter, 1996f).

There is also the problem of the duration of alliances. If similar investments in vessels are part of an alliance agreement, regulatory restrictions on the duration of the alliance[41] favour merger or acquisition over alliance, a point already noted by P&O Nedlloyd's Harris.

Returning briefly to Chapter 2, Figure 2.1 shows strategy in a two-way relationship with organization structure. The P&O Nedlloyd case provides an excellent example of how organization structure can also prod strategy. What P&O's strategy and Royal Nedlloyd's strategy each must be in the face of their respective common problem—a liner subsidiary's inability to deal with continuing poor financial performance—provides an elegant illustration of structure imposing strategy. Normally a parent would choose to set targets for the performance of subsidiaries and develop strategies to deal with lagging performance; such measures on the part of each parent failed to spur the desired outcome. Neither subsidiary was strong enough to spin-off or isolate from the parent (as Reynolds did with Sea-Land in 1983), and each subsidiary was seen by the parent as central to the overall organization's core activities. That is, the organization's diversification had been constrained[42] to business activities related to liner shipping. Ultimately, neither subsidiary in isolation could be a global player, and the existing alliances of each appeared to promise only more of the same; they were partial commitments, not full deployments of the total fleet available. Such partial alliances could not provide either the managerial savings needed to drive improved corporate financial performance or the asset commitment necessary to a unified operational strategy. A merger of the subsidiaries was probably seen as the only potentially successful strategy arising from the diversified organizational structure of each publicly-traded parent.

---

[40]   Bascombe (1998c:89). Also: http://www.nolweb.com, *1998 Annual Report*, Neptune Orient Lines confirms these numbers are still being used by the company.

[41]   Cosstick (1996) noted that DG IV limits alliances to three years.

[42]   To use Rumelt's (1974) classification system terminology.

Although the size of the P&O Nedlloyd joint venture made it a landmark deal for this industry at the time, the ownership structure of liner shipping companies may make such agreements difficult for other large players. Large scale mergers often require share exchange, an easier proposition with widespread shareholding and public trading. Acquisition on a smaller scale has been illustrated by CP Ships to be possible but, in those cases, the companies being acquired had intangible assets, but little else to inflate their book value. Such difficulties aside, there have been numerous mergers as well as acquisitions (Appendix B).

As already noted, market share maintenance appears to be difficult in mergers where one brand disappears. For example, the *Journal of Commerce* has pointed out that in the first quarter of 1996, P&O and Nedlloyd had a combined market share, as separate companies, of 10.7% in the trade between the US and north Europe; in the same quarter in 1998, the merged entity reported a share of 8.2%.[43] A similar outcome was reported for APL/NOL; the share of US-Asia trade pre-acquisition was 10.2% in the first quarter of 1997 and 9% post-acquisition in the same quarter one year later (Tirschwell, 1998a). The choice of whether to merge or to expand through alliances is dependent on costs and benefits, the trade-off of possible costs savings against the benefits of flexibility and broader market reach. The role of managerial preferences looms large in the decision.

As for the regulatory view of these arrangements, there is one continuing dilemma: how to deal with conferences and pricing. Conferences appear to have been unable to maintain pricing discipline, except for a brief period on the transatlantic eastbound and the transpacific westbound (see Figure 4.10). Alliances, however, go some way towards managing network structure and capacity through asset choice and deployment. If alliances remain within the conference system, they have the ability to impose pricing discipline only by limiting their use of revenue management principles.[44] Ultimately, the issue of whether conference pricing as an antitrust exempted activity should be retained in an era of stronger global alliances is an issue that must be addressed. The next two chapters examine appropriate regulation for this industry.

## Postscript

In July 1999, Maersk announced it was acquiring the assets of Sea-Land's newly created international operating company. The alliance had evolved into a sale as was long anticipated and predicted by many in the industry.

---

43  The article also pointed out that a number of lines had entered the trade in the intervening period and this may also account for the reduced share.

44  Sea-Land engages in "yield management" across multiple lanes to minimize equipment repositioning costs and maximize utilization.

# 8

# COMPETITION ISSUES IN LINER SHIPPING

*This objective of open competition clearly is tempered by the anti trust exemptions available...* (Creel Jr., 1998)

## INTRODUCTION[1]

All OECD countries accept that shippers want to move goods of any size and type at their convenience and that liner conferences are the most efficient way of doing this. In Canada and the US, liner conferences are exempt from competition (antitrust) regulation as long as they meet certain conditions; likewise, Council Regulation 4056/86 essentially exempts EC liner conferences from the Competition Rules (Articles 85 and 86) of the *Treaty of Rome*. Through periodic review, the industry has come under the regulatory microscope as shipper organizations press governments to remove antitrust exemption for conferences. In the last few years, however, strategic decisions have prompted closer scrutiny as firms attempted to become global in scope and the resulting organizational relationships have moved beyond those on the competitive end of the Continua of Alliances (Figures 3.6 and 3.7) towards those closer in effect to merger.

There has been a long-standing literature on the regulation of liner shipping conferences, the most competitive of these relationships. This was best reviewed by MacKenzie *et al.* (1985); their annotated bibliography included the very important early work of Marx (1953), Sturmey (1962), Deakin with Seward (1973), Sletmo and Williams (1981), and others who were so influential in evaluating the state of regulation in the liner shipping industry prior to the implementation of the US *Shipping Act of 1984*. Research did not stop with the passage of this Act, although there was a temporary lull in activity. The legislated five-year review of the Act (FMC, 1989), coupled with events in Europe, revived the debate about effective regulation both in the US (Sjöstrom, 1989; ACCOS, 1992; Clyde and Reitzes, 1995; Danas, 1989) and in Europe (Ruttley, 1991; Kreis, 1990). The Australians followed with their very thorough

---

[1] This chapter builds on a previously published article (Brooks, 1994). It also is grounded in work undertaken for Canada's Competition Bureau in 1995. In addition, this chapter incorporates conclusions arising from interviews with individuals at the Federal Maritime Commission in Washington; at DG IV of the Commission of the European Communities, the European Community Shipowners Association and the European Shippers Council in Brussels, at the Organization for Economic Cooperation and Development in Paris, and with both Transport Canada and the Canadian Transportation Agency in Ottawa.

examination (Part X Review Panel, 1993). Canada's review of liner shipping regulation was undertaken in 1993 but was only a small part of the broad ranging and relatively swift mandatory five-year review of transport regulatory reform (National Transportation Act Review Commission, 1993). The re-examination of policy in the US resulted in the 1995 to 1998 efforts to pass the *Ocean Reform Act of 1998*. In Europe the re-examination accompanied the implementation of the Commission's new consortia rules. The problem with many of these studies was their common theme—price;[2] although conferences have antitrust immunity to allow price-fixing, the nature of the competition in the industry has moved beyond pricing. So too must the policy focus; it must explore service competition and network competition. Traditional concepts do not seem to adequately address the global marketplace today.

The primary intention of this chapter is to identify the key issues of concern to competition regulators, building the foundation for Chapter 9 and assisting industry in its efforts to understand the regulators' points of view. It begins with a fundamental question: Should liner shipping be regulated like airlines, railroads or, for that matter, other industries in general?

It has been noted throughout the last three chapters that there are considerable similarities between railroads, airlines and liner shipping companies. Differences, however, are substantial. Liner shipping has both scale and traffic density economies but relatively inelastic market demand. There is also a limited ability to differentiate service, all the more so with slot-sharing. Differentiation then can only be made on the marketing or front office functions, relegating back office activities to the role of commodity, which may be outsourced, spun off or otherwise acquired at the lowest cost. The operation of the ship is a back office activity where ownership is not necessary for the execution of the strategy but control of the asset through a long-term charter may achieve equivalent or even better results.

Access to infrastructure is also not a limiting factor in the regulation of liner shipping. Ownership of terminal facilities is not essential to the execution of a successful strategy, although some carriers like Maersk and Sea-Land have not accepted that argument (based on their consistent investment in terminal facilities). The regulatory situation applicable to rail and air then has limited application. In rail, control of the asset is critical because, as noted in Chapter 5, it otherwise may be considered available as an acquisition target. The physical reality of the route encourages acquisition. Track investment may be partly offset by trackage and haulage rights but, from the view of the company, is the less desirable alternative; strategic control of the infrastructure dictates merger or acquisition as the growth strategy from the managerial decision-making perspective. In air transport, control of landing slots and gates likewise lends physical characteristics to the service route. However, it is the presence of ownership regula-

---

2    The studies evaluating cost structures and liner pricing include Bennathan and Walters (1969), Heaver (1972, 1973, 1977), Zerby and Conlon (1978), Jansson and Schneerson (1987) and Gilman (1983). Few of these studies have compared conference prices to non-conference prices on the same route, the exceptions being Bryan (1974) and Brooks and Button (1996). The flurry of activity examining liner pricing diminished in the early 1980s, only to be revived by the Federal Maritime Commission (1989) and Sjöstrom (1989, 1992, 1993) as noted in Chapter 2. These works on pricing were thoroughly reviewed in Brooks and Button's (1996) study of pricing in liner shipping on the north Atlantic.

tion which serves to restrict airline growth options to alliances. That is, regulation rather than managerial preference drives firm response, and therefore industry structure. These situations do not exist in liner shipping and so the regulatory climate influencing growth options and partner choice must balance government and business interests.

Is liner shipping sufficiently distinct to be treated separately from a regulatory point of view? Arguments in favour of liner shipping being treated as distinct from other industries have focused on a number of points. First, it is extremely capital-intensive with fixed costs often in excess of 80%. Second, the adjustment of supply to demand is extremely difficult because the market demands regular, weekly, fixed-day sailing schedules. Third, load factors are quite variable, with directional imbalances, and cyclical and seasonal variations. Fourth, supply must be maintained to service peak demand; the resultant reserve capacity tempts firms to engage in discounted pricing when demand is not at the peak. Fifth, as with other service industries, the value of unsold capacity is lost when not used (e.g., the value of a container slot drops to zero when the ship sails). Sixth, lower rates do not result in more demand, as has been experienced in the airline industry. There is little disagreement with these facts by either regulators or those in the industry. Furthermore, there is widespread political agreement that regulation should allow conferences to engage in price-fixing and be exempt from antitrust investigation; it is generally accepted that the conference systems lend some measure of stability to the industry, a measure that shippers seek in order to engage in long-term business relationships. The debate, therefore, lies in the substance of regulation: what aspects of conference activity should be allowed and what should be prohibited? how wide a scope should the regulation have?

To explore these questions, this chapter first examines the definition of a "conference" and then a "consortium," before discussing the key competition policy elements which would be investigated in determining if either would violate "usual" competition policy rules. The next chapter reviews where convergence and divergence of policies exist so as to identify where efforts to harmonize regulation might take place. The entire discussion over the two chapters is based on a detailed compendium of existing policy and regulations found in Appendix D after this chapter.

## PHILOSOPHY

Regulatory policy in some parts of the world has moved toward an approach of matching regulation to desired outcome rather than establishing fixed, but inflexible, standards. To use an analogy from the world of maritime safety, if the desired outcome is that a ship can be safely evacuated in a specific number of minutes, regulators should require shipowners to prove that the vessel can meet that goal, not dictate the exact number of lifeboats to be used. The onus to meet the standard falls to the owner, who may innovate to do so. To meet the needs of those whose interests are being protected by competition policy and regulation, the desired outcome is that shippers have effective and efficient alternatives (other ports, other routes to serve particular origin and destination points) and that captivity to a single service is minimized.

There are conflicting needs of regulatory policy. Carriers need one that provides a consistent framework within which to make strategic decisions, and prefer one that offers the ability to be innovative without fear of reprisal. Manufacturers need door-to-door prices in order to simplify comparison shopping (the desirable competitive environment), and long-term stability (so that prices to customers can be set for the duration of the sales contract and the distribution channel negotiated), and a choice of carrier. Regulators want to ensure that these conflicting needs are met but within a framework which discourages abuse of dominant position.

The US inherently distrusts conferences and therefore has opted for a system of open conferences unlike that existing elsewhere in the world, where conference membership is closed. Conferences serving the US are regulated by the Federal Maritime Commission, an entity specifically charged with oversight and with managing the regulatory processes applicable to conferences. The Commission is considered to be more pro-conference than the US Department of Justice, which would prefer that conferences lose their antitrust immunity.

Philosophy in Europe is somewhat different. Conferences are granted their antitrust immunity, and oversight of conference activity falls to DG IV, the Competition Directorate, rather than DG VII, the Transport Directorate. DG IV and its Commissioner, Karel Van Miert, are convinced that the EU's general competition policy should apply to liner shipping. He has been quoted as saying (Boyes, 1997) "It is not clear that self-regulation in shipping has been more successful and more beneficial to consumers than governments' regulation in other sectors." Ortiz Blanco and van Houtte (1996) have concluded that the possibility exists for the EC Courts to declare the exemption granted liner conferences illegal and for DG IV's competition rules to be extended.

Conference immunity from antitrust investigation in the EU is currently based on the notion of stability. That is, the immunity results in reduced volatility in prices; prices remain unchanged for longer than they might otherwise, thereby benefiting shippers by lessening the uncertainty about future prices. The buyers of shipping services are considered to obtain a fair share of the benefits arising from the immunity granted.[3]

The European Community Shipowners' Association argues that stability is needed if liner shipping is to continue to attract capital investment. In their view, funds spent trying to deal with competition rules would be better spent by governments investigating the protectionist practices of third countries (Boyes, 1997).

Canada has historically believed that the conference system provides the overall benefits of stability and reliability in the shipping services used by Canadian exporters and importers. Therefore the *Shipping Conferences Exemption Act 1987* prohibits only those practices viewed as anti-competitive. In 1992, the National Transportation Review Act Commission (NTARC) concluded that the reform of the SCEA 1987 had much less impact than was anticipated. They attributed this to the decline in the number of shipping conferences serving Canada and the

---

3   This philosophy is reiterated in the TACA decision of 16 September 1998 (referenced in Key Legal Citations), para. 329. It is a challenge to maritime economists that proof of stability has not been delivered.

strong presence of independent carriers (NTARC, 1993, II:110). NTARC concluded that, while the existence of conferences was in conflict with the competitive thrust of Canada's transport deregulation, it would serve no benefit and might harm Canada's competitive position to be the first to subject conferences to the full impact of Canada's *Competition Act*. The report signaled the interest of Canada in moving towards the abolition of conference exemption from antitrust regulation, but only in concert with its major trading partners (NTARC, 1993, I:138-9). NTARC recommended (Recommendation 29) such action take place when the US decided to do so.

Furthermore, NTARC's research on legal issues recommended that the SCEA be repealed as the legislation was not necessary to ensure security of supply (NTARC, 1993, II:190). Although abolition surfaced as an issue during the 1995 investigations by Canada's Bureau of Competition Policy and National Transportation Agency (NTA) into the acquisition of Cast Container Holdings by Canadian Pacific.

> *There is no indication that the* Shipping Conferences Exemption Act, 1987 *has had a significant impact on the level of service offered by liner operators to Canadian shippers during its first six years in force.*[4]

Conference regulation issues have not been a high priority for Canada, although, in the wake of the passage of the US *Ocean Shipping Reform Act of 1998*, Canada's current legislation is being reviewed.

## DEFINITION OF A CONFERENCE

There are various legal definitions to be considered (Appendix D). These definitions tend to be rather vague and therefore subject to differing interpretations.

In the wake of the 1992 TAA cutback on transatlantic capacity, the members of this capacity agreement retained 70% of their customers and controlled more than 80% of the traffic despite diversions to the non-TAA companies, Evergreen and Lykes, and to Canadian carriers such as Canada Maritime and Cast.[5] To meet European antitrust guidelines at the time, members were allowed to limit capacity or raise rates, but not both, and were not allowed to engage in price-fixing landside. Following the significant price increase by the TAA in January 1993, the Commission launched an investigation into shipper complaints with DG IV issuing a preliminary opinion that the TAA was in breach of the *Treaty of Rome*. The Commission did not approve of the TAA because it included both conference members, which already enjoyed exemption from antitrust guidelines via their membership and the significant independent operators (with

---

4   Abbott, R. A. (1994:viii), *Level of Service in the Canadian Liner Trades* (TP9868-E), Ottawa: Transport Canada. Reproduced with the permission of the Minister of Public Works and Government Services Canada, 1999.

5   Retention of members and 85% control reported by Matheson (1993). A smaller number for control—81.2%—was reported by Sansbury (1993); this latter number agrees with that published by the EC Commission, according to Middleton (1993). In 1992, the TAA control number was placed at 83.8%.

the exception of Evergreen and Lykes). Therefore, the inclusion of non-conference members meant that the TAA failed the EC's definition of a conference. It had met the American definition of a conference.[6]

## DEFINING A CONSORTIUM

The definitions of cooperative working agreements, in the case of the US, and consortia, in the case of the EU, appear in Appendix D. The first is very broadly defined and means that very few, if any, cooperative agreements will be subject to competition review. The second is vaguely defined, while Canada avoids the situation by failing to define them in liner shipping regulation. The result is confusion.

In Canada, the form a relationship between two or more firms takes does not affect the outcome of the Competition Bureau's investigation as the Bureau is more concerned about effect than structure; that is, Canadian philosophy is more closely related to the FMC philosophy than the EC's structural philosophy. The key focus is whether there is an undue lessening of competition and, therefore, the Bureau treats strategic alliances using principles similar to those it uses to examine mergers.

In the case of CP Ships' acquisition of Cast (discussed in Chapter 7), the Canadian Competition Bureau argued that the St. Lawrence Coordinated Service (SLCS) was "a consortium which may be treated for most purposes as a single competition" (Anonymous, 1997b). While the SLCS would meet both the European Commission definition of a consortium and the FMC definition of a cooperative working agreement, the inclusion of OOCL as inside a single entity went too far. OOCL marketed itself separately from CP's Canada Maritime, had its own sales force, and on all fronts competed against Canada Maritime. The SLCS was no more than a vessel and slot sharing agreement.

In the EU, a liner consortium holding more than 50% market share may not benefit from the block exemption. If the consortium is notified to the Commission and fulfills the conditions of Article 85 (3), it may be granted an individual exemption. This recognizes that there is little in practice to differentiate a conference from a consortium, so the Commission imposes the differentiation by structural terms (not more than 50%) rather than behavioural terms. Building on materials from Chapters 2 through 4, the two are differentiated by the purpose of the organizational structure, its location on cooperation and dependency continua and the elements of operating strategy that structure incorporates.

Therefore, while European regulators must be credited for recognizing the shift from conferences to consortia as the dominant form of business structure in this industry, Europe's consortia regulation is flawed as it fails to adequately reflect all elements upon which competition takes place. Second, the Europeans have not accepted that a consortium can be a disguised sale, or an evolution to a sale, and that neither a permanent nature nor an equity position is

---

6   As the TAA did not include Canada, the Canadian definition was not relevant at that time.

necessary for the abuse of market power to take place. Depending on where they are located on the cooperation and dependency continua (Figures 3.6 and 3.7), consortia may have more in common structurally with mergers and joint ventures than they do with conferences. It is the features of the consortia that are important.

## COMPETITION ISSUES—DEFINING THE RELEVANT MARKET

The primary issue in any competition investigation is the definition of "market." To illustrate, at stake in the Canadian investigation of CP Ships' acquisition of Cast was the definition of the relevant market and the ability of non-conference carriers to provide effective competition to conference carriers. At the National Transportation Agency hearings, it was argued by those against the acquisition that the merged companies would control approximately 75% of the TEUs shipped via Montreal, one of Canada's two North Atlantic gateways, not including the volumes shipped by other companies on Canada Maritime vessels. The company and its experts argued in favour of a broader market definition, pulling in the importance of considering Halifax and New York gateways as well as shippers from a broader hinterland. The debate underlined the importance of market definition and the difficulties that occur when the boundaries of the relevant market transcend more than one country's competition policy jurisdiction.

### Defining the Relevant Product Market

Identifying substitutes is one means of identifying the boundaries of the relevant product market. The European Commission has found, in its examination of air, tramp and breakbulk services, that these are incapable of being substitutes on the transatlantic route but may be so in trades with Africa (Ortiz Blanco and van Houtte, 1996:136, footnote 119). Substitution is highly route dependent; on main trades, these alternatives are substitutes only in the cases of extremely high and low value goods carried. For the majority of cargo carried, they are not feasible alternatives. Alternative routings are more likely to impose discipline on the market. Therefore, defining the relevant transport product market must necessarily include a geographic component; within Europe, individual routes affected by the agreement in question are examined to determine if other routes (including those by other modes) are substitutable; therefore the market is seen as a route or bundle of routes.[7] Overlap in geography must be present for a transport service to be a substitutable product .

Evidence of availability of substitutes is the presence of "splitting the business." It is critical to ask if the shipper who is splitting the business, and has a policy of doing so for risk reduction purposes, will continue to do so in the future. As discussed in Chapter 3, splitting the business may occur within a conference. Some transport buyers will split business conference/non-conference over more than one carrier or route to reduce risk in the trade lane. For example, shippers concerned about labour problems, delay due to weather, and so on, may split the

---

7    Case 66/86 *Ahmed Saeed* [1989] ECR 803:40; Commission Decision *Lufthansa/SAS* 16.01.96:31; Commission Decision *Eurotunnel* 13.12.94:62, 63.

business, thereby building a solid case for other carriers or routes providing effective competition. According to Canada's *Merger Enforcement Guidelines,* if the customer splits the business, the two or more companies are competing in the same market.

In addition to the more general concepts already applied in Chapter 3, the critical issues in defining the relevant product market are (1) the availability of competitors (those companies seen by shippers as competing for their business), (2) switching costs, and (3) the probability of switching in the face of a price rise.

**Competitors** may come in many forms: extra-conference or intra-conference, other modes, and so on. Evidence of competition may include cheating or "discounting" conference tariffs, rebating and "private arrangements." Carrier sales aggressiveness in getting the business indicates the level of competitive activity.[8]

**Switching costs** are low in this industry. Unlike manufacturing enterprises, there is no retooling and EDI, although proprietary for some shippers, is more frequently offered via value added network with the hardware platform being a personal computer usable for other activity or other carriers if the carrier is changed.

In order to assess the **probability of switching** in the face of a price rise, there needs to be an assessment of captivity or perceived captivity. Some shippers will be unlikely to switch in the face of a price rise because they perceive themselves to be captive; no port or carrier or route can offer them access to an existing market because of product transport requirements, service needs, or the value of the commodity is so low that the market ceases to exist with a rise in the delivered price. Every port will have its captive shipper group—that group of companies in such close proximity to the port that it makes little sense for them to ship via any other port. Carriers calling this port provide competitive service only in that they compete with each other; given the axiom that land-based transportation, for the most part, will cost more than ocean-based transport for a fixed distance, shippers close to these ports will find it uneconomic to move their shipments to another port and route for cost reasons. The issue is the extent of captivity, which is, in part, a function of the relationship between the value of the goods and the distance from the port in question.

There are some high volume shippers that will choose a carrier based on needs differing from those of a small occasional shipper or, for that matter, a freight forwarder or consignee. A price rise will not encourage switching behaviour in this group because they are seeking other benefits, such as space guarantees or special equipment.

---

8    The European Commission has argued that competition on the transatlantic is not as intense as might be supposed (Commission Decision of 19 October 1994 relating to a proceeding pursuant to Article 85 of the EC Treaty (IV/34.446 – Trans-Atlantic Agreement), *Official Journal of the European Communities*, L 376, 31.12.94, 48). Evergreen, in adopting a price follower strategy, was not seen as putting sufficient competitive pressure on TACA's prices. This position has been supported by the NITL (Jongkind, 1995).

The value of the goods available for carriage has a very strong role to play in the market dynamics of competition. Shippers of high value goods have many choices.[9] Because shipping prices have traditionally been based on a commodity tariff system, shippers of higher value goods have been charged more, and their prices have cross-subsidized the shipment of lower value commodities which would otherwise not move (Brooks and Button, 1996). However, shippers of low value goods have fewer choices. The cargo is not desirable, given its inability to pay an "adequate" contribution margin to the carrier. Although low value cargo has been viewed by many carriers as undesirable, it should not be forgotten that low-value cargoes, if sufficient in volume, may provide a mainstay for carriers which otherwise might not be able to ride out the storm of adverse economic conditions. (Many shippers of low value cargo are highly loyal to those carriers who serve them in better times.). Often seen as top-off cargo, the carrier with a better-paying customer in hand may leave the low-value shipper's boxes on the quay if the ship's capacity has been reached. Similarly, in cases where the value of the goods is quite high, shippers have often shown that they prefer to deal with the known operator rather than risk shipping with an unknown one. However, for most products, switching costs are low and buyer power reigns.

## Defining the Relevant Geographic Market

The hinterland of relevance to this issue should be the one currently served plus any that could probably be served in the near future; competition analysts do not tend to include the second of these in their deliberations. From an industry perspective, the hinterland for a port varies over time dependent on factors other than commodity mix—imbalances in a port's access to capital for facilities development, fiscal and regulatory policy as well as changes in the climate faced by its users, the shipping lines. Competition between shipping lines obviously takes place within a single port but competition between ports and shipping lines takes place on a trade lane basis.

The issue at the core of evaluating competitive activity is whether the potential trade route options offer effective competition to the one on which a merger, acquisition or joint venture is taking place between current competitors. If other routes do not service the total needs of shippers, then the relevant market is smaller; if they do, then more than one of the potential trade lanes is in the relevant geographic market.

Pirrong (1992:118) argued that port pairs do not accurately reflect the relevant market in liner shipping. He identified that port ranges become the key element as cargo frequently originates

---

9    The European Commission has argued that air cargo is a separate market from ocean shipping because the volume moving via air cargo is of limited volume (Commission Decision of 19 October 1994 relating to a proceeding pursuant to Article 85 of the EC Treaty (IV/34.446 – Trans-Atlantic Agreement), *Official Journal of the European Communities*, L 376, 31.12.94, 4.) More recently in the TACA decision of 16 September 1998 (see Key Legal Citations), the Commission concluded that air cargo is 20 times more expensive and up to nine times faster (para. 62) and that the parties agree that the two are not substitutes (para. 63). Likewise, the Commission also concludes that there is little substitution between breakbulk and container at the low value end of the market (para. 74).

inland (and is destined inland) and shippers have a choice of port pair combinations. To take the US midwest/Europe trade lane as an illustration, there is no doubt in the minds of Canadians that the Port of Montreal has long offered a cost-competitive routing to US midwest shippers. US shippers will argue that Canadian ports are not in the relevant geographic market because they suffer weather problems in winter. There has been debate[10] over whether the Port of Halifax is an effective competitor when the cost of inland rail service is included in the total delivered price paid by the same exporters and importers. The Ports of New York, Baltimore and Norfolk are all also within striking distance of being serious competitors for this high volume market.[11]

In Europe, for example, the smallest geographic market cannot be contemplated to include all European Union countries either, as the trade lanes serving the Mediterranean ports compete only marginally against those in the Hamburg–LeHavre range including UK. On the North Europe side, Felixstowe, LeHavre, Antwerp, Rotterdam and to some extent Hamburg would all argue that they are in the relevant geographic market to compete for this business. It is unlikely that a shipper would use LeHavre for Germany-destined goods or Felixstowe for those with a final destination on the continent. The European Commission concluded, in the inland transport case concerning ocean containers to and from Germany, that ports in the Antwerp–Hamburg range were competing in the market and that political barriers were not relevant.[12]

Conference trade lanes compete with non-conference routing options. Canadian ports compete for Canadian cargo with conference rates and via non-conference pricing against US ports for US cargo which might otherwise pay US conference rates. This implies, if considering the US midwest/Europe example, that the geographic market is limited by the ability to impose substantial rate increases. The relevant markets are not just trade lanes to or from Montreal, as argued by Canada's Competition Bureau in the CP acquisition of Cast case, but trade lanes to or from ports in the Norfolk to Montreal range. This also happens in Europe. Cargo from Scandinavian locations may travel to Canadian inland destinations as non-conference cargo or transhipped via a North Europe port as conference cargo on a port-to-port quote.

To illustrate how important it is that full consideration be given to trade lane competition, examine the *Containerisation International* survey (Eller, 1999). For a shipment of information technology equipment from Dublin to St. Louis, MO, Eller sought 18 quotations, receiving 13 (11 from lines plus 2 from forwarders). The range was from US$2570 to US$4125 and the transit time from 13 to 25 days. The fastest was not the most expensive, but was in fact a non-conference rate from TACA member ACL through a Canadian port, Halifax. Inland quotes and port ranges chosen accounted for much variation, but the exercise showed that port-range

---

[10]   During the investigations into the CP Ships' acquisition of Cast.

[11]   This has become more obvious in the 1998-99 fiercely contested battle between Baltimore, New York and Halifax for Sea-Land and Maersk's post-Panamax traffic.

[12]   See the HOV-SVZ/MCN Decision (1994), *Official Journal of the European Communities*, L104, 34, para. 52-71 at para. 68.

competition, intra-conference competition and intra-alliance competition are all thriving on the North Atlantic.

As marketers often say, "Perception is reality," and so the issue of effective competition is played out by both current use and contemplation of use in the future if faced with a significant price rise. Some routings have built in prejudices where perception outweighs reality. The Montreal routing is seen as problematic by some US shippers who think their cargo may be subjected to the most violent of weather, even in summer. Some Canadians have argued that American customs officials purposely target Canadian containers for delay as a protectionist activity. The internal dissension within Europe about the quality of service offered by port managers of particular nationalities is probably best left without additional detail. Perception clouds the economic reality of some routings to make them less effective competitors. The reality may also be that service standards on some routings are, in fact, substandard so that the routing is not seen as desirable. This implies that each case to be investigated will require a survey of shippers to explore their beliefs about relevant market options.

What can be concluded is that the trade lane is generally the most important unit of comparison; origin and destination are fixed, but the route between them is not.[13] This means that competition between ports and routes is a critical element in the examination of the relevant market for purposes of determining market power. There remain many options in the hands of regulators desirous of engendering competition on pricing, including service contracts and independent action. Consortium members, of course, have the freedom to generate appreciable and marketable differences among those with whom they share vessels—variation in land service provided, special boxes, tracking services, electronic data interchange or e-commerce, or other value-added services, and, most important, the quality of front-line personnel from booking clerks to sales personnel (Brooks, 1993). Competition is still alive and well among members in most vessel sharing consortia. Coordination of ocean service production (sailing schedules and slot charters) does not alter the extent of competition; it is the coordination of front office activities and add-on services that differentiate the competitors. The key issue then becomes how the consortium is structured and managed; if it markets itself as a single entity, it will likely be perceived as a single entity and should, therefore, attract greater regulatory attention.

## COMPETITION ISSUES—MARKET SHARE AND MARKET CONCENTRATION

The debate about market power and the existence, if not abuse, of dominant position is linked to the calculation of market share in the relevant market. The industry standard for calculating market share is the total annual TEU throughput on the trade lane country-to-country (e.g., Canada–Germany) via carriers operating in that lane. This method of calculating market share is preferable to alternatives based on total available capacity. Because this is a service industry,

---

13  In the TACA decision of 16 September 1998 (see Key Legal Citations), the European Commission agreed, defining the relevant market in this decision to include container shipping via points in northern Europe (not including Mediterranean ports) and ports in both Canada and the US (para. 84). Therefore, each market must be examined separately for the extent of substitution.

output is lost if the vessel sails with less than full capacity used. In addition, the vessel's full capacity may not be available for use; for example, on the North Atlantic, this occurs particularly on eastbound routes where, because of draught limitations at many Canadian and US ports, a vessel will reach its maximum loading capacity before it fills all slots available. There is no way of tracking whether a 4,000 TEU vessel sails with only 3,800 TEU because it has reached its draught limits in the port or because it failed to sell the remaining 200 TEUs in the market. For these reasons, the industry calculates market share on total actually moved rather than what might have been available for sale (i.e., capacity). Market share calculations using capacity on offer should be considered as misleading.[14]

Given both the wide variation in price possible[15] on a trade lane and that the industry has a standardized unit of service (the TEU) commonly used in statistical analysis of the market, the evaluation of market share by TEU sold is also more appropriate than by dollar of container revenue per TEU.

The definition of the market is important because it also becomes the base for considering the extent of "market" concentration. It is common practice to evaluate market concentration and, hence, the potential for abuse using the Herfindahl-Hirschman Index (HHI). Mathematically, this is expressed as

$$\text{HHI} = \sum_{i=1}^{n} S_i^2$$

where $S_i$ is the market share of the $i^{th}$ firm. The lower the HHI, the more competitive the market, and under perfect competition the HHI approaches zero. US DoJ guidelines for other industries set a HHI of greater than 1000 as worth an antitrust review and a HHI of greater than 1800 is deemed as a highly concentrated market. ACCOS (1992) identified a presumptive threshold of antitrust concern in liner shipping at a HHI of 1800.

Another common practice is to identify the market share held by the four largest firms—the four firm concentration ratio; when the four firm ratio exceeds 65%, antitrust regulators become interested.[16] This option would have rail and airline carriers subject to closer scrutiny by competition regulators than they currently face in either Europe or North America.

Mergers make HHI and four-firm ratios straightforward calculations; how should conferences and alliances be treated? Is there sufficient competition within an alliance to treat the alliance, for competition review, as a single entity in the market? Again, it depends on the features of the alliance.

---

14    Although this may have some similarities to the dilemma of overweight aircraft, and the air industry's use of ASM (available seat miles) to measure capacity, the shipping industry does not have the option of leaving baggage behind to secure an additional passenger. It can only lose the sale of the slot.

15    See Figure 4.11.

16    ACCOS (1992:88, footnote 141) sets the concentration ratio for this industry as six firms each controlling 18% of the market.

This calls for a subjective interpretation of the extent of participant competition or cooperation. If intra-alliance competition exists, there is a case for participating firms to be treated as individual lines and for them not to be grouped. If alliance partners are highly cooperative, for example, if there is revenue and cargo pooling, or if there is a joint marketing effort, it could be argued that they should be grouped as if they were a single company. ACCOS (1992) concluded that a higher HHI may be acceptable as liner shipping alliances are less complete than liner mergers and are capable of producing pro-consumer efficiencies.

In his examination of the transatlantic trades from 1983 to 1988 for Transport Canada, Davies (1990) concluded that the HHI was low, reflecting numerous firms (never less than 15) and their relative equality in size. At the time, independents held market shares ranging from 27% to 42%. The four-firm concentration ratio was in the upper moderate range, from 59% to 70%. His study of the transpacific noted a similar pattern even though non-conference carriers had a greater share of the market. He concluded that neither the introduction of the *Shipping Conferences Exemption Act 1987* in Canada nor the *Shipping Act of 1984* in the US had any material impact on market structure.

In Canada, a strategic alliance may be treated by the Competition Bureau as though it was a merger.[17] A consortium would be examined to evaluate its impact on the competitive environment of the business and determine whether or not there has been the development of sufficient market power to be abusive.

> *The Director generally will not challenge a merger on the basis that the merging parties will be able to unilaterally exercise greater market power than in the absence of the merger, where the post-merger market share of the merged entity would be less than 35 percent. Similarly, the Director generally will not challenge a merger on the basis that the interdependent exercise of market power by two or more firms in the relevant market will be greater than in the absence of the merger, where:*
>
> *(i) the post-merger share of the market accounted for by the four largest firms in the market would be less than 65 percent, or,*
>
> *(ii) the post merger market share of the merged entity would be less than 10 percent.[18]*

This brings the discussion to the imposition of structural limits on market share as a means of limiting potential for abuse of dominant position. Under EU competition policy, conference consortia are limited to 30% and non-conference consortia to 35% of a trade. (These limits may

---

17  For a more detailed explanation, see Brooks (1998).

18  Consumer and Corporate Affairs, Industry Canada (Competition Bureau) (1991:21). Reproduced with permission of the Minister of Public Works and Government Services Canada, 1999. ACCOS (1992:83) noted similar thresholds would be compatible with DoJ thinking.

be exceeded by application.[19]) Market share will be calculated on the basis of trade between port pairs or, overall, all ports on a particular route.

One of the reasons why the European approach is of particular interest is the absence of published public data to support regulatory review ceilings. In the United States, the *Journal of Commerce* Port Import-Export Reporting Service database enables the cross-checking of market share for those with the finances to buy the data. Neutral transparent industry statistics do not exist for all origin and destination pairs or networks in Europe or, for that matter, non-US countries (Canna, 1995). The European regulators therefore rely on the shipping lines to provide the data to define the share.

The European Commission's approach to determining share is based on traffic carried via specific port pairs.[20] The calculation does not rely on an average of the share of traffic carried by the consortium between individual port pairs, but rather on a calculation of the overall share of the aggregate of total traffic through the port pairs. The share calculation applies only to the ports the consortium serves, which belies the nature of route competition and feeder operations. The interplay among port competition (network competition), trunk route competition and line competition has not been fully considered in the European Commission's interpretation of the law.

There is room for a reexamination of this issue by all parties. Trade lane competition can be explored in a two-step market share evaluation process. In answering the question "which port pairs compete with which other port pairs?" regulators can identify market share overlap. After defining what constitutes overlap (based on the already discussed concept of surveying shippers about splitting the business), market share can be examined on the bundle of relevant routes. Ultimately, the issue is one of abuse of dominant position. Therefore, the approach should be to identify first the existence of dominance and then the abuse of position. Given the absence of data, regulatory authorities should require the lines to report at regular intervals their known volume on the monitored trade lane. Any under-reporting should be obvious when the data are aggregated and such an approach will provide regulators with the data necessary to determine if thresholds are being approached or exceeded.

Liner shipping alliances to date, even if considered as merged firms, have not yet garnered the market share requirements to exceed competition thresholds. For example, it has been reported that the five global alliances have still only acquired a collective market share in the order of 80% on the eastbound and 80% westbound on the transpacific. When the intra-alliance competition is considered, concern is diminished in the short-term. The realignment of mega-carriers that began in 1995 has shifted alliances from a trade route–focused scope toward those of two (or more) strong partners or of complementary equals with a global scope. Bleeke and

---

[19]   The market share thresholds within the EC consortia regulation meant that the cooperative working agreement between Sea-Land, Nedlloyd, P&O and Maersk was not automatically exempted as its 35.9% market share of the US/northern Europe container market exceeded the 30% threshold for conference carriers (Anonymous, 1997a).

[20]   This methodology is explained in detail in footnote 230, Ortiz Blanco and van Houtte (1996:159-60).

Ernst (1995) concluded that these types of alliances were stronger and more durable. The "virtual merger" seen in the airline industry could, in effect, have the market power of a merger. However, even with consolidation, alliance market share has not proven to be sufficiently high to enable the alliance to abuse its position in the trade. After the four alliances formed in the north Atlantic in 1995, the *Journal of Commerce* reported that the largest share was held by Sea-Land/Maersk at 20.0%, while the smallest share went to Hanjin–DSR–Cho Yang at 7.6% (Mongelluzzo, 1996). The total share held by the four alliances was 53.7%, leaving in excess of 40% for all the remaining players on the route, hardly a situation where alliance formation would warrant investigation by a competition authority.

## COMPETITION ISSUES—THE ABILITY TO IMPOSE A "PRICE" RISE

What is "price?" Although the service may be seen by many to be a commodity, liner pricing is highly complex with each box moved possibly charged a different price for a similar service. The ocean portion of the price quoted depends primarily on whether the move is a conference or non-conference move, the direction of the move (due to trade imbalances) and, most importantly, the commodity being moved (as higher value commodities cross-subsidize the carriage of lower value ones). Beyond this, there are price adjustments for special container needs (such as reefers, half heights, high cubes, and so on), "discounting" off conference tariffs, service contracts and independent action as well as currency and bunker adjustments. Finally, there are terminal handling charges and inland transport costs. In the eyes of the shipper, alternative suppliers are compared on the basis of total door-to-door cost. Therefore, the price is not just the one charged for the ocean leg.

In liner shipping, the relative price level and the ability to influence price are important indicators of market power. Because the demand for shipping is a derived demand, freight rates drop in recessions and grow in robust economies, both at rates exceeding the rate of decline or growth in the economies being served. Price rises and declines of more than 10% are not uncommon as the market is both competitive and dynamic.[21] Growth or decline in the economy is magnified by the highly responsive nature of freight rates (the demand side) coupled with lagged supply response (high barriers to exit and lengthy time to construct new vessels). Reserve capacity is demanded by buyers, surplus capacity is endemic and production capacity is lost with each sailing because it cannot be stored. Low production flexibility must be viewed as only a short-term difficulty; changes in asset utilization are possible through a serious examination of route scheduling, capacity management, asset sale or purchase and the potential benefits of strategic alliances. Better management of the yield from operations can lead to decisions to alter existing production capacity, although not necessarily in the timely fashion required. The structural downward pressure on prices eventually meets the floor, as ultimately there must be complete cost recovery. Few carriers or their shareholders are interested in merely postponing an inevitable bankruptcy. Price rises can occur naturally as a result of

---

21  For example, the Europe–Asia trades have experienced a decline of 20% westbound 1997 from 1995 (Fossey, 1997).

tightening supply or currency fluctuations, or unnaturally as a result of the exercise of market power by the carrier. Therefore, the examination of ability to sustain price increases in this type of market structure necessitates consideration of the impact of both the GNP growth of the countries at each end of the trade lane and currency fluctuations relative to the US dollar.[22]

It has been argued that the threat of a Section 6(g) investigation goes considerable distance towards limiting the ability of a conference to secure a substantial price rise, particularly if the rise results from the exercise of market power. This is illustrated in Figure 8.1. (Average rates, the solid line, decline over time as technology is introduced and productivity gains are shared with buyers.) Likewise, some believed that discussion agreements, by allowing all parties participating in the agreement to talk about conditions on the route, would serve to effect a price floor, preventing prices from dropping below a sustainable threshold.

While Figure 8.1 might offer an explanation of how pro-competitive provisions and the existence of section 6(g) dampen price declines and rises, chilling volatility in rates, there is no proof that the explanation is valid. Conferences and discussion agreements have appeared to promote solidarity in economic upswings, but have not necessarily set a price floor in recessionary times. In the late 1980s, the introduction of the Transpacific Stabilization Agreement appeared to stabilize the trade but that stability might have resulted more from the capacity management it was able to impose short-term than from ability to gain price solidarity.

### Figure 8.1: Limitations on Price Changes in US Trades

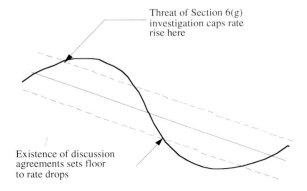

Threat of Section 6(g) investigation caps rate rise here

Existence of discussion agreements sets floor to rate drops

Even if it is possible to determine the base price, less likely in an era of confidential contracting and published as opposed to filed tariffs, the relevant issues are whether or not a price increase is (1) sustainable; (2) attributable to a lessening of competition (as distinct from a recovering

---

22  Given the dominance of US dollar transactions in this industry, the assessment of any price change must first take these pressures into account.

economy or an improving currency exchange); and (3) takes place in a market of sufficient size to warrant the expense of regulatory intervention. In many jurisdictions, only the first two are important as the third is, perhaps erroneously, assumed. The second will be explored in the next section of this chapter.

What is a sustainable increase? What factors will influence the price rise within the specified time frame?[23] Today's buyers are well aware of their options and continually erode the margins of conference pricing. Rate increases are only possible on well-utilized legs and in times of strong economic performance; that is, when demand may actually approach the supply available. This is not a frequent occurrence but happened in 1998 on the eastbound leg of the transpacific; here as the trade imbalance widened, westbound prices dramatically deteriorated but eastbound prices rose sharply.[24] Was this a short-term fluctuation or a sustainable price rise on the route?[25] Such circumstances may also occur when price is mandated or regulated by one end of the trade lane.[26]

At present, carriers still charge shippers of cognac a higher price than shippers of peat moss, and the differential is not fully accounted for by the differences in the marginal cost of handling each cargo.[27] Conference pricing continues to be built on crude yield management systems prevalent since the early days of conferences. As noted in Chapter 4, innovative pricing built on the service needs of the customer is one possible new direction carriers may examine in efforts to improve revenue generation. Through EDI, e-commerce and data mining, many carriers have the wherewithal to exploit revenue management principles individually but not within the conference structure. In fact, conference agreements tend to prevent carriers from exploring alternative pricing systems in any significant way. The result is more frequent consideration of non-conference alternatives and shipper disgruntlement with conference prices becoming more vocal. On many routes, the conference share has dropped to the level where the conference system is no longer able to stabilize the market or impose a substantial price rise.

The primary dilemma carriers face with any new pricing approach is its implementation. Many conference members have been unable to accept the inevitability of a time when conferences will cease to be effective. The few who have accepted this are gradually preparing to manage the transition. No buyer wants prices to go up, particularly not if existing markets for the product are a major share of the business and the company is competitive in these markets due to low transport costs. The ability to enter into confidential contracts rather than published

---

23  Under Canadian competition policy, lessening of competition has a two-year time frame associated with it. The difference in time frames was not explored in this study as it has an "air of hindsight" about it. One area for harmonization could be the agreed time frame for examining the issue of sustainability.

24  In the third quarter of 1998, the traffic eastbound Asia to the US, rose by 41.9% (http://www. schednet.com, 23 December 1998); the previous month, it was reported that prices since the beginning of the year had already risen 75% on the route (http://www.schednet.com, 9 November 1998).

25  The specific case of the transpacific eastbound pricing situation in the fall of 1998 is dealt with in Chapter 9.

26  For example, it remains unclear what the impact of the Shanghai Shipping Exchange will be on prices to and from China.

27  Brooks and Button (1994, 1996) provided a detailed examination of this issue.

tariffs is a necessity for successful transition and the passage of the *Ocean Shipping Reform Act of 1998* has brought the industry as a whole one step closer. Otherwise, the publication of tariffs defeats successful implementation of revenue management, because one of the foundations of successful revenue management is that the seller has better information than the buyer. The potential of that information platform is only now being understood by a few.

The final pricing issue is the competition analyst's view of price discrimination as it would unfold in a transition from conference pricing to revenue management as proposed in Chapter 4. The practice of discriminatory pricing (based on a conference tariff) eliminates or reduces wasteful inefficiency (as illustrated in Figure 4.15). Extreme price discrimination, however, extracts all the buyer's consumer surplus and raises equity issues (unfair pricing practices). This becomes a fine balance for the regulator and, according to Graham and Richardson (1997), may be addressed by improving market contestability.

In closing the discussion on price, Canada's National Transportation Act Review Commission noted in 1992 that "There is no evidence that conferences have abused their dominant position...."[28] Since then, alliances have become the dominant feature of liner shipping and it is unclear if the same will be said of them.

## WHAT CONSTITUTES LESSENING OF COMPETITION IN RELEVANT MARKETS?

Does the merger, alliance or other agreement increase barriers to entry or lessen competition? Evaluation of this question must include both the availability of substitutes and the barriers to entry for a new firm, both of which have already been discussed generically in Chapter 3. Alternative routes may also serve as substitutes as discussed earlier in this chapter.

The trading community is often split in its attitudes towards carrier availability. Some shippers have faith that there will always be a new entrant ready to come in while others do not. It is a matter of the cup being seen as half full or half empty. Confidence indicators can be a product of the media as much as a trading reality. The arrest of the vessels of a bankrupt carrier and the consequent delay of delivery of containers on board is a shipper's nightmare not easily overcome by a new entrant with no established reputation in the market. The number of failures experienced by shippers on a certain trade lane and the direct experience of the particular shipper are critical to defining the level of perceived competition by the shipper community. Competition may also be lessened if the acquisition of one firm by another eliminates an effective competitor. This last is situation-related because it has to do with the financial depth of the firms determined to be in the relevant market and their market share.

As noted in Chapter 2, there is considerable debate in the economic literature about barriers to entry in this industry and there is certainly no agreement among maritime economists about the issue. The ease of entry reflects more the experience of the entering firm; it is easier for an

---

[28]  NTARC (1993:II,110). Privy Council Office. Reproduced with permission of the Minister of Public Works and Government Services Canada, 1999.

already established firm with a knowledge of the business and other trade lanes to financially support development of a new trade lane than it is for a new company, as was concluded in Chapter 3. There always appear to be firms willing to enter and perhaps go bankrupt in trying. Davies (1986) may have concluded that the Canadian market was contestable in the period 1976-79, but there were also a few bankruptcies in the exit numbers.

Growth into a new market may be accomplished via slot charters but this should only be seen as a short-term situation. Successful entry (the ability to do more than snipe at entrenched companies for a few sailings) requires financial staying power to build the business. This implies (a) financial backer(s) with relatively deep pockets. In the rapidly expanding US economy of 1998, this was easier as new opportunities for investment were intensely sought in an overheated stock market in both Europe and the US. Four years earlier, capital was tight and return on investment more cautiously reviewed. Clearly, the ability to gain successful entry will be tied to the current state of the economies where investment funding is sought. On the other hand, an established firm might choose to redeploy small, older vessels currently operating elsewhere in the world and, with a small investment in new sales offices, begin operating tomorrow. Mega-carriers (those in global trades) with finely-tuned core business strategies may then take on the sniper role, seeking new routes with profit potential for redeployment of older, smaller vessels. The example that comes to mind is the one that stayed Canada's Competition Bureau investigation into CP Ships' acquisition of Cast. Sea-Land, P&O and Nedlloyd announced in the summer of 1997 their new **non-conference** service between Montreal and Europe, effectively proving that there was the potential for a new entrant to access a market that the Bureau was sure had insufficient competition. It merely proved that while barriers to entry for the industry are high, they can be relatively low for a well-known established carrier entering an additional market (new route).

While it is true that many service and infrastructure requirements are available from third parties, in the long-run it will be the ability of the carrier to maximize the yield obtained from the capacity it is able to offer to the market that will dictate which carriers are able to sustain operations in the face of continuing surplus capacity.

On the exit side, investments in terminals, inland facilities or agency networks intended to raise barriers to entry also raise significant barriers to exit. Furthermore the capital investment required to support EDI development, e-commerce IT networks or vertical integration increases barriers to exit. Extrication from a market may be costly. As more and more carriers sell vessels and then lease them back, extrication may be less difficult as the separation between ownership and operations grows.

## CONSTRAINTS ON THE DEVELOPMENT OF A DOMINANT POSITION[29]

Even though Canada and the EU have each developed their own set of competition policy principles to apply generally to industries and have opted to exempt liner shipping business structures from antitrust application, there are significant differences in the way each examines abuse of market power. Not only do the two differ in their views of what constitutes a potentially abusive business structure, but they have quite different philosophies about the ground rules for determining what constitutes a market in which the abuse of power may take place. The philosophy underlying EU attitudes can be found in the preamble to Council Regulation 4056/86 which states that

> *conferences should not, in respect of a given route, apply rates and conditions of carriage which are differentiated solely by reference to the country of origin or destination of the goods carried and thus cause within the community deflections of trade that are harmful to certain ports, shippers, carriers or providers of services ancillary to transport...*

It is important to note that, in Canada, market share or concentration in isolation cannot be used to challenge a merger. The Competition Bureau examines foreign competition, availability of substitutes, the existence of a failing firm as one of the partners, barriers to entry, effectiveness of the remaining competition, and whether or not the alliance removes, to use Bureau terminology, a vigorous and effective competitor.

> *The constraining influence of foreign firms on competition in Canada can range from non-existent to sufficient to ensure that the merger of the last two domestic firms in a market would ... [be permitted].*[30]

In the final analysis, however, if efficiency gains outweigh the reduction in competition, the merger or alliance will be approved.

In the experience of the European Commission, only two cases of abuse of dominant position have been found in the maritime transport sector, the first related to the Franco-African Shipowners' Committees and the second to the CEWAL liner conference. The former involved joint abuse of dominant position through cargo pooling between conference and non-conference shipowners excluding Danish shipowners and the second was a non-competition agreement existing with the same parties as the first case.[31] What constraints exist in the liner market to limit the likelihood that carriers will be able to achieve a dominant position? In addition to the availability of substitutes (previously discussed), this section reviews other constraints on the development of a position of market power.

---

[29]  Earlier thoughts on this topic appeared in an Invited Lecture, "Globalization and Liner Shipping," Bureau of Transport and Communications Economics, Canberra, Australia, 28 July 1995.

[30]  Merger Enforcement Guidelines, section 43. Industry Canada (Competition Bureau). Reproduced with permission of the Minister of Public Works and Government Services Canada, 1999.

[31]  Ortiz Blanco and van Houtte (1996:149, 142-3 respectively).

As noted in Chapter 4, **liner profitability** is poor. This situation is a symptom of the liner companies' inability to wrest market control away from competitors or from customers, or to impose a sustainable price rise.[32] Generally, greater return on investment is possible from investments in other industries and investment in shipping is often viewed as irrational. Such profitability problems cramp the shipping company's ability to raise finances for the capital investment required by "go-it-alone" service strategies in favour of some form of alliance or relationship.

**Excess capacity**, which has been well documented by many writers, also limits growth in the total fleet and new vessel purchases, particularly of the post-Panamax size, must clearly be based on assumptions of stealing market share from others in the market. The market upheaval that will result from anticipated investment in post-Panamax ships by ship owners is likely to be long-term.

Slot charters are problematic, providing difficulties in marketing carrier services. As the production of the ocean leg of the service is not necessarily under the control of the company marketing the service, the **differentiation of liner companies** moves more to the front office. Differences in marketing personnel and their ability to respond to problems, EDI and other obvious service elements become more important in acquiring a buyer's business. However, astute buyers who do not perceive the differences between competitors will differentiate between carriers on price, further encouraging the commoditization of the service. Inability to extract a premium price further contributes to poor liner profitability and to companies' willingness to seek other means of improving financial results, including the dream of a more efficient cost structure through asset investment.

The two most contentious issues for carriers in the *Shipping Act of 1984* were **service contracts** and mandatory **independent action** (IA) (Shashikumar, 1988 and 1989). Both provisions were seen as pro-competitive and pro-shipper; that is, they would act to reduce a carrier's ability to abuse its position. While service contracts and independent action may be seen as eroding conference solidarity on prices, it is interesting to note that the concept of independent action (IA) was originally developed by a shipping line, Sea-Land. Sea-Land had withdrawn from 13 conferences in the late 1970s, upset over the rigidity of conference pricing. They rejoined once IA was incorporated into conference provisions and then proceeded to push for its inclusion in the *Shipping Act of 1984* (Shashikumar, 1988:289, footnote 3).

Clyde and Reitzes (1995), in a report for the Federal Trade Commission, found no statistically significant relationship between freight rates and conference market share. They also found that the level of freight rates is significantly lower on routes where conference members are free to

---

32 Anonymous (1994) underscored this situation. The returns on equity of 69 major shipping companies publicly traded were reviewed and only 6 of the companies had dividend yields in excess of 5%. Of these 6, only one had a positive increase in share price in the previous year (P&O, a very diversified global company). Alternatively, an examination of share price increases shows that 26 of the 69 had share price increases of greater than 5%, and 19 had price increases of greater than 15%.

negotiate service contracts with individual shippers. To summarize, it was concluded (Clyde and Reitzes, 1995:39) that a

> *perfectly collusive outcome is unlikely even under favorable conditions that exist in ocean shipping. Liner conferences do not, or cannot, maximize joint profits, even when rate information is publicly available and a government agency attempts to prevent cheating on collusive pricing agreements.*

The existence of both confidential contracting and independent action may be seen from two viewpoints: from one, they enable revenue management principles to be implemented by individual carriers within the conference umbrella; from the other, they erode the solidarity of conference pricing encouraging destabilization of the conference. The Federal Maritime Commission (1989:684) concluded that carriers believed the existence of IA weakened the conference system. It is clear that both do serve to constrain the potential for abuse of dominant position. Confidential service contracts have been incorporated into the *Ocean Shipping Reform Act of 1998*.

Finally, there is the role of **shippers' councils or associations** to consider. The ability of shippers' associations to remedy abuse of conference power was first suggested by the *Royal Commission on Shipping Rings*. In Canada and the US, high volume, high value shippers like the auto parts manufacturers have considerable clout in the marketplace. Smaller shippers do not and they are seldom catered to, perhaps explaining the high use of freight forwarders, consolidators and other third party logistical service firms in both North America and Europe. As greater use is made of confidential contracting following regulatory reform in the US, the likelihood a smaller shipper will be able to secure a satisfactory deal is less.

What the individual small shipper is able to accomplish may be waning, but as part of a group, he or she may have a greater ability to counter the market power of the lines. However, the existence of shippers' councils have not necessarily rebalanced the situation. In Canada, the Canadian Shippers' Council has proven to be ineffective in limiting conference pricing; they often argue that they have insufficient information to conduct meaningful meetings with conference lines. The Canadian government has been disinclined to increase their power base through legislation. On the other hand, it appears that the Australian Peak Shippers Association has been more effective in leveraging its clout with conferences serving Australia (Part X Review Panel, 1993:17-33).

Further development of strategic alliances will diminish the need for conferences as operational efficiencies are resolved through cooperative effort and inter-company organizational learning. Although shippers benefit from the formation of alliances in the shorter term, in the long-term it may be that only large shippers have the clout to prevent abuse of dominant position on the pricing front. Small shippers may be forced into using forwarder networks in order to secure fair prices; they will definitely need to exercise greater due diligence in their choice of carrier.

## ARE ALLIANCES ANTI-COMPETITIVE?

Harrigan (1988) noted that alliances and joint ventures can act as change agents for industry; both can induce consolidation of excess capacity in mature industries (like shipping). Are they anti-competitive? For regulators, this is the key question.

However, before discussing the question about alliance anti-competitiveness, the anti-competitiveness of mergers must be discussed to provide a context. Eckbo (1983) argued that horizontal mergers are not anti-competitive. He sought to identify if they had collusive anti-competitive effects by examining abnormal stock returns to merging firms and their horizontal rivals. The rationale for the focus on stock returns was that future losses due to collusion might be offset by increased competition on non-price variables (such as quality of service); the stock price would reflect any expectation by the market of the effects of non-price competition on the firm's cash flow. He found that both bidder and target firms in mergers challenged by the Department of Justice and the Federal Trade Commission performed better than firms not challenged; there was no support for the collusion hypothesis.

As for alliances being anti-competitive, Gomes-Casseres (1996) argued they were not. In his study of 40 companies in the American, Japanese and European electronics sector, he concluded that alliances, rather than dulling the competition in the market, increase its intensity and pace. Companies continue to compete in those areas where they have a sustainable competitive advantage.

Furthermore, he reasoned that the essence of the new rivalry seen in the marketplace is found in the way in which competition and collaboration interact. The two take place at differing levels within a constellation. The collaboration within the network affects the competitive performance of the network as a whole. As a result, the performance of each individual firm within the network is directly dependent not only on its own capabilities and strategies but also on those of its allies (Gomes-Casseres, 1996:3). Alliances, therefore, have shaped business rivalry in that: (1) alliances as constellations[33] are new units of economic power; (2) constellations behave differently than single firms; (3) there has been, as a result of the evolution of collaborative behaviour, a restructuring of the way capabilities are controlled in an industry; and (4) collective competition has emerged which is more intense than competition between single traditional firms.[34]

---

[33] Gomes-Casseres (1996:35) argues that the alliance is not the unit of competition but the constellation is. The alliance is the negotiated relationship between the firms in a constellation, which he defined at page 6 as a loose collection of firms, each with disparate interests and capabilities.

[34] Gomes-Casseres (1996:10). Gomes-Casseres' six central findings are: (1) "constellations" of allied companies are new units of competition; (2) the advantage a constellation has over a single firm depends on which structure best controls the capabilities required for success in a specific context; (3) the design of the constellation determines its competitive advantage; (4) rivalry among a few competitors drives the spread of collaboration; (5) there are limits to the size of an effective constellation and to the spread of alliances in an industry; that is, there are diminishing returns to alliance formation; and (6) collective competition transforms the structure and dynamics of the industry and intensifies rivalry between constellations (Gomes-Casseres, 1996:205-9). Offensive strategies may then target the fragility of alliances or the pre-empting of their formation.

> *Multinationals can create highest value for customers and stakeholders by selectively sharing and trading control, costs, capital, access to markets, information, and technology with competitors and suppliers alike. Competition does not vanish.*[35]

Conferences are a cartel of firms but the market is such that non-conference suppliers may dampen the effectiveness of the cartel. Alliances encourage firms to combine resources in collective competition on operational elements—asset deployment and network configuration at a minimum. This still does not reduce competition because there remains intra-alliance competition at the brand level and non-conference suppliers still exist in the marketplace in which these alliances compete.

Gomes-Casseres' view of competing constellations is directly applicable to the liner shipping industry where collaboration is currently taking place in the areas of asset utilization and network configuration and competition occurs on service, pricing levels and inland transport packages. He believes that while some collaboration dulls competition, the primary benefit of constellation formation is to sharpen it; the outcome will depend on the configuration of the relationship between the parties, its intent and purpose. Gomes-Casseres' view is too genteel; there will always be alliances which compete internally. Not all are trusting collaborators.

## CONCLUSIONS

Liner shipping both inside and outside of conferences has faced a deteriorating revenue stream. For example, a 1993 study of shipping conference tariffs to and from Canada indicated that rates for a number of major commodities were below 1983 levels in real terms, although the changes in freight rate levels varied between trade routes (NTARC, 1993:II,120). Such poor earnings drive companies to contemplate restructuring in some form. A vessel sharing agreement that may or may not include a more extensive strategic alliance is seen by many liner companies as one solution.

Excess capacity also limits growth in the total fleet. The problem is exacerbated by buyers who do not perceive the differences between competitors, thereby encouraging the commoditization of the service. Inability to extract a premium price contributes to a further decline in liner profitability and, therefore, to companies' willingness to seek other means of improving financial performance. Alliances, vessel sharing agreements, and other forms of cooperative behaviour offer the dream of a more cost-efficient service delivery through production partnerships. The ability to increase departures per week while reducing the fleet required to deliver the service provides the economic justification for the formation of these relationships. It is quite clear that, for global service operators, the efficient economic size of the operation is larger than most companies are able to finance.

---

[35]    Bleeke and Ernst (1993), "The Death of the Predator," Bleeke, J. and D. Ernst (eds.), *Collaborating to Compete: Using Strategic Alliances and Acquisitions in the Global Marketplace*, New York: John Wiley & Sons Inc., 1-10. © 1993 John Wiley & Sons, Inc. Reprinted with permission.

Concurrently, global industries are seeking to reduce the number of suppliers they engage in order to streamline logistics operations. Alliances have become a competitive necessity for those seeking to serve global manufacturing operations. Whether they are anti-competitive will depend on how they are structured and what functions they incorporate. Even if they move towards the "virtual merger," do they have the ability to defend their position against others in the marketplace?

The key element to monitor will be alliance strength. Simple vessel and slot-sharing arrangements are hallmarks of weak alliances. A stronger alliance is one in which the members are not only able to agree on a network configuration and schedule, but are able to influence alliance members' investment decisions. The strongest alliance is one in which pricing and marketing decisions are made as a group. The next step is a virtual if not *de facto* merger. It is important for regulators to view the strongest alliances as substitutes for mergers and monitor them accordingly. Monitoring is a critical element of an even-handed regulatory climate. To use Bleeke and Ernst's (1995) typology, the alliances which should be scrutinized by competition analysts are the disguised sale, the evolution to a sale, and the alliance of complementary equals. All three of these have the potential to enable the alliance partners to secure a dominant position and, if circumstances are right, to abuse that dominant position. The key word, however, is "potential" and, if we accept Galbraith and Kazanjian's (1978) evolution of firm behaviour (Figure 2.1), regulators should expect that there will be other firms seeking to surpass the performance of the alliance under scrutiny through innovation in creative strategic thinking and a new organizational structure. Each growth option brings its benefits and its costs; the regulatory requirement is to monitor the development of these, without setting a climate which favours one organizational structure over another. In the era of network competition, a broader mind set is required than has been seen in the past.

# APPENDIX D

# A COMPENDIUM OF LINER REGULATION (US/EU/CANADA)

## PHILOSOPHY

US    The purpose of liner shipping regulation is international trade that is competitive. Activities that are deemed to be anti-competitive are listed; those not listed are considered permissible. There is a core set of regulations, embodied in CFR 46, to interpret the *Shipping Act of 1984*. The Federal Maritime Commission made the necessary modifications to CFR 46 to implement the *Ocean Shipping Reform Act of 1998* on 1 May 1999.[1] Conference immunity from antitrust is an acceptable policy given the pro-competitive provisions of an open conference system and the monitoring and enforcement capability inherent in the legislation.

The mandate for liner shipping regulation rests with the Federal Maritime Commission. In the FMC's five-year strategic plan issued September 1997, the organization set four goals, three of which are directly relevant to discussion here: to promote the efficiency of liner shipping by ensuring compliance with shipping statutes administered by the FMC; to do so in a balanced and equitable manner; and to promote a timely, efficient and decisive regulatory process.

EU    The EU's approach is also to support competitive international trade. Activities that are pro-competitive are listed; those not listed are prohibited. Exemption from antitrust is based on the belief that conferences provide the stability desired by shippers and that the sector would otherwise be unstable.

Transport, although generally falling under the purview of DG VII, the Transport Directorate, is scrutinized for its potential anti-competitive behaviour by DG IV, the Competition Directorate. Burden of proof falls on the carrier(s) to show why they should be exempt from competition rules. There are several regulations, each dealing with a different part of the maritime transport system: Council Regulation 4056/86 for conferences; Commission Regulation 870/95 for consortia and Council

---

[1]    Detailed changes to the regulations are available at http://fmc.gov/46CFR500.htm.

Regulation 1017/68 for inland transport. Exemptions from the application of competition rules are spelled out in these regulations.

Canada     The purpose of liner regulation is international trade that is competitive. The main legislation governing liner shipping activity is the *Shipping Conferences Exemption Act, 1987*. Under the *Canada Transportation Act, 1996*, the National Transportation Agency was renamed the Canadian Transportation Agency and lost its monitoring responsibilities to Transport Canada. Tariffs and agreements are still filed with the Agency but monitoring authority has moved. Transport Canada can ask the Agency for information from filings.

**Relevant Legislation and Regulations**

US         Prior to 1 May 1999: *Shipping Act of 1984*; after that date, the *Ocean Shipping Reform Act of 1998* and its regulations (in CFR 46). There is no review period written into the legislation.

EU         Council Regulation 4056/86 provides block exemption for conferences from Articles 85 and 86 of the *Treaty of Rome (1957)*; Commission Regulation 870/95 recognizes consortia and provides conditions for their block exemption from these articles. Commission Regulation 870/95 will be subject to review by 20 April 2000.

Canada     *Shipping Conferences Exemption Act of 1987* provides antitrust immunity to conferences by exempting conferences from the *Competition Act*. Conditions in liner shipping trades are "monitored" by Transport Canada and reported in its annual report, *Transportation in Canada*. The *Competition Act* is enforced by the Competition Bureau. Triggered by the passage of US reform for conferences, Canada commenced its review of SCEA in January 1999.

**Responsibility for Monitoring and Enforcement**

US         The Federal Maritime Commission accepts filing of agreements under the *Ocean Shipping Reform Act of 1998*. Under the *Shipping Act of 1984*, there were penalties for deviation from the filed tariff. Penalties still exist, and the FMC has ensured historical integrity of the publication system by requiring tariffs to be kept on-line for 2 years and accessible and accurate for a further 3 years (under Part 520.10).

EU         DG IV (Competition Directorate) of Commission of the European Communities.

Canada     The Canadian Transportation Agency accepts filing of tariffs and agreements under the *Shipping Conferences Exemption Act 1987*, Transport Canada monitors them. Industry Canada's Bureau of Competition Policy (staffed by Industry Canada and Department of Justice) may initiate an inquiry concerning the operations of shipping conferences and their effects on competition although responsibility for the administration of SCEA resides with the CTA.

## ECONOMIC/COMMERCIAL ISSUES

### Conferences

US          A conference, as defined in Section 3 (7) of the *Ocean Shipping Reform Act of 1998*,

> *means an association of ocean common carriers permitted, pursuant to an approved or effective agreement, to engage in concerted activity and to utilize a common tariff; but the term does not include a joint service, consortium, pooling, sailing, or transshipment arrangement.*

There were 71 conference agreements on file as of 30 September 1988 (Federal Maritime Commission, 1989a:134); by 1997 this number had dropped to 32 (Federal Maritime Commission, 1998:147). Conference membership in the US is open.

EU          As a signatory to the 1974 UNCTAD *Code of Conduct for Liner Conferences*, the EU has adopted the Chapter 1 definition of a conference:

> *a group of two or more vessel-operating carriers which provides international liner services for the carriage of cargo on a particular route or routes within specified geographical limits and which has an agreement or arrangement, whatever its nature, within the framework of which they operate under uniform or common freight rates and any other agreed conditions with respect to the provision of liner services.*

Conference membership in Europe is closed.

Canada      A conference is defined in Section 2(1) of the *Shipping Conference Exemption Act, 1987*, as

> *an association of ocean carriers that has the purpose or effect of regulating rates and conditions for the transportation by those ocean carriers of goods by water.*

Conference membership in Canada is closed.

In 1977, conference trade accounted for 69% of total Canadian liner tonnage inbound and outbound; more than 50 conferences served Canada. By 1988 the conference share had dropped to 52% (Abbott *et al.*, 1990) and 46.4% by 1997 (Transport Canada, 1999:258). In 1992, there were 23 tariff-filing conference agreements on five trade routes (National Transportation Agency, 1992:Appendix 6.3). In 1997, that number had declined to 19 (Transport Canada, 1998:133) where it remained in 1998 (Transport Canada, 1999:226).

### Alliances and Consortia

US          In the *Shipping Act of 1984*, Congress anticipated that new innovative structures would develop in the industry and so established the broad category of Cooperative

Working Agreements (CWAs).[2] Alliances are defined as CWAs with filing require-ments different from those of conferences. Any agreement to discuss rates; allocate cargo space; set conditions of service; pool traffic, revenue, earnings or losses; regulate sailings or volume of cargo; or set conditions on service contracts must be filed by CWAs. With the passage of the *Ocean Shipping Reform Act of 1998*, the definitions in this section of the act did not change.

EU

Article 1 of the Commission Regulation 870/95 defines a consortium as

*an agreement between two or more vessel-operating carriers which provide international liner shipping services exclusively for the carriage of cargo, chiefly by container, relating to a parti-cular trade and the object of which is to bring about cooperation in the joint operation of a maritime transport service, which improves the service which would be offered individually by each of its members in the absence of a consortium, in order to rationalize their operations by means of technical, operational and/or commercial arrangements, with the exception of price-fixing.*

Consortia have a "block exemption" from the application of competition rules under Commission Regulation 870/95. Notification is not mandatory (except as noted in the next paragraph and under the "notification" section of this Appendix). This means that the number of notifications, if they had been requested of DG IV, would likely understate the true level of activity.

The monitoring of consortia with large market shares was introduced in 1995 with Commission Regulation 870/95. Structural limits on market share are imposed to maintain this exemption, with conference members limited to 30% and non-confer-ence to 35%. A consortium that exceeds these limits must notify the Commission and request an application of the opposition procedures. Between 30 and 50% of market share, the Commission must oppose the exemption within six months or it is granted. If the Commission opposes the exemption, the consortium must disband. A consortium holding more than 50% market share may not benefit from the block exemption. If the consortium is notified to the Commission and fulfills the conditions of Article 85 (3), it may be granted an individual exemption.

Alliance procedures affecting liner shipping are different from those in the air industry because the Commission does not have the same base of authority; airline bilaterals provide for greater national authority than is the case for liner shipping.

Canada

Alliances and joint service agreements are not conferences and are not therefore covered by *Shipping Conferences Exemption Act, 1987* (Sletmo and Holste, 1991).

---

2   These are defined in the regulations, CFR 572.104 (i), as "an agreement which establishes exclusive, preferential or cooperative working relationships which are subject to the Shipping Act of 1984, but which do not fall precisely within the arrangements of any specifically defined agreement."

The Competition Bureau has issued a policy document about strategic alliances (all industries) being subject to merger guidelines; shipping alliances have not been investigated because once they file an agreement with the Agency, the *Competition Act* does not apply. For alliances which are not filed, the Act would apply. The market share cut-off for alliances is structural with a 35% threshold for the "merged entity" and 65% share for the four largest firms. Once triggered, the test is behavioural rather than structural and so a "merger" may be approved even if it triggers these thresholds.

Sea-Land, Maersk and P&O Nedlloyd did not file their joint non-conference Canada–Europe agreement with the Agency to seek the protection it would offer.

## Discussion Agreements

US          Discussion agreements are defined as Cooperative Working Agreements (see Alliances above).The key issue for the US is whether or not they are effective rate-setting mechanisms and whether capacity management practices within a discussion agreement are anti-competitive. Discussion agreements have been accepted by the FMC but are closely monitored.

The number of discussion agreements in US trades is not readily available as the statistics are included in the same category as agency and equipment interchange agreements, all of which totaled 69 in 1988 (Federal Maritime Commission, 1989a:31) and 122 in 1997 (Federal Maritime Commission, 1998:2).

EU          Discussion agreements are ruled by Article 85 of the *Treaty of Rome* and therefore are subject to antitrust investigation. As a result, they do not technically exist in European trades. Three discussion agreements between conference and non-conference lines—Eurocorde 1, the Eurocorde Discussion Agreement, and the Gulfway Agreement—have been presented to the Commission and all have been advised that exemption was not justified,[3] even though they had been accepted by the FMC. The view is that discussion agreements between outsiders and conference members serve to increase the market power of the conferences without concurrent commitment to stability on the part of the outsider.

Canada      When the *Shipping Conferences Exemption Act 1987* was created, there were a number of new restrictions imposed on the power of conferences. One of these was that agreements between conference carriers and independent operators were no longer specifically exempt (Sletmo and Holste, 1991). Discussion agreements are not conferences but, to be protected under the *Shipping Conferences Exemption Act 1987*, they must be filed with the Canadian Transportation Agency. The overriding premise is that discussion agreements exist primarily to control capacity, not to

---

3   Letter from the Commission to the TAA dated 30 January 1992. The Commission view of discussion agreements is detailed in Ortiz Blanco and van Houtte (1996:144-9).

discuss rates. For example, Sletmo and Holste (1991) noted that the Transpacific Stabilization Agreement was on file with the Agency and its parties believed they enjoyed exemption from the application of the *Competition Act*. The Canadian Transpacific Stabilization Agreement and the Eastern Canada/Mediterranean Discussion Agreement are illustrative of discussion agreements filed with the Agency.

The first discussion agreements were filed with the National Transportation Agency in 1989 (National Transportation Agency, 1990:90). In 1992, there were 14 other (i.e., not tariff-filing) agreements filed with the National Transportation Agency (National Transportation Agency, 1992:Appendix 6.3). No discussion agreements were filed in 1997, but two were filed in 1998.[4]

## Capacity Management

Capacity management programs may be instituted as part of an alliance, a discussion agreement or a conference. Rules may vary depending on the umbrella under which it is instituted and how regulators interpret those rules.

US          In the late 1980s and early 1990s, the FMC allowed capacity management within both the Transpacific Stabilization Agreement (TSA) and TAA/TACA. The philosophy is that capacity management programs work to benefit shippers if inefficient or old tonnage is removed so that carriers' costs are lower and prices drop. This effect may result if an alliance is able to remove the capacity and redeploy it on some alternative route. In the FMC's review of both the TSA and the TAA, it approved the agreements because they did not remove too much capacity; in each case, there remained a sufficient volume of excess capacity and, therefore, it was not believed that anticompetitive behaviour could force prices to rise. Continuous reporting was required as part of the monitoring process.

           In 1994, the FMC required TACA to suspend capacity management, and did the same with the TSA in 1995; in both cases, the FMC noted that conditions in the trade had changed.

EU          Apart from rate-fixing, Council Regulation 4056/86 authorizes, under Article 3, a variety of agreements including "the regulation of carrying capacity offered by each member." It was intended that such conditions would allow carriers to adjust sailing schedules and frequencies to deal with seasonal fluctuations and provide more efficient services. DG IV is generally opposed to capacity management agreements; its view is that the agreement will only bring benefits if there is a real withdrawal of inefficient or outdated capacity but not if the primary purpose is to increase rates for carriers. In 1994, the EC refused to grant immunity to the westbound-only capacity management program instituted by the TAA as its purpose was deter-

---

4    Judith Carigan (1999), Canadian Transportation Agency, correspondence with the author, 20 April.

mined to be the raising of rates and was not viewed as meeting the objectives of the Commission.[5]

Canada      The Agency does not have any jurisdiction over capacity management programs; they are not mentioned in SCEA and there is no obvious government policy on them.

## Maximum/Minimum Rates

US          Under the *Shipping Act of 1916*, carriers were for the first time required to file maximum rates with the US Shipping Board. Gradually, through legislative evolution, the filing of actual tariffs developed.[6] Under the *Shipping Act of 1984* the FMC required filing of rates and did not regulate minimum rates. Third party providers made available user-friendly versions of FMC e-tariffs to registered organizations (with access via password). The role of government is to ensure that filed tariffs are adhered to. Price regulation is not seen as desirable but an unreasonable increase could trigger an investigation; rates may therefore be psychologically "capped" by potential threat of FMC investigation. With the passage of the *Ocean Shipping Reform Act of 1998*, the requirement for tariff filing has become one of tariff publishing, moving the US closer to the models elsewhere.

EU          The Multimodal Group, a committee of advisors made up of representatives of shipping lines, shippers and neutral parties, was established by Commissioner Van Miert to explore the inland pricing issue. Known as the "Wise Men" in the trade press, the Group explored the concept that conferences should be allowed to adopt "not below cost" clauses. Some members believed that such clauses would be useful in preventing cross-subsidization of the inland rate by the ocean leg of the move. However, others in the group were concerned that this could be an anti-competitive practice and could restrict competition (Anonymous, 1998a). The question was moot as it was also noted that there was little interest within the industry for such clauses.

The UNCTAD Code (Articles 12 and 15) allows the use of promotional freight rates.

The Shanghai Shipping Exchange sets minimum rates for EU/China trade and its influence is being monitored by DG IV.

Canada      Tariffs are filed (hard copy or microfiche) with the Canadian Transportation Agency but not reviewed; monitoring is the responsibility of Transport Canada.

---

5   Commission Decision of 19 October 1994 relating to a proceeding pursuant to Article 85 of the EC Treaty (IV/34.446—Trans-Atlantic Agreement), *Official Journal of the European Communities*, L 376, 31.12.94, 1, para. 359-70.

6   Federal Maritime Commission (1989b:560-2 and Table 29-1) details this evolution.

Carriers must have hard copy available at offices for public review. There is no electronic filing service available. There are neither price floors nor caps.

## Inland Rates

US    The FMC allows point-to-point tariffs, recognizing the need for price quotation comparison and through bills of lading as part of a competitive marketplace. Under the *Shipping Act of 1984*, carriers cannot jointly purchase trucking and rail services.[7] The *Ocean Shipping Reform Act of 1998* allows rate and service negotiations for inland transport by groups of carriers, including cooperative working agreements, subject to antitrust laws.

On 30 April 1998, the FMC approved a new type of conference agreement, one covering only inland rates. The new Inland Shipping Service Association will give its six members the ability to quote uniform rates for cargo moving between inland points in the US and 27 countries in the Caribbean and Latin America (Anonymous, 1998b; Brennan, 1998). The argument in favour of this conference is that it will reduce the confusion on rate quotes for shippers with a common product passing through a common port but to differing overseas destinations, and enable speedier, more accurate billing. (The tariff is a zip-code tariff, geographical rather than commodity-based, with rates for 20′ and 40′ boxes.) Others have argued that this conference gives the lines the clout needed to acquire large discounts from inland transport suppliers. This development illustrates that the FMC is moving further away from the EU with respect to philosophy on inland pricing.

EU    The EU requires a separate tariff for inland transport. Joint inland tariffs by conferences are not allowed. Joint inland negotiations are not permitted as part of consortium regulation, but exemption may be possible (Damas, 1998). The Commission granted exemption to the Vessel Sharing Agreement (VSA), operated by Sea-Land, Maersk, P&O Nedlloyd and OOCL, from the EC's regulation governing inland cooperative practices; they still cannot engage in joint inland price-fixing but may cooperate on other aspects such as block train operations, container and equipment interchange, data systems, joint terminal usage and the like. The VSA did not meet the conditions for exemption as a liner consortium but the Commission noted that the VSA provided "the same benefits as those brought about by consortia falling within the scope" of Commission Regulation 870/95 (Anonymous, 1997a). The grounds noted were that the VSA's cooperation was "highly integrated" and yet the VSA was, in spite of its high market share, still exposed to effective competition on the North Atlantic trade.

Shipping executives argue that the benefits of conference pricing on the ocean are lost if the inland is not included. The European Commission has made proposals,

---

7    Donald Cameron of the NITL argued to the FMC that if shippers retained the right to deal with inland carriers directly, inland rate conferences would benefit shippers (Beargie, 1997).

aimed at consortia not conferences, to allow "certain groupings of shipowners—under strict conditions—to apply through an individual exemption to have joint inland prices." (Anonymous, 1997b). This may be used by carriers to assist with empty box repositioning costs (shippers are currently required to return boxes to the port and are charged for two-way transport) and the potential for inland depots to serve as hubs in a hub-and-spoke container management system. The view of DG IV is that such agreements will bring benefits to shippers (under Article 86) while continuing to encourage competition between carriers.

The Commission has adopted two formal decisions prohibiting inland pricing: the TAA decision[8] and the FEFC decision.[9] Both have been appealed to the court of First Instance. The court ruling in the SUNAG (the Scandinavia UK, North Continent Arabian Gulf) conference case, the first dealing with multimodal pricing, was never made because an out-of-court settlement was reached. The European Court of Justice will rule if Council Regulation 4056/86 allows conferences operating to and from Europe to agree on through rates or only on port-to-port rates.

The Multimodal Group advised Van Miert that conferences should not be exempt from inland price-fixing (Carsberg, 1997). It did, however, advise that a block exemption for conferences from Council Regulation 4056/86 might be considered for "fused services," those physically interdependent, where one service cannot be provided without the other.[10] The Group defined "economically joined" services as those where separate provision would cost more than joint provision. Problematic for TACA was the Group's view that neither TACA's existing inland arrangements nor its proposed hub and spoke system[11] could be considered fused services. The Group noted that there remained insufficient cooperation between TACA members as each continued to make inland arrangements individually.

The Group, supporting the views of the European Shippers' Council on inland pricing, concluded that TACA's hub-and-spoke system goes some considerable way towards meeting the conditions under which intermodal rate-making should be eligible for exemption (by improving the efficiencies of the system). They also concluded that the shipping lines failed to make a sufficient case for the necessity of including inland pricing in the range of permitted activities.

*If a group of shipowners wishes to have the benefit of being allowed to fix jointly inland rates within the context of a multimodal transport operation, it is essential for them to engage in*

---

8   Commission Decision of 19 October 1994 relating to a proceeding pursuant to Article 85 of the EC Treaty (IV/34.446–Trans-Atlantic Agreement), *Official Journal of the European Communities,* L 376, 31.12.94, 1.

9   Commission Decision of 21 December 1994 relating to a proceeding pursuant to Article 85 of the EC Treaty (IV/33.218 Far Eastern Freight Conference), *Official Journal of the European Communities,* L 378, 31.12.94, 17.

10  The example of this used in the report was LASH operations.

11  For a description, see Anonymous (1997b).

> *some sufficiently important on-shore co-operation between them.*
> (Carsberg, 1997:11)

Canada   Under the *Shipping Conferences Exemption Act 1987*, conference carriers may not collectively negotiate with inland carriers. They remain free to negotiate individually with inland carriers in order to develop point-to-point tariffs; this recognizes the need for price quotation comparison and through bills of lading but not on a conference-wide basis. What happens when one carrier believes that another carrier is discounting the conference tariff to get a competitive through rate (because it was unable to negotiate an acceptable inland rate)? The conference is left to investigate, and if necessary to sanction, a member for quoting a rate that may violate the conference tariff. The Canadian Transportation Agency has no jurisdiction to address this issue.

## Contracting—Service Contracts

US   The US has allowed **joint** service contracts under the umbrella of the conferences.

Under the *Ocean Shipping Reform Act of 1998*, US shippers are now able to enter into confidential service contracts with carriers, not unlike the situation already existing in Canada and the EU. While the NITL sought the removal of antitrust immunity for conferences as the means to gain this ability through the failed *Ocean Shipping Reform Act of 1995*, the compromise of confidential service contracts was acceptable (Damas, 1998). Confidential contracting is not available to ocean transportation intermediaries (such as NVOCCs). This change in the legislation clearly moved the US closer to the EU approach.

While conference **carriers** may have service contracts with shippers, NVOCCs and other ocean transportation intermediaries are not permitted the same. The FMC regards NVOCCs and other ocean transportation intermediaries as shippers rather than as carriers for the purposes of service contracts.

The number of service contracts filed with the Federal Maritime Commission in 1988 was 4,696 (Federal Maritime Commission, 1989a:135). By 1997, service contracts prevailed with that fiscal year reporting 10,565 new service contracts and 28,868 amendments to existing service contracts (Federal Maritime Commission, 1998:148).

EU   Conferences are allowed to enter into service contracts with shippers. Consortia must allow their members to offer individual service contracts. Damas (1998) pointed out that the EC would consider granting TACA an exemption for its joint service contracts if it met the following conditions: the conference permitted individual and confidential service contracts, independent action on service contracts was allowed and there were no guidelines on service contracts, even if voluntary.

NVOCCs and other transport intermediaries are permitted in principle to have service contracts with shippers (Damas, 1998). NVOCCs and other transport intermediaries are regarded as shippers for the purposes of service contracts.

Canada    Confidential service contracts are allowed in Canada. The majority are conference-wide and remain in effect for one year. Service contracts between individual conference carriers and shippers are permitted. Service contracts were traditionally not popular in Canada's trades but this appears to be changing. In 1998, 163 confidential service contracts were filed, compared with 181 in 1997, 140 in 1996, 175 in 1995 and 61 in 1994 (Transport Canada, 1999:226 and 1997), and only five in 1989.[12] Early speculation as to why service contracts numbered in the thousands in the US and so few in Canada included suggestions that their binding nature was not desirable on the part of the parties and that shipper awareness of the option might be poor (Sletmo and Holste, 1991). Greater adoption in recent years may reflect the general move towards more private contracting on the part of Canadian manufacturers, carriers and logistics intermediaries.

## Contracting—Loyalty Contracts

US    Under the *Shipping Act of 1984*, loyalty contracts (defined as percentage-based contracts) were subject to antitrust laws. Shippers are now able to enter into percentage-based contracts with carriers, but such contracts are subject to Department of Justice review for antitrust impacts. This can be as effective as continuing their prohibition for it is unlikely that a company would want to encourage the possibility of such a review. Service contracts are not considered to be loyalty agreements.

EU    The UNCTAD Code, under Article 7, contains provisions that permit conferences to institute and maintain loyalty contracts. Article 6 of Council Regulation 4056/86 allows conference carriers to offer immediate or deferred rebates to shippers under loyalty agreements.[13]

Canada    Loyalty agreements with specified commitment to carry 100% of the goods are prohibited. Non-conference carriers may have loyalty agreements with shippers and NVOCCs, but the Agency has no jurisdiction to deal with this issue.

## Contracting—Independent Action (IA)

US    Independent action by conference carriers was allowed but not required by the *Shipping Act of 1984*. Conferences were allowed to prohibit independent action on

---

12  National Transportation Agency (1990). The number of service contracts filed in 1988 and each year through to 1991 may be found in National Transportation Agency (1992:Appendix 6.5).

13  For further discussion see Ortiz Blanco and van Houtte (1996:123-6, 130).

·filed tariffs on listed exempt commodities. This changed with the *Ocean Shipping Reform Act of 1998* and conferences can no longer veto independent action on listed exempt commodities.[14]

More important, the ability of conference carriers to enter into independent action on service contracts without fear of a conference veto is a very pro-competitive move and consistent with the nature of supply chain management in today's trading environment. It too moves the US closer to existing EU policy.

EU       In the EU, there is mandatory independent action on service contracts.

Canada    In 1989, most IAs took the form of rate actions, with discounts ranging from an average of 6% in the Eastern Canada–Caribbean Rate Agreement to 30% in the case of the Transpacific Westbound Rate Agreement (National Transportation Agency, 1990:96). At the time, the Agency believed that the threat of IA influenced conferences to keep rates down (National Transportation Agency, 1990:95, 97). Moore (1990:19) noted that

> *it does not appear that the independent action provision contained in the* SCEA, 1987 *had a particularly greater impact on the operations of shipping conferences in 1989 than in 1988 nor that it has had an especially significant impact since its introduction.*[15]

## Treatment of State-Owned Carriers

US       The *Controlled Carrier Act of 1978* was incorporated into the *Shipping Act of 1984* to deal with the potential for unfair competition from state-owned carriers. The *Foreign Shipping Practices Act of 1988* amended the *Shipping Act of 1984* and gave investigative authority to the FMC.[16] Cosco is the only controlled carrier in the Top 20. Yangming, although state-owned, has been exempt under the US–Taiwan Most Favored Nation treaty. The *Ocean Shipping Reform Act of 1998* eliminates the flag loophole in the controlled carrier definition so that controlled carriers cannot avoid regulations by flagging out.

EU       Under Council Regulation 4057/86, with respect to unfair pricing practices, the European Commission investigated allegations that Hyundai Merchant Marine enjoyed unfair non-commercial advantages due to support by the Korean govern-

---

14  Exempt commodities under the *Shipping Act of 1984* are bulk cargo, forest products, recycled metal scrap, waste paper and paper waste. New assembled motor vehicles were added by the *Ocean Shipping Reform Act of 1998* and were defined by the FMC in Docket 98-29.

15  Moore, K. D. (1990), *Use of Independent Action by Shipping Conferences Providing Services To and From Canada 1989* (TP-9823-E), Ottawa: Transport Canada. Reproduced with permission of the Minister of Public Works and Government Services Canada, 1999.

16  See Section 10002 (b).

ment and concluded that such support had been injurious to the interests of Community shipowners.

Canada    This is not a policy issue in Canada.

## NVOCCs

US    Under the *Shipping Act of 1984*, NVOCCs were required to file tariffs with the FMC as carriers in respect of their relationship with shippers; on the other hand, NVOCCs were not given antitrust immunity as they were considered as shippers in their relationship with carriers. They are treated as a new type of entity (ocean transportation intermediaries) in the *Ocean Shipping Reform Act of 1998* (section 17). Ocean transportation intermediaries gained from the change from filing to publishing tariffs as did the carriers. NVOCCs must be licensed and bonded.

EU    As Article 3(1)(b) of Council Regulation 4056/86 defines a conference as "a group of two or more vessel-operating carriers," NVOCCs cannot avail themselves of the block exemption for conferences. A forwarder is considered as a shipper in Europe but may act as an agent for a carrier.

Canada    Third party logistics suppliers are heavily used by Canadian firms; they are not regulated and there are no bonding or licensing requirements, although it is recommended throughout the industry that shippers only use those that are members of CIFFA, a self-policing body. NVOCCs have no antitrust immunity, are not conferences and therefore do not file tariffs.

## Logistics Subsidiaries of Liner Carriers

There does not appear to be any regulation of these by the US, Europe or Canada; they exist outside the framework of the regulation of conferences and consortia. They may fall within FMC regulation in the US if they act as NVOCCs. Therefore, whether there is a conflict of interest between the subsidiary and its liner operations with respect to servicing the customer is not entirely clear.[17]

## Equitable Access

US    The principle of "common carriage" (that which is in short supply must be distributed equitably) has been long-standing in US transport regulation. However, the *Shipping Act of 1984* allowed service contracts and so gently breached this principle. Now that the *Ocean Shipping Reform Act of 1998* eliminates the require-

---

[17]  It is interesting to note that P&O Nedlloyd restructured their UK inland subsidiaries in January 1998 to separate them from the container line so that they, driven by their own profit responsibility, might be encouraged to seek third party business.

.ment for carriers to match service contract terms for "similarly situated" shippers, the principle of common carriage has been effectively abandoned in favour of less transparency and greater private contracting. Confidential contracting is a more common form of business practice in a business climate that emphasizes cooperative partnerships and alliances between organizations in the supply chain, and so can be expected to grow.

EU  If carriers participate in a conference, they must provide benefits to all. Article 13 of the UNCTAD Code is clear that conference tariffs should not differentiate between similarly situated shippers.

It is particularly interesting that the requirement of non-discrimination on the grounds of country of origin has enabled carriers serving the EU to institute port equalization practices in tariff-fixing, thereby making a discriminatory practice into one considered to be non-discriminatory from a legal point of view. Likewise, confidential contracting is not seen as violating the principles of common carriage.

Canada  Canada has the rhetoric of common carriage but not the practice, as confidential contracting is an entrenched principle in Canadian transport legislation and port equalization practices are allowed.

## Role/Power of Shippers' Councils

US  Industry associations do not have antitrust immunity and therefore cannot meet to discuss rates. There are no shippers' councils but there are non-profit shippers' associations which meet to negotiate with carriers regarding rates (TVRs and service contracts). In general, the US does not accept the view of the EC and Canada that shippers' organizations can counteract conference power.[18]

EU  Shippers' councils and associations can meet with the conferences to negotiate rates; they are a forum for discussion but not backed with legislated authority to negotiate group rates. As a practical matter, there is a *de minimus* philosophy about holding consultations (Ortiz Blanco and van Houtte, 1996:123).

Canada  The *Shipping Conferences Exemption Act 1987* gives the Minister of Transport the authority to designate shipper groups; the only so-designated group is the Canadian Shippers' Council (CSC). Conferences are required to provide the CSC with information sufficient for the adequate conduct of their meetings; the CSC has not always felt conferences met this obligation. CSC activity in 1996 focused on surcharges and ancillary charges (Transport Canada, 1997).

---

[18] As noted in Chapter 8, the author has serious reservations about whether shippers' organizations have been sufficiently strong to exercise any power against conferences.

## PROCESS ISSUES

### Filing/Publication of Tariffs: What and Why?

US          Under the *Shipping Act of 1984*, tariffs were filed and available through third party services, carriers/NVOCCs or the Automated Tariff Filing and Information System. The reasoning behind this approach was detailed in Part 4 of Federal Maritime Commission (1989b:483-607). Under the five-year review of the Act, the conclusion reached (Federal Maritime Commission, 1989b:604) was that

> *the tariff filing mechanism, in an open conference environment, promotes market efficiency, offers a pragmatic means of ensuring equitable treatment of shippers by carriers, and preserves equitable and fair competition between carriers.*

The *Ocean Shipping Reform Act of 1998* eliminates tariff filing with the Federal Maritime Commission but tariffs must still be made publicly available; this may include such means as private automated systems and web pages.[19] The philosophy behind this decision within the FMC is that service contracts account for a greater share of activity and they are still filed.

EU          The European Commission does not require tariff-filing by conferences. Rather they informally monitor sailing schedules and the trade press, and can seek further information from the conferences if desired. Under the *UNCTAD Code* of Conduct for Liner Conferences tariffs must be available and, under Article 54 of Council Regulation 4056/86, at reasonable cost. Tariff filing and enforcement are not viewed to be important features of their liner conference regulatory regime.

Canada      Conference tariffs must be filed with the Canadian Transportation Agency. Non-conference tariffs are not filed. Service contracts are filed on a confidential basis.

### Filing/Notification/Publication of Agreements: What and Why?

US          Under the *Shipping Act of 1984*, agreements (both conference and cooperative working agreements) were filed and available to the public. The *Ocean Shipping Reform Act of 1998* eliminates **tariff** filing with government but **agreements** must still be filed.

EU          Conference agreements and consortia agreements are notified as is anything which might be subject to Article 85 of the *Treaty of Rome*.

Under transport regulations, agreements decisions and practices need not be notified to the Commission, and therefore may be operated without declaration (Ortiz Blanco and van Houtte, 1996:215). However, the companies not notifying the

---

19   Tariff publication locations are identified for each entity publishing at http://servcon1.fmc.gov/fmc1db/ fmc1home.htm with publication sites hot-linked and entities ordered by alphabetized legal name.

Commission run the risk that their agreements will ultimately be voided and they will face fines. Exemption from notification is not exemption from the application of competition rules. Legal certainty therefore demands that companies notify the Commission of their practices and agreements. Given the Commission's particular interest in horizontal relationships, companies would be well advised to notify the Commission.

The Commission can request, *ad hoc*, copies of any agreements but it must be for purposes of investigation.

Canada Agreements must be filed with the Canadian Transportation Agency if they are to be exempt from the *Competition Act* under the *Shipping Conferences Exemption Act, 1987.*

## Process: Structural Trigger for Investigation

US There are two types of investigation: antitrust investigation (under Section 6 (g)) and investigation for unacceptable activities (under Section 10). Both are triggered by any information leading FMC staff to suspect violation.

EU An investigation is triggered when there is evidence that structural limits on consortium market share have been exceeded (30% maximum for conference members and 35% for non-conference carriers). Evidence of inland price-fixing or the announcement of a capacity management agreement by a conference may also trigger an investigation.

Canada Under Section 13 of the *Shipping Conferences Exemption Act 1987*, complaints in Canada may be filed with the Canadian Transportation Agency. The complaints must deal with a reduction of competition. The agency will then conduct an investigation and is under obligation to report in 120 days, unless both parties agree to an extension (Sletmo and Holste, 1991). The complaint must be deemed to be in the public interest. Canadian legislation is based on Section 6(g) of the US *Shipping Act of 1984* (Abbott, 1987).

Prior to the implementation of the *Canada Transportation Act, 1995*, the National Transportation Agency under Section 59 of the *National Transportation Act, 1987* had an obligation to investigate public interest complaints, such as those raised about surcharges on frozen meat in the Canada–New Zealand trade. The Agency's mandate to investigate such complaints disappeared with the new Act.

## Process: Burden of Proof

US The Bureau of Enforcement of the FMC is mandated to develop the case against the carrier(s) for Section 10 violations; for Section 6 (g) violations, the General Counsel will build the case for Federal Court.

EU     DG IV will issue a statement of objections; burden of proof falls on the carrier(s) to show why they should be eligible for immunity. As carriers have a block exemption up to a certain share, they are obligated to notify the Commission when the share is exceeded to seek the exemption.

Canada     The Canadian Transportation Agency or the Competition Bureau, as appropriate, develops the case against the carrier(s).

## Process for Resolution

US     Settlement of the case can be made at any time during the process through negotiation. There are two processes: for Section 10 violations there is a complaint process, while for Section 6(g) violations (substantially anti-competitive agreements), the FMC may seek injunctive relief via restraining order.

EU     The ability of an individual to bring an action is nil. The Commission must bring an action under Council Regulation 4056/86. EC hearings are before the parties without third party presence and with no Freedom of Information requirement; if the dispute goes to court, it is a public process.

Canada     Settlement can be made at any time during the process through negotiation as the parties are free to negotiate a resolution.

## Procedures: Information Requirements and Data Sources

US     Information requirements are defined in CFR 46; the information requirements imposed on carriers by the FMC have tightened over the years. The FMC reviews conference filings; PIERS; responses to requests or subpoenas for information; minutes; trade press; and may conduct shipper interviews. The scanning of minutes of meetings and the monitoring of market share have become more focused on potential abuse of market power.

EU     The commission may request, at any time, minutes, business plans, records and agreements.

Canada     Conferences are required to provide the Canadian Shippers' Council with information necessary for the conduct of the meeting. As for other data, PIERS does not cover Canadian trade, except that which moves through US ports. Statistics Canada collects commodity trade data in dollar value, tonnes, origin and destination from the Customs forms. TEU data are also collected by each port. No one collects **rate** data, which is considered to be between the shipper and the carrier, although Transport Canada has the authority to conduct rate studies on tariffs filed with the Agency. At present, no anticipatory research on rates is being conducted as resources have been allocated in support of legislation-in-process. Any citizen can gain access to filed tariffs at the Agency. As for the investigation of complaints, the

Agency may use any sources relevant to the circumstances of the complaint—minutes, business plans, records, trade press, shipper interviews, and so on.

### Procedures: Addressing Shipper Complaints

US      Shippers complain to the FMC, which may initiate investigation; the FMC can also initiate its own investigation.

There are three processes: informal verbal complaint (details noted and dealt with); a complaint to the Office of Informal Complaints which has an ombudsman role and may issue decisions on minor irritants (a US$10,000 threshold); and a formal complaint process with filing and adjudication before the Commission.

EU      There are no formalized procedures. DG IV believes it has more contact with shippers than the FMC has in the US.

Canada  The Canadian Shippers' Council may complain to the Canadian Transportation Agency. There have been complaints that the process is ineffective.

### Penalties

US      A conference member failing to comply with the *Shipping Act of 1984* is liable to a fine not exceeding US$5,000 unless the violation was willfully committed, in which case it may not exceed US$25,000. Each day of the violation is a separate offense.

EU      The Commission has the right to impose fines of up to 10% of turnover in the previous year against any company breaching European competition law. Notices may be found at the Commission's web site.[20] The two largest fines for individual companies were US$101 million equivalent in ECU on Volkswagen for impeding parallel importing and US$75 million equivalent in ECU on Tetrapak for tied selling.[21] The largest total fine, until the fine imposed on TAA/TACA members in September of 1998, was US$295 million on eight national cement associations and 33 European cement producers in 1994 (Anonymous, 1998c).

Canada  A conference member failing to comply with the *Shipping Conferences Exemption Act 1987* is liable to a fine not exceeding C$1,000. Each day may be declared a separate offense. To say that the penalty is not very severe is an understatement.

---

[20]  http://europa.eu.int/comm/dg04/merger/closed/en/peryear.htm

[21]  David Wood (1998), Personal interview, Commission of the European Communities, DG IV, Brussels, 8 July.

# 9

# THE REGULATORY DILEMMA: SEEKING A HARMONIZED REGULATORY ENVIRONMENT

## INTRODUCTION[1]

Governments exert significant influence on a firm's strategic choices through their competition rules and mergers policies. They also have additional influence on this industry through policies on liner shipping conferences. While most OECD countries provide conferences and alliances in the liner shipping industry with antitrust immunity, there has not been convergence in these policies or in their application. Neither has there been a concerted effort to ensure compatibility between alliance regulation and conference regulation. Finally, given the recent wave of mergers and acquisitions among global firms, competition policy must be modified to become more transnational in nature. Why has there been no progress towards developing a transnational competition policy for this industry?

The World Trade Organization has maritime services on its post-GATT agenda for new rules governing commercial practices but meetings have been discontinued; there has been some discussion about the resumption of these meetings before the end of 1999, but there is no sign yet that this will happen. The OECD has also provided a multilateral forum more generally in the area of competition policy (not just for this industry); it is studying deregulation in all sectors and has tried to find common ground across a large number of countries.

The achievement of common ground in the regulation of liner shipping requires competition analysts and transport policy analysts to agree, to shake hands across a gap of substantial

---

1  This chapter incorporates conclusions arising from interviews with individuals at the Federal Maritime Commission in Washington, at DG IV of the Commission of the European Communities, the European Community Shipowners Association and the European Shippers' Council in Brussels, at the Organization for Economic Cooperation and Development in Paris, and with both Transport Canada and the Canadian Transportation Agency in Ottawa.

philosophical width. Since 1994, the OECD's Maritime Transport Committee (MTC)[2] has achieved some measure of agreement on principles respecting the promotion of compatibility of competition policy as applied to this industry: that promotion of compatibility does not require standardization of competition rules, and that further efforts towards compatibility are desirable.[3] In addition to securing agreement on the need for adequate notice and dialogue at all junctures of decision-making with respect to the regulation of this industry (reviewing legislation, new commercial or technical agreements, and so on), the MTC members agreed on the following objectives: free and fair competition; maintenance of access to markets; economic efficiency; transparency; predictability of outcome; legal certainty; international compatibility; and responsiveness to changing circumstances which does not impinge on economic efficiency.[4] The OECD has now moved on to work on a new project to examine the interface between existing competition policies and regulations, and the complex business arrangements discussed throughout this book. In the long-term, however, the existence of this forum is very much dependent on the budget available and the restructuring options the OECD is currently considering.

In another area of relationship-building, there has been significant progress through bilateral agreements. Cooperation in competition policy is being promoted between the US, Canada and the European Commission with bilateral agreements between the first and third put in place in 1995[5] and between the second and third in 1999. The bilateral agreement between the US and Europe has resulted in cooperation on more than 300 cases, while that between Canada and the EU was signed 17 June 1999.[6] The two agreements are similar.

Such bilaterals are only a first step as they are easier between countries where convergent thinking is present as compared with countries where philosophies diverge significantly. The European Commission sees the World Trade Organization as the suitable agency to promote cooperation on an international framework for competition rules, and supported the setting up of the Working Group on Trade and Competition in Singapore in 1996 (Schaub, 1998). However, if most countries exempt conferences from competition rules, such cooperation is moot as far as this industry is concerned; shipping has been absent from this group's domain of discussion.

---

[2]    The member countries are Australia, Belgium, Canada, Denmark, Finland, France, Germany, Greece, Italy, Japan, Korea, Mexico, Netherlands, Norway, Poland, Sweden, Switzerland, Turkey, United Kingdom and United States. The EC also sits as a member.

[3]    Soft harmonization is the goal. Hard harmonization requires identical regimes; this is an unrealistic expectation in an international environment where some countries seek improved consumer welfare (e.g., the US) while others (e.g., Japan) seek community welfare or multilateral integration (e.g., Europe).

[4]    W. Hubner, Organization for Economic Cooperation and Development, personal interview, 6 July 1998.

[5]    Decision of the Council and Commission of 10 April 1995 concerning the conclusion of the Agreement between the European Communities and the Government of the United States of America regarding the application of their competition laws, *Official Journal of the European Communities*, L95, 27.4.95, 45.

[6]    The more than 300 cases cited were reported in 1998 in documents provided by D. Wood of DG IV.

Research to examine the issue of international harmonization of liner shipping competition rules has been surprisingly limited (Brooks, 1998; Weil, 1997; Jackson, 1997). Therefore, this chapter explores the philosophy of liner shipping regulation and the key issues with respect to industry regulation, identifying those areas where there has been greater convergence in regulatory thinking and those areas where divergence will continue to be an irritant to the industry and potentially restrict its ability to innovate to meet the needs of trading interests. To do so, it relies heavily on Appendix D at the end of the previous chapter. This chapter then identifies a set of guiding principles to narrow the regulatory gap, drawing conclusions that may serve as future discussion points for regulators. What remains is to establish an appropriate forum for discussion.

## THE REGULATORY DILEMMA

Figure 9.1 illustrates a hypothetical major trade. The small shaded circles represent shipping lines. The heavy line encloses those which belong to a conference while the thin lines enclose those belonging to one of the four alliances operating on the trade lane. Some carriers exist outside the conference and are not members of an alliance (the lonely circles at the bottom); they are the traditional non-conference competition. Other carriers are members of an alliance but not of a conference (the circles at the right of the conference box),[7] while still others are members of a conference but not of an alliance.[8]

### Figure 9.1: The Regulatory Dilemma

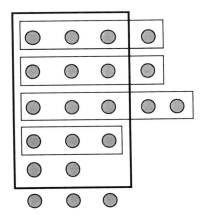

---

7    As an example, Hanjin, DSR-Senator and Cho Yang are alliance members, but only DSR-Senator is a member of the Far Eastern Freight Conference.

8    This illustration is not unrealistic as Sea-Land and Maersk are the only alliance completely within the conferences on the major trades (although they do operate on the north Atlantic outside the conference system in the service from Montreal).

The multi-layered dilemma becomes apparent when the rules applying to the industry are superimposed. First is the matter of jurisdiction. If the industry was confined to a single jurisdiction, this might not pose to be a problem if that jurisdiction declared its policy priorities by identifying whichever set of rules had precedence. The dilemma for shipping is that, with the exception of domestic trades, there is always more than one jurisdiction to be considered. In the case of the US and Europe for this industry, the jurisdictional conflict has moved from genteel to hot debate.

Second, one set of rules applies to conferences and a contradictory set applies to alliances. In Chapter 8 one simple illustration of this dilemma was presented—the definitions of a conference and a consortium. For example, if a consortium wishes to engage in price discussions, under EU law it must become a small conference; under US law it will then be required to be open to new members which defeats the managerial purposes of the consortium. It becomes an unbroken circle entrapping the lines, a perfect illustration of this regulatory dilemma.

Another illustration of the second dilemma is the divergence between European and US regulation with respect to multimodal pricing. Consortia in Europe must restrict their operations to the marine part of the move, as it is illegal to fix the price on inland, terminal or air transport parts of the journey. Yet, they are allowed to quote multimodal through rates under both the US and Canadian regulation. Ruttley (1991:17) concluded that

> *it is an unfortunate fact that the Council did not see fit to adopt the European Parliament's suggestion that the block exemption on liner conferences in Article 3 of Regulation 4056/86 be expanded to cover intermodal transport services.*

and that

> *A general criticism of the structure of competition law regime in this sector is the serious incompatibility between the multimodal nature of modern shipping services and the rigid distinction created by the Commission's interpretation of the scope of Regulation 1017/68 (inland transport), Regulation 4056/86 (international maritime services) and Regulation 17/62 (ancillary services to transport).*

Since he made these comments, Commission Regulation 870/95 has been implemented but failed to address this criticism. It is unfortunate that the consortia exemption rules under Commission Regulation 870/95 were not expanded to cover inland transportation services, given the business fact that a door-to-door service package is the way the buyer purchases the service and that intra-trade lane competition is the necessary unit under which to examine whether there is an abuse of market power or a lessening of competition. Should such an extension take place, transparency of all parts of the price would be necessary.

On the other hand, there appears to be nothing to prevent two or three separate lines, inside or outside an alliance, from setting up a logistics joint venture, with separate authority, to manage the inland service and compete against existing suppliers. Such a proposition would enable the carriers to avoid DG IV scrutiny but they would also lose the ability to undertake any cross-subsidization between inland legs and ocean legs. The signal delivered by the regulatory authority is that joint ventures are preferable to alliances.

Discussion agreements provide an excellent further illustration of the regulatory dilemma. They are considered cooperative working agreements by US authorities but are now prohibited under European law. The first discussion agreement was Eurocorde,[9] a voluntary agreement including conference carriers and independents like Evergreen and Polish Ocean Lines. In 1991, the FMC conducted a Section 6(g) audit of Eurocorde as it had more than 90% market share in the Europe–US east coast trade lane and found that, even with the high market share, the group of lines was unable to effectively raise rates. Eurocorde was replaced by the TAA and then TACA, with the European Commission concluding that discussion agreements were not conferences and therefore not able to avail themselves of antitrust immunity for their activities.

Are discussion agreements, as a form of alliance, anti-competitive? The findings of the FMC Section 6(g) investigation into Eurocorde would suggest not. This does not mean that discussion agreements could not, in future, provide the vehicle for anti-competitive activity. The FMC has continued to be concerned about discussion agreements as they may provide a means of abusing dominant position. To do so would require the group of companies in a discussion agreement to have much greater resolve to act in concert than has been evident to date. It would appear that current market conditions, with the significant excess capacity brought on by the injection of post-Panamax tonnage, are unlikely to encourage more than price maintenance efforts. Members of a discussion agreement would need to see capacity utilization rates rise (indicating that price rises might have a chance of sticking) before they would likely have that prerequisite resolve. Regulatory monitoring of circumstances and the activities of discussion agreement members through filing of minutes and reports is adequate; the threat of a Section 6(g) investigation is a sufficient deterrent to prevent abuse. Until recently, there appeared to be no evidence that DG IV's stand on discussion agreements was appropriate. Circumstances changed in 1998 and the antitrust immunity accorded discussion agreements came under scrutiny in the aftermath of the Asian currency crisis.

In Fact Finding Investigation 23 (Won, 1999), Commissioner Won looked into the practices of the Transpacific Stabilization Agreement during the 1998 eastbound peak shipping season (from July to November 1998). He found that members of discussion agreements can act in an anti-competitive manner once market conditions improve. At the time, there was the unusual situation at play—demand exceeded supply. Carriers within the TSA found vessel utilization to be at or near 100% on the eastbound leg while the westbound leg was depressed as a result of the Asian meltdown the previous fall. With large numbers of containers to reposition and no ability to increase revenue eastbound, carriers took advantage of the westbound situation to engage in a number of unacceptable practices. These included, for example, singling out NVOCC cargoes for rejection or space discrimination, refusing to carry cargo under existing contracts, mis-rating bills of lading, demanding bribes and entering into individual service contracts at higher rates not authorized by the conference. Commissioner Won reported that

---

9    FMC Agreement Number 202-10829.

the Transpacific Stabilization Agreement (a discussion agreement) replaced the conference agreement as the rate-making group on the trade lane and that the carriers did not meet the standard of reasonableness, equity and fairness desirable in apportioning the available cargo space under the current regulatory regime (the *Shipping Act of 1984*). Furthermore, it was clear that the minutes of all meetings were not filed with the FMC as required under the regulations. The Fact Finding Investigation concluded that abuse had taken place and that

> *the Commission must carefully examine the extent of its authority and resources to protect the public under circumstances where various layers of antitrust immunity (slot charters, alliances, conferences and TSA, in addition to other discussion agreements) combine with unusual economic conditions to permit carriers to extort price increases that would not otherwise be possible under competitive market conditions.* (Won, 1999:9)

Won concluded that competition was eliminated in the eastbound transpacific trade lane and not likely to be restored in the near future. A formal investigation has been initiated and if these findings are proved, penalties will result. Given the existence of confidential contracting after the implementation of the *Ocean Shipping Reform Act of 1998* on 1 May 1999, it is unclear whether the activities of the TSA will jeopardize the future of discussion agreements as an acceptable alliance in the US trades.

Finally, a third dilemma exists: should an alliance be treated as a merger? There is no reason to treat internally competitive alliances as though they had internalized all activities unless they cross the "brand" divide. The maintenance of separate identities, brands, sales forces and customer service departments leaves competition between alliance members still active. Brooks (1995) concluded that problem-solving capability of the sales force remains a key determinant of choice of carrier. When, as we currently see with American Airlines and Japan Air Lines, a swapping of sales staff and the signing of reciprocal agency agreements occurs, the line has been crossed. Has it been crossed with revenue sharing? Clear rules are needed to set the boundary of when an alliance becomes a virtual merger and therefore should be treated as such.

This dilemma should also be addressed at the multilateral level. As we have seen with airlines in Chapter 6, bilateral resolution is not satisfactory; it hampers efficient and innovative solutions by the companies working within the regulatory framework as the lowest common denominator applies.

## CONVERGENCE AND DIVERGENCE

### Convergence

Convergence has occurred on a number of fronts including **basic principles** such as the need for free and fair competition; maintenance of market access; economic efficiency; transparency of laws, regulations and the rule-making processes; and international compatibility.[10]

---

10    W. Hubner, Organization for Economic Cooperation and Development, personal interview, 6 July 1998.

Agreement that laws and regulations should adapt and respond to industry changes and result in a predictable outcome was also forthcoming from the member countries of the Maritime Transport Committee of the OECD. Most countries agree that shippers should have the freedom to enter into contractual arrangements with whichever carriers and modes of transport best serve their needs; this includes the freedom to make their own inland arrangements.

Convergence has tenuously occurred in the area of **self-regulation**. Liner conferences have largely been left to police themselves although there have been requirements in some jurisdictions for tariff-filing. Only in the US has there been a concerted effort to enforce tariffs filed. As the US moved closer to a model of self-regulation, by removing the requirement to file tariffs in favour of their publication under the *Ocean Shipping Reform Act of 1998*, DG IV is reconsidering its stance on self-regulation, as noted at the beginning of the last chapter. This would, in a deregulating world, be a step away from harmonization.

Many countries continue to accept that conferences should have **antitrust immunity**. Japan has reviewed its legislation and the Ministry of Transport and the Fair Trade Commission have agreed to retain the exemption from Anti-Monopoly Law for shipping conferences (but there will be a study team to establish standards for the granting of immunity). In particular, the Fair Trade Commission was concerned about discussion agreements, arguing that they strongly restrict competition (*Hong Kong Shipping Gazette*, 1998). While shipper groups in Canada, the US and the EU have called for an end to antitrust immunity, such immunity remains a cornerstone of the conference policy of these three countries. While there are signs that the case for immunity is weakening, with core theory proponents remaining adamant about its continuation, how long antitrust immunity will be the platform of choice is unclear.

With the passage of the *Ocean Shipping Reform Act of 1998*, the US moved closer to the European Commission and Canadian view of **confidential contracting**. Confidential service contracts will be allowed, as they are already in Europe and Canada. Service contracts have benefits for both parties and are seen as a win-win situation. Carriers are able to make a regular buyer out of one that previously only purchased services on a transaction-by-transaction basis, while time-volume rates secure the carrier's base business. Shippers believe that service contracts help them avoid future rate increases while providing guaranteed service.[11] What remains a divergence, however, is the position taken on whether joint service contracts are permissible.

There appears also to be general consensus on the **exclusion of capacity management** programs from accepted conference activities. While capacity management was initially allowed by the FMC, it has not been acceptable to the EU and the US has moved closer over time to the European position. This is not to say that FMC opposition to capacity management is written in stone. With the recent proposed reformulation of TACA as the North Atlantic Agreement, the FMC looked closely at its internal workings, raising questions about the possibility of it containing a capacity management program. Neither the FMC nor DG IV was

---

11    Shashikumar (1989:17, Table 4). Service contract rates were also perceived to be lower.

completely satisfied and, shortly after, the agreement was withdrawn. In Canada, a firm stance on capacity management has not materialized given the FMC and the EU moves against it.

Convergence has also occurred in the area of **independent action** as a pro-competitive tool to ensure greater intra-conference competition. The EU has made it mandatory while the US has allowed conference carriers to prohibit its use only on a short list of exempt commodities. Independent action is encouraged under SCEA. The three are quite close in agreeing on the ability of independent action to encourage intra-conference competition and act as a brake on anti-competitive behaviour. There is evidence that independent action has retained conference members, and stability, in conditions that would otherwise cause disintegration of a conference.

Finally, there is a general belief that the promotion of compatibility **does not require the standardization of competition rules worldwide.**[12] Extending professional courtesy, though intergovernmental notification of any planned public reviews of legislation, regulations, and commercial or non-technical agreements, is a start down the road towards harmonization. However, gaps remain in other elements of the policies affecting liner shipping and they will continue to be perilously large.

## Divergence

One critical area of divergence in competition policy with respect to liner shipping is the issue of **which authority** should regulate the industry nationally. In many countries, liner shipping is recognized as a unique sector and regulated by a particular agency viewed to have expertise in that industry. In the EU, however, there is no such special status and conferences are given a block exemption from competition rules. Here it is the competition authority that has the controlling hand. As long as this divergence exists, we are unlikely to see a meeting of minds on principles as competition policy analysts traditionally see no reason for this industry to be treated differently while transport agencies view it as an industry with high sunk costs, marginal costs below average costs, and tendencies to destabilization through price discounting.

Furthermore, the authority identified to regulate the industry in each country has sought to **impose its national philosophy** with exceptionally limited regard for the compatibility of that philosophy with that of its trading partners. The divergence is nowhere more clearly demarcated than between the US and Europe. The FMC focuses on the behaviour of parties to the agreement (conduct), while the European Commission looks at its structure. Both seek to intervene before the undesirable performance takes place.[13] While the US approach may be too political, the European preference for proscription has its flaws; proscription is subject to erosion of its effectiveness over time. It is better to set guidelines for outcomes rather than the

---

[12] W. Hubner, Organization for Economic Cooperation and Development, personal interview, 6 July 1998.

[13] Using the managerial framework of Figure 2.1 by Galbraith and Kazanjian (1978), the Europeans seek to intervene at the Market Structure element by providing market share thresholds while the FMC seeks to intervene during the Strategy Formulation stage. For both, evidence of potentially unacceptable behaviour can trigger an investigation but so can notification of exceeding thresholds in the cases of both Canada and Europe. The existence of behavioural triggers only is problematic.

method by which they will be achieved. There must be some clear middle ground. Structural thresholds offer the regulatory authority a clear signal that investigation is warranted while behavioural triggers encourage political interference. Neither end of the continuum is entirely satisfactory but some combination of the two could be highly effective.

A third key area of divergence is the **treatment of inland transport**. The details of this area of divergence are documented over several pages in Appendix D.[14] This divergence is growing rather than waning and is rapidly becoming a make or break regulation for shipping lines. Inland transport may account for as much as 75% of a line's cost base.[15] The EU has consistently opposed the development of joint inland tariffs by conferences while the US has allowed the quotation of a through rate and, ironically, recently supported the carriers operating to and from Latin American countries to develop joint inland tariffs (Anonymous, 1998a). This is an area of high priority to resolve.

Another area of divergence is the **treatment of agreements which are not strictly conference agreements**. The EU has developed separate regulation to recognize that alliances (consortia) are different from conferences and therefore should have specific regulation. On the other hand, Canada and other nations such as Australia have treated these agreements as simply another form of conference agreement without recognizing that such a path may present challenges if between conference and non-conference members. Discussion agreements, which have the potential to diminish competition and adversely affect shipper interests if effectively implemented, are accepted by most OECD countries but not by the European Commission. Antitrust immunity for discussion agreements was continued under the new US legislation. It is critical that this divergence be addressed in any harmonization move.

With the passage of Commission Regulation 870/95, the EU explicitly defined **market share thresholds** on both conference and non-conference consortia, moving down a path not followed by others. It is unclear if such limits may stifle alliance development or may indeed usefully serve to prevent abuse of dominant position. It is clear, however, that such structural limits have been imposed on cartels in other industries within the EC[16] and on mergers within the US.[17] Since 1996, the FMC has requested market share reports from those filing agreements;[18] this allows the FMC to identify when monitoring activity needs to become more focused. The use of market share thresholds as a trigger for monitoring is widely accepted by competition authorities. It may be adopted by those countries where other agencies regulate

---

14  Even Japan allows through rates so it appears that the EC stands alone on this issue. H. Yamada (1998); this correspondence with the author, 7 October, detailed Japanese rules with respect to inland transport.

15  This percentage is the one widely used in the trade press. Table 4.6 illustrated a smaller percentage for transpacific traffic. Without a doubt, inland transport accounts for a larger share of total costs than the ocean leg and, being beyond the control of most lines, becomes a cause for concern.

16  See Council Regulation 4064/89 of 21 December 1989 on the control of concentrations between undertakings, *Official Journal of the European Communities*, L395, 30.12.89, 1

17  *Hart-Scott-Rodino Antitrust Improvements Act of 1976*, Pub. L. 94-435, 90 Stat. 1383.

18  R. Blair, Federal Maritime Commission, personal interview, 20 January 1998. These reports supplement FMC use of the PIERS market share data and provide data in a form desired by the FMC.

conferences. With such a system, lines should be able to predict when their activities are likely to trigger investigation and therefore plan accordingly. There should be no surprises.

There is significant divergence on the scope of **service contracts**. Service contracts and time-volume rates provide stability for both carrier and shipper, and provide stability to the carrier as these commodities may form the base traffic for the route. Individual confidential service contracts are now allowed in all three. It remains problematic for conferences that the US allows joint service contracts while the EC sets stringent guidelines. In Canada, the conference controls terms and conditions. With the move towards more individual contracting in the US, conference solidarity will likely face further erosion.

While confidential contracting may be approximately compatible and the principle of common carriage effectively breached in all three jurisdictions, the sub-elements of **loyalty contracting** and **rebating** remain areas of divergence, with Canada and the US on one end of the continuum and the European Commission on the other. As the issue has not caused litigation problems for the lines, this divergence of philosophy on their appropriateness has not become a contentious issue. Should some of the larger issues be addressed through harmonization efforts, the importance of this issue will increase.

Finally, one last area of divergence is the whole subject of **filing (notification** in Europe), what is filed, why and the role filing plays in regulation. In Europe, agreements are notified so that regulators can monitor terms and conditions of service to ensure that prohibited activities do not take place; tariffs are not filed. In the US, under the *Shipping Act of 1984*, tariffs were not only filed but also monitored (and enforced) to ensure that similarly situated shippers received equal treatment. Tariff filing was to serve the purpose of ensuring that the principles of common carriage were upheld. The Canadian position has been to require filing but not enforce it. Given the US move under the *Ocean Shipping Reform Act of 1998* towards tariff publication and confidential contracting, the whole question of why tariffs are enforced becomes more difficult to answer. Regulatory reform in the US has narrowed the gap to some extent.

Current divergence in regulation results in the lowest common denominator—carriers respond to the regulatory agency with the heaviest hand on a particular issue. The net result is inefficiency when the desired outcome by all parties is an efficient industry with the flexibility to innovate and continuously improve. A climate of deregulation results in benefits passed on to cargo owners who can then take full advantage of the trade liberalization initiatives of their governments. Continuing squabbles over approaches and tools result in sub-optimal outcomes. Table 9.2 summarizes these areas of convergence and divergence for easy reference.

**Table 9.2: Summary of Convergence and Divergence in Liner Regulation**

| *Areas of Convergence* | *Areas of Divergence* |
| --- | --- |
| Basic principles regarding free and fair competition | Agency assigned authority for regulatory activities |
| The concept of self-regulation for conferences | National philosophies about regulation |
| Antitrust immunity | Treatment of inland transport |
| Confidential contracting | Treatment of discussion agreements and consortia |
| Exclusion of capacity management from accepted conference activities | Role of market share thresholds |
| Use of independent action as a pro-competitive regulatory tool | Scope of service contracts |
| Rule standardization not required | Treatment of loyalty contracts and rebating activities |
| | Regulatory administration re: tariff or agreement filing/notification/publication |

## Conclusions

*Like fire, competition should be the servant not the master.*[19]

The growth of international strategic alliances is a result of the evolution of the global economy with trade liberalization as its driving force. However, that liberalization has not been accompanied by a harmonization of regulation. In this global industry, national policies are no longer appropriate. The ability of regulators to manage anti-competitive behaviour is in serious doubt and unilateral action acts as a shot across the bow of trading partners. The "servant" has not been equipped to do its job. The current situation is untenable for both regulators and the industry.

The purpose of the conference system when founded in the 1870s was to counter destructive price competition through capacity regulation on the Europe–Far East trade route. The conference structure worked well until the balance of power in the buyer-supplier relationship shifted; early buyers had little bargaining clout and were not as sophisticated as those of today. Today, buyers of transport services are better informed and better able to use their market power against ocean carriers. As greater reliance on market mechanisms is encouraged, the role of antitrust immunity comes into question. There is a philosophical disconnect.

---

19  Standing Committee on Transport (1985), December hearings into Transport Canada's White Paper, *Freedom to Move: Change, Choice, Challenge*:4 as reported by National Transportation Act Review Commission (1993, 1:17). Reproduced with permission of the Minister of Public Works and Government Services Canada, 1999.

In 1998, Karl-Heinz Sager of DSR-Senator was reported as believing the conference system would come to an end within the three years (J. Porter, 1998). He was probably not far off the mark. With the introduction of single line confidential contracting and the removal of the "similarly situated" shipper provision through the *Ocean Shipping Reform Act of 1998*, that demise is expedited. In late October 1998, APL resigned from the Transpacific Westbound Rate Agreement (TWRA), following in the footsteps of P&O Nedlloyd and Hapag Lloyd, both of whom dropped out earlier in the year. This reduced the conference share of westbound trade to northeast Asia to less than 40% and to southeast Asia to less than 48% (Burnson, 1998:27). The ability of the TWRA to impose any stability on the route was completely undermined. John Clancy of Sea-Land has highlighted the importance of confidential service contracts under the new US regulatory climate and concluded that Sea-Land will belong to discussion agreement and not conferences in future (Boyes, 1998:53). The days of conferences as the predominant business structure for the liner industry are extremely limited.

What will be the alternative? To managers, organic growth may be dissatisfying when larger-scale opportunities through alliances or mergers present themselves. With so many players in the market, stability must be found through organizational restructuring.

Mergers and acquisitions can provide greater control and additional benefits; capacity management can, for example, be effected within a merged entity without regulatory burden or threat of intervention found in alliances. At a minimum, alliances are necessary for the efficient service and global coverage required by manufacturers competing in the global market. They enable carriers to choose the right assets for the trade and allocate them more effectively through appropriate schedules; the only missing ingredient of the operational strategy is pricing. Within the conference system, crude yield management is available. It is only alliances operating outside the conference system that have the ability to engage in finely-tuned revenue management strategies over the longer term.

As more carriers enter into consortium arrangements, they will seek greater pricing flexibility than the conference system allows—pricing that is responsive and innovative. The interplay of asset utilization, network configuration and revenue management as carrier management tools, discussed in Chapter 4, will entice alliance partners to draw the same conclusion. The effect of the conference system on dampening a carrier's or alliance's ability to innovate new approaches to pricing will chafe. As a result, the conference system will no longer be seen as the system innovative companies want and will fail as the price stabilization mechanism. The conference system will only last until a Top 20 carrier perfects revenue management the way the airlines have. Until such innovation occurs, the conference system will remain a poor managerial substitute.

The bases of competition will also continue to evolve. Competition is moving towards, if not there already, network competition; large shippers have greater clout and carriers, to service them, need to be able to compete door-to-door, either through a fully owned and integrated network, or a cooperative network that is integrated and seamless. The nullification of location as a source of competitive advantage for clusters (M. E. Porter, 1998) and their focus on greater cooperation will also move the mindset of these businesses seeking global reach towards more cooperative activities. The introduction of single line confidential contracting in the *Ocean Shipping Reform Act of 1998* will hasten the development of global contracts further altering the base of competition as shippers negotiate pricing and service delivery on a worldwide scale.

It is likely that alliances will be able, once ocean coordination is secured and partnerships consolidated globally, to move inland and develop cooperative rather than competitive packages of services, thereby ultimately building the case for the antitrust exemption they seek for inland operations. Not all alliances will evolve in so genteel a manner, however. The lack of a cohesive conference membership policy within the current global alliances indicates that many liner alliances are not as cooperative as they should be. Some carriers will be concerned about their loss of market identity, and this will be particularly problematic when cooperation moves inland, becoming more visible to the buyer of the services. Furthermore, many carriers view their information systems as competitive weapons, making systems integration an unlikely element of a competitive alliance. For these reasons, some alliances will continue to be highly competitive internally, no more than simple vessel- or slot-sharing arrangements. For some, competition will still take place intra-alliance, as carriers will be unwilling to concede all control to the alliance and many buyers will still engage in carrier choice on the service offered and the way they are treated by sales staff.

Not all carriers will restrict their relationships to simple alliances. While such simple alliances enable partner firms to address tangible assets for network reconfiguration, to use the terminology of resource-based economists, it is the addressing of intangible assets that truly attracts carriers seeking global reach. This can only be done through complex integrative alliances or mergers. The structure of the relationship is then key to its regulation.

In this emerging marketplace, niche carriers and snipers will continue to play a role, taking care of specialized or unserved needs. The global carriers cannot be all things to all purchasers, nor will they want to be. Like other market leaders in other global industries, the largest carriers will focus on core business and then, because they erode that focus, will broaden their market scope thereby creating opportunities for snipers and those who focus on serving a niche well. Some of the more successful carriers in today's transport markets are niche players and there is no reason to assume that focus strategies, if properly implemented, will fail. CP Ships' multi-trade multi-brand niche strategy has been a successful one for the company to date. They have taken advantage of the back room savings possible from some rationalization, particularly in the equipment management area, while gaining dominance in niche markets through each subsidiary's focus on core business and professional execution of a narrow differentiation strategy.

Those liner operators with the deepest pockets will endure in the short and medium term but only because they have the ability to finance a transition to new approaches to doing business. However, the absence of vision, or the managerial talent and energy to achieve that vision, may result in their failure in the long-term. Both professional operating management (as discussed in Chapter 4) and vision are required to survive the consolidation process.

In sum, liner shipping has both scale and density economies but relatively inelastic market demand. There is also limited ability to differentiate an individual company's service, particularly with slot-sharing. The differentiation then can only be made on the marketing or front office functions while the back office has become commoditized. This lends itself, at a minimum, to the use of alliances to secure operational savings but, more likely, to the merging of back office operations, coupled with the branding of front office operations, an approach which sounds remarkably similar to that pursued by CP Ships.

Access to essential infrastructure is not a limiting factor in the liner shipping market. It is in rail (due to track investment, which is partly mitigated by trackage and haulage rights) and in airlines (with landing slots and gates to control entry). Because such access is not limited, the liner market is more competitive and less protected than these other two industries. It is this environment that has seen the rise of global strategic alliances and urged this re-examination of appropriate regulatory policy.

Liner shipping explored cooperation in its early development through the formation of conferences and regulators generally agreed that antitrust immunity was appropriate for conference activities. As the marketplace evolved through growth, alliances have developed and eventually moved companies to the right along the continua of cooperation and interdependency. In the coming decade, these arrangements will mature; given the current number of players, this maturity is unlikely to be accompanied by firms capable of abusing their market share. Alliances will only become efficient and effective if the regulatory environment allows them also to be innovative. Through innovation, alliance members will also likely develop their own unique strategic characters and so challenge the boundaries of the industry. Regulators should ensure that companies are not discouraged from innovation as this will result in greater efficiency, but they must recognize that it is the outcome that is to be regulated and not the means of getting there. Multilateral harmony in liner regulation should be embraced as the ideal.

Is such multilateral harmony possible? As liberalization has strengthened, regionalism has also grown, as illustrated by the formation of trading blocs, particularly in Europe through the Single European Market and the Americas through both the *Canada–US Trade Agreement* and the *North American Free Trade Agreement*. The debate about whether we will ultimately see a world that is more multilateral or one that is more regionally oriented is well presented by Kobrin (1995). He argued that multilateralism has reached its limits,[20] noting the importance of a common set of rules with regard to public goods and the flows of trade and investment. Without common guiding principles by which anti-competitive activity may be addressed, full liberalization will move beyond the grasp of even the most committed free market advocates. It is possible to argue that culture and philosophy will prevent a common global set of guiding principles to deal with anti-competitive activity, but those common principles are still a

---

[20]  This point of view is anchored by the considerable difficulty with which new issues may be put on the agendas of multilateral fora. Few nations want to risk giving up the gains already made in order to put new issues on the table.

prerequisite to realizing real gains in trade liberalization. The goal must be to find common ground, and expeditiously. A set of guiding principles is needed.

## GUIDING PRINCIPLES[21]

The following principles express conclusions about the ideal not the existing. How the ideal becomes reality is the content of the final section of this chapter.

### Principle 1: Harmonization does not require a common philosophy; it does imply rules that are compatible and consistently applied.

It is highly unlikely that there will ever be agreement with respect to the general principle of whether conferences, or indeed consortia and other cooperative working agreements, should be dealt with by a separate regulatory body or as exceptions to standard rules of competition. There is agreement that they need a regulatory framework which recognizes that liner shipping has some unique features that render it unsuitable to be regulated by rules applying to most other industries. There must be multilateral efforts to ensure that the two ends of a trade route have rules with consistent compatibility or the current situation will not be ameliorated.

### Principle 2: Innovative business structures must be encouraged to develop.

In the past two decades there has been a transition in the role of government; it has been demonstrated that the business sector can evolve to offer, in a deregulated environment, a myriad of services which meet the needs of its customers. The nature of the business too is no longer clear cut. In place of what were once shipping lines whose core business was ocean carriage, now there are shipping lines whose core business may also include terminal operations, logistics services companies, or inland operations. The core business no longer has a clear, definable boundary. Such innovation is good, however, as it delivers the range of benefits sought by the market and the wide range of needs is better served. Regulation needs to incorporate a more flexible view of business structures and focus on ensuring that the outcome is in the public interest, not that the structure is proscribed.

### Principle 3: Conferences do not serve the same purposes as alliances. There is scope to regulate them differently, recognizing that a hierarchy of regulatory regimes must be established so that the order of the application of the regulations is clear when both apply.

From its inception in the 1870s to the early 1980s, the conference system worked relatively well to provide stability for buyers of its services. With the growing power of buyers and the

---

21  For the purpose of these principles, the terms alliance and consortium are used interchangeably. The term cooperative working agreement is not used, except in its broadest sense as including all agreements for cooperation.

shipping business and regulatory climate, the role of conferences has diminished in the past 15 or so years as alliances have been introduced. The two do not serve the same purposes.

The conference system is a mechanism for pricing and crude revenue management in the face of excess capacity; conferences serve to suppress short-run price competition thereby providing some measure of short-term stability to the market. (Conferences do not fully suppress price competition because of the existence of non-conference carriers and the potential for conference members to cheat on the agreement, or take independent action.) They also establish a standard set of terms and conditions for the transaction.

Alliances and joint ventures are mechanisms that strengthen asset utilization and encourage optimization of the network configuration; the result should be capacity appropriate for the strategic scope of the business. An alliance competes against other alliances **as a network** and therefore includes the inland component of the network. In other words, these business structures serve to improve the conditions of long-run competition.

While there is no justification for similar regulation for both conferences and consortia, the regulation must be compatible. Europe is correct to have regulatory rules (Commission Regulation 870/95) that discriminate between the two forms of business conduct but Europe's existing regulation fails to recognize the network as the basis of competition. It has been called by Farthing and Brownrigg (1997:139) a confused and rigid instrument; its expiration on 21 April 2000 provides the opportunity for the European Commission to revise its regulation of consortia and recognize the need for some migration towards greater harmony and the competitive base of a network.[22]

The drivers for alliances and joint ventures are similar to each other and to those for merger, but are dissimilar to the drivers for conference participation. Different purposes, different organizational structure, different corporate conduct, different outcome, and different competition concerns should spell distinct regulatory approaches.

Regulatory oversight for alliances, joint ventures and mergers should be internally consistent. If structural or behavioural limits are imposed on mergers, the same limits should apply to alliances as a network. This becomes particularly critical once alliances engage in joint marketing activities and cease to compete in the front office—the interface with the buyer. While Europe has set an individual market share trigger for further monitoring, it is worth contemplating an approximately similar threshold for firms seeking to use alliances.

It is important that a hierarchy of the two sets of regulation be established, that is, that one takes precedence over the other and that this precedence be harmonized multilaterally as well as clearly enunciated. Without this condition, the divergence between the sets of regulation

---

[22] On 28 January, DG IV released a working paper *Report on Commission Regulation No. 870/95*, as a discussion document laying out a timetable for this review process. The document concluded that the Commission will likely review the retulation, possibly with minor modifications. 15 January 2000 is the deadline set for reaction.

becomes unmanageable and inconsistently applied. Consistency and clarity are the highest priorities for business planning and investment.

**Principle 4: The law should be "outcome neutral" with respect to the structural choice of merger, acquisition, joint venture or alliance as a growth option.**

Mergers in the industry are driven by economies of scale and the ability to internalize the benefits of both alliances and conferences. Therefore, they already have an intrinsic benefit over alliances in that, once cleared by the Department of Justice in the US or DG IV in Europe, the two participants become a single entity without the need to become embroiled in litigation with regulators about activities now internal to the firm: prices charged to customers or management of capacity. The speed with which mergers can surmount regulatory hurdles is clear from the P&O Nedlloyd case discussed in Chapter 7. Alliances can engage in capacity management through reconfiguration of service patterns and the overall redeployment of assets, but will always be subject to regulatory oversight as they rationalize activities.

The alliance umbrella affords the carrier the opportunity to manage capacity and improve vessel utilization without the financial or relationship commitment inherent in the merger, acquisition or joint venture alternatives. The alliance umbrella also offers the carrier market reach, as do marketing agreements and vessel sharing agreements. There is concern expressed in some quarters that if the regulation of consortia becomes too onerous, it will encourage merger activity, which may be less desirable from a regulatory point of view than a pro-competitive alliance.

Butz (1991) identified an important element to remember in examining liner shipping conferences and alliances: intrafirm competition is foreclosed with a merger while, with conferences and alliances, rivalry between participants remains an important source of competition. Regulation should not promote the formation of alliances over mergers (and vice versa) so that carriers will make alliance versus merger decisions on the grounds of managerial preference and the commercial benefits afforded by the chosen option. Regulatory burden should not be the primary driver of commercial decisions.

**Principle 5: Conferences and consortia should be required to file (notify) agreements to competition authorities in return for antitrust immunity, but tariff publication should be reviewed as a principle.**

If tariff publication or filing no longer serves to uphold a regulatory regime based on principles of common carriage, effective enforcement of policy objectives mandates the filing of agreements (along with meeting minutes and other decision documents as requested). Carriers may choose to publish tariffs for the information of their customers. Carriers may also choose to publish tariffs in the belief that such publication maintains market discipline. Such publication may also serve as a signal to another carrier that a trade lane is ripe for a new entrant because the price holds the promise of profitability. As there is no "similarly situated" shipper to protect under any legislation currently in force in the US, Canada or Europe, the purpose of tariff publication, except to meet the entrenched regulatory requirement,[23] is in doubt. A multilateral discussion about its purpose would prove worthwhile.

**Principle 6: The definition of the relevant market should focus on the trade lane with port ranges at either end.**

New infrastructure developments such as the Channel Tunnel can alter routing decisions. So can new technology, such as FastShip Atlantic, a high-speed catamaran service for cars and other high value goods. Government policies, such as the US imposition of a replacement tax for the Harbour Maintenance Tax, or increases in user fees for government services, all drive the dynamic restructuring of network configurations by competing lines. Likewise, as proposed in Figure 3.2, changes to the strategies used by competing lines, be they market followers, state-supported lines, or other modes of transport, can alter the state of competition on a trade lane. With the increasing importance of network competition, we can only be certain that the interpretation of the relevant geographic market as the route between a port-pair is too narrow.

**Principle 7: Capacity management by consortia should be allowed but not by conferences or wider cooperative agreements.**

As a consortium is an organizational structure enabling its members to optimize network configuration, the members fail to achieve their desired objective if they are prevented from participating in capacity management activities within the consortium. For the purposes of back office activities, such as vessel operations, the consortium should be treated as a single entity rather than as a group. Only then will the benefits of alliance cooperation be felt. This does not mean that capacity management activity is desirable in a conference or a discussion agreement. There remain, at the alliance level of consolidation on a route, a sufficient number of other players to limit any anti-competitive effects arising from such capacity management.

**Principle 8: The activities of discussion agreements should be severely proscribed and monitored.**

Discussion agreements should have antitrust immunity so long as their activities do not include price-fixing, capacity management or such anticompetitive practices. Discussion agreements, it has been concluded by the Federal Maritime Commission (Hsu, 1998), make it possible for carriers to establish broad networks with more service routes and faster transit times, a very pro-shipper outcome. Discussion agreements also serve a useful forum for the determination of service standards for a route; filing or notification of their agreements facilitates regulatory scrutiny. If the FMC investigation proves Won's findings in Fact Finding Investigation 23 (Won, 1999), the role played by discussion agreements should be revisited, strictly regulated and monitored to prevent participants from engaging in predatory practices in a rising market.

---

[23]  The UNCTAD Liner Code requires tariff availability but how that availability is executed should be discussed.

**Principle 9: Price-fixing by conferences should continue to be exempt from antitrust regulation for the short to medium term only.**

Antitrust immunity for conference price-fixing activity grants some measure of short-run stability, albeit tempered by confidential service contracts and mandatory independent action. While conferences have generally not been able to control trade sufficiently to impose significant and sustainable price rises, they have served the purpose of slowing, if not limiting, rate wars in times of declining volumes. The antitrust immunity has served this useful purpose.

The remaining question then becomes whether to allow consortia to engage in price-fixing via conference participation or to allow price-fixing to take place under the consortium umbrella. Preventing non-conference consortium members from discussing prices with conference consortium members is difficult to police.

Conference members agree to a standard set of practices to govern pricing and membership affords an opportunity to stabilize service in what might be an otherwise unstable environment. Through internal discipline, self-regulating conferences have the ability to stabilize prices without the destructive competition inherent in highly capital-intensive industries. The days of conferences as a stabilizing mechanism are as limited as the days of conference existence. If antitrust immunity for conferences OR consortia but not both is legislated, conferences will not survive. However, if we extend antitrust immunity to revenue management activities within a consortium, conferences may fail but the system will be stabilized by the benefits of alliance participation.

Now is not the time to remove antitrust immunity from conferences. The day will come, however, when it will no longer be necessary. The strategic alliances now strengthening will continue to do so, and be encouraged further if a harmonized regulatory environment can be put in place; ultimately alliances will replace conferences as the dominant means of cooperation to ensure market stability. When that happens, antitrust immunity for consortia will be all that is required and authorities can agree to eliminate immunity for conferences and discussion agreements. The potential for abuse of dominant position by alliances would be limited by the application of structural guidelines and close monitoring by regulatory authorities.

**Principle 10: Until antitrust immunity is withdrawn, conference membership should be closed.**

Only the US has open conferences. Butz (1991:E30) argued that the US should consider adopting closed conferences for five reasons: (1) closed conferences tend to be smaller than open ones, (2) closed conferences are in a better position to exploit efficiency gains possible from cooperation, (3) they are in effect in all other jurisdictions, (4) ending both independent action and instituting closed conferences would make it easier to identify anti-competitive behaviour, and (5) firms should be able to form binding agreements with other firms of their own choosing, not then possible under US regulation.

The closed conference system ensures that parties agree to the terms or face sanctions, whatever may be legal. It enables its members to impose price discipline. The open conference system with independent action, service contracts and confidential contracting is no longer required as these three mechanisms are sufficient to counter any potential for abuse inherent in the closed system, particularly if shippers' associations have antitrust immunity for their dealings with conferences.

**Principle 11: Price-fixing by consortia should be allowed if they do not exceed an established market share threshold and do market their services as if they were a single entity with a single sales force.**

The key feature of a cooperative as opposed to competitive alliance is one in which the participants cease to trade on their individual brand identities. If the service is marketed as a single service, the price charged to the buyer should be uniform. How the participant secures its longer-term place in the market will depend on its productive capacity and its managerial skill on the operations side. As a group, they will succeed in branding the alliance and securing customers or the alliance will inevitably fail to extract all the possible advantages available to it, facing the commercial consequences of diminished competitiveness.

**Principle 12: The component parts of the door-to-door price paid by shippers should be transparent.**

The ability to ensure that abuse of dominant position does not take place partly rests with providing the buyer of the service with sufficient information to undertake its own analysis of its market situation. Shippers, if component prices are readily observable, are able to undertake comparison shopping, securing on their own account that which they do not find at an acceptable price in the marketplace. If invoices are transparent, with all elements of the price tallied, they are able to compare both the total door-to-door delivered price and any part of that price. It also enables shippers to determine if they are better served by a third party service— the value added by each supplier should become clearer. Such transparency also enables regulators to undertake confidential audits and encourages lines to be accountable to their customers. Such transparency should make the market operate more efficiently and encourage lines to compete on the services desired by customers. This transparency does not prevent inland joint prices by consortia as there will remain plenty of non-consortia prices available.

**Principle 13: The regulatory process should be timely.**

In today's global and dynamic trading environment, and with the capabilities available through electronic media for communication, there is no excuse for slow and burdensome regulation. Timeliness is an essential requirement in today's global business environment and it should be incumbent upon regulatory authorities to ensure that decision-making is undertaken in a timely manner in all regulatory processes. To encourage timeliness, the burden of proof will likely need to be imposed on the carrier.

**Principle 14: National regulation of conferences and consortia is undesirable.**

This is an era of global trade; national regulation runs counter to the liberalization of trade and its attendant benefits. Nowhere is this more critical than in the area of competition policy, irrespective of the industry under discussion. A global regulatory scheme for this industry is necessary to its future well-being. While some might argue that the availability of the UNCTAD Code is sufficient, the absence of the US from its list of signatories and its lack of applicability to consortia limits its further consideration.

There is still a role for conferences, that of an industry association responsible for setting standards for its members, lobbying on behalf of the industry for international uniformity of interpretation of harmonized policies by national governments, and serving as an umbrella organization for the development of support services, particularly in the terminal development and hardware sharing areas where trade imbalances make investments particularly costly. It can also play its traditional role of encouraging short-term stability.

It is equally clear that consortia or alliances in this industry need a broader regulatory climate than is afforded by national regulation. To regulate one end of a trade lane is to perpetuate the current regulatory dilemma. The industry is changing rapidly and participants need encouragement to adopt technological change and innovate in the way they do business. The current situation has a chilling effect on innovation and encourages the lines to channel funds towards government relations activities and political lobbying instead of towards making their activities more efficient and customer-focused.

**Principle 15: In the longer term, a supranational regulatory agency should be established to provide regulatory oversight for the industry.**

If not national regulation of either conferences or consortia, then a new mechanism for the international regulation of liner shipping is needed. This will require a new role for national governments and establishment of an appropriate forum for development of the regulatory policy. The guidelines for such a regulatory agency, perhaps as part of the World Trade Organization, would be negotiated by governments recognizing Principle 14.

### SETTING A NEW COURSE

Dunning (1997:364) pointed out the critical paradox of the global economy:

*Globalization is not reducing the role of national governments. But it is changing its raison d'être and its content ... a free market needs strong government.*

As markets have become more liberalized, resources have been allocated more efficiently through market mechanisms. The need for an interventionist role for government in the allocation of resources has diminished. However, as globalization of trade has gained ground, there is also the dilemma that a by-product of more efficient resource allocation is a widening gap between the wealthy and those not so fortunate, both within a single nation and between the developed and developing world. As the gap widens, the role of the state in developing human resources and commercial infrastructure grows ever more important to prosperity in the face of declining protectionism. As explained by Dunning, a single nation's competitiveness rests now on its ability to supply location-bound assets to attract or retain firm-specific mobile assets.

*The Economist* argues that even if all trade barriers were abolished, some markets would still not have free trade (Anonymous, 1998b). Liberalization of trade and foreign direct investment policies must be balanced by strengthening of competition policy to prevent private firms from erecting replacement barriers for those dismantled by governments. While certainly the argument exists to provide countermeasures to the disparity that freer trade yields socially, it is also the regulatory dilemma discussed in this chapter that presses this industry towards a speedier resolution of the issues. What is needed from governments is a commitment and a political will to develop an agreed framework that promotes an efficient industry, along with a dispute resolution mechanism to deal with infractions and regulatory concerns. The needs of industry and the role of government need to find a new balance.[24]

Dunning (1997:57) also noted that most large multinationals have restructured their organizations to respond to the demand of globalization, but there is little evidence that governments have yet made this move. He attributed this reluctance to the inflexibility and intransigence of established regimes, arguing that there is room on the WTO agenda to add issues of supranational importance. Whether liner shipping regulation is a high priority for that agenda is very doubtful.

Litigation is untenable as it presses national policy on a subject of multilateral jurisdiction. What would, therefore, serve as an appropriate forum for development of a new global regulatory policy? The OECD was one which held promise but failed to follow through.[25]

Another possibility would be to mediate resolution between the US and Europe on the assumption that such a mediated resolution between the extremes would find a common ground more closely approximating what the rest of the world might adopt. Given its significant investment in understanding the issues through its Part X Review, Australia is a highly respected country which could lead the discussions as "honest broker." This may be reinforced by its ranking as the "most fair" competition policy country by the IMD World Competitiveness Report (Anonymous, 1998c).

The World Trade Organization has two possible avenues: the Competition Policy agenda and the Maritime Transport Services agenda. The WTO failed to gain agreement on the Maritime Transport Services negotiation at Marrakesh but negotiations are to resume by the year 2000. So far it has been the US' position—in particular its unwillingness to put the protection

---

[24]  Mintzberg (1996) provided a thoughtful book on the role of government in future.

[25]  The OECD Maritime Transport Committee had the opportunity to develop a solution but failed to show leadership by leaving its discussions in an "Official Use" format thereby denying the opportunity for wider public debate.

provided by the *Merchant Marine Act of 1920*, commonly called the Jones Act[26] on the table—that has derailed these talks, but perhaps a whole new agenda on liner shipping regulation could free the logjam. As for the Competition Policy discussions, the process is considered by many as likely to be long and arduous and not at all in the foreseeable future (Anonymous, 1998d). There are many issues already on the agenda for these discussions and to choose this path would not be timely. Furthermore, according to Graham and Richardson (1997:559), the absence of political will to build an institutional framework for international law and enforcement limits the likelihood of this outcome occurring.

Whatever the process, it is clear that governments have accepted that the nature of the liner shipping is unique. It therefore seems most logical that a sector-specific multilateral agreement is most appropriate, one that provides a global set of regulations cognizant of both the evolution of transport business structures and the global scope of the aspirations of shipping industry participants.

To date, governments have done little more than sign bilateral agreements and agree to disagree. One only needs to contemplate the situation facing the airline industry discussed in Chapter 6. While positive comity through competition bilaterals is a first step, much more needs to be accomplished. The industry needs to support a process of multilateral regulatory development. With more than 50% of the world's liner capacity owned by 20 companies, it may be far easier to get bureaucratic progress if it becomes a priority for the majority of these key players. Otherwise, resolution by litigation is promoted and planning for healthy business growth is less important than a good VP Regulatory Affairs.

---

26  *Merchant Marine Act*, 46 U.S.C.A. § 863 (1920).

# BIBLIOGRAPHY

**Author's Note**: This bibliography does not include web site citations, press releases, company brochures, company *Annual Reports*, personal interviews or minor legal citations. These appear only in the footnotes. Significant legal citations appear at the front of the book (following the Table of Contents).

## REFERENCES FOR CHAPTER 1

ACCOS (1992), Report of the Advisory Commission on Conferences in Ocean Shipping, Washington, DC, April.

Anonymous (1990), "EC Shipping Policy Flagging," *Lloyd's Shipping Economist*, February, 5.

Beargie, T. (1994), "Carriers Paid a Price for TACA," *American Shipper*, December, 17.

Bellamy, C. and G. D. Child (1987), *Common Market Law of Competition*, London: Sweet & Maxwell.

Bonney, J. (1995), "Hanjin, Tricon Tighten Global Alliance," *American Shipper*, August, 36.

Booz-Allen & Hamilton Inc. (1990), *Strategic Shifts in World Liner Markets*, Presentation at Halifax Port Days, 10 September.

Bott, A. (1990), "Playing Field Imbalances," *Transport*, September, 207-11.

Brooks, M. R. (1998), "Competition in Liner Shipping: Are National Policies Appropriate?" *Ocean Yearbook*, 13, 142-66.

Brooks, M. R., R. G. Blunden and C. I. Bidgood (1993), "Strategic Alliances in the Global Container Transport Industry," R. Culpan (ed.), *Multinational Strategic Alliances*, Binghamton, NY: Haworth Press, 221-48.

Brooks, M. R. and K. J. Button (1992), "Shipping Within the Framework of a Single European Market," *Transport Reviews*, 12, 3, 237-51.

Canna, E. (1994), "Notes and Comments," *American Shipper*, December, 43.

Canna, E. (1995), "Van Miert Moves Towards TACA Fines," *American Shipper*, August, 21.

Clancy, J. P. (1995), "Seeking Better Returns," *International Container Review*, London: Contract Communications, 9-11.

Consumer & Corporate Affairs (1991), *Merger Enforcement Guidelines*, Ottawa: Supply and Services Canada.

*Containerisation International*, various issues.

*Containerisation International Yearbook*, various years.

Davison, D. (1998), "Transatlantic Transition," *Containerisation International*, December, 45-49.

Drewry Shipping Consultants (1996), *Global Container Markets: Prospects and Profitability in a High Growth Era*, London: Drewry Shipping Consultants.

Erdmenger, J. and D. Stasinopoulos (1988), "The Shipping Policy of the European Community," *Journal of Transport Economics and Policy*, 22, 3, 355-60.

European Communities Commission (1985a), *Progress Towards a Common Transport Policy – Maritime Transport*, (COM (85) 90 Final), Brussels: Office for Official Publications of the European Communities.

European Communities Commission (1985b), *Completing the Internal Market*, (COM (85) 310 Final), Brussels: Office for Official Publications of the European Communities.

Evans, A. (1994), *The Law of the EC Including the EEA Agreement*, Stockholm: Balder.

Fabey, M. (1998), "TACA Losing Out," *Journal of Commerce*, 20 April, electronic version.

Federal Maritime Commission (1989), *An Analysis of the Maritime Industry and the Effects of the 1984 Shipping Act*, Washington, DC: Federal Maritime Commission.

Fossey, J. (1990), "Top 20 Carriers Consolidate," *Containerisation International*, June, 46-51.

Fossey, J. (1995), "Top Shots," *Containerisation International*, November, 55-9.

Fossey, J. (1998), "Winds of Change," *Containerisation International*, February, 35-8.

Freundmann, A. (1998), "TACA Evolves, Will Cease as a Conference," *Journal of Commerce*, 9 September, 1A, 14A.

Götting, H.-P. and W. Nikowitz (1990), "EEC Merger Control: Distinguishing Concentrative Joint Ventures from Cooperative Joint Ventures," *Fordham International Law Journal*, 13, 185-204.

Høj, J., T. Kato and D. Pilat (1995), "Deregulation and Privatisation in the Service Sector," *OECD Economic Studies*, Paris: OECD, 25, 2, 37-74.

House Committee on Merchant Marine and Fisheries (1914), *Report on Steamship Agreements and Affiliations in Foreign and Domestic Trade*, H. Doc. 805, 63rd Congress, Second Session.

Industry Canada (1995), *Strategic Alliances Under the Competition Act*, Ottawa: Supply and Services Canada.

Jennings, E. (1980), *Cargoes: A Centenary Story of the Far Eastern Freight Conference*, Singapore: Meridian Communications (South-east Asia) Pte Ltd.

Kreis, H. W. R. (1990) "European Community Competition Policy and International Shipping," *Fordham International Law Journal*, 13, 41-5.

Levitt, T. (1983), "The Globalization of Markets," *Harvard Business Review*, 61, 3, 91-102.

Mahoney, H. (1990), "Reading Between the Lines," *Containerisation International*, March, 29-39.

Maloney, S. (1995), "Call for End to Liner Conference Exemption, *Lloyd's List*, 16 December, 1.

Ortiz Blanco, L. and B. van Houtte (1996), *EC Competition Law in the Transport Sector*, Oxford: Oxford University Press.

Part X Review Panel (1993), *Liner Shipping Cargoes and Conferences*, Canberra: Australian Government Publishing Service.

Porter, J. (1994), "TAA Overhauls Pact to Appease Shippers, EU," *Journal of Commerce*, 6 July, 1A, 10A.

Porter, M. E. (1980), *Competitive Strategy: Techniques for Analyzing Industries and Competitors*, New York: Free Press.

Roberts, A. S. (1992), "Race is on to Lure N. Europe Ship Pacts," *Journal of Commerce*, 4 November, 1A, 10A.

Toll, E. (1992), "Lines to Cut Atlantic Capacity," *Journal of Commerce*, 16 April, 1A.

Transport Canada (1998), *Transportation in Canada 1998: Annual Report* (TP13198E), Ottawa: Transport Canada.

Ullman, G. (1995), *U.S. Regulation of Ocean Transportation Under the Shipping Act of 1984*, Centreville, MD: Cornell Maritime Press.

UK House of Lords Select Committee on the European Communities (1986), *European Maritime Transport Policy*, London: HL Paper 106, Her Majesty's Stationery Office.

UK House of Lords Select Committee on the European Communities (1990), *Community Shipping Measures*, London: HL Paper 90, Her Majesty's Stationery Office.

United Kingdom (1909), *Report of the Royal Commission on Shipping Rings*, Cd. 4668.

UNCTAD (1998), *Review of Maritime Transport 1997*, Geneva: UNCTAD.

Weil, R. T. (1995), "Conference Regulation in the European Community," *Survey of Maritime Administrative Law*, 4, June, 47-54.

Wilks, S. (1992), "The Metamorphosis of European Competition Policy," *Russell Working Papers No. 9*, Exeter, UK: University of Exeter.

## REFERENCES FOR CHAPTER 2

Alberts, W. A. and N. P. Varaiya (1989), "Assessing the Profitability of Growth by Acquisition," *International Journal of Industrial Organization*, 7, 133-49.

Allen, J. W., S. L. Lummer, J. J. McConnell, and D. K. Reed (1995), "Can Takeover Losses Explain Spin-Off Gains?" *Journal of Financial and Qualitative Analysis*, 30, 4, 465-86.

Andrews, K. R. (1971), *The Concept of Corporate Strategy*, Homewood, IL: Dow-Jones Irwin.

Anonymous (1997), "Why Too Many Mergers Miss the Mark," *The Economist*, 342, 7998 (4 January), 57-8.

Axelrod, R. (1984), *The Evolution of Cooperation*, New York: Basic Books.

Bain, J. S. (1959), *Industrial Organization*, New York: John Wiley.

Barney, J. B. (1986), "Types of Competition and the Theory of Strategy: Toward an Integrative Framework," *Academy of Management Review*, 11, 4, 791-800.

Barkema, H. G. and F. Vermeulen (1997), "What Differences in the Cultural Background of Partners Are Detrimental for Joint Venture Partners?" *Journal of International Business Studies*, 28, 4, 845-64.

Bartlett, C. and S. Ghoshal (1989), *Managing Across Borders: The Transnational Solution*, Boston: Harvard Business School Press.

Baumol, W. J., J. C. Panzar and R. D. Willig (1982), *Contestable Markets and the Theory of Industry Structure*, New York: Harcourt Brace Jovanovitch.

Beamish, P. (1988), *Multinational Joint Ventures in Developing Countries*, London: Routledge.

Bleeke, J. and D. Ernst (1993a), "The Death of the Predator," *Collaborating to Compete: Using Strategic Alliances and Acquisitions in the Global Marketplace*, Bleeke, J. and D. Ernst, eds., New York: John Wiley & Sons Inc., 1-10.

Bleeke, J. and D. Ernst (1993b), "The Way to Win in Cross-Border Alliances," Bleeke, J. and D. Ernst (eds.), *Collaborating to Compete: Using Strategic Alliances and Acquisitions in the Global Marketplace*, New York: John Wiley & Sons Inc, 17-34.

Bleeke, J. and D. Ernst (1995), "Is Your Strategic Alliance Really a Sale?" *Harvard Business Review*, 73, 1, 97-105.

Bleeke, J., D. Ernst, J. A. Osono and D. D. Weinburg (1993), "Succeeding at Cross-Border Mergers and Acquisitions," Bleeke, J. and D. Ernst (eds.), *Collaborating to Compete: Using Strategic Alliances and Acquisitions in the Global Marketplace*, New York: John Wiley & Sons Inc, 79-90.

Bradley, M., A. Desai and E. H. Kim (1983), "The Rationale Behind Interfirm Tender Offers: Information or Synergy?" *Journal of Financial Economics*, 11, 183-206.

Brouthers, K. D., P. van Hastenburg and J. van den Ven (1998), "If Most Mergers Fail Why Are They So Popular?" *Long Range Planning*, 31, 3, 347-53.

Brush, T. H. (1996), "Predicted Change in Operational Synergy and Post-Acquisition Performance of Acquired Businesses," *Strategic Management Journal*, 17, 1, 1-24.

Buckley, P. J. and M. Casson (1976), *The Future of the Multinational Enterprise*, New York: Holmes & Meier.

Burgers, W. P., C. W. L. Hill and W. C. Kim (1993), "A Theory of Global Strategic Alliances: The Case of the Global Auto Industry," *Strategic Management Journal*, 14, 6, 419-32.

Button, K. J. and P. Nijkamp (1998), "Economic Stability in Network Industries," *Transportation Research Part E: Logistics and Transportation Review*, 34E, 1, 13-24.

Caves, R. E. (1980), "Industrial Organization, Corporate Strategy and Structure," *Journal of Economic Literature*, 18, March, 64-92.

Chandler, Jr., A. D. (1962), *Strategy and Structure: Chapters in the History of the American Industrial Enterprise*, Cambridge: M.I.T. Press.

Chatterjee, S. (1992), "Sources of Value in Take-overs: Synergy or Restructuring—Implications for Target and Bidder Firms," *Strategic Management Journal*, 13, 5, 267-86.

Chatterjee, S., M. H. Lubatkin, D. M. Schweiger and Y. Weber (1992), "Cultural Differences and Shareholder Value in Related Mergers: Linking Equity and Human Capital," *Strategic Management Journal*, 13, 5, 319-34.

Ciborra, C. (1991), "Alliances as Learning Experiments: Co-operation, Competition and Change in Hightech Industries," L. K. Mytelka (ed.), *Strategic Partnerships and the World Economy*, Rutherford, NJ: Fairleigh Dickinson University Press, 51-77.

Coase, R. (1937), "The Nature of the Firm," *Economica*, 4, 386-405.

Contractor, F. J. and P. Lorange (1988), "Why Should Firms Co-operate? The Strategy and Economic Basis for Co-operative Ventures," Contractor, F. J. and P. Lorange, eds., *Co-operative Strategies in International Business*, Lexington, MA: Lexington Books, 3-28.

Cyert, R. M. and J. G. March (1963), *A Behavioural Theory of the Firm*, Englewood Cliffs, NJ: Prentice Hall.

Datta, D. K. (1991), "Organizational Fit and Acquisition Performance: Effects of Post-Acquisition Integration," *Strategic Management Journal*, 12, 4, 281-97.

Datta, D. K., G. E. Pinches and V. K. Narayanan (1992), "Factors Influencing Wealth Creation from Mergers and Acquisition: A Meta-Analysis," *Strategic Management Journal*, 13, 1, 67-84.

Davies, J. E. (1984), *Pricing in the Liner Shipping Industry: A Survey of Conceptual Models*, Ottawa: Canadian Transport Commission.

Davies, J. E. (1986), *The Theory of Contestable Markets and Its Application in the Liner Shipping Industry*, Ottawa: Canadian Transport Commission.

Davies, J. E. (1990), *Legislative Change on the North American Liner Trades: A Study of Causes and Consequences*, Ottawa: Transport Canada Economic Analysis.

Dunning, J. (1979), "Explaining Changing Patterns of International Production: In Defence of the Eclectic Theory," *Oxford Bulletin of Economics and Statistics*, 41, 4, 269-96.

Dunning, J. (1997), *Alliance Capitalism and Global Business*, New York: Routledge.

Easterbrook, P. and G. A. Jarrel (1984), "Should Tender Offers Be Rejected?" *New York University Law Review*, 59, 277-95.

Federal Maritime Commission (1989), *An Analysis of the Maritime Industry and the Effects of the 1984 Shipping Act*, Washington, DC: Federal Maritime Commission.

Galbraith, J. R. and R. K. Kazanjian (1978), *Strategy Implementation: Structure, Systems and Process* (2d edition), St. Paul, MN: West Publishing Company.

Gardner, B. (1985), "The Container Revolution and Its Effects on the Structure of Traditional U.K. Liner Shipping Companies," *Maritime Policy and Management*, 12, 195-205.

Gilman, S. (1994), "Contestability and Public Policy in Liner and Short Sea Shipping," H. J. Molenaar and E. Van de Voorde (eds.), *Competition Policy in Liner Shipping*, Antwerp: University of Antwerp, 45-64.

Gomes-Casseres, B. (1996), *The Alliance Revolution: The New Shape of Business Rivalry*, Boston: Harvard University Press.

Goold, M. and A. Campbell (1998), "Desperately Seeking Synergy," *Harvard Business Review*, 76, 5, 130-43.

Grabher, G. (1993), "Rediscovering the Social in the Economics of Interfirm Relations," Grabher, G. (ed.), *The Embedded Firm: On the Socioeconomics of Industrial Networks*, New York: Routledge, 1-31.

Håkansson, H. and J. Johanson (1993), "The Network as a Governance Structure: Interfirm Co-operation Beyond Markets and Hierarchies," Grabher, G. (ed.), *The Embedded Firm: On the Socioeconomics of Industrial Networks*, New York: Routledge, 35-51.

Hamel, G. (1991), "Competition for Competence and Inter-Partner Learning Within International Strategic Alliances," *Strategic Management Journal*, 12, Special Issue (Summer), 83-103.

Hamel, G. and A. Heene (1994), *Competence-Based Competition*, New York: Wiley.

Hannah, M. T. and J. Freeman (1977), "The Population Ecology of Organizations," *American Journal of Sociology*, 82, 5, 929-64.

Harrigan, K. R. (1983), "Strategic Alliances: Their New Role in Global Competition," *Columbia Journal of World Business*, 22, 2, 67-70.

Harrigan, K. R. (1988), "Joint Ventures: a Mechanism for Creating Strategic Change," A. Pettigrew (ed.), *The Management of Strategic Change*, Oxford: Basil Blackwell, 195-230.

Harrigan, K. R. and W. H. Newman (1990), "Bases of Interorganization Co-operation: Propensity, Power, Persistence," *Journal of Management Studies*, 27, 4, 417-34.

Hart, O. (1995), "An Economist's Perspective on the Theory of the Firm," O. E. Williamson (ed.), *Organization Theory: From Chester Barnard to the Present and Beyond*, New York: Oxford University Press.

Heaver, T. D. (1993), "Workable Competition, Politics and Competition Policy in Liner Shipping," Gwilliam, K. M. (ed.), *Current Issues in Maritime Economics*, Dordrecht: Kluwer Academic Publishers, 68-84.

Heflebower, R. B. (1954), "Towards a Theory of Industrial Markets and Prices," *American Economic Review*, May, 121-39.

Helper, S. (1993), "An Exit-Voice Analysis of Supplier Relations: The Case of the US Automobile Industry," Grabher, G. (ed.), *The Embedded Firm: On the Socioeconomics of Industrial Networks*, New York: Routledge, 141-60.

Hirschman, A. O. (1970), *Exit Voice and Loyalty*, Cambridge, MA: Harvard University Press.

Hofstede, G. (1980), *Culture's Consequences: International Differences in Work-Related Values*, Beverly Hills, CA: Sage.

Hofstede, G. (1991), *Culture and Organizations: Software of the Mind*, Berkshire, UK: McGraw-Hill.

Jansson, J. O. and D. Schneerson (1987), *Liner Shipping Economics*, London: Chapman and Hall.

Jankowski, W. B. (1989), "Competition, Contestability and the Liner Shipping Industry," *Journal of Transport Economics and Policy*, 23, 2, 199-203.

Killing, J. (1982), "How to Make a Global Joint Venture Work," *Harvard Business Review*, 60, 3, 120-7.

Kitching, J. (1967), "Why Do Mergers Miscarry?" *Harvard Business Review*, 45, 6, 84-101.

Kogut, B. (1988a), "Joint Ventures: Theoretical and Empirical Perspectives," *Strategic Management Journal*, 9, 4, 319-32.

Kogut, B. (1988b), "A Study of the Life Cycle of Joint Ventures," *Management International Review*, 28, April (Special Issue), 39-52.

Kogut, B. (1989), "The Stability of Joint Ventures Reciprocity and Competitive Rivalry," *Journal of Industrial Economics*, 38, 2, 183-98.

Lorange, P., J. Roos, and P. Simcic Brønn (1992), "Building Successful Strategic Alliances," *Long Range Planning*, 25, 6, 10-17.

Lu, Y. and D. Lake (1997), "Managing International Joint Ventures: An Institutional Approach," Beamish, P. W. and J. P. Killing (eds.), *Co-operative Strategies: European Perspectives*, San Francisco, CA: New Lexington Press, 74-99.

Lundvall, B.-A. (1993), "Explaining Interfirm Cooperation and Innovation: Limits of the Transaction Cost Approach," Grabher, G. (ed.), *The Embedded Firm: On the Socioeconomics of Industrial Networks*, New York: Routledge, 52-64.

Mason, E. S. (1939), "Price and Production Policies of Large-Scale Enterprise," *American Economic Review*, Supplement, March, 61-74.

Mason, E. S. (1949), "The Current State of the Monopoly Problem in the United States," *Harvard Law Review*, June, 1925-85.

McConville, J. (1994), "Competition Policy in Liner Shipping: Synopsis of the General Discussion," Molenaar, H. J. and E. Van de Voorde (eds.), *Competition Policy in Liner Shipping*, Antwerp: University of Antwerp, 95-124.

Mintzberg, H. (1978), "Patterns in Strategy Formation," *Management Science*, 24, 9, 934-48.

Morosini, P. (1998), *Managing Cultural Differences: Effective Strategy and Execution Across Cultures in Global Cultural Alliances*, Oxford: Pergamon Press.

Mytelka, L. K. (1991), "Crises, Technological Change and the Strategic Alliance," L. K. Mytelka (ed.), *Strategic Partnerships and the World Economy*, Rutherford, NJ: Fairleigh Dickinson University Press, 7-34.

Normann, R. and R. Ramírez (1993), "From Value Chain to Value Constellation: Designing Interactive Strategy," *Harvard Business Review*, 71, 4, 65-77.

Ohmae, K. (1989a), "The Global Logic of Strategic Alliances," *Harvard Business Review*, 67, 2, 143-54.

Ohmae, K. (1989b), "Managing in a Borderless World," *Harvard Business Review*, 67, 3, 152-61.

Parkhe, A. (1991), "Interfirm Diversity, Organizational Learning, and Longevity in Global Strategic Alliances," *Journal of International Business Studies*, 22, 579-601.

Parkhe, A. (1993a), "Strategic Alliance Structuring: A Game Theoretic and Transaction Cost Examination of Interfirm Cooperation," *Academy of Management Journal*, 36, 4, 794-829.

Parkhe, A. (1993b), "Partner Nationality and the Structure-Performance Relationship in Strategic Alliances," *Organization Science*, 4, 2, 301-24.

Perlmutter, H. V. and D. A. Heenan (1986), "Cooperate to Compete Globally," *Harvard Business Review*, 64, 2, 136-52.

Pilling, B. K. and L. Zhang (1992), "Cooperative Exchange: Rewards and Risks," *International Journal of Purchasing and Materials Management*, 28, 2, 2-9.

Pirrong, S. C. (1992), "An Application of Core Theory to the Analysis of Ocean Shipping Markets," *Journal of Law and Economics*, 35, 89-131.

Porter, M. E. (1979), "How Competitive Forces Shape Strategy," *Harvard Business Review*, 57, 2, 137-45.

Porter, M. E. (1980), *Competitive Strategy: Techniques for Analyzing Industries and Competitors*, New York: Free Press.

Porter, M. E. (1985), *Competitive Advantage: Creating and Sustaining Superior Performance*, New York: Free Press.

Porter, M. E. (1986), "Competition in Global Industries, A Conceptual Framework," Porter, M. E. (ed.), *Competition in Global Industries*, Boston: Harvard Business School Press, 15-60.

Porter, M. E. (1987), "From Competitive Advantage to Competitive Strategy," *Harvard Business Review*, 65, 3, 43-59.

Pralahad, C. K. and G. Hamel (1990), "The Core Competence of the Corporation," *Harvard Business Review*, 68, 3, 79-91.

Ravenscraft, D. J. and F. M. Scherer (1987), *Mergers, Sell-Offs and Economic Efficiency*, Washington: Brookings Institution.

Ravenscraft, D. J. and F. M. Scherer (1989), "The Profitability of Mergers," *International Journal of Industrial Organization*, 7, 101-16.

Richardson, G. B. (1972), "The Organization of Industry," *Economic Journal*, 82, 883-96.

Ring, P. S. and A. H. Van de Ven (1992), "Structuring Cooperative Relationships Between Organizations," *Strategic Management Journal*, 13, 7, 483-98.

Rugman, A. M. (1981), *Inside the Multinationals: The Economics of Internal Markets*, London: Croom Helm.

Rugman, A. M. and A. Verbeke (1993), *Global Competition: Beyond the Three Generics*, Greenwich, CT: JAI Press.

Sanchez, R. and A. Heene (1997), "Reinventing Strategic Management: New Theory and Practice for Competence-Based Competition," *European Management Journal*, 15, 3, 303-17.

Scherer, F. M. (1970), *Industrial Market Structure and Economic Performance*, Chicago: Rand McNally College Publishing Company.

Scherer, F. M. and D. Ross (1990), *Industrial Market Structure and Economic Performance* (3d ed.), Boston: Houghton Mifflin.

Schmidt, D. and K. Fowler (1990), "Post-Acquisition Financial Performance and Executive Compensation," *Strategic Management Journal*, 11, 7, 559-69.

Shleifer, A. and R. W. Vishnay (1991), "Takeovers in the '60s and '80s: Evidence and Implications," *Strategic Management Journal*, 12, Special Issue (Winter), 51-9.

Sjöstrom, W. (1989), "Collusion in Ocean Shipping: A Test of Monopoly and Empty Core Models," *Journal of Political Economy*, 97, 5, 1160-79.

Sosnick, S. H. (1958), "A Critique of Concepts of Workable Competition," *Quarterly Journal of Economics*, August, 416-23.

Teece, D., G. Pisano and A. Shuen (1990), *Firm Capabilities, Resources and the Concept of Strategy*, CCC Working Paper 90-8, Berkeley, CA: University of California.

Thorelli, H. B. (1986), "Networks: Between Markets and Hierarchies," *Strategic Management Journal*, 7, 1, 37-51.

Trautwein, F. (1990), "Merger Motives and Merger Prescriptions," *Strategic Management Journal*, 11, 283-95.

Varadarajan, P. R. and M. H. Cunningham (1995), "Strategic Alliances: A Synthesis of Conceptual Foundations," *Journal of the Academy of Marketing Science*, 23, 4, 282-96.

Vernon, R. (1983), "Organizational and Institutional Responses to International Risk," R. Herring (ed.), *Managing International Risk*, New York: Cambridge University Press.

Vickers, J. (1985), "Pre-emptive Patenting, Joint Ventures, and the Persistence of Oligopoly," *International Journal of Industrial Organization*, 3, 261-73.

Williamson, O. (1975), *Markets and Hierarchies: Analysis and Anti-Trust Implications*, New York: Free Press.

Williamson, O. (1985), *The Economic Institutions of Capitalism*, New York: Free Press.

Yoshino, M. Y. and U. S. Rangan (1995), *Strategic Alliances: An Entrepreneurial Approach to Globalization*, Boston: Harvard Business School Press.

Zerby, J. A. and R. M. Conlon (1978), "An Analysis of Capacity Utilisation in Liner Shipping," *Journal of Transport Economics and Policy*, 12, 1, 27-46.

## REFERENCES FOR CHAPTER 3

Anonymous (1999), "Share and Share Unalike," *The Economist*, 352, 8131, 18-20.

Armistead, C. (1985), "Capacity Management," Voss, C., C. Armistead, B. Johnson and B. Morris (eds.), *Operations Management in Service Industries and the Public Sector*, New York: John Wiley and Sons.

Bangsberg, P. T (1991), "Lines Veer from Intermodal Services in Effort to Cut Costs, Report Says," *Journal of Commerce*, 4 December, 1B.

Boeing (1996), *1995/1996 World Air Cargo Forecast*, Seattle: Boeing Commercial Airplane Group.

Boeing (1997), *1996/1997 World Air Cargo Forecast*, Seattle: Boeing Commercial Airplane Group.

Brennan, J. (1989), *Intermodalism in the 1990's*, Speech: Halifax Port Days, 18 September.

Broadwater, M. K. (1992), "Globalization: Its Importance as a Carrier Strategy and Likely Impact on Ports," Presentation: Halifax, September.

Brooks, M. R. (1985), "An Alternative Theoretical Approach to the Evaluation of Liner Shipping, Part II: Choice Criteria," *Maritime Policy and Management*, 12, 2, 145-55.

Brooks, M. R. (1990) "Ocean Carrier Selection Criteria in a New Environment," *Logistics and Transportation Review*, 26, 4, 339-55.

Brooks, M. R. (1993), "International Competitiveness—Assessing and Exploiting Competitive Advantage by Ocean Container Carriers," *Logistics and Transportation Review*, 29, 3, 275-93.

Brooks, M. R. (1995), "Understanding the Ocean Container Carrier Market—A Seven Country Study," *Maritime Policy and Management*, 22, 1, 39-50.

Brooks, M. R. (1998), "Performance Evaluation in the North American Transport Industry: Users' Views," *Transport Reviews*, 18, 1, 1-16.

Brooks, M. R. (2000 forthcoming), "Performance Evaluation of Carriers by North American Companies," *Transport Reviews*, 20, 2.

Brooks, M. R., R. G. Blunden and C. I. Bidgood (1993), "Strategic Alliances in the Global Container Transport Industry," R. Culpan (ed.), *Multinational Strategic Alliances*, Binghamton, NY: Haworth Press, 221-48.

Contractor, F. J. and P. Lorange (1988), "Why Should Firms Co-operate? The Strategy and Economic Basis for Co-operative Ventures," Contractor, F. J. and P. Lorange (eds.), *Co-operative Strategies in International Business*, Lexington, MA: Lexington Books, 3-28.

Crum, M. J. and B. J. Allen (1991), "The Changing Nature of the Motor Carrier-Shipper Relationship: Implications for the Trucking Industry," *Transportation Journal*, 31, 2, 41-54.

Damas, P. (1998), "Who's Making $" *American Shipper*, July, 54-9.

Denham, M. (1991), "Strategic Alliances: Partnering for Global Success," *McKinsey on Management*, Winter, 32-6.

Drewry Shipping Consultants (1996), *Global Container Markets: Prospects and Profitability in a High Growth Era*, London: Drewry Shipping Consultants.

Fossey, J. (1998), "Winds of Change," *Containerisation International*, February, 35-8.

Ghemawat, P. (1986), "Sustainable Advantage," *Harvard Business Review*, 64, 5, 53-8.

Gibson, B. J., H. L. Sink, and R. A. Mundy (1993), "Shipper-Carrier Relationships and Carrier Selection Criteria," *Logistics and Transportation Review*, 29, 4, 371-82.

Intermodal Association of North America (1993), *The 1992 Intermodal Index*, Lexington, MA: Mercer Management Consulting.

Kleinsorge, I. K., P. B. Schary and R. D. Tanner (1991), "The Shipper-Carrier Partnership: A New Tool for Performance Evaluation," *Journal of Business Logistics*, 12, 2, 35-57.

Lado, A., N. G. Boyd, S. C. Hanlon (1997), "Competition, Cooperation and the Search for Economic Rents: A Syncretic Model," *The Academy of Management Review*, 22, 1, 110-41.

LaLonde, B. J. and A. B. Maltz (1992), "Some Propositions About Outsourcing the Logistics Function," *International Journal of Logistics Management*, 3, 1, 1-11.

MacMillan, I. C. (1984), "Seizing Competitive Initiative," Lamb, R. B. (ed.), *Competitive Strategic Management*, Englewood Cliffs, NJ: Prentice-Hall Inc., 272-96.

Mongelluzzo, B. (1998), "Sea-Land, Maersk to Cut Capacity in Pacific," *Journal of Commerce*, 11 February, 1A, 11A.

Moreby, D. (1990), "Survey," *Seatrade Business Review*, May/June, 29-33.

OECD, *Maritime Transport*, various years.

Phillips, L. T. (1991), "Contractual Relationships in the Deregulated Transportation Marketplace," *Journal of Law and Economics*, 34, October, 535-64.

Pocock, C. (1999), "Ship Shape," *Cargovision*, June, 7-9.

Porter, M. E. (1979), "How Competitive Forces Shape Strategy," *Harvard Business Review*, 57, 2, 137-45.

Porter, M. E. (1985), *Competitive Advantage: Creating and Sustaining Superior Performance*, New York: Free Press.

Porter, M. E. (1998), "Clusters and the New Economics of Competition," *Harvard Business Review*, 76, 6, 77-90.

Sclar, M. L. and D. L. Blond (1991), "Air Cargo vs. Sea Cargo Trends," DRI/McGraw-Hill Conference *World Sea Trade Outlook,* London, 25 September.

Svensson, R. (1995), Presentation: *Fast, Efficient, Safe*, Halifax, 12 September.

UNCTAD (1998), *Review of Maritime Transport 1997*, Geneva: UNCTAD.

## REFERENCES FOR CHAPTER 4

Ahlander, K. and A. Spanholtz (1998), "Organizationally Challenged," *Containerisation International*, July, 43-5.

Anonymous (1998), "Airline Alliances: Mergers in Mind," *The Economist*, 26 September, 68.

Anonymous (1999), "How to Merge: After the Deal," *The Economist*, 350, 8181, 21-3.

Ariño, A. and J. de la Torre (1998), "Learning From Failure: Towards an Evolutionary Model of Collaborative Ventures," *Organization Science*, 9, 3, 306-25.

Bendall, H. B. and A. F. Stent (1998), "Longhaul Feeder Services in an Era of Changing Technology: An Asia-Pacific Perspective," presentation to the World Conference on Transport Research, Antwerp, July.

Boyes, J. R. C. (1998), "Consolidation Continues," *Containerisation International Yearbook 1998*, 5.

Broadwater, M. K. (1992), "Globalization: Its Importance as a Carrier Strategy and Likely Impact on Ports," Presentation: Halifax, September.

Brooks, M. R. (1985), "An Alternative Theoretical Approach to the Evaluation of Liner Shipping, Part II: Choice Criteria," *Maritime Policy and Management*, 12, 2, 145-55.

Brooks, M. R. (1990) "Ocean Carrier Selection Criteria in a New Environment," *Logistics and Transportation Review*, 26, 4, 339-55.

Brooks, M. R. (1992), *Canada Maritime Limited* (392-046-1), Cranfield, UK: European Case Clearing House.

Brooks, M. R. (1995), "Understanding the Ocean Container Carrier Market—A Seven Country Study," *Maritime Policy and Management*, 22, 1, 39-50.

Brooks, M. R. (1998), "Performance Evaluation in the North American Transport Industry: Users' Views," *Transport Reviews*, 18, 1, 1-16.

Brooks, M. R. (1999a), "Performance Evaluation by North American Carriers," *Transport Reviews*, 18, 1, 1-16.

Brooks, M. R. (1999b), "Performance Evaluation of Carriers by North American Logistics Service Firms," *Transport Reviews*, 19, 3, 273-84.

Brooks, M. R. (2000 forthcoming), "Performance Evaluation of Carriers by North American Companies," *Transport Reviews*, 20, 2.

Brooks, M. R. and K. J. Button (1994), "Yield Management: A Phenomenon of the 1980s and 1990s?" *International Journal of Transport Economics*, 21, 2, 177-96.

Brooks, M. R. and K. J. Button (1996), "The Determinants of Shipping Rates: A North Atlantic Case Study," *Transport Logistics*, 1, 1, 21-30.

Brouthers, K. D., L. E. Brouthers, and T. J. Wilkinson (1995), "Strategic Alliances: Choose Your Partners," *Long Range Planning*, 23, 3, 18-25.

Cauley de la Sierra, M. (1995), *Managing Global Alliances: Key Steps for Successful Collaboration,*. Wokingham, UK: Addison-Wesley Publishing.

Cooper, M. C. and J. T. Gardner (1993), "Building Good Business Relationships—More than Just Partnering or Strategic Alliances?" *International Journal of Physical Distribution and Logistics Management*, 23, 6, 14-26.

Damas, P. (1998), "Container Carriers' Margins Disappear," *American Shipper*, July, 60-2.

Damas, P. and C. Gillis (1997), "Maersk's World," *American Shipper*, March, 48-9.

Davies, J. E. (1990), *Legislative Change on the North American Liner Trades: A Study of Causes and Consequences*, Ottawa: Transport Canada Economic Analysis.

Devlin, G. and M. Bleackley (1988), "Strategic Alliances—Guidelines for Success," *Long Range Planning*, 21, 5, 18-23.

Doz, Y. L. and G. Hamel (1998), *Alliance Advantage: The Art of Creating Value Through Partnering*, Boston: Harvard Business School Press.

Drewry Shipping Consultants (1996a), *Global Container Markets: Prospects and Profitability in a High Growth Era*, London: Drewry Shipping Consultants.

Drewry Shipping Consultants (1996b), *Post-Panamax Containerships: 6000 TEU and Beyond*, September.

Duysters, G., A. P. de Man, L. Wildeman (1999), "A Network Approach to Alliance Management," *European Management Journal*, 17, 2, 182-7.

Falkenberg, J. (1992), "Cooperation in Shipping: Managing Strategic Alliances," Bergen, Norway: SNF (Centre for Research in Economics and Business Administration).

Feldman, J. M. (1998), "Making Alliances Work," *Air Transport World*, 35, 6, 26-35.

Håkansson, H. and J. Johanson (1993), "The Network as a Governance Structure: Interfirm Co-operation Beyond Markets and Hierarchies," *The Embedded Firm: On the Socioeconomics of Industrial Networks*, G. Grabher ed., New York: Routledge, 35-51.

Harvey, M. G. and R. F. Lusch (1995), "A Systematic Assessment of Potential International Strategic Alliance Partners," *International Business Review*, 4, 2, 195-212.

Hauser, J. and G. Katz (1998), "Metrics: You Are What You Measure," *European Management Journal*, 16, 5, 517-28.

Inkpen, A. C. and A. Dinur (1998), "Knowledge Management Processes and International Joint Ventures," *Organization Science*, 9, 4, 454-68.

Jansson, J. O. and D. Schneerson (1987), *Liner Shipping Economics*, London: Chapman and Hall.

Kanter, R. M. (1994), "Collaborative Advantage," *Harvard Business Review*, 72, 4, 96-108.

Kaplan, R. S. and D. P. Norton (1996), *The Balanced Scorecard: Translating Strategy into Action*, Boston: Harvard University Press.

Kumar, R. and K. O. Nti (1998), "Differential Learning and Interaction in Alliance Dynamics," *Organization Science*, 9, 3, 356-67.

Main, J. (1990), "Making Global Alliances Work," *Fortune*, 122, 15, 121-26.

McLellan, R. G. (1997), "Bigger Vessels: How Big is Big?" *Maritime Policy and Management*, 24, 2, 193-211.

Medcof, J. W. (1997), "Too Many Alliances End in Divorce," *Long Range Planning*, 30, 5, 718-32.

OECD, *Maritime Transport*, various years.

Saxton, T. (1997), "The Effects of Partner and Relationship Characteristics on Alliance Outcomes," *Academy of Management Journal*, 40, 2, 443-61.

Swan, W. M. (1998), "Spill Modeling for Airlines," presentation to the World Conference on Transport Research, Antwerp, July.

Tretheway, M. and T. H. Oum (1992), *Airline Economics*, Vancouver, BC: Centre for Transportation Studies, University of British Columbia.

UNCTAD (1998), *Review of Maritime Transport 1997*, Geneva: UNCTAD.

Verma, R., G. M. Thompson and J. L. Louviere (1999), "Configuring Service Operations in Accordance with Customer Needs and Preferences, *Journal of Service Research*, 1, 3, 262-74.

Vollman, T. E. and C. Cordon (1998), "Building Successful Customer-Supplier Alliances," *Long Range Planning*, 31, 5, 684-94.

Zerby, J. A. and R. M. Conlon (1978), "An Analysis of Capacity Utilisation in Liner Shipping," *Journal of Transport Economics and Policy*, 12, 1, 27-46.

## REFERENCES FOR CHAPTER 5

Anonymous (1994a), "UP Offer Complicates BN/Santa Fe Merger Plans," *Traffic Management*, 33, 11, 20.

Anonymous (1994b), "Union Pacific's $3.4 bil Offer for Santa Fe is Rejected," *Corporate Growth Report Weekly*, 17 October, 815, 7496.

Anonymous (1995a), "Merger Gets Mixed Reviews," *Transportation and Distribution*, 36, 12, 18.

Anonymous (1995b), "Shipper Wary as Railroads Settle Gaps Over Merger," *Purchasing*, 15, 118, 10, 61.

Anonymous (1995c), "Burlington Northern Increases Bid by 17% for Santa Fe RR," *Corporate Growth Report Weekly*, 2 January, 825, 7616.

Anonymous (1995d), "UP + SP: Intriguing Possibilities, Intriguing Questions," *Railway Age*, 196, 9, 20.

Anonymous (1995e), "Union Pacific Agrees to Buy Chicago & North Western," *Corporate Growth Report Weekly*, 20 March, 836, 7748.

Anonymous (1995f), "Union Pacific is Set to Acquire Southern Pacific for $3.9 Billion," *Corporate Growth Report Weekly*, 14 August, 856, 7988.

Anonymous (1996a), "Justice Raises Antitrust Concerns over UP/SP Merger," *Logistics Management*, 35, 5, 22.

Anonymous (1996b), "Enemy Down," *Distribution*, 95, 4, 16.

Anonymous (1996c), "Conrail, KCS Enter the UP-SP Merger Debate," *Railway Age*, 197, 2, 21.

Anonymous (1996d), "Conrail, CSX Still Have to Persuade Shareholders," *Financial Post Daily*, 22 November, 9, 168, 10.

Anonymous (1996e), "Opposing the Merger," *Distribution*, May, 95, 6, 15.

Anonymous (1996f), "Out of Crisis, a New Strategy," *Railway Age*, 197, 5, 67-8.
Anonymous (1996g), "Rail Capital Expansions," *Transportation and Distribution*, 37, 2, 10.
Anonymous (1996h), "Norfolk Southern Ups Its Hostile Bid for Conrail," *Financial Post*, 11 November, 90, 45, 19.
Anonymous (1996i), "CSX Buys Conrail for US$8.4b," *Financial Post Daily*, 16 October, 9, 146, 3.
Anonymous (1996j), "Bids by CSX and Norfolk Southern for Conrail Draw Mixed Reviews," *Iron Age New Steel*, 12, 12, 16.
Anonymous (1996k), "Steaming," *The Economist*, 19 October, 341, 7988, 66-71.
Anonymous (1997a), "Conrail Split Good News for Shippers—Eventually," *Purchasing*, 3 April, 54-5.
Anonymous (1997b), "Norfolk Southern Gains Upper Hand over CSX in Conrail Battle," *Containerisation International*, March, 31.
Anonymous (1997c), "Conrail Approves Joint Takeover by CSX and Norfolk Southern," *Weekly Corporate Growth Report*, 17 March, 936, 8926A.
Anonymous (1997d), "CSX and NS Agree to Split Up Conrail," *Containerisation International*, May, 25.
Anonymous (1997e), "NS and CSX Agree to Split Conrail," *Containerisation International*, April, 22.
Anonymous (1997f), "CSX Extends Deadline As Conrail Battle Drags On," *Financial Post*, 18/20 January, 91, 3, 17.
Anonymous (1997g), "BNSF: Merger Conditions 'Working As Intended' – Almost," *Railway Age*, 198, 8, 25.
Anonymous (1997h), "Why CN Fears a Conrail Split-Up," *Railway Age*, 198, 8, 29.
Anonymous (1997i), "Application for Acquisition of Conrail Due This Month," *World Wide Shipping*, June, 18.
Anonymous (1997j), "Conrail Shareholders Derail CSX Merger," *Financial Post*, 15/17 February, 91, 7, 12.
Anonymous (1998a), "Sharing the Wealth to End a Fight," *Mergers and Acquisitions*, 31, 6, 5.
Anonymous (1998b), "CSX & NS: Last Minute Maneuvering Secures Approvals," *Transportation and Distribution*, 39, 7, 16.
Anonymous (1998c), "The Wreck of the Union Pacific," *Fortune*, 137, 6, 94-102.
Bascombe, A. (1998) "Perfecting the Mousetrap," *Containerisation International*, April, 47-51.
Berman, P. and R. Khalaf (1990), "A Game of Chicken," *Forbes*, 28 May, 145, 1, 38-40.
Berman, P. and R. Khalaf (1993), "Sweet-talking the Board," *Forbes*, 15 March, 151, 6, 51-2.
Blaze, J. (1998), "The Conrail Transition: Getting Ready for Year 1998–2003 & Beyond," presentation to the NYC Chapter of the Transportation Research Forum, June.
Bradley, P. (1996a), "UP/SP Merger Unites Railroads, Divides Shippers," *Logistics Management*, 35, 8, 19.
Bradley, P. (1996b), "Transportation League Speaks Out Against UP/SP Marriage," *Logistics Management*, 35, 4, 25-6.
Brooks, M. R. and K. J. Button (1995), "Separating Track from Operations: A Typology of International Experiences," *International Journal of Transport Economics*, 22, 3, 235-260.
Burke, J. (1998), "Mergers Mark a Turbulent First-half," *Railway Age*, 199, 7, 37-39.
Byrnes, N. (1994), "The Waiting Game," *Financial World*, 13 September, 163, 19, 32-34.
Calderwood, J. A. (1996), "Rail Mega Merger: Let the Conflict Begin," *Transportation and Distribution*, 37, 2, 97.
Caves, D. W., L. R. Christensen and J. Swanson (1981), "Productivity Growth Scale Economies, and Capacity Utilization in US Railroads," *American Economic Review*, 71, 994–1002.
Caves, D. W., L. R. Christensen, M. W. Tretheway and R. J. Windle (1985), "Network Effects and the Measurement of Returns to Scale and Density in US Railroads," Daugherty, A. (ed.), *Analytical Studies in Transport Economics*, Cambridge: Cambridge University Press.
Chatterjee, S. (1992), "Sources of Value in Take-overs: Synergy or Restructuring—Implications for Target and Bidder Firms," *Strategic Management Journal*, 13, 5, 267-86.
Conrail (1996), "CSX and Conrail Sue NS for Tortious Interference," Press Release 5 December.
Edgerton, J. (1995), "Increasing Volume and Falling Payrolls Clear the Track for Rail Stocks," *Money*, 24, 6, 71-2.
Else, P. (1993), "Allocative Efficiency and the Proposed Restructuring of British Rail," *Fiscal Studies*, 14, 65-73.
Fairley, P. and G. Morris (1996), "Closer Ties in Road and Rail," *Chemical Week*, 8 May, 158, 18, 61.
Feder, B. J. (1996), "Not All Aboard: A Rail Merger and Its Critics," *New York Times*, 28 June, C1, D4.
Friedlaender, A. F., E. R. Berndt, J. Chiang, M. Showalter and C. A. Vellturo (1993), "Rail Costs and Capital Adjustments in a Quasi Regulated Environment', *Journal of Transport Economics and Policy*, 27, 131–52.

Gilbert, N. (1995), "The Road Not Taken," *Financial World*, 14 March, 164, 7, 28-30.
Gratwick, J. and T. Heaver (1985), "CN: A case study," T. E. Kierans and W. T. Stanbury (eds.), *Papers on Privatisation*, Montreal: Institute for Research on Public Policy.
Griffiths, D. (1996), "Winner Takes All," *Container Management*, December, 41-3.
Grimm, C. and J. Plaistow (1998), "Competitive Effects of Railroad Mergers," Presentation: Transportation Research Forum, Philadelphia, 30 October.
Hanscom, J. (1996), "A CSX-Conrail Combine—Implications for Liner Shipping," *Seatrade Review*, December, 27-29 at 29.
Harrington, L. (1998a), "All Eyes on the Railroads," *Transportation and Distribution*, 39, 1, 81.
Harrington, L. (1998b), "Railroads: Merger Woes," *Industry Week*, 247, 1, 53-56.
Helm, D. and D. Thompson (1991), "Privatised Transport Infrastructure and the Incentive to Invest", *Journal of Transport Economics and Policy*, 25, 231–47.
Isidore, C. (1997), "CSX Reports Healthy Earnings in 2nd Quarter," *Journal of Commerce*, 23 July, 14A.
Jansson, J. O. and P. Cardebring (1989), "Swedish Railway Policy 1979–88," *Journal of Transport Economics and Policy*, 23, 329–337.
Keeler, T. E. (1983), *Railroads, Freight, and Public Policy*, Washington: Brookings Institution.
Kessides, I. N. and R. D. Willig (1998), *Restructuring Regulation of the Rail Industry for the Public Interest*, OECD: Competition Policy Roundtable No. 15 (DAFFE/CLP (98) 1).
Laabs, J. (1996), "Conrail to Cut Hundreds of Jobs—Sagging Revenues to Blame," *Personnel Journal*, 75, 4, 11.
LaMonica, P. R. (1995), "From Sea to Shining Sea," *Financial World*, 5 December, 164, 25, 44-6.
Lewis, J. (1996), "The Biggest Guns in the West," *Containerisation International*, March, 59-65.
Mance, H. O. (1940), *The Road and Rail Transport Problem*, London: Pitman.
Martin, J. (1996), "The Great Train Game," *Fortune*, 11 November, 134, 9, 151-4.
Martin, J. (1997), "Surviving a Head-on Collision," *Fortune*, 14 April, 159-60.
Miller, L. S. (1994), "The Economy Came on Like Gangbusters...," *Railway Age*, 195, 7, 30-4.
Miller, L. S. (1995), "Confident Yes—Complacent No," *Railway Age*, 196, 12, 43-46.
Miller, L. S. (1996), "Collision Course," *Railway Age*, 197, 11, 23-30.
Miller, L. S. and W. C. Vantuono (1994), "A Good Marketplace... A Good Railroad," *Railway Age*, December, 195, 12, 31-8.
Minahan, T. (1995), "Merger Mania Drives Rumours of Coast-to-Coast Rail Lines," *Purchasing*, 14 December, 119, 9, 65-7.
Minahan, T. (1996), "Green Light for UP-SP Merger has Shippers Seeing Red," *Purchasing*, 15 August, 21, 2, 57-59.
Moore, T. (1996), "Working on the Railroad," *Fleet Owner*, 91, 9, 12.
Morosini, P. (1998), *Managing Cultural Differences*, Oxford: Pergamon Press.
Morris, G. (1994), "North American Railroads Couple Up," *Chemical Week*, 19 October, 155, 14, 23-4.
Morris, G. (1995a), "Railroad Merger Comes to a Head," *Chemical Week*, 1 February, 156, 4, 27.
Morris, G. (1995b), "BN, Santa Fe Merger Approved," *Chemical Week*, 2 August, 157, 4, 45.
Morris, G. (1995c), "UP-SP Concentrate Chemicals," *Chemical Week*, 23 August, 157, 7, 48.
Morris, G. (1996a), "SPI Sticks to Merger Opposition," *Chemical Week*, 13 March, 158, 10, 27-9.
Morris, G. (1996b), "Western Railroads: Down to Two," *Chemical Week*, 25 September (Coping with Consolidation Supplement), T19-22.
Morris, G. (1996c), "CSX Raises Bid for Conrail," *Chemical Week*, 13 November, 158, 44, 97.
Morris, G. (1997), "STB Upholds Shipper's Choice," *Chemical Week*, 22 January, 159, 3, 48.
Morris, G. (1998a), "Eastern Rail Mergers Under New Scrutiny," *Chemical Week*, 11 March, 160, 9, 25.
Morris, G. (1998b), "UP Settles Suits; Conrail Split Approved," *Chemical Week*, 5 August, 160, 29, 15.
Morton, P. (1996), "When Railroads Collide: Canadian Carriers Are Quietly Watching the Birth of a Titanic American Competitor," *Financial Post*, 20 April, 90, 16, 8.
National Transportation Act Review Commission (1993), *Competition in Transportation: Policy and Legislation in Review*, Ottawa: Supply and Services Canada.
Norfolk Southern Corporation (1998), *Annual Report 1997*.
Norman, J. R. (1994), "Choose Your Partners!" *Forbes*, 21 November, 154, 12, 88-9.
Nowicki, P. E. (1997), "A Carrier Perspective," Presentation: Session 44: *Rail Mergers: Transportation in the Wake of BN-SF and UP-SP Mergers*, Transportation Research Board Annual Meeting, 13 January.

Palmeri, C. and A. Marsh (1995), "Can Drew Lewis Drive the Golden Nail?" *Forbes*, 18 December, 156, 14, 52-64.

Starkie, S. (1993), "Train Service Coordination in a Competitive Market," *Fiscal Studies*, 13, 2, 53-64.

Waters, W. G. (1985), "Rail Cost Analysis," K. J. Button and D. E. Pitfield (eds.) *International Railway Economics*, Aldershot, Gower.

Watson, R. (1996), "Vague 'Volume' Definition a Boon to UP," *Journal of Commerce*, 21 August.

Watson, R. (1997a), "15,000 Pages on How to Split Up Conrail," *Journal of Commerce*, 24 June, 1A, 8B.

Watson, R. (1997b), "Rumours Roil About Rail Mega-Merger," *Journal of Commerce*, 22 May, 1A, 4B.

Weber, J. and S. Chandler (1994), "The Merger Union Pacific is Out to Derail," *Business Week*, 14 November, 3398, 100-1.

Welty, G. (1994), "A New Colossus of the West," *Railway Age*, 195, 8, 25-8.lty, G.

Welty, G. (1995a), "BN and Santa Fee Contemplate the Rewards of Merger," *Railway Age*, 196, 3, 22.

Welty, G. (1995b), "For SP, BNSF was 'the Handwriting on the Wall'," *Railway Age*, 196, 10, 18.

Welty, G. (1995c), "For Union Pacific, 'Unprecedented Problems With Service'," *Railway Age*, 196, 12, 20.

Welty, G. (1996), "Railroaders of the Year: Matchmakers Rob Krebs, Jerry Grinstein," *Railway Age*, 197, 1, 31-3.

Wilner, F. N. (1998a), "Good-bye Conrail. Hello, Competition!" *Railway Age*, 199, 7, 29-36.

Wilner, F. N. (1998b), "Reconsidering Conrail," *Traffic World*, 255, 8, 15.

## REFERENCES FOR CHAPTER 6

Abbott, K. and D. Thompson (1991), "Deregulating European Aviation—The Impact of Bilateral Liberalization," *International Journal of Industrial Organization*, 9, 125-40.

Anonymous (1995), "Airline Alliances: Flying in Formation," *The Economist*, 22 July, 59-60.

Anonymous (1997a), "Lufthansa Profits Decline Ahead of STAR Pact," *Airfinance Journal*, 196, 22-3.

Anonymous (1997b), "STAR Alliance Unlikely to Impact on Airline Cost Cutting," *Airfinance Journal*, 196, 18.

Anonymous (1998), "Airline Alliances: Mergers in Mind," *The Economist*, 26 September, 68.

Anonymous (1999), "Star and oneworld in Thai Battle," *Airfinance Journal*, 216, 16.

Argyris, N. (1989), "The EEC Rules of Competition and the Air Transport Sector," *Common Market Law Review*, 26, 1, 5-32.

Berry, S. T. (1990), "Airport Presence as Product Differentiation," *American Economic Review*, 80, 394-9.

Beirne, M. (1999), "Star Pushes to Stay Ahead of Air Consortia," *Brandweek*, 40, 7, 6.

Blöndal, S. and D. Pilat (1997), "The Economic Benefits of Regulatory Reform," *OECD Economic Studies*, Paris: OECD, 28, 1, 7-48.

Brueckner, J. K. and P. T. Spiller (1994), "Economics of Traffic Density in the Deregulated Airline Industry," *Journal of Law and Economics*, 6, 45-73.

Bureau of Transport and Communications Economics (1994), *International Aviation: Trends and Issues (Report 86)*, Canberra: Australian Government Publishing Service.

Button, K. J. (1997), *Why Don't All Aviation Marriages Work?* George Mason University, Fairfax, VA: Institute of Public Policy.

Button, K. J. and D. Swann (1989), "European Community Airlines—Deregulation and Its Problems," *Journal of Common Market Studies*, 27, 4, 259-82.

Caves, D. W., L. R. Christensen and M. W. Tretheway (1984), "Economies of Density Versus Economies of Scale," *RAND Journal of Economics*, 15, 471-89.

Caves, D. W., L. R. Christensen, M. W. Tretheway and R. J. Windle (1986), "An Assessment of the Efficiency Effects of US Airline Deregulation Via an International Comparison," E. Bailey (ed.), *Public Regulation: New Perspectives on Institutions and Policies*, Cambridge, MA: MIT Press.

Dressner, M., S. Flipcop and R. Windle (1995), "Transatlantic Airline Alliances: A Preliminary Evaluation," *Journal of the Transportation Research Forum*, 35, 1, 13-25.

Dressner, M. and R. Windle (1998), "Assessing Competitive Behavior by US Air Carriers," *Transportation Research Forum Proceedings*, 2, 423-444.

Dwyer, R. (1998), "Airlines Disappointed over EU's Alliance Conditions," *Airfinance Journal*, 209, 24.

Eckel, C., D. Eckel and V. Singla (1997), "Privatization and Efficiency: Industry Effects of the Sale of British Airways," *Journal of Financial Economics*, 43, 2, 275-298.

Feldman, J. M. (1996), "Trying to Raise the Crossbar," *Air Transport World*, 33, 6, 23.

Feldman, J. M. (1998), "Making Alliances Work," *Air Transport World*, 35, 6, 26-35.

Findlay, C., G. C. Hufbauer and G. Jaggi (1996), "Aviation Reform in the Asia Pacific," G. C. Hufbauer (ed.), *Flying High: Liberalizing Civil Aviation in the Asia Pacific*, Washington: Institute for International Economics, 11-32.

General Accounting Office (1990), *Airline Competition: Higher Fares and Reduced Competition at Concentrated Airports*, GAO/RCED 90-102, Washington, DC.

General Accounting Office (1993), *Airline Competition: Higher Fares and Less Competition Continue at Concentrated Airports*, GAO/RCED 93-171, Washington, DC.

General Accounting Office (1996), *Domestic Aviation: Changes in Airfares, Service, and Safety Since Airline Deregulation*, GAO//T-RCED-96-126, Washington, DC.

General Accounting Office (1998), *International Aviation Alliances and the Influence of Airline Marketing Practices*, GAO/RCED-98-131, Washington, DC.

Grimm, C. M. and H. B. Milloy (1993), "Australia Domestic Aviation Deregulation," *Logistics and Transportation Review*, 29, 3, 259-74.

Hill, L. (1999), "Wishing on a Star," *Air Transport World*, 36, 1, 42-3.

Høj, J., T. Kato and D. Pilat (1995), "Deregulation and Privatisation in the Service Sector," *OECD Economic Studies*, Paris: OECD, 25, 2, 37-74.

International Civil Aviation Organization (1998), *Annual Civil Aviation Report 1997*, http://www.icao.org.

Jebb, F. (1998), "Survival of the Biggest," *Management Today*, November, 52-7.

Kayal, M. (1997a), "Momentum Shifts on BA-AA Merger," *Journal of Commerce*, 27 May, 1A.

Kayal, M. (1997b), "BA, AA Flying into Rough Skies," *Journal of Commerce*, 23 July, 1A.

Kayal, M. (1997c), "United Deal Spans Three Continents," *Journal of Commerce*, 15 May, 1B.

Killgren, L. (1998), "Flying Colours," *Marketing Week*, 21, 21, 26-7.

Leung, J. (1996), "Winging Their Way to Global Might," *Asian Business*, 32, 12, 24-34.

Morrison, S. A. and C. Winston (1987), "Empirical Implications and Tests of the Contestability Hypothesis," *Journal of Law and Economics*, 30, 1, 53-66.

Morrison, S. A. and C. Winston (1990), "The Dynamics of Airline Pricing and Competition," *American Economic Review*, 80, 2, 389-93.

Morrison, S. A. and C. Winston (1995), *The Evolution of the Airline Industry*, Washington, DC: Brookings Institution.

Nyathi, M. Z. (1996), *Strategic Alliance Partner Choice in International Aviation*, Unpublished PhD Thesis: University of Sydney.

Ortiz Blanco, L. and B. van Houtte (1996), *EC Competition Law in the Transport Sector*, Oxford: Oxford University Press.

Oum, T. H. and C. Yu (1998a), "Cost Competitiveness of Major Airlines: An International Comparison," *Transportation Research Part A: Policy and Practice*, 32A, 6, 407-22.

Oum, T. H. and C. Yu (1998b), "An Analysis of Profitability of the World's Major Airlines," *Journal of Air Transport Management*, 4, 4, 229-237.

Park, J-H. (1997), "The Effects Airline Alliances on Markets and Economic Welfare," *Transportation Research Part E: Logistics and Transportation Review*, 33E, 3, 181-95.

Park, J-H. and A. Zhang (1998), "Airline Alliances and Partner Firms' Output," *Transportation Research Part E: Logistics and Transportation Review*, 34E, 4, 245-56.

Prokesch, S. E. (1995), "Competing on Customer Service: An Interview with British Airways' Sir Colin Marshall," *Harvard Business Review*, 73, 6, 100.

Reguly, E. (1999), "Airline Merger: Ottawa Blew It," *Globe and Mail* (www.globeinvestor.com/archive/gam/19990916/RERIC.html).

Reiss, P. C. and P. T. Spiller (1989), "Competition and Entry in Small Airline Markets," *Journal of Law and Economics*, 32, 2, 179-202.

Saunders, L. F. and W. G. Shepherd (1993), "Airlines: Setting Constraints on Hub Dominance," *Logistics and Transportation Review*, 29, 3, 201-20.

Strassman, D. L. (1990), "Potential Competition in the Deregulated Airlines," *Review of Economics and Statistics*, 72, 4, 696-702.

Transportation Research Board (1999), *Entry and Competition in the Airline Industry: Issues and Opportunities (Special Report 255)*, Washington: National Research Council.

Tretheway, M. W. (1984), "An International Comparison of Airlines," *Proceedings of the Canadian Transportation Research Forum*, 653-76.

Tretheway, M. W. (1990), "Globalization of the Airline Industry and Implications for Canada," *Logistics and Transportation Review*, 26, 357-67.

Tretheway, M. W. (1991), *The Characteristics of Modern Post-Deregulation Air Transport*, Vancouver, BC: Faculty of Commerce and Business Administration, University of British Columbia.

Tulley, S. (1996), "Northwest and KLM: The Alliance from Hell," *Fortune*, 133, 12, 64-72.

Upbin, B. (1997), "Teaching an Airline to Fly," *Forbes*, 160, 13, 86-93.

US Department of Transportation (1990), *Airline Marketing Practices: Travel Agencies, Frequent Flyer Programs, and Computer Reservation Systems*, Secretary's Task Force on Competition in the US Domestic Airline Industry.

Van de Voorde, E. (1992), "European Air Transport After 1992: Deregulation or Re-regulation?" *Antitrust Bulletin*, 37, 2, 507-528.

Windle, R. and M. Dressner (1999), "Competitive Responses to Low Cost Carrier Entry," *Transportation Research Part E: Logistics and Transportation Review*, 35E, 1, 59-75.

Wines, L. (1996), "Robert Crandall and Colin Marshall: The Big Air Link," *Journal of Business Strategy*, 17, 5, 36.

Yarrow, G. (1995), "Airline Deregulation and Privatization in the UK," *Keizai Bunseki*, 143, 3, 49-83.

Youssef, W and M. Hansen (1994), "Consequences of Strategic Alliances Between International Airlines: The Case of Swissair and SAS," *Transportation Research Part A: Policy and Practice*, 28A, 5, 415-31.

## References for Chapter 7

Abrams, A. (1993), "Nedlloyd Stock Surges on Rumours of Possible Merger With Sea-Land," *Journal of Commerce*, 6 August, 1A.

Anonymous (1983), "RJR Prepares for Sea-Land Divestiture," *American Shipper*, October, 17-18.

Anonymous (1985), "Sea-Land Extends its Family Again," *American Shipper*, January, 4.

Anonymous (1989), "Sea-Land Striving to Regain Brand Leadership," *Lloyd's Shipping Economist*, August, 26-31.

Anonymous (1991a), "Nedlloyd Battles Against Losses," *Port Development International*, January-February, 51.

Anonymous (1991b), "Nedlloyd Defers Box Building," *Cargoware International*, March, 7.

Anonymous (1991c), "Maersk/Sea-Land Joint Asia/North America Service Takes Shape," *Canadian Sailings*, April 22, 22.

Anonymous (1991d), "Society Wedding," *Journal of ICHCA Cargo Systems*, May, 29.

Anonymous (1993a), "P&O Containers Stretches Service Across the Pacific," *Distribution*, 92, 4, 20-2.

Anonymous (1994a), "Nedlloyd's Mixed Results," *Containerisation International*, June, 24.

Anonymous (1995), "Key Year Ahead for P&O Containers," *Lloyd's List*, 24 August, 6.

Anonymous (1996a), "Nedlloyd's Turbulent Year," *Containerisation International*, January, 26.

Anonymous (1996b), "New Merger is Full of Promises that Need to be Kept," *International Container Review*, Autumn/Winter, 9-13.

Anonymous (1996c), "Nedlloyd-P&O Merger Will Create Mega-Carrier," *Logistics Management*, October, 22.

Anonymous (1996d), "Maersk's Thomsen Cuts Costs," *Traffic World*, 26 August, 42.

Anonymous (1996e), "P&O/Nedlloyd Emerge In Force," *Container Management*, October, 12.

Anonymous (1997a), "Sea-Land Drives CSX Profits," *Containerisation International*, March, 25.

Anonymous (1997b), CP Could Spend up to US$200m for Lykes Line," *Financial Post Daily*, 15 January, 6.

Anonymous (1997c), "CP Ships' Ray Miles Dismisses Merger Option," *Containerization International*, January, 7.

Anonymous (1997d), "NOL Plans to Buy APL," *American Shipper*, May, 8-10.

Anonymous (1997e), " Crossed Lines," *Port Development International*, May 22-5 at 23.

Anonymous (1997f), "APL/NOL Tie Approved," *Container Management*, October, 12.

Anonymous (1998), "NOL Contemplates Next Acquisition," http://www.schednet.com, 1 June.

Anonymous (1999), "Apollo's Big Buy," *Container Management*, April, 37.
Armbruster, W. (1990), "Sea-Land's Reorganization Is a Part of Carrier's Wider Profit Strategy," *Journal of Commerce*, 9 May, 6B.
Armbruster, W. (1991), "Three Ship Lines Expand Chassis Pool Experiment," *Journal of Commerce*, 6 May, 1B.
Baldwin, T. (1996a), "Lykes Chief Entertains Potential Suitors," *Journal of Commerce*, 1 November, 1A, 2B.
Baldwin, T. (1996b), "Canadian Pacific Plans to Buy Lykes," *Journal of Commerce*, 31 December, 1A, 6B.
Baldwin, T. (1997), "Agreement Covers Lykes Debt to Parent Firm, Three Banks," *Journal of Commerce*, 2 January, 1A, 2B.
Bangsberg, P. T. (1997), "Profit Hunger Drove NOL Hunt," *Journal of Commerce*, 16 April, 2B.
Barnard, B. (1988a), "Ship Lines Bolster Land Legs to Stay Competitive in Europe," *Journal of Commerce*, 5 October, 3B.
Barnard, B. (1988b), "Nedlloyd Looks to Unify Operations," *Journal of Commerce*, 22 December, 10B.
Barnard, B. (1990a), "Nedlloyd Chairman Predicts Reorganization Will Boost Profits," *Journal of Commerce*, May 11, 10B.
Barnard, B. (1990b), "Royal Nedlloyd Posts Steep Slump in Profit for First-Half 1990," *Journal of Commerce*, 24 August.
Barnard, B. (1991a), "Nedlloyd Considers Restructuring Proposals," *Journal of Commerce*, 1 February, 1B.
Barnard, B. (1991b), "Embattled Royal Nedlloyd Braces for Today's Shareholders Meeting," *Journal of Commerce*, March 14.
Barnard, B. (1993), "Hagen Received Incentive Before Quitting Nedlloyd," *Journal of Commerce*, 10 February, 1B.
Barnard, B. (1995), "P&O Navigation's Profit Rose Slightly in First Half," *Journal of Commerce*, 10 September, 1A.
Bascombe, A. (1998a), "Mr. Halliwell Comes to Town," *Containerisation International*, April, 69-73.
Bascombe, A. (1998b), "A Changing World," *Containerisation International*, July, 40-1.
Bascombe, A. (1998c), "A Changing Scene," *Containerisation International*, October, 85-9.
Beargie, T. (1987), "1988 Looks Good for APL and Sea-Land," *American Shipper*, September, 32.
Bleeke, J. and D. Ernst (1995), "Is Your Strategic Alliance Really a Sale?" *Harvard Business Review*, 73, 1, 97-105.
Bonney, J. (1993), "Lykes Plans Four New Containerships," *American Shipper*, December, 31.
Boyes, J. R. C. (1997), "Back to Basics," *Containerisation International*, February, 39-42.
Boyes, J. R. C. (1998), "Consolidation Continues," *Containerisation International Yearbook 1998*, 5.
Bowman, R. J. (1995), "A New Dimension to Shipping," *Distribution*, July, 94, 7, 79-82.
Brennan, T. (1998), "Lykes in the Black: Line See First Profit in 8 Years," *Journal of Commerce*, 11 June, electronic edition.
Brooks, M. R., R. G. Blunden and C. I. Bidgood (1993), "Strategic Alliances in the Global Container Transport Industry," Culpan, R. (ed.), *Multinational Strategic Alliances*, Haworth Press, 221-48.
Burroughs, B. and J. Helyar (1990), *Barbarians at the Gate: The Fall of RJR Nabisco*, New York: Harper & Row.
Buxton, P. (1998), "Chaos on Forecourts as Oil Giants Merge," *Marketing Week*, 21, 41, 22.
Canada Newswire (1998), "Canadian Pacific to Acquire Australia New Zealand Direct Line," 22 September, electronic version.
Canna, E. (1987), "Nedlloyd Reveals Strategy," *American Shipper*, December, 26.
Canna, E. (1989), "Sea-Land Closes Global Loop," *American Shipper*, March, 32-4.
Canna, E. (1995a), "Canadian Pacific Buys Cast," *American Shipper*, May, 18-20.
Canna, E. (1995b), "Orderly Transition," *American Shipper*, August, 28-30.
Cauthen, S. (1996), "Anticipate Alliance Will Reduce Costs," *World Wide Shipping*, December/January, 26-30.
*Containerisation International Yearbook*, various years.
Cauthen, S. (1997), "APL-NOL Merger," *World Wide Shipping*, September, 29.
Cosstick, H. (1996), "Unity Fare," *Container Management*, November, 25.
Crichton, J. (1991), "P&O Rules the Waves," *Containerisation International*, September, 49-53.
Crichton, J. (1996), "Costs of Living," *Containerisation International*, June 49-52.
Crichton, J. (1997), "P&O Nedlloyd Picks Grand Alliance," *Containerization International*, August, 9.
Crichton, J. (1998), "Harris' *State of the Union* Address," *Containerization International*, October, 61-3.

Damas, P. and C. Gillis (1997), "Maersk's World," *American Shipper*, March, 48-9.
Dow, J. (1998), "Urge to Merge Shows No Sign of Stopping," *Journal of Commerce*, 22 June, electronic version.
Drewry Shipping Consultants (1996), *Global Container Markets: Prospects and Profitability in a High Growth Era*, London: Drewry Shipping Consultants.
Fabey, M. (1995), "Lykes Charts Survival Course," *Journal of Commerce*, 20 December, 1A, 6A.
Fossey, J. (1994), "Lykes' New Focus," *Containerisation International*, June, 50-1.
Fossey, J. (1996), "Big, Blue and Beautiful," *Containerisation International*, March, 73-7.
Fossey, J. (1997a), "A Rising Force," *Containerisation International*, December, 42-3.
Fossey, J. (1997b), "NOL's Bid to Survive," *Containerisation International*, May, 6-7.
Fossey, J. (1997c), "NOL/APL Shockwaves," *Containerisation International*, December, 6-7.
Fossey, J. (1998), "Hit and Miss," *Containerisation International*, April, 55.
Freudmann, A. (1998), "CP Ships, TMM Form Shipping Venture," *Journal of Commerce*, 30 July, electronic edition.
Galbraith, J. R. and R. K. Kazanjian (1978), *Strategy Implementation: Structure, Systems and Process* (2d edition), St. Paul, MN: West Publishing Company.
Glass, J. (1995), "Sea-Land Chairman Dismisses Rumours of Sale to A P Møller," *Lloyd's List*, 21 September, 1A.
Haigh, D. (1999), "Mergers Will Fail Unless the Focus is on Marketing," *Marketing*, 11 February, 20.
Hall, K. G. (1998), "TMM denies CP Ships Venture is First Step Towards Eventual Sale," *Journal of Commerce*, 31 July, electronic edition.
Hardwicke, R. (1985), "Does Sea-Land's CCF 'Nest Egg' Invite Plunder?" *American Shipper*, September, 35-6.
Lim, S.-M. (1998), "Economies of Scale in Liner Shipping," *Maritime Policy and Management*, 25, 4, 361-74.
Machalaba, D. (1995), "CSX Expects to Post Gains for 4th Quarter; Cost Controls on Railroad, Strong Grain Shipments at Barge Unit Are Cited," *Wall Street Journal*, 17 November, 7B.
Magnier, M. (1981), "Mighty Sea-Land Has to Attack the Pacific Shipping Conference to Save It," *Fortune*, 1 June, 83-6.
Magnier, M. (1990), "Nedlloyd Picks San Francisco Over LA as Hub," *Journal of Commerce*, 23 August, 1A.
Middleton, W. (1990), "Sea-Land Goes Global," *Container Management*, October, 12.
Mottley, R. (1997), "NOL Completes Purchase of APL," *American Shipper*, December, 6.
Porter, J. (1991a), "Nedlloyd Posts Loss for 1990," *Journal of Commerce*, 19 April, 1A, 1B.
Porter, J. (1991b), "Nedlloyd Chief Sees no Pressure to Resign," *Journal of Commerce*, 9 July, 1A, 8B.
Porter, J. (1991c), "P&O Trafalgar Reticent About Rumored Deal," *Journal of Commerce*, 1 July, 3B.
Porter, J. (1991d), "P&O Talks Could Create Box Giant," *Journal of Commerce*, 2 July, 1A.
Porter, J. (1991e), "P&O Acquires Container Interests of Cunard Ellerman in Complex Deal," *Journal of Commerce*, 19 July, 8B.
Porter, J. (1992a), "Nedlloyd Moves Draw Industry Praise as Recovery Nears," *Journal of Commerce*, 31 March, 1B.
Porter, J. (1992b), "Nedlloyd Board Seeks Suspension of Norwegian Tycoon Hagen," *Journal of Commerce*, 24 December.
Porter, J. (1993a), "P&O Containers Gears Up to Branch Out," Journal of Commerce, 26 January, 5B.
Porter, J. (1993b), "Nedlloyd Group Set to Raise $154 Million in Bond Issue," *Journal of Commerce*, 8 February, 8B.
Porter, J. (1993c), "Nedlloyd to Reduce Staff by 10%," *Journal of Commerce*, 22 April, 1A.
Porter, J. (1995a), "P&O-Maersk Europe-Asia Link Will End in '96," *Journal of Commerce*, 10 May, 1A.
Porter, J. (1995b), "Nedlloyd Lines Performance Blamed for Parent's Decline in Stock Price," *Journal of Commerce*, 11 October.
Porter, J. (1995c), "Nedlloyd's Shares Plunge on Lower Profit Forecast," *Journal of Commerce*, 18 October.
Porter, J. (1996a), "Troubled P&O Running Out of Steam as Investors Target Container Shipping," *Journal of Commerce*, 9 August, 1A.
Porter, J. (1996b), "Gigantic Box Line Emerging," *Journal of Commerce*, 10 September, 1A.
Porter, J. (1996c), "P&O, Nedlloyd Seem to be Good Cultural Fit," *Journal of Commerce*, 11 September, 1A, 2B.
Porter, J. (1996d), "Merger Casts Doubt on Consortia's Future," *Journal of Commerce*, 12 September, 1A, 2B.
Porter, J. (1996e), "Merger Stirs the Waters," *Journal of Commerce*, 23 September, 1C, 6C.

Porter, J. (1996f), "P&O Nedlloyd Plans Expansion in Pacific Trades," *Journal of Commerce*, 9 October, 1A, 3B.
Reier, S. (1990), "Viking Virtue," *Financial World*, 20 February, 159, 4, 74.
Reiss, C. (1985), "The Mighty Urge to Merge: Big-Name Buyers Bag Brands," *Advertising Age*, 56, 84, 1.
Roberts, A. S. (1993a), "For Nedlloyd Chief, It's Do-or-Die on Righting the Ship, Analysts Say," *Journal of Commerce*, 8 February, 8B.
Roberts, A. S. (1993b), "Nedlloyd to Maintain Transport Business," *Journal of Commerce*, 3 March, 1A.
Roberts, A. S. (1993c), "P&O and Nedlloyd Bucking a Trend in Attempt to Offer Customers More," *Journal of Commerce*, 8 March, 8B.
Roberts, W. (1997), "Marad Approves Milestone Ship Deal," *Journal of Commerce*, 17 October, 1A, 5A.
Rumelt, R. P. (1974), *Strategy, Structure, and Economic Performance*, Boston: Harvard University.
Schultz, S. (1997), *World Maritime News*, electronic service, 18 April.
Tirschwell, P. (1997a), "Shotgun Marriage," *Journal of Commerce*, 21 October, 1A, 5A.
Tirschwell, P. (1997b), "NOL-APL: What Now?," *Journal of Commerce*, 15 April, 1A, 4B.
Tirschwell, P. (1998a), "Brand Name Loyalty," *Journal of Commerce*, 5 June, electronic edition.
Tirschwell, P. (1998b), "For APL, NOL a Year of Learning, Sharing," *Journal of Commerce*, 13 April, 1A, 11A.
Toll, E. (1991), "P&O to Raise $1 Billion, Reports 45% Profit Drop," *Journal of Commerce*, 22 August, 8B.
Vail, B. (1988), "Sea-Land Breaks the Ice," *American Shipper*, March, 28-30.
Wastler, A. R. (1991), "Sea-Land Services Drops APL for Maersk to Form New Service," *Journal of Commerce*, 1 February, 1A.
White, D. F. (1989), "Nedlloyd Ship Plan Stirs Fear," *Journal of Commerce*, 6 February, 1A, 10B.

## REFERENCES FOR CHAPTER 8

Abbott, R. A. (1994), *Level of Service in the Canadian Liner Trades* (TP9868-E), Ottawa: Transport Canada.
ACCOS (1992), *Report of the Advisory Commission on Conferences in Ocean Shipping*, Washington, DC, April.
Anonymous (1994), "Competition Affects Returns on Equity," *Lloyd's Shipping Economist*, October, 11-13.
Anonymous (1997a), "Transatlantic VSAs Seek Exemptions," *American Shipper*, August, 22.
Anonymous (1997b), "CP Fights Cast Divestiture," *American Shipper*, March, 26.
Bleeke, J. and D. Ernst (1993), "The Death of the Predator," Bleeke, J. and D. Ernst (eds.), *Collaborating to Compete: Using Strategic Alliances and Acquisitions in the Global Marketplace*, New York: John Wiley & Sons Inc., 1-10.
Bleeke, J. and D. Ernst (1995), "Is Your Strategic Alliance Really a Sale?" *Harvard Business Review*, 73, 1, 97-105.
Bennathan, E. and A. Walters (1969), *The Economics of Ocean Liner Freight Rates*, New York: Praeger Press.
Boyes, J. R. C. (1997), "Laying Down the Law," *Containerisation International*, December, 60-1.
Brooks, M. R. (1993), "International Competitiveness—Assessing and Exploiting Competitive Advantage by Ocean Container Carriers," *Logistics and Transportation Review*, 29, 3, 275-93.
Brooks, M. R. (1994), "Competition Policy in Liner Shipping: Policy Options—A Commentary," H. J. Molenaar and E. Van de Voorde (eds.), *Competition Policy in Liner Shipping*, Antwerp: University of Antwerp, 83-94.
Brooks, M. R. (1998), "Competition in Liner Shipping: Are National Policies Appropriate?" *Ocean Yearbook*, 13, 142-66.
Brooks, M. R. and K. J. Button (1994), "Yield Management: A Phenomenon of the 1980s and 1990s?" *International Journal of Transport Economics*, 21, 2, 177-96.
Brooks, M. R. and K. J. Button (1996), "The Determinants of Shipping Rates: A North Atlantic Case Study," *Transport Logistics*, 1, 1, 21-30.
Bryan, I. A. (1974), "Regression Analysis of Ocean Liner Freight Rates on Some Canadian Export Routes," *Journal of Transport Economics and Policy*, 8, 161-73.
Canna, E. (1995), "Framework for Consortia," *American Shipper*, June, 30-8.

Clyde, P. S. and J. D. Reitzes (1995), *The Effectiveness of Collusion Under Anti-Trust Immunity: The Case of Liner Shipping Conferences*, Washington: Federal Trade Commission.

Consumer & Corporate Affairs (1991), *Merger Enforcement Guidelines*, Ottawa: Supply and Services Canada.

Creel Jr., H. (1998), Speech to the Containerisation International 30th Anniversary Conference, London, 25 February.

Danas, A. M. (1989), "Europe 1992 and the Rise of the Pacific Rim: Do Changing World Trade Patterns Require a Change in United States Shipping Laws?" *Vanderbilt Journal of Transnational Law*, 22, 1036-96.

Davies, J. E. (1986), *The Theory of Contestable Markets and Its Application in the Liner Shipping Industry*, Ottawa: Canadian Transport Commission.

Davies, J. E. (1990), *Legislative Change on the North American Liner Trades: A Study of Causes and Consequences*, Ottawa: Transport Canada Economic Analysis.

Deakin, B. M. with T. Seward (1973), *Shipping Conferences: A Study of Their Origins, Development and Economic Practices*, Cambridge: Cambridge University Press.

Eckbo, B. E. (1983), "Horizontal Mergers, Collusion and Stockholder Wealth," *Journal of Financial Economics*, 11, April, 241-73.

Eller, D. (1999), "Dublin-St. Louis Rates Mystery," *Containerisation International*, February, 42-3.

Federal Maritime Commission (1989), *Section 18 Report on the Shipping Act of 1984*, Washington, DC.

Fossey, J. (1997), "Suicidal Tendencies," *Containerisation International*, May, 37-41.

Galbraith, J. R. and R. K. Kazanjian (1978), *Strategy Implementation: Structure, Systems and Process* (2d edition), St. Paul, MN: West Publishing Company.

Gilman, S. (1983), *The Competitive Dynamics of Container Shipping*, Aldershot, UK.: Gower Press.

Gomes-Casseres, B. (1996), *The Alliance Revolution: The New Shape of Business Rivalry*, Boston: Harvard University Press.

Graham, E. M. and J. D. Richardson (1997), "Issue Overview," in Graham, E. M. and J. D. Richardson (eds)., *Global Competition Policy*, Washington, DC: Institute for International Economics, 3-4.

Harrigan, K. R. (1988), "Joint Ventures: a Mechanism for Creating Strategic Change," A. Pettigrew (ed.), *The Management of Strategic Change*, Oxford: Basil Blackwell, 195-230.

Heaver, T. D. (1972), "Trans-Pacific Trade, Liner Shipping and Conference Rates," *Logistics and Transportation Review*, 8, 3-28.

Heaver, T. D. (1973), "The Structure of Liner Conference Rates," *Journal of Industrial Economics*, 21, 3.

Heaver, T. D. (1977), *Report on a Review of Overseas Cargo Shipping Legislation*, Australia: Department of Transport.

Industry Canada (1995), *Strategic Alliances Under the Competition Act*, Ottawa: Supply and Services Canada.

Jansson, J. O. and D. Schneerson (1987), *Liner Shipping Economics*, London: Chapman and Hall.

Jongkind, R. J. (1995), *Some Policy Implications of the North Atlantic Liner Trades*, Unpublished Masters Thesis: Erasmus University.

Kreis, H. W. R. (1990) "European Community Competition Policy and International Shipping," *Fordham International Law Journal*, 13, 41-5.

MacKenzie, C. H. C., M. E. Power, and T. L. McDorman (1985), *Liner Shipping Conferences: An Annotated Bibliography* Lexington, MA: D. C. Heath and Company.

Marx Jr., D. (1953), *International Shipping Cartels: A Study of Industrial Self-Regulation*, Princeton: Princeton University Press.

Matheson, R. (1993), "Capacity Management Threat to Conferences?" *Canadian Sailings*, 13 September, 17.

Middleton, I. (1993), "A Different Ball Game," *Seatrade Review*, August, 6-9.

Mongelluzzo, B. (1996), "Alliances in Infancy," *Journal of Commerce*, 8 January, 45.

National Transportation Act Review Commission (1993), *Competition in Transportation: Policy and Legislation in Review*, Ottawa: Supply and Services Canada.

Ortiz Blanco, L. and B. van Houtte (1996), *EC Competition Law in the Transport Sector*, Oxford: Oxford University Press.

Part X Review Panel (1993), *Liner Shipping Cargoes and Conferences*, Canberra: Australian Government Publishing Service.

Pirrong, S. C. (1992), "An Application of Core Theory to the Analysis of Ocean Shipping Markets," *Journal of Law and Economics*, 35, 89-131.

Ruttley, P. (1991), "International Shipping and EEC Competition Law," *European Competition Law Review*, 12, 1, 5-18, London: Sweet and Maxwell.

Sansbury, T. (1993), "US Shippers Ready to Launch Attack on Atlantic Conference," *Journal of Commerce*, 24 June, 1C.

Shashikumar, N. (1988), "Mandatory Independent Action: A Legislative Paradox," *Maritime Policy and Management*, 15, 4, 283-90.

Shashikumar, N. (1989), "Service Contracts: A Study of Unfulfilled Promises," *Maritime Policy and Management*, 16, 1, 13-26.

Sjöstrom, W. (1989), "Collusion in Ocean Shipping: A Test of Monopoly and Empty Core Models," *Journal of Political Economy*, 97, 5, 1160-79.

Sjöstrom, W. (1992), "Price Discrimination by Shipping Conferences," *Logistics and Transportation Review*, 28, 2, 207-215.

Sjöstrom, W. (1993), "Antitrust Immunity for Shipping Conferences: An Empty Core Approach," *Antitrust Bulletin*, 38, 2, 419-23.

Sletmo, G. K. and E. W. Williams, Jr. (1981), *Liner Conferences in the Container Age: U.S. Policy at Sea*, New York: MacMillan Publishing.

Zerby, J. A. and R. M. Conlon (1978), "An Analysis of Capacity Utilisation in Liner Shipping," *Journal of Transport Economics and Policy*, 12, 1, 27-46.

## REFERENCES FOR APPENDIX D

Abbott, R. A. (1987), *Regulation of Liner Conferences in Canada and the United States*, Transport Canada: TP8691E, September.

Abbott, R. A., L. Goa and B. Conlin (1990), *Market Share of Conference and Non-Conference Shipping Lines in Canadian International Trade* (Economic Research TP 10693), Ottawa: Transport Canada.

Anonymous (1997a), "EU Approves VSAs' Inland Cooperation," *American Shipper*, November, 22.

Anonymous (1997b), "Shippers React Cautiously to TACA Plan," *American Shipper*, March, 10.

Anonymous (1998a), "EC "Wise Men" Narrow Scope," *American Shipper*, February, 14.

Anonymous (1998b), "FMC Approves Inland-Only Conference," *American Shipper*, July, 16.

Anonymous (1998c), "The Irritating Commissioner," *The Economist*, 346, 8053 at 72.

Beargie, T. (1997), "Zip-code Conference," *American Shipper*, August, 18-20.

Brennan, T. (1998), "Inland Freight Conference Approved," *Journal of Commerce*, 28 May.

Carsberg, B. (1997), *Final Report of the Multimodal Group*, Luxembourg: Office for Official Publications of the European Communities.

Damas, P. (1998), "FMC and EC Move Closer," *American Shipper*, May, 8-12.

Federal Maritime Commission (1989a), *27th Annual Report for Fiscal Year 1988*, Washington, DC.

Federal Maritime Commission (1989b), *Section 18 Report on the Shipping Act of 1984*, Washington, DC.

Federal Maritime Commission (1998), *36th Annual Report for Fiscal Year 1997*, Washington, DC.

Moore, K. D. (1990), *Use of Independent Action by Shipping Conferences Providing Services To and From Canada 1989* (TP-9823-E), Ottawa: Transport Canada.

National Transportation Agency (1990), *NTA Annual Review 1989*, Ottawa: National Transportation Agency.

National Transportation Agency (1992), *The Shipping Conferences Exemption Act, 1987: A Staff Report to the National Transportation Act Review Commission*, Ottawa: National Transportation Agency

Ortiz Blanco, L. and B. van Houtte (1996), *EC Competition Law in the Transport Sector*, Oxford: Oxford University Press.

Sletmo, G. K. and S. Holste (1991), *The Canadian Shipping Conferences Exemption Act: Issues and Roles for Shippers and Shipping Conferences*, Ottawa: External Affairs and International Trade Canada, August.

Transport Canada (1997), *Transportation in Canada 1996: Annual Report*, Ottawa: Transport Canada.

Transport Canada (1998), *Transportation in Canada 1997: Annual Report*, Ottawa: Public Works and Government Services Canada.

Transport Canada (1999), *Transportation in Canada 1998: Annual Report* (TP13198E), Ottawa: Transport Canada.

## REFERENCES FOR CHAPTER 9

Anonymous (1998a), "FMC Approves Inland-Only Conference," *American Shipper*, July, 16.

Anonymous (1998b), "Commerce and Contestability," *The Economist (World Trade Survey)*, 349, 8088, 14-16.

Anonymous (1998c), "Competition Laws," *The Economist*, 347, 8068, 113.Boyes, J. R. C. (1998), "A New World," *Containerisation International*, December, 51-3.

Anonymous (1998d), "The Borders of Competition," *The Economist*, 348, 8075, 69-70.

Boyes, J. R. C. (1998), "A New World," *Containerisation International*, December, 51-3.

Brooks, M. R. (1995), "Understanding the Ocean Container Carrier Market—A Seven Country Study," *Maritime Policy and Management*, 22, 1, 39-50.

Brooks, M. R. (1998), "Competition in Liner Shipping: Are National Policies Appropriate?" *Ocean Yearbook*, 13, 142-66.

Burnson, P. (1998), "Maritime Reform May Rewrite Liner Conference System," *Canadian Sailings*, 2 November, 27-8.

Butz, D. A. (1991), *Report to the Advisory Commission on Conferences in Liner Shipping*, 9 December in ACCOS (1992), *Report of the Advisory Commission on Conferences in Ocean Shipping*, Washington, DC, April.

Dunning, J. (1997), *Alliance Capitalism and Global Business*, New York: Routledge.

Farthing, B. and M. Brownrigg (1997), *Farthing on International Shipping*, Colchester, UK: LLP Limited.

Galbraith, J. R. and R. K. Kazanjian (1978), *Strategy Implementation: Structure, Systems and Process* (2d edition), St. Paul, MN: West Publishing Company.

Graham, E. M. and J. Richardson (1997), "Conclusions and Recommendation," *Global Competition Policy*, Graham, E. M. and J. D. Richardson, eds., Washington, DC: Institute for International Economics, 547-80.

*Hong Kong Shipping Gazette* (1998), "Japan to Allow Anti-Trust Immunity to Continue," www.schednet.com, 17 April.

Hsu, M. C. (1998), *Regulating an Industry in Transition*, speech to the International Trade Club of Southern California, 17 February.

Jackson, A. E. (1997), "Strategic Alliances and Strategic Mergers in 1997," *Survey of Maritime Administrative Law*, 6, June, 33-44.

Kobrin, S. J. (1995), "Regional Integration in a Globally Networked Economy," *Transnational Corporations*, 4, 2, 15-33.

Mintzberg, H. (1996), "Managing Government, Governing Management," *Harvard Business Review*, 74, 3, 75-83.

National Transportation Act Review Commission (1993), *Competition in Transportation: Policy and Legislation in Review*, Ottawa: Supply and Services Canada.

Porter, J. (1998), "Sager Predicts Demise of the Conferences," *Lloyd's List*, February 4, 3.

Porter, M. E. (1998), "Clusters and the New Economics of Competition," *Harvard Business Review*, 76, 6, 77-90.

Ruttley, P. (1991), "International Shipping and EEC Competition Law," *European Competition Law Review*, 12, 1, 5-18. London: Sweet & Maxwell.

Shashikumar, N. (1989), "Service Contracts: A Study of Unfulfilled Promises," *Maritime Policy and Management*, 16, 1, 13-26.

Schaub, A. (1998), "International Co-operation in Anti-Trust Matters: Making the Point in the Wake of the Boeing/MDD Proceedings," http://europa.eu.int/en/comm/dg04/speech/eight/en/sp98004.htm

Weil, R. T. (1997), "Harmony and Dissonance in International Liner Shipping Regulation," *Survey of Maritime Administrative Law*, 6, June, 25-32.

Won, D. J. H. (1999), *Summary of the Report Issued in Fact Finding Investigation No. 23*, Washington, DC: Federal Maritime Commission.

# Index